Infinitive Constructions
with Specified Subjects

Recent Titles in
OXFORD STUDIES IN COMPARATIVE SYNTAX
Richard Kayne, *General Editor*

Infinitive Constructions
with Specified Subjects

A Syntactic Analysis
of the Romance Languages

GUIDO MENSCHING

OXFORD
UNIVERSITY PRESS
2000

OXFORD
UNIVERSITY PRESS

Oxford   New York
Athens   Auckland   Bangkok   Bogotá   Buenos Aires   Calcutta
Cape Town   Chennai   Dar es Salaam   Delhi   Florence   Hong Kong   Istanbul
Karachi   Kuala Lumpur   Madrid   Melbourne   Mexico City   Mumbai
Nairobi   Paris   São Paulo   Singapore   Taipei   Tokyo   Toronto   Warsaw

and associated companies in
Berlin   Ibadan

Copyright © 2000 by Guido Mensching

Published by Oxford University Press, Inc.
198 Madison Avenue, New York, New York 10016

Oxford is a registered trademark of Oxford University Press

Library of Congress Cataloging-in-Publication Data
Mensching, Guido.
Infinitive constructions with specified subjects : a syntactic
analysis of the Romance languages / Guido Mensching.
p.   cm. — (Oxford studies in comparative syntax)
Includes bibliographical references and index.
ISBN 0-19-513303-X; ISBN 0-19-513304-8 (pbk.)
1. Romance languages—Infinitive. I. Title. II. Series.
PC162.M46   2000
440'.045—dc21   99-38156

1 3 5 7 9 8 6 4 2

Printed in the United States of America
on acid-free paper

To Isabel

Preface

Specified subjects of Romance infinitive clauses have been a topic of discussion in generative grammar at least since Rizzi's (1982) famous Aux-to-Comp analysis. Since then, a small number of articles has been published on similar phenomena in Portuguese, Romanian, Sardinian, French, Occitan, and Spanish. However, each of these languages was dealt with in a quite isolated fashion: the striking fact that almost all Romance languages permit the subject of an infinitive clause to be overtly realized, even in the nominative case, was not addressed. Outside the generative framework, the phenomenon of specified subjects in infinitive clauses has received quite extensive attention since the last century, particularly by scholars of historical Romance linguistics and recently also within linguistic typology. Many valuable studies have been produced on different languages, and there have been various attempts to explain the origin and the development of these structures, even from a cross-linguistic Romance view. However, these pieces have never been put together. I therefore decided to dedicate a book to specified subjects in infinitive clauses that takes into account all Romance languages, in both the present-day and past stages, and their geographical varieties.

This book is a slightly reduced English version of a manuscript in German (Mensching 1997), which I submitted to the faculty of philosophy of the University of Cologne on January 31, 1997, as part of my appointment as a university lecturer (Habilitation). Some changes were made in the original version to adapt the book to the purposes of this series. In particular, two rather large chapters in which the data are presented and analyzed through a taxonomic approach were omitted; part of this material is summarized in chapter 2 of the present book. Other parts have been included and extended in articles by Mensching and Popovici (1997) and Mensching (1998,1999).

Most of this book, then, was originally written in 1996. For the present version, I have slightly updated the theoretical assumptions by including some work that appeared after that time, without, however, aiming at completeness. Among the studies that could not be included in the final version, I would particularly like to mention an article by Adam Ledgeway (1998), which mainly focuses on inflected forms in Calabrian that do not derive from the Latin infinitive but are nevertheless argued to be infinitives. In addition, in his introductory remarks, Ledgeway (who developed his theories completely independently from my own work) hits on some of the same ideas that I develop in detail in chapters 5 and 6 of this book. I take this as independent confirmation for my hypotheses, showing that I am on the right track. This article can be recommended for further reading about the southern Italo-Romance varieties.

When I began to work on the subject of Romance infinitive clauses in 1994, the discussion within generative grammar was still mainly focused on nonminimalist linguistic theory. It therefore seemed to me that the main focus of this book should be on an analysis within the traditional principles and parameters paradigm, so that I dedicated a rather large chapter (chapter 6) to a nonminimalist interpretation and a smaller one to minimalism (chapter 7). Note that this procedure is not a necessary one because the minimalist program does not presuppose an analysis in the preceding model. However, it still seems appropriate to me to include the nonminimalist interpretation in order to compare and unify, for the first time, the scattered attempts to explain the phenomenon of specified subjects in Romance infinitive clauses, which appeared mainly during the 1980s. In addition, it should be observed that case theory is one of the core modules in this framework, so the study of case assignment to the subject of nonfinite constructions is quite an important point. Finally, even today the minimalist program has not been accepted by all scholars of generative grammar, so the approach presented in chapter 6 can still be considered a valid solution.

The phenomena discussed in this book originally attracted my attention many years ago during my studies of Spanish and other Romance languages. My curiosity became even greater when I was writing my Sardinian grammar (Mensching 1994) and again encountered structures of the same kind. My interest in generative grammar has been greatly stimulated by my work in computational linguistics at the department of linguistic data processing of the University of Cologne, and many of the results of the present book owe much to our attempts to implement generative grammar for machine translation, and above all to discussions with my colleagues of this department, particularly Jürgen Rolshoven, Jean-Yves Lalande, Tobias Schoofs, and Eva Remberger, to whom I would like to express my thanks. Our research in the field of computational linguistics was supported by the central public funding organization for academic research in Germany (Deutsche Forschungsgemeinschaft), which also financed my Habilitation project through a research grant.

Furthermore, I express my gratitude to Hans Dieter Bork of the department of Romance philology of the University of Cologne, who supported my work from the very start and who has been my teacher and counselor in questions of historical linguistics and has also provided some additional data. My special thanks go to Michael Allan Jones for having proposed my book for this series, to its general editor Richard S. Kayne for having accepted it, to the reviewers, and to Peter Ohlin, Cynthia L. Garver, and the other staff of Oxford University Press who directed the technical part of publishing this book. Moreover, I thank Daniela Fink and Alexander Foith (Cologne), who corrected the German version, and Jeroen van de Weijer (Leiden), who corrected the English manuscript. This book would not have been possible without the aid of numerous speakers of Romance languages who offered to serve as informants, either in real life or "virtually" through the Internet. Unfortunately, I cannot mention all of them here. As "representatives" I would like to thank Victoria Popovici (Cologne) for her judgment on the Romanian data and for her help with Old Romanian and, for Spanish, my wife, Isabel, who during various years may have had the impression that all she said was important to me just because it contained infinitive clauses with subjects (in which she would be totally wrong!). I especially thank her for our regular discussions on language and literature and her invaluable advice on the linguistic structures of her mother tongue.

Cologne, Germany   G. M.
April 1999

Contents

Abbreviations

A	adjective	INF	infinitive
ACC	accusative	Infl	inflection
A.c.I.	accusitavus cum infinitivo	INTERR	interrogative (particle)
		IP	inflection phrase
A CL	adverbial clitic	LCA	linear correspondence axiom
Adv	adverb		
AdvP	adverbial phrase	LEX	lexical
Agr	(subject) agreement	M	masculine
AgrO	object agreement	ME	Modern English
AgrOP	object agreement phrase	MF	Modern French
AgrP	(subject) agreement phrase	MG	Modern Galician
		MGe	Modern German
AgrS	subject agreement	MI	Modern Italian
AgrSP	subject agreement phrase	MidF	Middle French
		MP	Modern Portuguese
AP	adjective phrase	MP(B)	Modern Portuguese (Brazilian)
Aux	auxiliary		
C	complementizer	MP(E)	Modern Portuguese (European)
CF	Classical French		
CFC	core functional category	MR	Modern Romanian
CL	clitic	MS	Modern Spanish
Comp	complementizer	N	noun
COND	conditional tense	N.c.I.	nominativus cum infinitivo
CP	complementizer phrase		
CS	Classical Spanish	NP	noun phrase
D	determiner	Neg	negation
DAT	dative case	NegP	negation phrase
DP	determiner phrase	NOM	nominative Case
ECM	exceptional case marking	NP	noun phrase
		obj	object
ECP	empty category principle	OF	Old French
		OI	Old Italian
EMF	early Modern French	OR	Old Romanian
F	feminine	OS	Old Spanish
FUT	future tense	P	preposition
GEN	genitive case	PART	particle
GP	Galician-Portuguese	PL	plural
GTC	government transparency corollary	PP	prepositional phrase
		R CL	reflexive clitic
I	inflection	RF	regional French

R P	reflexive pronoun	T	tense
S	sentence	Tns	tense
Sard	Sardinian	TOP	topic(alisation)
SC	small clause	TopP	topic phrase
SG	singular	TP	Tense Phrase
Sic	Sicilian	V	verb
Spec	specifier	VP	verb phrase
subj	subject		

Infinitive Constructions with Specified Subjects

1

Introduction

One of the basic characteristics of infinitive constructions, according to standard assumptions, is the fact that they lack an overt subject. This property has repeatedly been emphasized in generative grammar, and it has influenced the development of common theories about phenomena like empty categories, raising, and case assignment. Some regular exceptions have been noted, however, and these fitted quite well into the assumptions concerning infinitives, such as exceptional case marking (ECM) and the insertion of the preposition *for* in English, where the infinitival subject appears in the accusative case. However, as demonstrated by studies like Rizzi (1982) and Raposo (1987), some Romance languages permit specified subjects in a far broader range of infinitive constructions, remarkably also in the nominative case, which would definitely fall prey to the case filter in languages like English and German. For these phenomena, scholars in generative grammar have usually emphasized the language-specific properties involved in such constructions. What has not been sufficiently underlined is the fact that specified subjects in infinitival environments can be considered a common property in most Romance languages and can be found right from the first texts, appearing in the Middle Ages.

This book has the following aims: first, to systematically describe Romance infinitive constructions with specified subjects, taking into account diachronic and dialectal varieties, and, above all, to interpret the facts within a generative framework, examining how overt subjects in infinitive clauses are licensed and what determines their position and their case. The short descriptive part of the book in chapter 2 presents the phenomenon of infinitive clauses with specified subjects in most of the Romance languages. In this part, based on the evaluation of a large amount of data in Mensching (1997), the major differences between the languages and/or their diachronic and dialectal varieties are pointed out. The analytical part in the other chapters interprets these and other linguistic phenomena, deriving them from a small number of abstract principles in the sense of modern approaches to the theory of language. It is shown that most of the underlying syntactic mechanisms can be derived from recent standard assumptions in the generative framework. Nevertheless, the data to be analyzed call for a thorough revision of the principles assumed for Romance languages.

The languages discussed are mainly Italian, French, Spanish, and Portuguese, although minor paragraphs deal with Sardinian, Romanian, Occitan, and Catalan. In Rhaeto-Romance, the relevant infinitive constructions could not be detected. It is interesting that this group of varieties licenses specified subjects in gerund constructions (cf. Rolshoven 1998), but I do not pay much attention to gerunds here (but see section 4.3.3.2). In general, it can be said that overt subjects of gerunds are much more widespread than those of infinitive constructions. Note that modern English and French allow the subject of gerunds, but not of infinitives, to be expressed in the nominative case. This will be an interesting point for future research. For the moment, the reader is referred to works like Rizzi (1982), Battistella (1983), Emonds (1986), Johnson (1988), Belletti (1990), and Roberts (1993). Moreover, in this book I do not concentrate on causative and similar constructions like the ones studied by Pearce (1990) and infinitival matrix clauses (absolute infinitives) since these have been sufficiently accounted for.[1]

1.1   Some basic problems of Romance infinitive clauses

To become familiar with the subject of this book, consider the following example from French:

(1)   Pierre a   acheté les tiquets [pour aller à Paris].
       P.   has bought the tickets   for   to-go to P.
       'P. bought the tickets (in order) to go to P.'

Here two actions are expressed—(i) 'to buy tickets' and (ii) 'to go to Paris'—although only in (i) is the agent of the action represented by a lexical element (*Pierre*). Speakers of French usually interpret this example by assuming that the performer of action (ii) is the same as that of (i). Note that the overt expression of the person who performs the action expressed in the infinitive is ungrammatical in standard French (for the reader's convenience, I represent infinitival subjects in bold letters throughout the book):

(2)   ⋆Pierre a   acheté les tiquets [pour **moi** aller à Paris].
       P.   has bought the tickets   for   I/me to-go to P.
       'P. bought the tickets (in order) for me to go to P.'

As the translation shows, this is grammatical in English. It is interesting that (2) is also grammatical in some regional varieties of French (Walloon and Lorraine), and similar structures existed in the historical stages of French, at least until the eighteenth century. Moreover, it is noteworthy that in earlier periods structures like (2) were possible in a far wider range of configurations than in the modern varieties of French. Consider the following example from Old French:

(3)   [A l' esmouvoir l' ost   le roy] rot   grant noise de trompes.
       on the to-start   the enemy the king began great noise of trumpets
       'When the king's enemy started, a great noise of trumpets began.' (Joinv. 231, pp.
       112–14; cf. A. Haase 1888:103; E. Stimming 1915:123; Lewent 1925:224)

Within the theory of syntax, it is an interesting question what determines the grammaticality of infinitive clauses like the ones in (2) and (3) from both a diachronic and a synchronic perspective.

Until now I have said that the characteristic property of the last two examples is the fact that the performer of the action expressed by the infinitive is lexically realized. But note that this generalization is not correct, as the following sentence with a passive infinitive, grammatical in standard French, shows:

(4) Ces tiquets spéciaux sont vendus [pour être utilisés **par les visiteurs**
     these tickets special   are sold   for to-be used   by the visitors
     japonais].
     Japanese
     'These special tickets are sold (in order) to be used by the Japanese visitors.'

The agents of the action 'to use' are 'the Japanese visitors', overtly expressed in the infinitive construction by the PP *par les visiteurs japonais*. The special point about the infinitives in examples (2) and (3), therefore, has nothing to do with theta roles but rather with the fact that it is the subject that is expressed overtly. This claim is confirmed by the observation that those linguistic varieties in which (2) is grammatical also allow for the theme of a passive predicate (which surfaces as a subject) to be expressed:

(5) Et y   fu du   pére envoiez, / [Pour **nous** estre a Dieu   MidF
     and there (he) was by-the father sent   for   we/us to-be to God
     ravoiez].
     sent
     'And he was sent there by the Father in order for us to be sent to God.' (Mir. N.D.,
     XXXIX, 1065ff., vol. VII, p. 231; cf. Tobler 1921:93; E. Stimming 1915:124)

We can therefore reformulate the question mentioned above: What determines the grammaticality of specified subjects in infinitive clauses? Note that we cannot simply answer this question by assuming that the preposition assigns case to the subject, as is usually proposed for the English *for* construction. First, in a French example like (2), the morphological case of the subject cannot be recognized and, second and more important, the Romance languages do not behave uniformly with respect to case properties. Consider the following examples from Portuguese:

(6) Ele trouxe um sanduíche [para **eu** / (*)**mim** comer].
     he brought a   sandwich for   I /   me   to-eat
     'He brought a sandwich for me to eat.' (Thomas 1969:185)

Whereas the nominative form *eu* is generally the only grammatical solution in Portuguese, some Brazilian varieties admit the accusative form *mim*. It is important to remember that nominative subjects in infinitive clauses are not unproblematic within syntactic theory because nominative assignment has usually been interpreted as connected with finiteness. Strikingly, nominative subjects in infinitive constructions are grammatical in most Romance languages. To account for examples like (6) and the cross-linguistic variation involved, one of the basic issues in this book is a revision of case theory.

In the examples reviewed so far, the referee of the overt infinitival subject is different from the one of the main clause. It has to be noted that this is not necessarily the case. Consider the following examples:

(7) a. Moi$_i$, je$_i$ veux [aller **moi**$_i$-même / *toi$_j$ même avec lui].   MF
         I   I want to-go I   myself / you yourself with him
         'I want to go with him personally.'

     b. (Io$_i$) credevo [di aver   vinto io$_i$ / *tu$_j$].   MI
         I   believed *di* to-have won I /   you
         'I believed that it was me who had won.'

These are cases of so-called emphatic pronouns (*pronoms distinctifs*, according to Ronat 1979), which need to be coreferential with an element in the matrix clause. As can be seen in (7), they are grammatical in standard French, in contrast to (2), and this can be observed in all Romance languages. Emphatic pronouns are not the focus of the present book. There has been a quite satisfying account for this phenomenon, which is presented and slightly modified in chapter 3.

Apart from the construction type represented by examples (1) to (6), nonemphatic subjects, which are the main theme of this study, have been grammatical in Romance in a considerable number of configurations, as I show in chapter 2. Besides the case properties already mentioned, Romance infinitive constructions with specified subjects display other cross-linguistic differences that need to be explained. First, the grammaticality of overt subjects seems to depend on the function of the infinitive clause within the sentence. Consider the following contrast between Spanish and Italian:

(8) a. [Haberse   **Julia** presentado a las elecciones] fue un error.   MS
         to-have-herself J.   presented   at the elections   was a   mistake
         'The fact that J. presented herself at the elections was a mistake.'

     b. *[Essersi **Giulia** presentata alle elezioni] è stato un'errore.   MI

     c. [Affaticarsi **l' uomo** nel bene] non è merito.   OI
         to-labor   the man in-the good not is merit
         'The fact that human beings strive hard to do good things is not a merit.'
         (Giord. Riv., 17; cf. Segre 1991:119)

Here the infinitive clause functions as the subject of the sentence. In contrast to Modern Italian, specified subjects are grammatical in this configuration in Spanish, as well as in Old Italian. As we will see, the Modern Italian example becomes grammatical when the subclause is a complement of certain verbs or when a determiner precedes the infinitive. It is interesting that, as will be shown, structures like (8c) can still be found in other Italo-Romance varieties.

Second, in the examples given so far, the reader will have discovered another difference: whereas the subject occurs to the left of the infinitive in examples (2),

(5), and (6), it is situated to its right in (3), (7), and (8). As I show in the course of the book, this is not arbitrary. Although some varieties allow both possibilities, in others only one of them is grammatical. Languages that allow both possibilities do not behave in a uniform manner, however. For example, the preverbal subject of an infinitive is the unmarked case in Portuguese, whereas it is a marked option in Spanish. In languages that behave like Portuguese, the postverbal subject is usually focalized, similar to what occurs in finite environments. Although I offer a general explanation for this contrast, the exact pragmatic conditions that regulate word order in these cases are not discussed at length in this book. The reader is referred to Vallduví (1992a,1992b) for a discussion of this issue. The fact that word order is sometimes dependent on the way in which the infinitive clause is embedded into the sentence is relevant for our interpretation of the licensing of either subject position however. Consider the following facts from Spanish:

(9) a. [Para **yo** presentarme a las elecciones] sería necesario mucho
         for I   to-present-R CL to the elections would-be necessary much
         dinero.
         money
         'To present myself at the elections, a lot of money would be necessary.'

     b. ⋆[**Yo** presentarme] a las elecciones fue un error.
         I   to-present-R CL to the elections was a mistake.
         'The fact that I presented myself at the elections was a mistake.'

Although postverbal subjects are grammatical in both examples, the adverbial infinitive clause with a preposition in (9a) licenses a preverbal subject, whereas the infinitival subject clause in (9b) does not.

Finally, it has to be noted that the licensing of infinitival subjects can depend on the properties of the infinitive itself:

(10) a. per essere **Rosaria** arrivata   a'. ⋆per arrivare **Rosaria**   MI
         for to-be R.   arrived   for to-arrive R.
         'because R. arrived'   'because R. arrives'

     b. para **as mulheres** chegar*em*   b'. ⋆para **as mulheres** chegar   MP
         for the women   to-arrive-3PL   for the women   to-arrive

Whereas Italian allows a specified subject only with the infinitive of an auxiliary, in Portuguese the overt subject regularly co-occurs with inflected forms of the infinitive that show agreement with the subject.

Some of the relevant data have been known right from the beginning of Romance linguistics, as I point out in section 1.2. However, the exact syntactic properties of these constructions and their diachronic and diatopic distribution have for a long time remained unknown and are partly uncovered here for the first time. In spite of the fragmentary knowledge about these phenomena, scholars in descriptive and historical grammar have repeatedly tried to relate the appearance of specified subjects in infinitive constructions to other phenomena, like the inflected infinitive and its origin. On the same basis, insufficient from a syntactic point of view, hypotheses were formulated about a possible survival of the Latin *Accusativus cum Infinitivo* (A.c.I.), even in the shape of infinitives with nominative subjects. I review some of these accounts later in this chapter. It is clear, however, that problems of this kind cannot be resolved in a satisfactory way until the underlying syntactic principles are investigated from a more general point of view, taking into account all Romance languages and, most of all, the way in which language itself functions. I would like to contribute to this end with this book, without pretending to resolve all the questions of interest to the scholar of historical linguistics.

Above all, specified subjects in infinitive constructions confront some core assumptions of generative grammar with a series of partially nontrivial problems, a fact that makes the present study of interest to general linguistic theory. One of the questions that concerns us in the following chapters is the issue of how case assignment works and how it is related to movement processes that yield the differences in word order. Following the idea of the case filter introduced by Vergnaud (1979) and Chomsky (1980), it has usually been claimed that finiteness is crucial for nominative case assignment, where finiteness is understood as a series of properties of the functional head I(nfl), recently interpreted as consisting of various functional categories like tense and agreement. Although such an account can be quite easily extended to Portuguese examples like (10b) along the lines of Raposo (1987)—remember that the infinitive has overt agreement similar to a finite verb—an Italian structure like (10a) or the Spanish ones in (9) seem to have nothing to do with finiteness.

Up to now, there have been few articles dealing with specified subjects in various Romance languages, which I briefly characterize in section 1.2 and discuss in detail in chapter 4. Generally it can be said, however, that each of them is concerned with the most striking phenomena of one individual language, and usually these accounts do not aim at a revision of case theory but treat the facts observed as a kind of language-specific exceptions. During the 1990s, the assumptions within case theory, as well as the facts about movement elaborated in the 1980s, have been reformulated by means of properties of the functional categories T and Agr (e.g., Roberts 1993, 1994; Chomsky 1992 seqq.; cf. sections 3.2.3 and 7.1). Although there have been some quite interesting proposals about infinitives and related verbal forms, the discussion about subjects, their case, and their position usually focused on finite structures. This is generally legitimate, given the fact that many languages do not license overt subjects in infinitive clauses but only in a very restricted way. However, as will be clear from what I have said so far, the Romance languages are extremely interesting in this respect, so that we can now examine more thoroughly how some of the principles assumed function in nonfinite contexts. This is what I attempt here. As we will see, the recent theoretical approaches toward clause structure and related facts are in principal compatible with our data, although most of the assumptions have to be modified to some degree on the basis of the Romance evidence.

1.2 On the study of Romance infinitival subjects

I have already alluded to the fact that the analysis of specified subjects in Romance infinitive constructions within generative grammar has been fragmentary, both in the linguistic varieties involved and the phenomena described. In particular, diachronic and diatopic varieties have hardly been included. Most important of all, none of the existing studies, perhaps with the exception of those referring to ECM, has endeavoured to review the situation from a pan-Romance perspective. Most of the studies I discuss in chapter 4 describe some interesting facts about a single language, mentioning at most some parallels and divergences in Italian and Portuguese, as described by Rizzi (1982) and Raposo (1987). Note that this is not sufficient because the licensing of overt subjects in infinitive clauses has to be regarded as an extremely widespread phenomenon within the group of languages under discussion. Moreover, the empirical basis of most approaches is rather small and thus insufficient for detecting the whole range of configurations in which this kind of phenomenon occurs. In addition, as I show in chapter 4, some of the accounts given are not compatible with the data I present in chapter 2. Finally, many approaches, though interesting and in part even excellent, reflect rather older phases of linguistic theory. As a consequence of these factors, there is now a series of diverging accounts for partially very similar phenomena.

At this point, it is convenient to look at the study of our problem within other frameworks. In contrast to what has just been mentioned, the phenomena at issue have received a great deal of attention from scholars outside generative grammar. Works in descriptive and even normative grammar, as well as studies of historical linguistics and linguistic typology, have provided a large amount of data that has never been analyzed within any framework of formal syntax.[2] Many of these have been used in this book, as can be seen from the references included with most of the examples. In addition, a few scholars tried to interpret their data in a comparative way. Within the framework of historical grammar, we mention Diez (1882), Lewent (1925), Meier (1955), and Maurer (1968). For linguistic typology, I would like to point out the studies by Körner (1983, 1987a), and M. Haase (1995). Generally, it can be said that the problem with these studies is the fact that little attention is paid to word order and case properties, both of which are, of course, crucial for the present analysis. However, for the purpose of further elucidating some of the problems involved in the type of constructions under discussion, I briefly review the most important points.

Fiedrich Diez, who is usually considered to be the founder of Romance philology as a field of scientific research, found the Romance tendency to express the subject of an infinitive striking, particularly in comparison with German. Diez (1882:943–47) offers some isolated examples from Italian, French, Occitan, Spanish, and Romanian, distinguishing between subjects appearing in the accusative case (pp. 943–46) and the nominative case (pp. 946–47) and observing the existence of inflected infinitives in Portuguese. Further comments are made by Meyer-Lübke (1899:§388, §546), who provides some data, which he subsumes in part under the construction known as A.c.I. Note that this generalization, obviously due to the influence of Latin grammar, is problematic because some of the examples he gives for Spanish and Portuguese must be assumed to have nominative subjects, as is shown in the following chapter. The type of construction represented by example (2) here is discussed by Lewent (1925), with a particular emphasis on its history in French. Although some of these data are extremely interesting, the differences in the case of the subject are not taken into account.

The endeavor to emphasize the similarities between infinitive constructions of various varieties of Romance without paying too much attention to the syntactic differences is quite symptomatic even for later works. However, there are some exceptions, like a quite interesting article by Meier (1955). Meier is the first scholar to compile a considerable number of phenomena from various languages, and he offers a first attempt to roughly classify the syntactic environments in which specified subjects appear in Romance infinitive clauses. He distinguished between infinitives after prepositions and after declarative, epistemic, and volitional verbs; infinitival subject clauses in impersonal sentences; and constructions introduced by a definite article. As we see in chapter 2, some of these distinctions are extremely relevant for our analysis, although, naturally, their exact structure still has to be determined. This will be done in chapters 3 to 7. Moreover, Meier calls our attention to word order facts, stating that in prepositional infinitive clauses we generally find the sequence subject + infinitive in Old French and Portuguese and frequently in Old Spanish, whereas the reverse order is found in Modern Spanish, Italian, and Catalan. This might be admitted as a rough approximation, although we see in the following chapters that it has to be refined and amplified on the evidence of other varieties not mentioned.[3] Another quite interesting point in Meier's article is the idea, intended for future research, that these word order facts might correspond to two different traditions, which might be traced back to a remote epoch, reflecting two different regional tendencies of Vulgar Latin. Obviously, this idea is intriguing for scholars of generative grammar, in the sense that here different parameter settings may be involved. Unfortunately, Meier does not pay attention to case properties. He thus proposes that most of the Romance infinitive structures with specified subjects may have a common origin and that they might be interpreted as a survival of the Latin A.c.I.[4]

Meier's (1955) article can be said to be the summit of the nongenerative approaches toward the phenomena we are discussing. The remaining studies are rather loose collections of data, which seem to be parallelled by superficial observation. This is the case with a quite frequently quoted section of Maurer's extensive study on the inflected infinitive of Portuguese, in which the author tries to find parallels in various Romance languages.[5] Differences in word order are not taken into account, and the issue of the case of the subject is disposed of with the comment that frequently the subject shows nominative case, although, naturally, in most examples this case cannot be distinguished from the accusative (1968:71). Although this is obviously true for the morphological case, I show in the course of this book that abstract case, as postulated in our framework, is absolutely necessary to account for the distribution of word order and the configurations in which a subject is allowed to be overt in the different languages.

As far as studies in linguistic typology are concerned, case properties are also frequently neglected. Similarly to Maurer (1968), Körner (1983, 1987a) compares infinitive constructions with different word orders without distinguishing between accusative and nominative subjects. Among other things, he postulates a corollary according to which those Romance languages in which accusative complements referring to humans are realized by a prepositional case marker, like Spanish and Portuguese, also show a strong tendency to overtly express the subject of infinitives, in contrast to French and Italian. This corollary does not seem to hold, however. As I show, Old Italian behaves essentially like Ibero-Romance but does not generally license prepositional accusatives.

Finally, a rather interesting typological approach is that of M. Haase, who proposes that infinitives with specified subjects are something in between finite and nonfinite constructions. Evidently, his statement that, on these grounds, it is irrelevant to distinguish between subjects in accusative and nominative case (1995:140) must be rejected from a syntactic point of view. However, the issue of finiteness, its relationship to the overt realization of subjects, and the way in which it can be expressed by means of specific properties of functional categories is an essential point in our discussion.

1.3   Some methodological observations

To conclude this introduction, I first consider the research procedure and the framework chosen for the interpretation of the data. Finally I offer some brief comments on the question of syntactic imitation and borrowing and the notion of subjects.

An appropriate description and analysis of syntactic phenomena must be founded on an ample empirical basis. For the present study I took into account about 2,500 examples from numerous Romance varieties. A large part of these data was provided by the works mentioned in the preceding section and other, mostly descriptive, studies. Those data concerning older stages of the Romance languages were confirmed by consulting modern editions, whenever possible, and some gaps were filled by retrieving new data. For instance, the approximately 150 examples known for Old Spanish could be more than doubled. Some other varieties, like Old Sardinian, are considered here for the first time. Since my study does not aim at a numerical evaluation, no fixed corpus was used. Nevertheless, some texts were systematically scrutinized.[6] Most of the relevant data were included in Mensching (1997). Obviously, only a small part of the material can be included here. For the diachronic level, I examined various stages for each language: at the very least, the oldest documented phase and the contemporary situation. For the languages that this book focuses on (Italian, French, Spanish, and Portuguese), intermediate stages were considered as well. The contemporary varieties of the Romance languages are based both on written and oral sources. For the latter, I considered some existing corpora and studies.[7] The speakers' judgments on the grammaticality of the relevant constructions are based, in part, on existing work, such as the accounts summarized in chapter 4, and, in addition, on my own inquiries (cf. Mensching 1997: 314–24 for a complete listing).

I now turn to the linguistic theory chosen for the analysis. At the present time, there are essentially two competing models within generative grammar. The first, corresponding to the principles and parameters (P&P) theory founded principally by Chomsky (1981, 1986a), with important impulses through the work by, for instance, Abney (1987), Baker (1988), Sportiche (1988b), Pollock (1989), Belletti (1990), and Rizzi (1990a). The second is the minimalist program, introduced by Chomsky in 1992 and extended in 1994 and 1995. The assumptions made within the traditional P&P framework[8] have been founded on the analysis of numerous languages, whereas for the minimalist program much empirical work is still to be done, as Chomsky (1995:ch. 4, especially) repeatedly emphasizes, and it is not yet clear how to reinterpret the vast amount of theoretical results of the preceding phase in linguistic theory. In this book, I therefore concentrate on a traditional P&P approach, particularly in chapter 6, but I offer an alternative solution to our data within the minimalist framework in chapter 7. The structural position of constituents that I elaborate on in chapter 5 is essentially valid in both approaches. At the end of the book, we will then have two solutions, one that is more complex but based on principles that have proved their validity in many years of generative studies, and another one, which I consider as experimental but which has the advantage of occupying only a few pages, in conformity with the aims of the minimalist program.

Following Lenerz (1984:7, 51–54), generative grammar is particularly appropriate for examining linguistic variation, both on a synchronic, language-internal level and in the diachronic dimension. With respect to the latter, which is an important factor in the present publication, the interesting point is that in a generative approach the structures of a language do not coexist in an isolated way but can be considered different, but related, realizations of similar underlying phenomena (1984:24). For this reason, some of the problems and hypotheses formulated by scholars of historical grammar, as reviewed in section 1.2, will appear in a new light in view of the results achieved in the present book. I return to this point on various occasions and in the outlook presented in chapter 8. As has been said, not all the issues relevant to historical linguistics can be resolved here.

One of the points of discussion in traditional historical grammar is the question of whether some of the constructions I examine were borrowed from Latin. We see in the next chapter that this has been postulated at least for the A.c.I. construction selected by declarative and epistemic predicates. Although I make some comments on this matter, I consider this issue tangential to the purposes of this book. As we can see in the French material offered by E. Stimming (1915), this type of construction, although perhaps oriented toward Latin models at the beginning, became established at least in certain registers of the language, where it was used for many centuries. If syntactic borrowing was really involved originally (a point put into doubt, for instance, by Meier 1955) we must therefore consider that this functioned in a way similar to lexical borrowing: a word once borrowed enters into the speakers' competence, although it may only be used in certain registers. Evidence that this was also the case for the infinitive constructions under discussion is the fact that the matrix verbs by which they are licensed do not coincide 100 percent with the Latin facts.[9] The learned character and the restriction of these and some other constructions to literary or formal levels of language can be considered within the notion of stylistic markedness, which has been of some importance in generative grammar.[10]

Finally, since this book is about subjects, some points have to be cleared up before we start reviewing the data. When I refer to subjects I mean, of course, the so-called *grammatical subject* (Jespersen 1924:145–54; Buyssens 1975:29–32; Blumenthal 1980:4–6), in accordance with the common generative terminology. The definition of "subject" is a structural one; that is, it is a constituent with a specific base position in a tree structure that moves to various S-structural landing sites according to cross-linguistic variation (Radford 1988:112–13; Vater 1994:124,127–29; see chapter 3). The constituent that is the subject of a sentence is determined by the subcategorization of the verb, in the sense that some theta roles preferably show up as the subject if the verb is in the the the active voice. Nevertheless, I examine facts from historical varieties in which the lexical properties of verbs do not necessarily correspond to the modern ones. Therefore, the question might arise of how we can recognize the subject status of a constituent, even more so because subjects of infinitive clauses behave differently than finite structures.

The notion of "subject" is a basic issue in various directions of linguistics, and it cannot be discussed exhaustively here. The reader is referred to the relevant literature, such as the studies just mentioned, as well as Keenan (1975) and Sasse (1978, 1987). Here I just discuss some of the most important points. Buyssens (1975:31) proposes that subjects should be identified on the paradigmatic level, that is, by testing if a constituent can be substituted for by an element belonging to the set that is usually designated as that of the nominative pronouns, like the Italian *io* 'I', *tu* 'you', *egli* 'he', *ella* 'she', and so on, or in the Spanish *yo, tú, él,* and *ella,* respectively. This criterion is not sufficient because it can also be applied to predicate nominals, and, especially for infinitive constructions, it is rather problematic. Note that in an A.c.I. configuration like the Latin *Antonius dixit [Marcum venisse],* the accusative form *Marcum* is usually considered to be a subject, although it cannot be substituted for by any element of the nominative paradigm. If we still maintain that it is a subject, we obviously do so by comparing the situation of nonfinite constructions with finite ones, where nominatives are usually found.

Similar difficulties arise for positional facts. In most (nonergative) languages, the subject is usually the first nominal phrase in a clause in the unmarked case (cf. Sasse 1978:223–24 and the literature cited there). This holds for the Romance languages, but, as we shall see, usually this is not the case in infinitive clauses since preverbal subjects are not always grammatical, as we have already seen in section 1.1. Moreover, the word order subject + infinitive is often the marked option, as in the Spanish in example (9a), where the unmarked case is *para presentarme yo,* with the subject occurring postverbally. To maintain a subject criterion like the sentence-initial position, we have to transform the infinitive clause into a finite one and see how the putative subject behaves.

By following Sasse (1978, 1982, 1987), it can be said that usually more than one criterion applies. In the ideal case, a subject has the following properties: for pragmatics it fulfills a topic function; semantically, it is the realization of a determined theta role (e.g., agent); morphologically, it bears a certain case, usually nominative; and, finally, it agrees with the predicate in person, number, and sometimes gender. Constituents to which only a number of these criteria apply might be argued to have a somewhat reduced subject status. In this sense, many of the subjects I am examining here might be considered "semisubjects" (Sasse 1982). I return to this point at certain occasions later on in this book, where we see how such a notion can be interpreted within generative grammar and why the reduced subject status is rather typical for infinitive constructions.

2

The Basic Data

This chapter presents the fundamental data, outlining in a comparative way the most important environments in which specified subjects in infinitive constructions have been possible in present and past Romance varieties. More details are offered in the discussion of existing generative accounts (chapter 4) and in the course of the subsequent analysis. This is especially the case for data concerning the extraction of the subject to the main clause, which I do not consider at this point. This chapter is essentially descriptive. To achieve a description that is not too dependent on the framework used in the interpretation and to make the data accessible to readers who are accustomed to other syntactic theories, I mostly use a terminology based on traditional grammar.

Sections 2.1 to 2.4 deal with Italian, French, Spanish, and Portuguese, and section 2.5 summarizes some facts from other Romance varieties. For each language, I show in which kind of infinitive constructions specified subjects can occur, as well as the basic facts regarding case and word order. To simplify matters, I subsume various cases in which the subject occurs to the right of the infinitive under the term postverbal. A more detailed description and analysis are provided in chapter 5.

Before starting with the description of the languages, however, I first present the major syntactic environments in which specified subjects of infinitives are grammatical or, for the earlier stages of Romance languages, could be found by documentary evidence. The exact nature of these and other constructions are analyzed later in this book. The most important construction types are presented in examples (1) to (9). Most of the labels refer to the function traditionally attributed to the infinitive clause. I give examples from different languages for illustrative purposes only; as seen in the following sections, most of these types are grammatical in numerous varieties.

Subject

(1) a. Suffist [l' **une partie** estre vraye].   MidF
         suffices the one part   to-be true
         'It is sufficient that one part is true' (Rabelais, 406; cf. E. Stimming 1915:166)

15

    b. et [cantar **augeletti**], [et fiorir   **piagge**], / e . . . atti   OI
        and to-sing little-birds and to-flower meadows and   gestures
        soavi / sono un deserto
        gentle are   a desert
        'and the singing of little birds, and the flowering of meadows, and gentle ges-
        tures . . . are a desert' (Petr. Son., 269; cf. Diez 1882:944, fn.)

Direct object

(2) a. Lo Schiller disse [**la musica** esprimere l' anima].   MI (19th c.)
        the S.   said   the music to-express the soul
        'S. says that the music expresses the soul.' (Graf, 236; cf. Schwendener
        1923:53)

    b. Ho   sentito [ritornare **le bambine** a casa].   MI
        (I) have heard   to-return the girls   to home
        'I heard the girls coming back home.'

Prepositional complement

(3) Esta é a   razão [de se   repetirem **as cortes**].   CP
    This is the reason of R CL to-repeat-3PL the C.
    'This is the reason the Cortes repeated themselves.' (Vieira Serm., IV, 45; cf.
    Flasche 1948:706)

Adverbial

(4) Lors [por revenir **sa color**] / Le comancierent a beigner. /   OF
    then for to-return his color   him (they) began to to-bathe
    'Then, in order to make her color come back, they began to bathe her.' (Erec, 5220;
    cf. Tobler 1921:93; Nyrop 1930; Körner 1983:80)

Attribute

(5) En el momento [de alzarse **el telón**] se escucha el piano . . .].   MS
    at the moment   of to-rise the curtain R CL hears   the piano
    'At the very moment when the curtain rises, one hears the . . . piano.' (Grillo 61; cf.
    Skydsgaard 1977:710)

Apposition

(6) Isto só basta pera fugir do   mundo, [serem **os homens**   CP
    this only suffices for   to-flee from-the world   to-be-3PL the men
    julgados pelos homens].
    judged   by-the men
    'This alone is sufficient in order to flee from the world, namely the fact that men are
    judged by men.' (H.P., I,326; cf. da Silva Dias 1954:218)

Predicate Nominal

(7) O melhor é [**tu** dares   o braço à Sra.   D. Cândida].   MP
    the best   is you to-give-2SG the arm   to Senhora D. C.
    'The best is that you offer your arm to Senhora. D. C.' (Osório, Ambições, 121; cf.
    Sten 1952:104)

Introduced by a determiner

(8) Aquí fué [el desmayarse **Preciosa**].   CS
    here was the to-faint-R CL P.
    'Here P. fainted.' (Cerv. Nov., 10; cf. Diez 1882:946)

The examples in (1) are usually interpreted as subject clauses. In our context, the most important type is (1a), where the infinitive clause is the subject of impersonal predicates. In this construction, also known as a dependent subject clause in descriptive and historical grammar, specified subjects appear very frequently in the Romance languages, particularly in earlier varieties. The construction occurs after impersonal verbs (e.g., French *il faut* and Portuguese *calha* 'it is necessary'); complex predicates, which consist of a copula and a predicate nominal (e.g., Portuguese *é difícil* 'it is difficult' and Old Italian *è cosa manifesta* 'it is manifest'); or a verb of movement followed by a PP, usually denoting mental activity (e.g., Old Italian *viene alla memoria* 'it comes to memory'). The languages that allow this kind of construction also license specified subjects in infinitive clauses selected by passive predicates, which can be subsumed under this type. From this we can distinguish a "real" subject clause like (1b), characterized by its preverbal position and the fact that the verb can appear in the plural when the clause is coordinated with another constituent, as can be seen in the example. This difference is relevant for our purposes because not all Romance languages permit both types.

The kind of complement clause represented in (2a) is usually selected by declarative, epistemic, or volitional predicates. This type must be distinguished from those Romance infinitive constructions that occur after causative, permissive, and perceptional verbs, represented by (2b). The latter type is not the focus of this book because it has been the subject of many publications inside and outside of generative grammar. For the purposes of this chapter, it is important to keep in mind that the indications on case and the subject positions given here do not take into account this construction. Some of the relevant data and various proposals about their interpretation are discussed in section 4.1. By contrast, the type of object clause represented in (2a) is extremely important in this book, and we see some of the critical data in this chapter. In this configuration not only does the well-known Italian Aux-to-Comp construction (cf. Rizzi 1982; see our discussion in section 4.3.2) appear, but it is also, together with (1a), the main context of a special type of Romance A.c.I. construction. This type, to which the examples given in (1a) and (2a) seem to belong, is known in Romance historical linguistics as the "learned A.c.I construction," which, according to E. Stimming (1915), Schwendener (1923), and others, was adapted from Latin.[1]

The other types, exemplified by (3) to (8), do not need to be discussed at this point. We examine their properties in the course of this chapter. Let us now proceed with the detailed description of each individual language.

2.1   Italian

The basic facts about Modern Italian are well known in generative grammar from Rizzi (1982) and have been the subject of studies within other frameworks as well (e.g., Skytte 1983; Renzi and Salvi 1991). As compared with other Romance languages and, as we shall see, with earlier phases of Italian and with other Italo-Romance varieties, in Modern Italian the grammaticality of lexical subjects is restricted, both from a stylistic and from a syntactic point of view: first, it is limited mainly to the literary language; second, it only occurs with the infinitives of *essere* 'to be' and *avere* 'to have';[2] third, it is possible only in a small subset of infinitive constructions, namely the types represented by examples (2a), (4), and (8). The type in which the infinitive clause functions as an adverbial is restricted to infinitive constructions introduced by the preposition *per* (with final or causal sense).

Italian infinitive clauses that function as complements of declarative and epistemic predicates are usually introduced by the preposition *di*. Note, however, that this preposition is possible only when the infinitival subject is either empty (cf. Rizzi 1982; Skytte 1983:115–74, 293–98) or an emphatic pronominal subject (Renzi and Salvi 1991:529). Otherwise, the preposition is ungrammatical and disappears, as in (9c):

(9) a. Credevo [*di* aver vinto].
         (I) believed *di* to-have won.
         'I believed that I had won.'

     b. Credevo [*di* aver vinto **io**].
         (I) believed *di* to-have won I
         'I believed that it was I who had won.'

     c. Credevo [avere **egli** vinto].
         (I) believed to-have he   won
         'I believed that he had won.'

This situation can already be observed in Old Italian, but, in addition, the preposition was usually not present either when the infinitive construction actually functioned as a prepositional complement.[3] The suppression of the preposition does not seem to have been obligatory, however, as is illustrated in (10a), in contrast to (10b):

(10) a. Lagrimando dimostro / quanto   *si*   *dolga* con ragione il core /
         crying   (I) show   how-much R CL hurts with reason the heart
         [*d'* esser tradito   sotto fede **Amore**]. /
         of to-be betrayed under trust Love.
         'Crying, I show how much the heart justly grieves about the fact that Love has been betrayed under trust.' (Bocc. Dec., IV, Concl., p. 268)

     b. alcuni che diranno non *dolersi*   [**Sofronia** esser moglie di Tito],
         some who will-say not to-hurt-R CL S.   to be wife   of T.
         ma *dolersi*   *del*   modo . . .
         but to-hurt-R CL of-the manner
         'some people who will not say that they complain about the fact that S. is T.'s wife, but that they complain about the manner . . .' (Bocc. Dec., X, 8, p. 550)

It has to be noted that (10a) and (10b) display different subject positions. This is an important point explained in chapters 5 and 6.

The constructions given in (10) would both be ungrammatical today because of the restrictions mentioned above. This fact strongly suggests that Old Italian behaved differently than does Modern Italian. This assumption turns out to be true if we consider some more data. It can, in fact, be shown that all the syntactic restrictions mentioned did not hold in earlier stages of the language. First, the appearance of specified subjects was not restricted to auxiliary and copulative verbs; second, the syntactic environment of the infinitive clause was not limited to the three types mentioned at the beginning of this section. These characteristics are demonstrated in the following examples:

(11) a. El non è vergogna [a essere l' uomo abbattuto].
   it not is shame   to to-be the man knocked-down
   'It is not a shame for a man to be knocked down.' (*La tavola ritonda*, in Prosa, 720; cf. Dardano 1963:123, fn. 60)

   b. /... troverete   il passo / possibile [a salir   persona viva]. /
      (you) will-find the passage possible   to to-go-up person living
      '... you will find the passage through which it is possible for a living person to go up.' (Dante Div. Com., 11.49–51, pp. 516–17; cf. Tobler 1921)

   c. Alessandro ... [senza sapere alcuno ove la notte dormito si
      A.   without to-know anybody where the night slept   R CL
      fosse] ... con l' abate ... rientrò   in cammino.
      (he) was with the abbot   (he) returned on way
      'Without anybody knowing where he had slept that night, A. continued his way with the abbot.' (Bocc. Dec., II, 3, p. 83)

These properties can partially still be found in the nineteenth century, as is illustrated in (12):

(12) che il Gualteruzzi ammetteva [appartenere il Proemio allo stesso
   that the G.   admitted   to-belong the preface to-the same
   autore]
   author
   'that G. admitted that the preface belonged to the same author' (Biagi, Intr., p. XXIII; cf. Schwendener 1923:48)

Although here the infinitive construction is selected by a declarative verb, the infinitive *appartenere* without an auxiliary would be ungrammatical today.

   Another striking difference between present-day Italian and the earlier stages of the language is that in the former, the subject must follow the infinitive, whereas this was not always the case in the older stages, as can be seen in example (10b), where the subject is preverbal.[4] From the fifteenth century onward, preverbal subjects are restricted to those infinitive constructions which appear in the configurations exemplified by (1a) and (2a). Today, the subject can occur only in postverbal position, immediately following the auxiliary or copulative verb, as in (9c) and (13c).

   In contrast to the other Romance languages I discuss in the following sections, in Italian the subject could appear either in the accusative or in the nominative case, the latter being the only grammatical solution today. Note, however, that both cases are in complementary distribution, in the sense that postverbal subjects appear in the nominative and preverbal subjects appear in the accusative case,[5] as illustrated in (13) and (14), respectively:

(13) a. [Il volere **io** le mie poche forze sottoporre a gravissimi   14th c.
the to-want I   the my few   forces to-put-under to very-heavy
pesi]   m' è di questa infermità stata cagione.
burdens me is of this   illness   been reason
'The fact that I wanted to place my small strength under such a heavy burden has been the reason of my present illness.' (Bocc. Dec., X, 7, p. 542; cf. Diez 1882:946; Maurer 1968:71)

   b. Non ti   puoi mantenere amici quelli . . . [per non poter   16th c.
not you (DAT) can maintain   friends those   for not can (INF)
tu   usare contro di loro medicine forti].
you (NOM) to-use against of them medicines strong
'You cannot maintain their friendship anymore . . . because you cannot use strong medicine against them.' (Mach. Principe, III; cf. Meier 1954:281)

   c. Tu non ti   rallegri [aver **io** incontrata una morte].   19th c.
you not R CL delight to-have I found   a   death
'You are not glad that I have found death.' (D'Azeglio, ch. 18, p. 222; cf. Schwendener 1923:72)

(14) a. Negar non voglio esser possibile, [**lui** essere beato . . .].[6]   13th c.
to-deny not (I) want to-be possible   him to-be   blessed
'I do not want to deny that it is possible that he is blessed . . .' (Bocc. Dec., I, 1; cf. Schwendener 1923:82)

   b. che confessi   [**me** solo esser felice]   16th c.
that (you) confess me alone to-be lucky
'that you confess that I am the only one to be lucky' (Orl. Fur., V, 36; cf. Schwendener 1923:51)

   c. affermando [**sé**   essere Opimio . . .]   19th c.
affirming   himself to-be O.
'affirming that he was O . . .' (Carducci, vol. 3, p. 145; cf. Schwendener 1923:48)

These facts, which have not been made explicit in the literature consulted, are discussed in chapter 6.[7]

2.2   French

The first contrast with Italian is that in all stages of French the syntactic environments in which our construction occurs are even more restricted. Specified subjects have never been possible in infinitive clauses introduced by a determiner (see example 8), although determined constructions with nonovert subjects were frequent until the sixteenth century.[8] The only exception to this regularity is the temporal construction with the preposition à (limited to Old French), as can be seen in example (3) of chapter 1. Another syntactic environment where specified subjects never seem to have occurred are infinitival subject clauses of the type in (1b) and configurations in which the infinitive clause functions as a predicate nominal, as in (7). However, during the history of French we frequently find subjects in impersonal constructions and in infinitival complement clauses:

(15) a. Est bone chose et deleitaule [habiteir **les freres** en un].[9]   OF
         is good thing and delightful to-live   the brothers in one
         'It is a good and a delightful thing for brothers to live in unity.' (Serm. S. Bern.,
         34, p. 133; cf. Diez (1882:945)

     b. comme il soit de bonne costume . . . [**les roys** estre conseilliez   MidF
         as   it is of good   custom   the kings to-be counseled
         par les prelas]
         by the prelates
         'as it is customary that the kings are counseled by the prelates' (Christine de
         Pisan, 273, 22; quoted by E. Stimming 1915:165)

     c. Or ne penses [de **ce** plus auenir].   OF
         now not think   de this more to-happen
         'Now do not think that this will happen anymore.' (Auberi, 55, 21; cf. Tobler
         1921:92)

     d. Il pourra dire [**cette faute** partir d' une ame enyvrée de   MidF
         he can (FUT) to-say this defect to-stem from a   soul inebriated of
         sa bonne fortune].
         his good   fortune
         'He will be able to say that this misbehavior stems from a soul that is inebriated
         by his good fortune.' (Montaigne B, I, 47, vol. 1, p. 348; cf. Gougenheim
         1951:156; Junker and Martineau 1992:136)

Although overt subjects in the impersonal construction may have already been archaic in the seventeenth century,[10] their use in infinitival complement clauses that function as a direct object can still be observed now and then in the literature of the nineteenth century.[11] Today, both constructions are generally considered ungrammatical (cf. section 4.1).

In Old French, the constructions illustrated in (15) could optionally be introduced by a preposition, as can be seen in (15c). Note that this is in clear contrast to Italian. In fact, the use of specified subjects in prepositional infinitive clauses of different types seems to be a further characteristic of French as compared with Italian. Consider the following examples, where the infinitive construction is used as an attribute and as a prepositional complement of a noun, respectively:

(16) a. et quant vint li *termines* [*de* naistre **l' enfançon**]   OF
         and when came the date   of to-be-born the child
         'and when the date on which the child should be born arrived' (Cygne, 25; cf.
         E. Stimming 1915:123)

b. Vous donneriez *occasion* [*de* s'   esmouvoir **grans tumultes**   EMF
    you   would-give occasion   of R CL to-rise   great   tumults
    sans   profit].
    without profit
    'You would give people the opportunity to arise great tumults without need.'
    (Calvin Lettres, 2, 380; cf. A. Haase 1890:214; Lewent 1925:231)

However, overt subjects in these kinds of prepositional infinitive constructions
are rather rare and seem to have disappeared during the early Modern French
period.[12] This is not the case for those prepositional constructions in which the
infinitive clause functions as a sentence adverbial, which was extremely frequent.
Consider the following Old French examples:

(17) a. J'ocit ma char [por **l' ame** vivre].
      I kill my flesh for the soul to-live
      'I kill my flesh, so that my soul can live.' (Bal., 4024, p. 120; cf. E. Stimming
      1915:123; Lombard 1936:223)

    b. Asaillir fait   [ains **la tierce**   passer].
      to-attack (he) makes before the third-office to-pass
      'He ordered the attack before the third office had passed.' (Garin le Lorrain, 1,
      198; cf. Lachmund 1878:25; Lewent 1925:224)

Most examples from Old French show the preposition *por/pour*, although the
construction can now and then be found with temporal *à* and with *sanz/senz*
'without' and less frequently with other prepositions, of which we have an example in (17b). More or less the same situation holds for Middle French. However,
in Classical French we can find little documentary evidence, and that exclusively
with the preposition *pour*.[13] According to Lewent (1925) and Nyrop (1930), the
same construction with *pour* was still used in the nineteenth century in judicial
language.[14] This construction is still grammatical today in some diatopic varieties, in an area that extends from northeastern France almost down to the river
Loire:[15]

(18) a. Je m'   adresse à vous [pour **vous** me donner quelques
      I myself address to you   for you me to-give some
      renseignements . . .]
      information-PL
      'I apply to you in order for you to give me some information . . .' (Regional
      French, Walloon, APG; cf. Frei 1929:94, letter written by a person from Pas-
      de-Calais)

    b. ʒã   be'ty   oʒ'dy [por **no** li'ø   dõ   søl][16]
      we-have threshed today for us to-bundle of-the rye
      'We have threshed today so that we can pack the rye.' (Lorraine, dialect of
      Moncheux; cf. Franz 1920:36)

In contemporary standard French, this construction is not grammatical.

There is only one configuration in which present-day French generally allows specified subjects. This kind of construction was studied by Vinet (1985), as we see in detail in section 4.3.1.2. Consider example (19a), in which the preposed infinitive clause has the function of a conditional clause. It is structurally similar to the temporal construction in (19b), found in the documentary evidence of Middle French (Biedermann 1908:719–21; Lombard 1936:244–56; Gougenheim 1951: 176–77):

(19) a. [**Le frigidaire** tomber en panne], on aurait vraiment   MF
      the fridge   to-fall in failure one would-have really
      l' air   fin.
      the aspect fine
      'If the fridge broke down, we would really have bad luck.' (Vinet 1985:408)

    b. [Et **lui** estre venu], envoya la charette en son hostel.   MidF
      and he to-be come (he) sent the coach to his lodging
      'And after he had come he sent the coach to his lodging.' (Chron. G. de C., 51;
      cf. Biedermann 1908 and Lombard 1936:250)

Let us now consider word order. In contemporary French, in both the dialectal construction mentioned in (18) and the common structure in (19a), the subject is always preverbal. However, as can be observed in the examples in (15) and (16) of this section, the earlier stages of French show both preverbal and postverbal subjects. In contrast to what has been stated about Italian, there seems to have been hardly any restriction on the grammaticality of either position. The only detail that can be mentioned in this respect is the fact that postverbal subjects cannot be found with infinitives of transitive verbs in the material considered here, a situation that is similar to Portuguese, as we see in section 2.4. Postverbal subjects were already extremely rare from the seventeenth century onward, and in the known examples from the nineteenth century, the preverbal subject position is the only one that could be found.

A crucial difference from Italian and, as is shown later in this chapter, most other Romance languages is that the subject always seems to bear the accusative case. In Old French, we find the oblique form (cf. A. Stimming 1886; Lerch 1929:155), independently of where the subject appears:

(20) a. / La pucelle le tint l' estrier / [A descendre **le chevalier**]. /
      the girl   him held the bridle to to-get-off the knight (ACC)
      'The girl held the bridle for him in order for the knight to dismount.' (Perceval,
      13405–6, vol. 2, p. 238; cf. Meyer-Lübke 1899:511; A. Stimming 1886:555;
      Lewent 1925:223; Lerch 1929:154)

    b. Vinrent [a **cest conte**   mouvoir].
      (they) came to this count (ACC) to-move
      'They came to the count's departure.' (Esc., 157, p. 5; cf. Tobler 1921:94)

In later texts, the case cannot be determined on morphological grounds. However, the use of the third-person reflexive pronoun in examples like the following clearly shows that in Middle French the subject was still in the accusative (recall that these pronouns have no nominative forms):

(21) Il pouvoit cognoistre [soy   estre en évident péril . . .].
    he could   recognize   himself to-be in evident danger
    'He could recognize that he evidently was in danger . . .' (G. Chast., ch. 1, p. 30; cf.
    E. Stimming 1916:145)

In chapter 6, I argue that the assumption of the accusative being the only possible case for infinitival constructions in French (except for cases like those in 19) is necessary, too, on both structural and theoretical grounds.

2.3   Spanish

In the preceding two sections, it has been shown that both Italian and French show certain restrictions for the syntactic environments in which overt subjects can appear in infinitive clauses. In both languages, we find even more restrictions in the modern varieties than in the earlier stages. In Spanish, by contrast, there have always been fewer restrictions, and there are more construction types that show a specified subject (basically all the types mentioned in 1 to 8). Moreover, the data are much more homogeneous from a diachronic perspective. In (22), I present some examples for configurations that have disappeared in Modern Italian and French, or which have never been documented in those two languages, but can be found in Spanish from the Middle Ages until today. In (22a), the infinitive construction is used as a subject clause in nonimpersonal environments; in (22b), it functions as an apposition; in (22c), the infinitive construction is an attribute:

(22) a. E [affogar   omne sus fijos]   es dalles   de pequennos   OS
      and to-suffocate man   his children is to-give-them as little-ones
      et assoora grandes sennorios.
      and in-time great   possessions
      'And for a man to suffocate his children means to give them great possessions in
      their early childhood and at the right time.' (Cron., 145b43; cf. Beardsley
      1921:259)

   a'. [Irse   Maribel a Alemania] supone   que su marido se   MS
      to-go-R CL M.   to Germany presupposes that her husband R CL
      quede al   cuidado de los niños.
      remains at-the care   of the children
      'The fact that M. goes to Germany means that her husband must stay in order to
      take care of the children.' (cf. Hernanz Carbó 1982:337)

b. Las cuales (gracias) son: [conocerse   **el home** et de   qué   OS
    the which blessings are: to-know-himself the man and from which
    parte viene].
    part (he) comes
    'These (blessings) are that the human being knows himself and the place where
    he comes from.' (Cast. de D. Sancho, 88a, cf. Diez 1882:944)

b'. Lo mejor sería   [ir **yo** también].   MS
    the best would-be to-go I also
    'The best thing would be that I also go.' (cf. Hernanz Carbó 1982:343)

c. Díssolis   a la ora [de **la alma** essir]: "..."   OS
    (he) said-them at the hour of the soul to-leave
    'At the time at which the soul was leaving, he said to them: "..."' (Berceo, S.
    Mill., 299; cf. Diez 1882:946; Beardsley 1921:260)

c'. En el momento [de alzarse **el telón**] se escucha el piano ...   MS
    at the moment   of to-rise the curtain R CL hears   the piano
    'At the very moment at which the curtain rises, one hears the piano ...' (Grillo,
    61; cf. Skydsgaard 1977:710)

As in the other languages, prepositional adverbial clauses have been the most frequent configuration for the appearance of specified subjects. For the prepositions
allowed in those contexts, we find the reverse tendency of French and Italian,
where the number of prepositions was reduced in the course of time. In Spanish,
there is a continuous increase of prepositions in the documentary evidence (cf.
Mensching 1998). As Fernández Lagunilla (1987:131–32) notes, the construction
is potentially possible with all prepositions in present-day Spanish.[17]

In Old Spanish, the infinitive clauses in impersonal constructions and some
other configurations could be used either with or without the preposition *de*,[18]
and in both cases an overt subject was possible, similar to Old French but different from Italian:

(23) a. Mas ligera cosa es [meterse   **omne** a las grandes aventuras].
         more easy thing is to-put-R CL man in the great   adventures
         'It is easier for a man to join the great adventures.' (Cal. e D. *A*, 216; cf. Diez
         1882:944)

     b. Natural cosa es [*de* cobdiciar **los omnes** saber   los fechos ...]
         natural thing is *de* to-wish   the men   to-know the events
         'It is a natural thing that humans want to know the events ...' (Gen. Est., 1r)

I now turn to the position of the subject. As can be seen in example (22c),
earlier stages of Spanish allowed preverbal subjects in addition to the postverbal
position, although the latter already prevailed in Old Spanish and its frequency is
even higher in Classical Spanish. Unlike Italian, there were no restrictions in the
environments where either position occurs. Here are some Classical Spanish
examples, which show preverbal subjects in different types of infinitive clauses:

(24) a. / . . . fué fuerza / [la tierra ceder   al   mar]. /
              was force   the earth to-give-way to-the sea
              '. . . it was necessary for the earth to give way to the sea.' (Cald., HD, 1, 2100a,
              14)

      b. Yo debia   tener por cierto [tú ser anegado].
           I   must (PAST) hold for   certain you to-be drowned
           'I had to consider it as a fact that you had drowned.' (Clareo, XV, p. 121)

      c. [después de Vuestras Altezas   haber dado fin á la guerra . . .]
           after   of your   Highnesses to-have given end to the war
           'after your Highnessess had stopped the war . . .' (Colón Diario, II, 15; cf.
           Nyrop 1930:220)

From the eighteenth century onward, however, preverbal subjects no longer occur in almost any infinitival environments. The only constructions where preverbal subjects are still grammatical today are adverbial clauses (cf. Gili Gaya
1985:189; Fernández Lagunilla 1987:127,132–33).[19] These cases are characteristic for the spoken language. It is symptomatic that the following examples,
though taken from literary texts, occur in direct speech:

(25) a. No me sorprendería tener algún tío   ricacho en América, [sin
           not me would-surprise to-have some uncle rich   in A.   without
           yo saberlo].
           I   to-know-it
           'It would not surprise me if I had a rich uncle in A. without my knowing it.'
           (Belarmino, 102; cf. Skydsgaard 1977:864)

      b. Todo por culpa de cosas que   pasaron [antes de yo nacer].
           all   by guilt of things which happened before of I to-be-born
           'All that (was) due to things which happened before I was born.' (Muchachos,
           18; cf. Skydsgaard 1977:655)

This construction is not restricted to the prepositions *sin* 'without' and *con* 'with',
as claimed by Fernández Lagunilla (1987), but the documentary evidence and the
inquiry of speakers shows that it can frequently be found with *por* 'because of',
para 'for' and '*antes de* 'before', as in (25b). There are, however, some interesting restrictions, which will be discussed in chapter 6.
    A last striking difference between Spanish and Italian and French is that in the
former the case is always nominative, as can be seen in the data containing a pronominal subject in different positions (cf. 22b', 24b, and 25 above). Consider also
the following example from Old Spanish:

(26) los quales creerían   [yo no haber leido las reglas . . .]
      the which would-believe I   not to-have read the rules
      'who would believe that I had not read the rules . . .' (Santillana Prov., 23; cf. Diez
      1882:946)

This is interesting in comparison to Old Italian, in which the subject would bear the accusative case in the same configuration, as shown in 2.1.

2.4 Portuguese and Galician

A well-known fundamental difference between the languages discussed so far and the Luso-Romance varieties Portuguese and Galician is that in the latter two languages the infinitive has inflected forms that reflect agreement morphology. The inflected infinitive is an old phenomenon of the language, and it almost always shows up when the infinitive has an overt subject.[20] This is demonstrated by the following examples from various diachronic and diatopic varieties:

(27) a. [pera **seus criados** dormir*en*]   GP
      for   his   servants to-sleep-3PL
      'in order for his servants to sleep' (Devanceiros, vol. 2, doc. 40; cf. Gondar 1978:65)

  b. dizendo [ser*em*   **aquellas cousas** engano]   CP
      saying   to-be-3PL those   things   deception
      'saying that those things were due to deception' (Barros, Déc. I, III, 10, I, 238; cf. Said Ali 1971:342, 345)

  c. [pra loitar*es*   **ti** comigo]   MG
      for to-fight-2PL you with-me
      'in order for you to fight with me' (Saco y Arce 1967; Gondar 1978:52)

  d. E   Jacinto lamentava [não estar*em* ali   com ele **os janotas**   MP
      and J.   deplored   not to-be-3PL there with him the dandies
      da   cidade].
      of-the city
      'And J. deplored the fact that the dandies of the city were not there with him.'
      (Costa, Solar, 262; cf. Sten 1952:113)

Apart from this, the Portuguese and Galician facts are very similar to Spanish in terms of the types of constructions in which infinitival subjects have been grammatical until today, which are essentially the same as in Spanish.[21] For example, consider the following constructions in different prepositional environments, which are still grammatical today in all varieties of Portuguese:

(28) a. Somos ledas [*de* **tu**   padeceres   por Christo].   CP
      (we) are glad   of you (NOM) to-suffer-2SG for Christ
      'We are glad that you suffer for Christ.' (Nunes, Crest., 2, 218; cf. Said Ali 1971:342)

  b. Por Portalegre chegou aviso [*dos*   **castelhanos** haverem   CP
      at P.   arrived notice of-the Castilians   to-have-3PL
      intentado tomar   Valença].
      tried   to-conquer V.
      'At P. a notice arrived according to which the Castilians had tried to take V.'
      (Vieira Cartas, II, 154; cf. Flasche 1948:706)

    c. Porque desce o divino a cousa humana? / [Para subir o   CP
       why   lowers the divine the thing human   for to-rise the
    humano a ser   divino].
    human   to to-be[22] divine
    'Why does the divine lower the human affairs? In order for the human being to
    rise and be divine.' (Camões, Son., 198; cf. Otto 1891:383)

Portuguese and Galician also behave like Spanish in case properties. They have
always shown nominative subjects (see 28a for an example). There is only one
construction that allows the use of the accusative, already mentioned in chapter 1,
and which is limited sociolectally to some lower varieties of Brazilian Portuguese
(cf. Thomas 1969:185; Roth 1979:20, Lemos Monteiro 1994:85–86, Scotti-Rosin
1994:312a). Consider the following example, repeated from chapter 1:

(29) a. Êle trouxe um sanduíche [para **mim** comer].
       he brought a   sandwich for me to-eat
       'He brought a sandwich for me to eat.' (Thomas 1969:185)

    b. ⋆Êle trouxe um sanduíche [para comer **mim**].

This construction is limited to the preposition *para* 'for'. As demonstrated by
example (29b), the subject is always preverbal in this construction.

On the other hand, the usual construction with a nominative subject admits
postverbal subjects. An extremely striking syntactic difference, especially in
comparison to Spanish, is the high frequency of preverbal subjects, which the
reader will already have noticed in some of the examples given here. In general,
the preverbal position is preferred in Modern European and Brazilian Portuguese,
a fact that already seems to have been the case in the oldest medieval texts. In
most constructions, both positions are possible, the postverbal one being rather
marked and used for focalizing and emphasizing purposes.

Given the general preference for preverbal subjects in infinitive clauses, it is
rather surprising that there are cases in which this position is not available, and
the subject must occur after the infinitive. This is the case of infinitival complement clauses selected by epistemic and declarative verbs (see the summaries of
Raposo 1987 and Ambar 1994 in sections 4.3.2.2 and 7.2). As illustrated in (30),
this restriction did not apply in earlier stages of the language, and today preverbal
subjects sometimes appear to be more acceptable in Brazilian than in European
Portuguese:

(30) a. Creemos [a **santa trinidade** seer padre e   filho e   spiritu   GP
      (we) believe the holy trinity   to-be father and son and spirit
      santo . . .].
      holy
      'We believe that the Holy Trinity is the Father, the Son, and the Holy Spirit
      . . .' (Crônicas Breves e Memórias Avulsas de Santa Cruz de Coimbra, ch. 3,
      quoted in Maurer 1968:97)

b. ?O aluno compreendeu [**isto** ser inútil]. MP (B)
    the pupil understood   this to-be useless
    'The pupil understood that this was useless.'

In impersonal constructions, both Brazilian and Portuguese speakers prefer the preverbal position, excluding infinitive clauses that are complements of *parecer* 'to seem'. According to Raposo and Uriagereka (1990:532–34), (31b) is ungrammatical, although to speakers I consulted it seemed more or less acceptable, particularly in Brazilian Portuguese.

(31) a. Parece [serem **essas actividades** úteis para o país].
    seems to-be-3PL these activities   useful for the country
    'It seems that these activities are useful for the country.'

    b. ?Parece [**essas actividades** serem úteis para o país].

In addition, it should be noted that in European Portuguese and in Galician the preverbal subject position is possible (though not very frequently used) in infinitive constructions introduced by a determiner (cf. Gondar 1978:75–76). In contrast, the speakers of Brazilian Portuguese that I consulted did not accept the preverbal subject at all in these contexts, in conformity to what was observed by Thomas (1969:5). The following example, rejected by Brazilian speakers, is grammatical in European Portuguese:

(32) *[O **ele** ganhar as eleições] significa uma mudança radical. MP (B)
    the he to-win the elections means a   change   radical
    'The fact that he wins the elections means a radical change.'

Unlike these constructions, where the postverbal position is the better and sometimes the only grammatical option, there are cases in which the situation is the opposite. The following grammaticality facts, which hold both for European and Brazilian Portuguese, show that with an infinitive of a transitive verb the postverbal subject is less acceptable than with intransitive verbs:

(33) a. Aconteceu [*entrarem* **outras nações aqui**].
    happened to-enter-3PL other   nations here
    'It happened that other nations entered here.'

    b. ?Aconteceu [*interromperem* **eles** as comunicações].
    happened to-interrupt-3PL they the communications
    'It happened that they interrupted the communications.'

This is rather a property of the spoken language. Literary Portuguese does not reject the use of a subject following a transitive verb (see chapter 4, example 56). Furthermore, this restriction did not hold in earlier stages, as is shown by example (34) from Classical Portuguese:

(34) Entre os homens [*dominarem*   **os brancos** aos   pretos],
     among the men   to-dominate-3PL the white   ACC PART-the black
     é fôrça.
     is violence
     'Among human beings, the fact that the white dominate the black is violence.'
     (Vieira Serm., III, 133; cf. Flasche 1948:691)

Finally, it has to be pointed out that the phenomenon observed for spoken Modern Portuguese is not characteristic of infinitive clauses but is also found in finite clauses, so that it is not directly relevant to the present study. See section 6.3.1.2 for further discussion.

2.5   Other Romance varieties

2.5.1   Italo-Romance

In northern Italy none of the constructions under discussion could be found. It must be kept in mind that the historical varieties discussed in section 2.1, as well as contemporary Italian, are based on Tuscan. It is therefore not surprising that in other Central Italian varieties similar phenomena can be detected. Consider the following data from the fifteenth century, from southern Umbria and Romagna, respectively:

(35) a.   Or pensa come è   honestà [**li chierici** andare in processione
           now think how (it) is honesty   the clericals to-go   in procession
           contra la Chiesa].
           against the Church.
           'Now think how honest it is that the clericals go for procession against the
           Church.' (Testi non tosc. Qu., 10, 56, p. 27; text from Spoleto, A.D. 1419)

     b.   E   qui pare che al nomico de l· omana natura ie mostrase la
           and here seems that the enemy of the human nature him showed   the
           via spinosa . . . mostrandie la via . . . [de hogne male **lui** potere   fare].
           way thorny   showing-him the way   of every evil he can (INF) to-do
           'And here it seems that the enemy of the human nature showed him the thorny
           path, showing him the way in which he could do all sorts of evil.' (Testi non
           tosc. Qu., 118, 1, p. 144; text from Forlì, A.D. 1496).

Whereas example (35a) is similar to constructions that can be found in the earlier stages of Italian (cf. 2.1), (35b) is somewhat more interesting because this configuration, in which the infinitive clause is a prepositional complement of a noun, could not be found in the documentary evidence of (Tuscan) Old Italian. Another diverging property in this example is the preverbal subject after prepositions, no longer common in Old Italian at the end of the fifteenth century (see 6.1.1.2 for discussion).

    A clearer picture emerges from the data for southern Italo-Romance varieties.[23] In Sicilian, specified subjects in infinitive clauses are still frequent today and can even be found in the regional Italian spoken on the island (Leone 1982:137). The following examples (36a), (36b), and (36d) show a similar word order as does (35). Moreover, consider the examples in (36a), (36b), and (36c), where a specified subject co-occurs with a preposition, in contrast to (9). [24]

(36) a. Si dícinu   [di **tu**   mangiarimi, mi mangi].
        if (they) say *di* you (NOM) to-eat-me   me (you) eat
        'If they told you to eat me, then eat me!' (19th c.; Pitrè 4, 165, cf. Rohlfs
        1949:539, Maurer 1968:71)

     b. 'jiu rispar'mjavu i   mi 'soɾdi [pi **mi 'paʈɾi**ka't:arisi a 'mak:ina]
        I   saved   the my money for my father to-buy-R CL the car
        'I saved my money in order for my father to buy the car.' (Corleone, Palermo)

     c. [ri 'ʒi:ri **mi 'paʈɾi** 'sempri a 'k:j:εza] um mi 'pjatʃi
        di to-go my father always to church   not me pleases
        'The fact that my father always goes to church does not please me.' (Corleone,
        Palermo)

     d. um pɔ 'εs:iri ['**jíu** 'ʒi:ri 'kju a 'k:jeza][25]
        not can to-be I   to-go more to church
        'It is impossible that I do not go to church anymore.' (Corleone, Palermo)

The preverbal position of the subject, which can be seen in (36a), (36b), and (36d), is the most usual word order in Sicilian infinitive clauses.[26] Moreover, the postverbal position is also grammatical, as shown in (36c). Another difference from Italian is that in Sicilian the subject is always in the nominative case, even when it appears preverbally, as in example (36a), which is similar to what I demonstrated for Spanish and Portuguese. Furthermore, the examples show the use of nonauxiliary verbs. Though similar to Old Italian, this is another difference from contemporary Italian.

Another southern Italian variety in which specified subjects can be found is Old Neapolitan. It is interesting that this dialect had inflected infinitive forms, showing number and person agreement with the subject, similar to Portuguese (cf. Savj-Lopez 1900; Meier 1955; Loporcaro 1986):

(37) a. p(er) tanta pizola accaysune [de esser*enno* licenciati **li Greci**]
        for   such small occasion of to-be-3PL dismissed the Greek
        'for that small occasion of the Greeks' being dismissed' (Cronaca di Partenope,
        5r, 1–3, quoted by Loporcaro 1986:202)

     b. vedendo li Grieci [**tanta   copia de cavalieri armati** esser*no*
        seeing the Greek so-much crowd of knights   armed   to-be-3PL
        venuti . . .]
        come
        'the Greek, seeing that such a great crowd of armed knights had come . . .'
        (Cronaca di Partenope, 58v, 23–24, quoted by Loporcaro 1986:203)

c. Tenemo,   secundo   la santa fè catholica, [essere*no* stati non
(we) consider according-to the holy faith catholic   to-be-3PL been not
homicidi **li occidituri**].
murderers the doomed
'We consider, according to the Holy Catholic Faith, that the doomed men are
not murderers.' (Del Tuppo Lett. D.C.; quoted by Savj-Lopez 1900:502 and
Meier 1955:274)

d. Et era a loro necessario donare la terra a lo inimico, [et de po
and was to them necessary to-give the land to the enemy   and then
loro essere*no* **tucti** morte].
they to-be-3PL all   dead
'And it was necessary that they gave the land to the enemy and that then they
were all killed.' (Del Tuppo Fab., XXX, quoted by Savj-Lopez 1900:502 and
Meier 1955:275)

These examples indicate that the infinitival subject could show up in various
configurations. The subject occurs either preverbally or postverbally. Because of
the small number of known examples, we cannot identify the case of the subject,
although the parallel to Portuguese might suggest that it is nominative.

Let us finally turn to Sardinian. As in the other languages discussed so far,
infinitive clauses with specified subjects have been possible since the earliest
texts, as can be seen in the following examples from Old Campidanian and Old
Logudorese, respectively:

(38) a. pro dari   lli **deus et Sanctu Jorgi** sanidadi assa filia
for to-give her God and St.   George health   to-the daughter
'in order for God and St. George to give health to the daughter' (CVC, VIII,
401)

b. pro aver   inde **su Pisscopatu** pro su populo sa iustithia
for to-have hence the bishopric   for the people the justice
'so that henceforth the bishopric would meet out justice to the people' (DV, II,
420)

This construction, in which the prepositional infinitive clause functions as an
adverbial, is still frequent today with various prepositions (cf. Pittau 1972:93;
Blasco Ferrer 1986:159; Jones 1992, 1993; Mensching 1994:91). Consider the
following data from Nuorese and Logudorese:

(39) a. At   segadu sos pratos [pro non mandigare*(s)* **tue**].
(he) has broken the plates   for not to-eat(-2SG)   you (NOM)
'He broke the plates in order for you not to eat.' (cf. Blasco Ferrer 1986)

b. Isetta [fintzas de andàre*(po)* **deo**].
wait   until   of to-go(-1SG) I
'Wait until I go.' (cf. Pittau 1972:93; Mensching 1994:91)

c. Su postinu est colatu [prima de arrivare **jeo**].
the postman is passed before of to-arrive I
'The postman passed before I arrived.' (cf. Jones 1992:295)

Apart from this, Sardinian allows specified subjects in all the major configurations presented in (1) to (8) at the beginning of this chapter, with the exception of determined infinitive constructions (cf. Jones 1993:284–85). The fact that the constructions under discussion are usually found in prepositional contexts (even subject clauses are introduced by the preposition *a*) is due to a general property of Sardinian infinitive clauses (cf. Jones 1993:260–70, Mensching 1994:42, 1996), and thus not restricted to the occurrence of specified subjects.

As the data show, the subject is always in the nominative case and postverbal, a preverbal subject being completely excluded (see the grammaticality facts mentioned in Jones 1992:299). As can be seen from the examples, some Logudorese and Nuorese varieties have inflected infinitive forms, although they are not obligatory (cf. Wagner 1938–39; Pittau 1972:93ff; Blasco Ferrer 1986:159, Jones 1992, 1993; Mensching 1994:91).

2.5.2 Occitan

Although infinitive constructions with specified subjects do not appear as often in the Old Occitan documents as in Old and Middle French (cf. Dittes 1903 and Lewent 1925), there is enough evidence for the existence of constructions that are similar to the Old French data. The following examples show overt subjects in infinitival subject, object, and adverbial clauses:

(40) a. aquel que sent [**lo rey** esser son frayre carnal]
     that who feels the king to-be his brother carnal
     'the one who feels that the king is his carnal brother' (Tratt. penit., Appel 1930:no. 120, 10f.; cf. Dittes 1903:15)

   b. Plus leugiera cauza es [passar **lo camel** per   lo caus dell' agulha]
     more easy   thing is to-pass the camel through the eye of-the needle
     quel   ric intrar el regne de dieu.
     than-the rich to-enter the kingdom of God
     'It is easier for a camel to go through the eye of a needle, than for a rich man to enter into the kingdom of God.' (GO, 58b; cf. Diez 1882:944; Lerch 1929:154)

   c. L'agres fuy [al   **dous** parer].
     the acid flees on-the sweet to-appear
     'Acid flees when sweetness appears.' (Raimb. Vaqu., 41,21, cf. Dittes 1903:3; Lewent 1925:225)

The subject is usually located to the left of the verb, but the postverbal position was also possible, as (40b) shows.[27] The case of the subject, when this can be recognized, is always the accusative.

Examples similar to (40a) are found now and again in the literature of the nineteenth century. According to Ronjat (1937:595), this is to be considered an exceptional literary device. However, Camproux (1958), who examined Gévaudanais, a northern variety of Languedocian, claims that this type of construction is extremely popular.[28] Some of his examples, which have recently been confirmed by Sauzet (1989) for other Languedocian varieties as well, are shown in (41); see Camproux (1958:273–83):

(41) a. Pensabion   [**las bachos** manja soun dadoul].
       (they) thought the cows   to-eat their feed
       'They thought that the cows were eating their feed.'

   b. Es arribat [**las trufos** si   peri   tout am un cop].
      is happened the jugs   R CL to break all   with one blow
      'It happened that the jugs broke at one blow.'

   c. Ieu trabalha [per **elo** s'   amusa].
      I   work   for her R CL to-amuse
      'I work for her to amuse herself.'

The data show essentially the same configurations as the Old Occitan examples in (40).[29] The subject is always preverbal. Note that the case of the subject cannot be determined because personal pronouns have the same form for the nominative and the accusative case (Alibèrt 1976:61–63). As for other Occitan varieties, a construction similar to (41c) is mentioned by Miremont (1976) for Limousin, which is geographically near the zone studied by Camproux (1958).

   Finally, Ronjat (1937:595) presents some data from Gascon, which is usually considered to be a variety of Occitan. All his examples are adverbial clauses with prepositions:

(42) a. sense l' aué   **digun** bist
       without him to-have anybody seen
       'without anybody having seen him' (Armagnac; BT, 96, 2, 3)

   b. [en dura   toustems **era guerro**] e' [n presenta-s   **d' autes**
      in to-last still   the war   and in to-present-R CL of other
      dificultats . . .]
      difficulties
      'by the fact that the war still went on and that other difficulties . . . appeared'
      (Luchon; BDM, 1917, 1)

As can be seen from these data, the subject is postverbal in Gascon, which can thus be said to clearly behave distinctly from Occitan in a strict sense, whereas it seems to be close to the Iberian Peninsula languages, particularly to Spanish, as well as to Catalan, as we see immediately.

2.5.3   Catalan

As I demonstrated in Mensching (1999), Old Catalan shows a picture similar to Old Spanish for the construction types, the position of the subject, and case properties:

(43) a. que el ballester   dega primer provar [**la sageta** ésser sua]
        that the crossbowman must first   to-prove the arrow   to-be his
        'that the crossbowman must first prove that the arrow is his one' (Evast, 29)

    b. Molt gran argument es [**natura** jutjar   tant grans coses].
        very great argument is nature to-judge so great things
        'It is a very important argument that nature judges about so great things.'
        (Bernat Metge, 584; quoted by Par 1923:297)

    c. Fortuna alre no em consent [per ésser-me **vós** marit   e   senyor].
        fate   other not me consents for to-be me you husband and lord
        'Fate does not allow me anything else, because you are my husband and lord.'
        (Tirant lo Blanch, 29)

    d. [Al   venir **los homines** de   Vilafranca] albe(r)garen als   Pujals.
        On-the to-come the men   from V.   (they) stayed   at-the P.
        'When the men from V. came, they stayed at the P.' (Martí, 27; cf. Breilmann-
        Massing 1990:145–55)

As the examples show, the subject is preverbal or postverbal, and as far as this
can be judged, it is always nominative (see Mensching 1999). Thus, Old Catalan
behaves comparably to the other Ibero-Romance languages, Spanish and Portuguese.

In Modern Catalan, the acceptability of specified subjects in infinitive clauses
seems to be slightly less than for Spanish, but the general situation for word order
is almost identical to Spanish, the postverbal subject usually being the only grammatical option (Badia i Margarit 1962:450; Hualde 1992:64; Brumme 1997:378;
Mensching 1999). However, the preverbal position of the subject is allowed in
adverbial infinitive clauses with some prepositions (similar to Spanish) and in
infinitive clauses that function as an apposition:

(44) a. No em sorprendria   tenir   algun oncle ric a l' Amèrica [sense
        not me would-surprise to-have some uncle rich in the A.   without
        jo saber-   ho].
        I to-know it.
        'It would not surprise me to have a rich uncle in America without knowing it.'

    b. Això seria   increïble, [**el meu marit**   trobar feina a Grècia]!
        this would-be unbelievable the my husband to-find work in Greece
        'For my husband to find work in Greece, that would be unbelievable!'

In these cases, this is the preferred word order, the postverbal subject being
slightly less acceptable. For further data, see Mensching (1999).

2.5.4 Romanian

Meyer-Lübke (1899:§388) mentioned a few biblical passages from one of the
oldest literary Romanian documents, *Codicele Voronețean*, in which an A.c.I.
construction in complement clauses (the type in example 2a) appears. As shown
in Mensching and Popovici (1997), these are mere word-by-word translations of

the Old Church Slavonic Bible. However, we could find some isolated examples, apparently authentic, chiefly from the sixteenth and seventeenth centuries, with preverbal subjects in infinitive clauses selected by impersonal predicates and declarative and epistemic verbs. For the latter, consider example (45), which is parallel to the construction mentioned for the earlier phases of the other Romance languages and for contemporary Occitan:

(45) Iară unii grăescŭ [cămila   a fi funea   ceaia mai groasă ce e la
     but   some say   camel-the to be rope-the the   most thick   that is in
     corabie].
     sailing-vessel
     'But some say that the camel is the thickest rope that can be found on a sailing ves-
     sel.' (Coresi, Carte cu învățătură; quoted by Diaconescu 1977:121)

This kind of construction seems to have been extremely rare, however. Among the few data gathered and presented in Mensching and Popovici (1997), no examples that would allow the determination of the case of preverbal subjects could be found.

    In contrast, postverbal subjects are regularly seen in the whole documentary evidence of the history of Romanian, usually in infinitival subject clauses selected by impersonal predicates and adverbial clauses introduced by prepositions and less frequently in other prepositional contexts. Here are some examples for the types mentioned, which are still accepted today:

(46) a. E o absurditate [a se   bate **cineva** pentru ochii   unei   actrițe].
         is a absurdity   to R CL fight someone for   eyes-the a (GEN) actress (GEN)
         'It is absurd for someone to have a fight for the eyes of an actress.' (Negruzzi, I,
         211; cf. GLR 1966:I, 227)

     b. [Înainte de a veni **zăpada**] a   bătut un vânt puternic.
         before   of to come snow-the has beaten a wind   terrible
         'Before the snow came a terrible wind was blowing.'

     c. Vine vremea [de a pricepe   **omul**   ce- i bine și ce- i rău].
         comes time-the of to understand man-the   what is good and what is bad
         'The time will come when the human beings will understand what is good and
         what is bad.' (Creangă, A. 35; cf. GLR 1966:I, 227)

As shown by Motapanyane (1988) and Dobrovie-Sorin (1994), the subject is always in the nominative case. Preverbal subjects are entirely excluded, as illustrated in (47):

(47) *[Înainte de **zăpada** a veni] a bătut un vânt puternic.

The situation of Romanian is somewhat special because in almost all environments the subjunctive has thrust aside the infinitive. Where it is still possible, it is usually stylistically marked. Thus, speakers accept examples like (46a) and (46c) less readily than the type represented in (46b) because, among the constructions mentioned, only the latter is still in use to a certain degree (cf. Mayerthaler et al. 1993). Generally, it seems that whenever speakers accept an infinitive construction, they also accept the fact that it may have a specified subject.

2.6   Summary

In this chapter I present the most important data from old and modern Romance languages. I show that almost all Romance languages license specified subjects in infinitive clauses (or did so in the past) in a considerable number of configurations other than causative constructions. The cross-linguistic variation for the case and the position of infinitival subjects, roughly characterized in chapter 1, is presented in a detailed fashion. Whereas the most usual Romance pattern is the word order infinitive + NP_{subj}, where the subject bears a nominative case, some varieties allow preverbal subjects and/or subjects marked as accusative case.

3

Foundations of Romance Syntax

In this chapter, I present some basic assumptions of generative grammar that will be crucial for the explanation of specified subjects in infinitive clauses in the following chapters. Most of the following discussion is devoted to a review of the state of the art in the field of Romance syntax. Many of the principles discussed in this chapter are reexamined and partially modified in the course of this book in the light of the infinitive constructions at issue. In this chapter, I concentrate on those assumptions that were developed in the principles and parameters (P&P) theory originally proposed by Chomsky (1981, 1986a), but I emphasize the theoretical innovations of the late 1980s and early 1990s. Some points of the theoretical background outlined here are particularly relevant for the approach adopted in chapter 6. Some differences concerning the minimalist program (Chomsky 1992 and seqq.) are mentioned in this chapter, but a detailed discussion is postponed until chapter 7, in which I outline a minimalist approach to account for our data.

The chapter is organized as follows: in section 3.1, I discuss syntactic structure, with special emphasis on the basic approaches toward clause structure in the Romance languages. The second part of this chapter (3.2) concerns some essential points of case theory. This part may be considered the core of the chapter because a discussion of case-assigning mechanisms, especially for the nominative case, is needed for understanding the following chapters, which concentrate on how specified subjects of infinitives are licensed. Section 3.3 focuses on some important points concerning the analysis of Romance infinitive constructions. However, the state of the art for specified subjects in infinitive clauses is not discussed here because chapter 4 is devoted exclusively to this topic.

3.1   Basic assumptions

3.1.1   Clause structure and movement

Throughout this book, I assume that the structure of finite and nonfinite clauses in Romance languages is in conformity with the Split-Infl hypothesis (Chomsky 1989; Pollock 1989), following the ordering of categories proposed by Belletti (1990), in which AgrP dominates TP and TP dominates VP. This order has been borne out for Romance languages and has been prevailing in the literature (cf. Belletti 1990:27–28; Haegeman 1994:598–602), although it has to be noted that this is probably a simplified structure: there is considerable evidence for claiming that at least one further category, probably AgrO (object agreement, introduced by Chomsky 1989), is needed to account for the syntax of Romance languages.[1] In chapters 5 and 6, I use the abbreviated structure because AgrO is largely irrelevant for the phenomena to be discussed within nonminimalist principles and parameters theory. However, AgrO is included and applied to our data in the minimalist account in chapter 7. Unless stated otherwise, I use the label Agr as an abbreviation for AgrS.[2]

I also assume that the subject of a clause is base-generated inside VP, more precisely, in its specifier position. One of the original arguments for this assumption, namely, that quantifiers can surface either inside VP or in AgrP, with the quantified subject remaining in VP (Sportiche 1988b; Haegeman 1994:530), has been shown to hold in most Romance languages, for example, by Fontana (1993: 87) for Spanish, Belletti (1990:67–70) for Italian, Motapanyane (1988:87) for Romanian, and Mensching (1996) for Sardinian. The relationship between nominative case assignment and VS(O) structures, which is discussed in section 3.2, contains another strong argument in favor of this assumption. In the course of my analysis of infinitive constructions, the mechanisms for licensing specified subjects examined in chapters 5 to 7 provide considerable additional evidence for the claim that the subject is base-generated inside VP. I usually assume that its position is at the left-hand side of VP. As I demonstrate in chapters 5 and 6, this property is suggested by the data. This point of view coincides with Kayne's claim that "specifier-head-complement, and not the reverse, is the only order available to the subcomponents of a phrase" (1994:36).[3]

As far as verb movement is concerned, the most usual pattern in the Romance languages is illustrated in the following simplified structure of a finite clause in Italian:

(1)

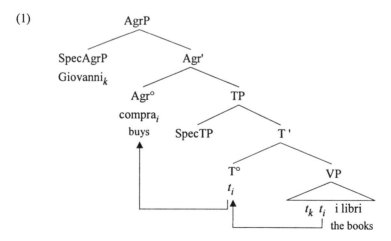

As illustrated, the finite verb moves from its base position to T° and then up to Agr°, where it picks up the information about inflectional morphology through incorporation. Moreover, for the discussion of Romance clause structure both in this chapter and throughout the book, Pollock's (1989) proposal for NegP, situated between AgrP and TP, according to Belletti (1990), is relevant (see Haegeman 1995 and Rowlett 1998 for further discussion). Neg° is a cliticlike element, which usually moves to Agr°, where it is incorporated together with other elements such as verbs or clitics.[4] These assumptions make it possible to capture several cross-linguistic differences within the Romance languages, as is illustrated by the following examples:

(2) a. Copilul n -o mai caută des pe   maică-sa.   MR
         child-the not her more seeks often ACC. PART mother his
         'The child does not often search for his mother any longer.'

     b. L' enfant ne cherche plus souvent sa mère.   MF
         the child not seeks   more often   his mother
         'The child does not often search for his mother any longer.'

According to Motapanyane (1988:78), from whom these examples are taken, V° only moves up to T° in Romanian, in contrast to French and other Romance languages, where it moves on to Agr° (Pollock 1989; Belletti 1990):

(3) a. [$_{AgrP}$ Copilul$_i$ n-o$_k$ [$_{NegP}$ t_k mai [$_{TP}$ caută$_j$ [$_{VP}$ des t_i t_j pe maică-sa]]]].

     b. [$_{AgrP}$ L'enfant$_i$ ne$_k$ cherche$_j$ [$_{NegP}$ t_k plus [$_{TP}$ t_j [$_{VP}$ souvent t_i t_j sa mère]]]].

Moreover, adverbs are also important indicators for movement. Compare the following:

(4) a. ⋆Jean souvent vient.   a'. Jean vient souvent.   MF
     b. ⋆Gianni spesso viene.   b'. Gianni viene spesso.   MI
     c. John often comes.   c'. ⋆John comes often.   ME

Following Pollock (1989), I assume that VP-modifying adverbs like *souvent/ spesso/often* are located in a position that is left-adjoined to VP in examples like these. The cross-linguistic diversity in the word order observed in the examples can thus be explained by postulating a difference in the behavior of V°: in the Romance languages, the finite verb moves out of VP, as shown in (5), whereas it remains in its base position in English.

(5) Jean vient$_i$ [$_{VP}$ souvent t_i]

According to Rohrbacher (1994:28), European Portuguese behaves like French, Italian, and also Spanish, whereas Brazilian Portuguese optionally allows the English structure with V° in situ, as illustrated in (6b):

(6) a. Ninguém telefonou provavelmente.   MP (E/B)
         nobody   telephoned probably

     b. Ninguém provavelmente telefonou.   MP (B)
         nobody   probably   telephoned

More arguments for the Split-Infl hypothesis and for the analysis of NegP and of adverbs are found in section 3.3. The data from Romance infinitive constructions discussed in this book provide further evidence for these assumptions, as is shown in chapters 5 to 7. Recently, Cinque (1999) offered a more thorough examination of adverbs from a cross-linguistic perspective. He assumes numerous functional categories above VP, which appear in a fixed order, identical in all languages. Adverbs are located in the specifiers of functional categories, and their exact location depends on the type of the adverb. Cross-linguistic differences in word order for adverbs are explained exclusively by a different range of verb movement, in the spirit of Pollock (1989). I generally do not assume so many functional categories here, but I sometimes return to Cinque's theories for adverbs.

For the rest, unless stated otherwise, I follow standard assumptions that can be found in introductory works like Haegeman (1994) and, with particular reference to Romance languages, Müller and Riemer (1998). Some important points that are taken into consideration here are the empty category principle (ECP),[5] the DP analysis (Abney 1987; see also Brame 1982; Szabolcsi 1983, 1987; Vater 1990), incorporation (Baker 1988), and relativized minimality (Rizzi 1990a),[6] although it must be noted that some of these principles are modified or even abolished in the minimalist approach presented in chapter 7.

In the following sections, I discuss some characteristic properties of Romance languages, most of which are crucial for the analysis of specified subjects.

3.1.2   Some properties of CP and AgrP

In the nonminimalist part of this book, particularly in chapter 6, I claim that government, together with Rizzi's (1990a) relativized minimality, is able to account for some interesting cross-linguistic differences concerning infinitival CPs. I argue that the assumption that C° has language-specific properties has considerable explanatory power. Let me illustrate this point in a quite simplified way, using the following data with finite constructions:

(7) a. ¿Quién crees   [que venderá el libro]?   MS
         who (you) think that will-sell the book
         'Who do you think will sell the book?'

     b. Chi credi [che venderà il libro]?   MI
     c. Cine crezi [că vinde cartea]?   MR
     d. ★Qui crois-tu [que vendra le livre]?   MF
     e. ★Who do you think [that will sell the book]?   ME
     f. ★Wer glaubst du [daß das Buch verkaufen wird]?   MGe

For the Spanish example in (7a), the simplified structure in (8) can be assumed:

(8) Quien$_i$ crees [$_{CP}$ t_i que [$_{AgrP}$ t_i venderá$_j$ [t_i t_j el libro]]]?

As shown by the data in (7), this movement is also possible in Italian and in Romanian but not in French, English, and German. The problem seems to be the complementizer (observe that 7 is grammatical in English, French, and German when *that* is not present). According to one of the components of Rizzi's (1990a: 32) conjunctive ECP, the trace of the DP extracted to the main clause must be properly head-governed. In the Spanish example above, we must assume that this is the case since movement has applied, so we assume that t_i in SpecAgrP is governed by C° (*que*), whereas the trace t_j in SpecCP is governed by V° (*crees*). How can the ungrammaticality in other languages be explained? According to Rizzi (1990a:6), only heads of certain categories are governors, namely, A, N, P, V, T, and Agr. As a first approach to solving our problem, we can assume that, in addition to these elements, C° is a governor in Spanish, Italian, and Romanian but not in French, English, and German. For the latter group of languages, we must still prohibit V° from governing the trace in SpecAgrP. This is achieved by the minimality condition, which states that there must not be any c-commanding X° element between the supposed governor (here: V°) and the governed element (here: t_i in SpecAgrP), although the intervening c-commanding element does not have to belong to the class of governors. Such an X° element is a "potential governor"[7] according to Rizzi (1990a:7). For our purpose, we could thus assume the following distribution:

(9) a.   ¿Quién$_i$ ... [$_{V°}$ crees [t_i [$_{C°}$ que] t_i [venderá el libro]]]?   MS
                       | |
                  governor   governor

b. *Qui$_i$ ... [$_{V°}$ crois-tu [t_i [$_{C°}$ que] [vendra le livre]]]?   MF
                   | |
              governor   ~~governor~~

C° is not a governor in French, but it is a potential governor, so government by V° is excluded. I do not pursue this issue here any further. What I want to illustrate is that the governing capacity of heads may be considered a language-specific property. In chapter 6, I use a similar account to explain some case assignment and movement processes in Romance infinitive clauses. This is in conformity with the following observation made by Rizzi (1990a:60): "C° is, in many languages, inert for government but sufficient to block government by a higher governor under Minimality."

Some further properties of C° are relevant for our discussion. Rizzi (1990a: 51–60) argues that C° can contain an agreement feature, which I call [+Agr] throughout this book. This can be seen in some languages on the evidence of overt agreement morphology on complementizers (see, e.g., Bayer 1984), and further support for this claim comes from a number of languages in which an overt C° is modified when *wh* movement to SpecCP takes place in such a way that C° agrees with the *wh* element.[8] For Romance languages, Rizzi (1990a:56) argues that this is the case in constructions of the following type, which are grammatical for some speakers of French (cf. Pesetsky 1982):

(10) l' homme [que   je crois [*qui* viendra]].
     the man   whom I think   that will-come
     'the man who I think will come'

The selection of *qui* instead of the usual conjunction *que* is interpreted here as agreement between the *wh*-moved subject and C°[+Agr]:[9]

(11) L'homme que$_i$ je crois

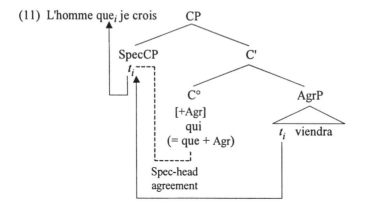

I return to this point concerning infinitive constructions in the next chapter; in chapter 6 I present further evidence from infinitive clauses, which leads to a slight modification of Rizzi's ideas about [+Agr] in C°.

I now turn to SpecCP. In the Romance languages, too, one of the main functions of SpecCP is to serve as a landing site for *wh* elements. Consider the following examples:

(12) a. *Qué* compras?   a'. *⋆Libros* compras?   MS
        what (you) buy   books (you) buy
        'What do you buy?'   'Is it books you buy?'

    b. *Cosa* compri?   b'. *⋆Libri* compri?   MI
    c. *Qu'*achètes-tu?   c'. *⋆Des livres* achètes-tu?   MF
    d. *Itte* comporas?   d'. *Libros* comporas?   Sard

Whereas Spanish, Italian, and French allow only for constituents inherently possessing *wh* features to appear in SpecCP, Sardinian licenses the movement of other elements to this position.[10] Another kind of fronting can be found in the Old Romance languages. Consider the following example from Old French:

(13) *Quatre saietes* ot li bers au   costé.
     four   boats   had the baron at-the side.
     'The baron had four boats at his side.' (Charroi de Nîmes, 1, 20; quoted by Roberts 1993:85)

To follow the argument, it is important to keep in mind that in German, and in other Germanic languages, the properties of CP are held responsible for the fol-

lowing complementary distribution of word order in main clauses and subordinate clauses:

(14) a. Ich fahre nach Hause.
         I go   to   home

     a'. *daß ich fahre nach Hause
             that I go   to   home

     b. *Ich nach Hause fahre.
          I   to   home go

     b'. daß ich nach Hause fahre
            that I to   home go

     c. Nach Hause fahre ich.
          to   home go   I

     c'. *daß nach Hause fahre ich
            that to   home go   I

Given the assumption that German is a verb-final language, these data can be
accounted for by assuming that C° is not permitted to remain empty. In the main
clause, this condition is fulfilled by verb movement to C°, as in (14a). In the
subordinate clause (14b'), C° is occupied by the complementizer *daß*, and the
verb remains in Agr°, which is clause-final in German. If C° is occupied by a
verb, then SpecCP is not supposed to remain empty either, so that the subject or
some topicalized nonsubject constituent will be found there (V2 effect), as in
(14a) and (14c). These properties of German can partially be interpreted by
claiming that the subject is moved to SpecCP in order to be case-marked because
in certain configurations C° is the functional head that contains the feature responsible for nominative assignment (see N. Müller 1993:71–81, Roberts
1993:52–64, and Wilder 1995).[11] Although SpecCP is an A-position in this case,
in other cases, such as those involving *wh* movement or the topicalization in
(14c), it behaves as an A'-position, so that SpecCP can be said to have a dual
status (cf. Taraldsen 1986; N. Müller 1993:49–56, 71–81) in German.

Let us now return to the French example in (13). Because of the V2 effect,
Adams (1987) interpreted such constructions as being parallel to the German
structure, assuming that the topicalized complement *quatre saietes* is located in
SpecCP, the verb *ot* in C°, and the subject in SpecAgrP. The problem is, however, that the V2 phenomenon can also be found in subordinate clauses, which is
excluded in German, in accordance with the mechanisms already outlined:

(15) *quant* a aus est li rois venus
         when to them is the king come
         'when the king came to them' (Chrétien de Troyes, 573; quoted by Dupuis 1989)

For this reason, Adams (1988) and Dupuis (1989) proposed an alternative analysis, which can roughly be summarized in the following way: in Old French,
SpecAgrP was accessible either to a subject or to a fronted nonsubject constituent; in other words, it had a dual status, like SpecCP in German, functioning both
as an A-position and an A'-position. They therefore assumed the structure of (15)
to be roughly as represented in (16), similar to Diesing's (1990) analysis of word
order in Yiddish:

(16)

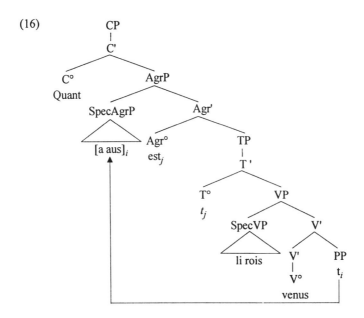

According to Roberts (1993), the same phenomenon can be explained by assuming Agr recursion. The difference is that instead of assuming one and the same position both for A-moved and for A'-moved constituents, Agr recursion provides various landing sites inside AgrP. This obviously has the advantage of being able to explain cases in which no V2 phenomenon is observed (which can be found, according to the documentary evidence), although there is a topicalized constituent. The basic approach, however, is similar to the assumption of a dual status of SpecAgrP, the important point being that in Old French AgrP was accessible both to A-movement and to A'-movement. Since the exact nature of the mechanism is not important for our purposes, for reasons of simplicity I do not consider Agr recursion here.

This property of SpecAgrP was not restricted to Old French but seems to be a general property of the older stages of most Romance languages. Fontana (1993) uses a similar explanation to account for the Old Spanish word order in examples like (17), and, as I claimed in Mensching (1999), the same holds for Old Catalan. The data presented in (18) and (19) show the same properties for Old Italian and Galician-Portuguese, respectively:[12]

(17) a. *Esto* he   yo en debdo.
      this have I in debt
      'This is what I owe.' (Cid, 225)

   b. ca   *çerca* viene el plazo[13]
      because near   comes the deadline
      'because the deadline is approaching' (Cid, 212)

   c. quando *esto* entendio pharaon
      when   this heard   Pharaoh
      'when the Pharaoh heard this' (Gen. Est., 48r)

(18) a. *Questo* tenne   lo re   a   grande maraviglia.
     this   considered the king as great   miracle
     'The king considered this a great miracle.' (Novellino, 7)

     b. E   *tutte queste cose*   fece Dio nostro padre.
     and all   these   things did God our   father
     'And God our father did all these things.' (Bestiario, 19)

     c. ciò che *di voi* adussemi Ser Monaldo.
     this that of you told-me   S.   M.
     'the things that S. M. told me about you' (Guitt., 33, 3)

(19) *Este gloriosio castello* achou o   rrey . . . assy prazivell e   deleitoso.
     this glorious   fortress   found the king   so   pleasant and delightful
     'The king found this glorious fortress so pleasant and delightful.' (Textos arcaicos,
     47; cf. Huber 1933:254)

In chapters 5 to 7, I support the assumption on the A'-bar properties of SpecAgrP in the Old Romance languages with further arguments.

3.1.3 Clitics

Romance clitics are one of the most widely discussed phenomena in generative grammar of the Romance languages. In a few cases, the behavior of clitics is included in the discussion of the structure of infinitive constructions, so that some basic remarks on their interpretation are necessary. The question of clitics cannot be discussed at length here, so I concentrate on some important points. I start by comparing the following examples from Italian and French:

(20) a. Non *lo* vedo più.   a'. per non veder*lo* più
     Not   it (I) see more   for   not   to-see-it more
     'I do not see it anymore.'   'in order not to see it anymore'

     b. Je ne *le* vois plus.   b'. pour ne plus *le* voir
     I   not it see   more   for   not more it to-see
     'I do not see it anymore.'   'in order not to see it anymore'

According to Kayne (1991), T° is empty in infinitive clauses, and the infinitival inflectional ending is generated in a special inflectional head (Infn), which projects a phrase (InfnP) located between TP and VP. By Kayne's account, Italian clitics are base-generated adjoined to T°. Italian infinitives first move to Infn° and then further up, passing by the clitic in T°, which remains in its place, so that the enclitic structure in (20a') is produced. Still assuming that clitics are base-generated adjoined to T°, Kayne states that the proclitic position in finite clauses like (20a) can be predicted, given that InfnP is absent and the verb moves to T° instead. This will also hold for French finite clauses like (20b). Since the clitic is incorporated into T°, it will move together with the verb on its way up to Agr°. In French infinitive clauses, the situation is different. Here, Kayne argues, clitics are base-generated adjoined to Infn°, the final landing site of the infinitive, so that the proclitic position follows. Interpreting Kayne's InfnP as Chomsky's AgrOP, we see that this will yield the following structure for French infinitive clauses, according to Hegarty (1993), as quoted in Rohrbacher (1994:245):[14]

(21)

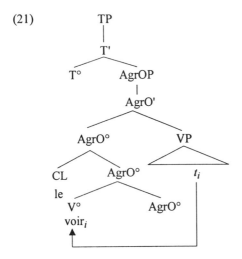

A problem in this account is that in examples like (20) the clitic is the direct object of the verb, so that it must be assumed that it is base-generated in the complement position of the verb.[15] This is not a real problem, since it can be claimed that the base positions assumed here are in reality derived positions. As an alternative solution, the following structure, taken from Rolshoven et al. (1998) is proposed:

(22)

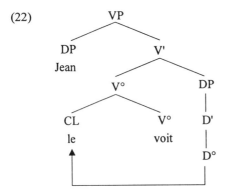

Here, the clitics are adjoined to V° in its base position, so that the verb will al-ways move together with the clitic, according to the type of verb movement, which depends on language-specific settings. In this model, it is claimed that in Italian and Spanish, nonfinite V° does not allow the incorporation of clitics. Yet, they have to cliticize onto some node, so it is assumed that they are incorporated into AgrO° or T°, so that V°[–finite] will left-adjoin to the AgrO°/T° + clitic complex, which yields the postverbal clitic position.[16]

It has to be noted, however, that not all clitics are generated as complements of verbs. Adverbial clitics like French *ne* and *y* are adjuncts, whereas the clitics in the so-called reflexive passive construction (Italian *si parla* 'is spoken') are to be interpreted as passive markers (the question of where they are generated is left open here). In the case of the so-called pronominal verbs (Italian *andarsene* 'to go away'), the clitics come from the lexicon together with the verb itself. Moreover, I consider clitic-doubling phenomena (see the Romanian example in 3a) as marking of object agreement (cf. Kaiser 1992).

Further comments about clitics are made at various points later in this book, especially for the earlier stages of Romance languages (see 5.2.1.2, 5.2.2.2, 5.2.3.2, and 6.4.1.1).

3.2 Case theory: Principles of nominative case assignment

3.2.1 Foundations

It has been a common assumption that in the Romance languages transitive verbs and prepositions assign the accusative case, whereas finite inflection I°[+finite] assigns the nominative case, presumably in a similar way to English.[17] Roughly speaking, until the end of the 1980s, case marking was usually considered to take place exclusively in government configurations. A definition of government that is based on strict c-command can account for accusative assignment, as is illustrated in the following Spanish examples:

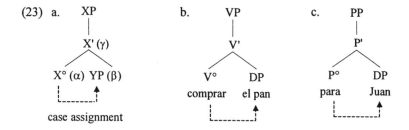

Given the assumption that the subject of a clause is base-generated in the specifier position of VP, the same mechanism can be applied to postverbal subjects in Romance languages, as was assumed by many scholars, for example, E. Bonet (1989) for Catalan; Contreras (1991) and Fontana (1993) for Spanish; Cresti (1990), Saccon (1992), and Roberts (1993, 1994) for Italian; Dobrovie-Sorin (1994) and Motapanyane (1988, 1994) for Romanian; and Mensching (1996) for Sardinian. Thus, a Spanish sentence like (24a) can be assigned the simplified structure in (24b):[18]

(24) a. Compró Juan una casa.
      bought J.   a   house
      'J. bought a house.'

b.

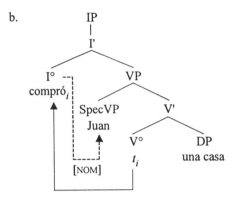

Further support for the idea that postverbal subjects can remain in their base position is given by Cinque (1999); see also section 5.4 in this book.

In contrast, case assignment to preverbal subjects, which are located in the specifier of IP in this simplified structure, cannot be accounted for under the strict c-command condition, according to which the first branching node of the governor must dominate the governed element. Traditionally, this problem was avoided by extending the government relationship to include SpecIP in the governing domain of I°. This was usually achieved by assuming m-command, so that it was not the first branching node but the first maximal projection that had to dominate the governed element (cf. Haegeman 1994:135–38). An alternative solution to the problem was proposed in Chomsky (1981:172):

> While assignment of nominative Case under government by AGR is natural for English on the assumption that the base structure is NP-INFL-VP, it may be that this should be regarded as a special case, and that the general property is that nominative is assigned as a concomitant of agreement (i.e. the NP-Agr relation), which may or may not involve government.

It was not before the end of the 1980s that such an account was generally accepted. After works like Sportiche (1988a) and Koopman and Sportiche (1988, 1991), it is now usually assumed that case assignment to preverbal subjects is not accomplished by government but through a specifier-head relationship that holds between the nominative assigner I°[+finite] and the subject DP (*Spec-head agreement*):

(25) Case assignment by Spec-head agreement

> Let H be a Case assigning head. Then, if it is a Case assigner by agreement, it may assign Case to an NP in its specifier position, as a reflex of the general process of specifier-head agreement. (Koopman and Sportiche 1991:229)

I therefore assume that m-command is not necessary for case theory and that government can be reduced to strict c-command, in conformity with Sportiche
(1988a) and Roberts (1993).[19]

Returning to the assumption that there are two case-assigning mechanisms, an
interesting point is that Koopman and Sportiche (1991:231) assume a parameter
according to which I° assigns nominative case through government in some languages (e.g., Welsh and Gaelic; see also McCloskey 1991), whereas in others
Spec-head agreement is the only configuration available. The latter can be assumed for French and English, so that the ungrammaticality of the VS(O) order is
predicted. An interesting idea that follows from this theory is that in some languages, e.g., Arabic (according to Koopman and Sportiche 1991:231) and Italian
(Cresti 1990; Roberts 1993:19ff, 1994; see the discussion later in this chapter), I°
permits both mechanisms. This view can be extended to the other Romance languages in which subjects are permitted to remain in their base position.[20] I return
to this issue in section 3.2.3 because it still has to be shown how such an approach can work within the Split-Infl hypothesis. It is important to keep in mind
that in these languages subjects usually appear postverbally when they are focalized. It can be assumed, with Vallduví (1992a, 1992b), that usually only focalized subjects are permitted to remain in their base position, whereas nonfocalized
subjects move to AgrP.[21]

3.2.2   Nominative assignment by tense or by agreement?

Clauses that contain a finite verb include such information as tense, number, and
person. In earlier accounts these are claimed to be encoded inside I° by the features [+Tns] and [+Agr]. In the Split-Infl framework assumed here, this information is contained in the functional heads T° and Agr°. In the history of case theory, there has been some discussion about whether tense or agreement is responsible for nominative assignment. This issue is extremely important in the framework assumed here because it has to be decided which of the two functional
heads is a nominative assigner.

In Chomsky (1980:10), a finite clause was still considered to have the structure [s̄ Comp [s NP Tense VP]]. Since agreement does not appear in this structure, it is obvious that tense was the only possible candidate for being the nominative assigner:

(26) NP is nominative when governed by Tense.   (Chomsky 1980:68)

A similar point of view can be found in Rizzi (1982:86)[22] and Vergnaud (1982).

The assumption that the nominative is assigned by agreement can be traced
back to Chomsky (1981:258–59):

(27) AGR is co-indexed with the NP that it governs (namely, the subject), assigning it nominative Case and sharing its grammatical features.

The logic in this approach is that [+Agr] contains the information about number
and person of the subject, so that, in contrast to [+Tns], it is closely related to the

subject.[23] The assumption of nominative assignment through Spec-head agreement can be considered a logical continuation of this idea. However, there have been objections to the claim that nominative case is assigned by agreement. Koopman observes, about Vata, that I° does not contain [+Agr], so that the nominative must be assigned in another way.[24] Given the fact that there are other languages in which nominative subjects are licensed even when I° is [+Agr, –Tns] (e.g., Portuguese; see 3.3.1 and 4.3.1.1), Koopman (1984:188–93), who tries to find a universal principle, concludes that [+Tns] is not a nominative assigner either. On the basis of an examination of verb positions, she concludes that I° assigns nominative case when it is occupied by a verb.[25] This may work in some languages, and similar assumptions help to explain certain constructions in the Romance languages (see 4.3.2.1 and 6.1.1.1), but generally it is problematic in a more recent framework, in which it is assumed that in some languages (e.g., English) verbs remain in their base position but still allow nominative subjects.

Iatridou (1993) shows that in modern Greek [+Tns] can assign the nominative: in subordinate clauses introduced by the particle να, she observes the following distribution of nominative/accusative and tenses:

(28)   *Case of the subject*   *Permitted tenses*
    a.   accusative   present
    b.   nominative   present, tenses referring to the past

Present tense in the case of (28a) does not refer to the speaker's present, but its meaning is determined by a *consecutio temporum*, depending on the tense of the main clause; in (28b), however, the interpreted time corresponds to the tense of the verb. In both cases, there is subject-verb agreement, so that subordinate clauses of type (28a) have I°[+Agr, –Tns], and those of type (28b) have I°[+Agr, +Tns]. Since the nominative case cannot be assigned in (28a), Iatridou assumes that [+Tns] is the feature responsible for nominative assignment. I would like to suggest that an even clearer example of nominative assignment by [+Tns] can be found in the so-called absolute infinitive of Ancient Hebrew. In this language, there were two different infinitive forms (cf. Bergsträsser 1928:40–41 and Gesenius 1896:118):

(29)   a.   b.

      מְלֹךְ   מָלוֹךְ
      məlōk̲   mālōk̲
              'to reign'

Whereas the form in (29a), the so-called *infinitivus constructus*, was mainly used in subordinate clauses, the form in (29b), which is traditionally called *infinitivus absolutus*, had the following main functions: first, it served as a kind of reinforcement of the finite verb (cf. Gesenius 1896:334–37), as in (30a), and, second, it could be used instead of the finite verb in infinitival main clauses, as in (30b). These clauses can have specified subjects (cf. 1896:337–39):

(30) a. ‏הֲמָלֹךְ תִּמְלֹךְ עָלֵינוּ:‏

    ha-   malōk timəlōk   ᶜālēnū ?

    INTERR to-reign reign-2SG-M over-us ?

    'Do you (really) want to reign over us?' (Gen. 37:8)

b. ‏וְשַׁבֵּחַ אֲנִי אֶת־הַמֵּתִים ....:‏

    wə-šabbēaḥ 'anī   'et   ha- mmētī m.

    and-to-praise I (NOM) ACC PART the dead

    'And I praised the dead . . . .' (Eccl. 4:2)

It seems that in both functions the absolute infinitive has something to do with finiteness: in (30a) it accompanies a finite verb, and in (30b) the infinitive itself assumes the function of a finite verb. Since the infinitive has no agreement morphology, we can interpret this by saying that, in contrast to the *infinitivus constructus* (29a), the infinitive form (29b) is specified for [+Tns] and that this feature assigns the nominative. We can thus fill the following gap noted by Iatridou (1993:180): "Unfortunately, I do not know of any languages which permit the combination of features [+T] [–A]." I discuss absolute infinitive constructions in Romance, which also license overt subjects, in section 4.3.3.3.

To summarize the results of this section, it seems obvious that tense and agreement may both assign the nominative case. It also seems that for some languages only one of them is a valid case assigner.

3.2.3 Agr° *and* T° as nominative assigners

If both [+Agr] and [+Tns] are capable of assigning the nominative case, as is suggested by the preceding discussion, some more concrete principle is expected to emerge from the Split-Infl hypothesis. This line is followed by Roberts (1993, 1994). Like Koopman and Sportiche (1991), Roberts claims that universal grammar provides two mechanisms for nominative assignment, namely, nominative assignment by Spec-head agreement and nominative assignment through government. The nominative assigning heads are T° and Agr°, but languages differ about whether T° and/or Agr° assign the nominative through government and/or Spec-head agreement. The cross-linguistic variation is thus driven by a parameter (Roberts 1993:27). The available possibilities are summarized in the following table:[26]

(31)

Nominative assigner	Government	Spec-head agreement
Agr°	+/-	+/-
T°	+/-	--------

Nominative assignment through governing T° is typically found in VS(O) structures: in strict VS(O) languages, this is the only option available for nominative assignment. Consequently, some of these languages lack agreement between the subject and the verb. Roberts argues that in these languages the verb remains in T° and is not moved on to Agr°, so that agreement with the subject is not established. Such phenomena can be observed, for example, in Welsh and Arabic. Classical Arabic allows for both VS(O) and SV(O) structures, but only in the former does the verb agree with its subject, as demonstrated in (32):[27]

(32) a. تشتري البنات بيتاً

taštarī   l- banātu   baitan
buys SG the girls NOM house ACC

b. البنات تشترين بيتاً

al- banātu   taštarī   baitan
the-girls NOM buy PL   house ACC

The earlier account mentioned (nominative assignment to the base-generated subject by governing I°) can now be described more precisely by assuming that T° is the relevant case assigner in this configuration. Furthermore, I assume, following Roberts (1993), that in those Romance languages that regularly allow both VS(O) and SV(O), two nominative assignment mechanisms are available: (i) Agr° assigns the nominative under Spec-head agreement with the subject and (ii) T° assigns the nominative to a DP that it governs.[28] Roberts's assumption is summarized here:

(33)

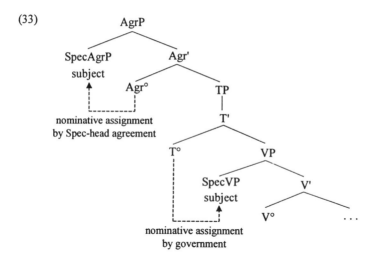

The difference between the word order "Gianni arriva" versus "arriva Gianni" in Italian (both meaning 'John arrives') can thus be explained as follows:[29]

(34) a. Gianni arriva.

[CP [AgrP [Spec Gianni$_i$] [Agr' [Agr° arriva$_j$] [TP t_j [VP t_i t_j]]]]]

[NOM]

b. Arriva Gianni.

[CP [AgrP [TP [T° arriva$_j$] [VP [Spec Gianni] t_j]]]]

[NOM]

An interesting point is that the lack of agreement between the postverbal subject and the verb, mentioned above as a characteristic of some Celtic and Semitic languages, can sometimes be observed in Romance languages, too. A well-known example quoted in the generative literature concerns French structures of the following type:[30]

(35) Il venait   *deux jeunes filles.*
     it came (SG) two young girls
     'There came two young girls.'

This phenomenon is frequently observed in Old Romance languages, for example, Old French, Old Italian, Old Spanish, and Galician-Portuguese:[31]

(36) a. Parmi Paris en va   *trois paire.*   OF
         Through P.   A CL goes three pairs
         'Three pairs run through P.' (Ruteb., 326, 88)

     b. Morì   *tre fratelli* di nostro padre.   OI
         died (SG) three brothers of our   father
         'Three brothers of our father died.' (Morelli, 305)

     c. No nos espanta *tus westes.*   OS
         not us terrifies your armies
         'Your armies do not terrify us.' (Recontamiento, 437, 14)

     d. Les sucedió   *cosas.*   CS
         them happened (SG) things
         'Things happened to them.' (Quij., II, 8/2, 140)

     e. E   hi   morreo *grandes gentes.*   GP
         and there died (SG) great   people
         'And great people died there.' (Nunes, Crest., 52)

The fact that most of these examples have intransitive verbs might be interpreted in a way that would take into account the properties of unaccusatives (cf. Burzio 1986; Belletti 1988; Raposo and Uriagereka 1990). For example, we could try to apply Belletti's theory that unaccusative verbs assign partitive case. However, as example (36c) shows, this structure was possible with transitive verbs, too, at least in Old Spanish.[32] Moreover, such an assumption would not account too well for the parallel to VS(O) languages concerning the lack of agreement.[33] Roberts's (1993) idea that this is due to case assignment by T° receives further support from some other phenomena, which are outlined in the discussion of our data (e.g., the situation in Modern Galician; cf. section 6.3.1.1).

I return to Roberts's (1993) account in the next chapter because it contains an interesting interpretation of nonfinite structures. In chapter 6, I argue that most of the data presented in chapter 2 can be explained by accepting the basic ideas presented in this section, although some points of Roberts's theory have to be revised.

3.3   Romance infinitive constructions

3.3.1   Basic properties

Just like finite clauses, infinitive constructions can project a complete clause structure, including CP. Evidence for the existence of CP in some constructions is provided by *wh* elements, whereas other constructions lack this property. Consider the following contrast in Italian (cf. Graffi 1994:123):

(37) a. Gianni non sa   [*dove* trovare Maria].
        G.   not   knows where to-find M.
        'G. does not know where to find M.'

     b. ⋆Gianni vuole [*che cosa* fare]?
        G.   wants what thing to-do

     c. ⋆Conviene   [*che cosa* fare]?
        is-convenient what thing to-do

One way of explaining this contrast is to note that in examples like (37b) and (37c) the position SpecCP that is necessary for *wh* movement is missing; that is, these constructions are possibly AgrPs or VPs. I return to infinitival CPs in section 3.3.3. It is not always easy to decide on the exact status of an infinitive construction, and there is cross-linguistic variation involved. As we see in the following chapters, the position and the properties of subjects in infinitive clauses often provide some hints on this issue. Whenever the exact status cannot be determined or is irrelevant, I use the notation CP/AgrP.

A basic difference between infinitive constructions and finite clauses is that the node known as I° in the earlier framework is usually characterized by [–Agr, –Tns]. This is not necessarily so, as we have already mentioned in 3.2.2 concerning the observations made by Koopman (1984). Examples for I° with [+Agr, –Tns] are the inflected infinitive constructions of Portuguese, Sardinian, and Old Neapolitan, mentioned in chapter 2. As I point out in 3.2.2, there may be languages in which infinitive constructions are specified with [–Agr, +Tns]. To summarize, it can be said that a construction traditionally considered to be nonfinite is characterized by the fact that at least one of the two features of I° is negative. Note, however, that a negative specification for one of these features does not necessarily imply that the functional head that bears this feature is absent. On the contrary, the presence of T° and Agr° in infinitive clauses has been used in the Split-Infl hypothesis to account for some striking word-order phenomena, such as the following contrast of French and Italian (cf. Pollock 1989; Belletti 1990:73):

(38) a. *souvent* paraître triste   a'. ⋆*spesso* sembrare triste
        often   to-seem sad

     b. paraître *souvent* triste   b'. sembrare *spesso* triste
        to-seem often   sad

     c. *ne plus*   paraître triste   c'. ⋆*non più* sembrare triste
        not anymore to-seem sad

     d. ⋆*ne* paraître *plus*   triste   d'. *non* sembrare *più* triste
        not to-seem anymore sad

On the assumption that the adverb in these examples is left-adjoined to VP and that NegP is located between AgrP and TP, these data can be explained as follows:

(39) a. [$_{VP}$ souvent [$_{VP}$ paraître triste]]

　　b. paraître$_i$ [$_{VP}$ souvent [$_{VP}$ t_i triste]]

　　c. [$_{NegP}$ ne plus [$_{TP}$ paraître$_i$ [$_{VP}$ t_i triste]]]

　　d. [$_{AgrP}$ non$_j$ sembrare$_i$ [$_{NegP}$ t_j più [$_{TP}$ t_i [$_{VP}$ t_i triste]]]]

Whereas the verb remains inside VP in (39a), V° movement has to be postulated in (39b), which seems to be obligatory in Italian. The landing sites can be determined on the basis of our assumptions concerning NegP. We can thus assume that in infinitive clauses the verb may move to T° in French, whereas in Spanish and Italian movement is continued up to Agr°, where the verb is incorporated together with Neg°.[34] As Motapanyane (1988) shows, Romanian behaves similar to French in this respect, and we see in chapter 6 that Portuguese seems to admit both options.[35] Although it is obvious that the assumptions made within the Split-Infl framework imply that functional categories must be assumed for infinitive clauses, we cannot necessarily conclude (as we have done) that they must be the same ones as in finite constructions. The results presented in chapters 6 and 7 of this book strongly suggest, however, that this assumption can be supported.

For the structural position of the types of infinitive clauses described at the beginning of chapter 2, I mostly follow standard assumptions, which do not have to be mentioned here. However, some of the configurations deserve more discussion. First, I assume that infinitive clauses that function as attributes are adjuncts to N', similar to that which can be assumed for adjectives and restrictive relative clauses. Consider the following example from Classical Spanish:

(40) [$_{DP}$ el [$_{NP}$ [$_{N'}$ [$_{N'}$ punto] [$_{PP}$ de [$_{CP/AgrP}$ partirse　　　el amigo]]]]]
　　　　 the　　　　　point　　　 of　　　 to-go-away-R CL the friend
‘the moment at which the friend left’ (Cerv. Nov. 9, quoted by Diez 1882:946)

Second, infinitival appositions are separated from the rest of a sentence by a pause or, orthographically, by a comma. Furthermore, this construction is usually coindexed with some element of the main clause. These constructions are considered to be dislocations and can be argued to be adjuncts (cf. Haegeman 1994), perhaps to CP, as in the following example from Classical Portuguese:

(41) [$_{CP}$ [$_{CP}$ Isto$_i$ só　basta　pera fugir do　　　mundo, [$_{CP/AgrP}$ serem　os
　　　　　　　　 this　only suffices for　to-flee from-the world　　　　 to-be-3PL the
homens julgados . . .]$_i$]]
men　　 judged
‘This alone is enough to flee from the world, namely the fact that humans are judged . . .’ (H.P., I, 326)

Third, I would like to mention here infinitive clauses found in impersonal constructions, for example, after impersonal verbs like ‘to happen’, or ‘to be convenient', impersonal expressions consisting of 'to be' plus a DP or an AP, and passive predicates (see the examples in 42). In all these constructions, the infinitive clause has been considered to be the subject of the main clause in traditional grammar. In contrast to "real" subject clauses, its unmarked position is after the predicate, whereas the preverbal subject position is occupied by an expletive element, which is phonetically empty in most Romance languages, although in some varieties it may be overt, as in the following examples:

(42) a. [*Il*] se   trouve [assez   de vaillants hommes être   prêts . . .].   CF
         it R CL finds   enough of valiant   men   to-be ready
         'It is found that many valiant men are ready . . .' (Malh. Épîtres, LVII, II, 472;
         cf. A. Haase 1965:207)

    b. [*Il*] avint   [gentz montez estre veuz].   OF
         it happend people riding   to-be seen
         'It happened that riding people were seen.' (Bible Rq., I, 741; quoted by Diez
         1882:945)

    c. [*Egli*] era impossibile [l' uomo in fiera transformarsi].   OI
         it   was impossible   the man   in beast to-transform-R CL
         'It was impossible for the man to become transformed into a beast.' (Giov. da
         Prato, II, 174; cf. Schwendener 1923:80–81)

I claim that the structural position of these infinitive clauses is similar in all three examples. Example (42a) is a so-called reflexive passive construction (cf. 3.1.3), and, similar to passive structures constructed with the auxiliary 'to be' (which are found in the same contexts), it has to be assumed that the infinitive construction is the complement of the verb. A similar assumption holds for unaccusative verbs, to which impersonal verbs like 'to happen' in (42b) can be argued to belong (cf. Grewendorf 1989; Hoekstra 1984). As can be seen in these examples, the infinitive construction that occurrs after the copula + predicate nominal in (42c) shows the same behavior as the other two examples. Assuming, with Burzio (1986) and others, that structures that consist of a copula and a predicate nominal are small clauses (SCs), I assume the following D-structure:

(43)

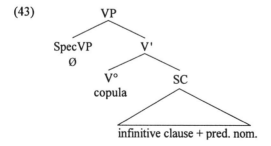

The similarity observed in the syntactic behavior of this construction as compared with (42a) and (42b) can be related to the fact that here, too, the infinitive clause is c-commanded by V°. To make the small clause structure compatible with X-bar theory, it has been assumed that the adjective is the head of the SC (so that the SC can be reinterpreted as an AP) and that the subject (the infinitive clause in our case) is in its specifier position (cf. Radford 1988). If the predicate nominal is a DP, it should then be assumed that the SC is a projection of D°. This is quite interesting with respect to our data: it can be observed in our material that the determiner is usually missing in Old Romance (e.g., Old Spanish *natural cosa es*; see examples 23a and 23b of chapter 2). This could be explained by assuming that these varieties selected an NP small clause instead of a DP one. More recent accounts interpret SCs as AgrPs with a phonetically empty head Agr°, which is responsible for agreement in gender, number, and person between the SC subject and its complement (the predicate nominal); cf. Haegeman (1994:122–26) and Chomsky (1995:175). In such a framework, my hypothesis about the Old Romance languages can be reformulated by saying that Agr° usually selected an NP complement instead of a DP.

3.3.2   PRO and emphatic pronouns

The empty category PRO is not a central subject of this book because we focus on infinitival contexts with overt subjects, which, in contrast to PRO, are assumed to be case-marked. When there is an empty subject that co-occurs with an overt subject in the same syntactic configuration, we obviously have to assume this empty category to be *pro* and not PRO. However, we have to take into account emphatic pronouns in infinitive constructions (cf. 1.1). Emphatic pronouns have been studied in detail by Ronat (1979), Burzio (1986:106ff), and Piera (1987).[36] Consider the following contrast in Spanish, mentioned by Piera:

(44) a. [Telefonear **tú**   primero] sería   un error.
         to-phone   you (NOM) first   would-be a mistake
         'It would be a mistake if you phoned first.'

     b. Julia quería [telefonear **ella**].
         J.   wanted to-phone   she
         'J. wanted to phone by herself.'

Whereas the subject in (44a) is not coreferential with any element in the sentence, the pronoun *ella* in (44b) is coreferential with the subject of the main clause. In contrast to (44a), R-expressions are not allowed in (44b):

(45) a. [Telefonear **Julia** primero] sería un error.
     b. ∗Julia quería [telefonear **Julia**].
     c. ∗Julia quería [telefonear **Paula**].

Since these pronouns appear in syntactic contexts usually occupied by PRO, Piera (1987) assumes the following structures, in which the emphatic pronouns are obligatorily coindexed with PRO:

(46) a.   Julia$_i$ queria [PRO$_i$ telefonear **ella**$_i$]

    b.   Julia$_i$ prometió a Marta$_j$ [PRO$_i$ encargarse   **ella**$_i$ del   asunto].
        J.   promised to M.   to-attend-R CL she   of-the matter
        'J. promised to M. to attend to the matter personally.'

    c.   Julia$_i$ animó   a Marta$_j$ a [PRO$_j$ encargarse   **ella**$_j$ del   asunto].
        J.   encouraged to M.   to   to-attend-R CL she   of-the matter
        'J. encouraged M. to attend to the matter personally.'

Piera furthermore assumes that the theta role is assigned to PRO, so that the pronouns under discussion are located in a nontheta position. Since they obviously follow principle A of binding theory, these pronouns have to be considered as anaphors (Ronat 1979; Burzio 1986). According to Piera (1987:161), the post-verbal position of the overt subject is a general property of emphatic pronouns, which is not restricted to infinitive clauses.[37]

The assumption that emphatic pronouns are bound with PRO can be traced back to Burzio (1986:106ff). This assumption implies that emphatic pronouns need no case, which is a reasonable assumption because these elements are non-arguments.[38] For the case properties, Piera (1987) suggests a modification of Burzio's account by assuming that anaphors in nontheta positions will be assigned to be nominative when they are coindexed with a c-commanding subject.

Emphatic pronouns deserve some further discussion against the background of nonemphatic specified subjects in infinitive constructions. In contrast to nonemphatic subjects in the Aux-to-Comp structures discussed by Rizzi (1982; cf. 4.3.2.1), emphatic subjects are allowed to co-occur with the preposition *di*:

(47)   *Non-emphatic*   *Emphatic*

a. *Credevo [*di* essere **lui** arrivato ieri].   a'. Credevo [*di* essere arrivato io ieri].
   (I) believed *di* to-be   he   arrived yersterday   (I) believed *di* to-be   arrived   I   yesterday

b. Credevo [essere **lui** arrivato ieri].   b'. *Credevo [essere arrivato io ieri].
   (I) believed to-be   he   arrived   yesterday   (I) believed to-be   arrived   I   yesterday

What I would like to point out here is the fact that the emphatic pronoun behaves exactly like PRO, for both coindexation facts and the construction types where it is allowed:

(48) a.   Gianni$_i$ credeva [di PRO$_i$ essere arrivato].
    a'.   Gianni$_i$ credeva [di essere arrivato **lui**$_i$].
        'G. believed to have arrived (personally).'

    b.   *Gianni$_i$ credeva [di PRO$_j$ essere arrivato].
    b'.   *Gianni$_i$ credeva [di essere arrivato **lui**$_j$].
        'G. believed that he (= another person) arrived (personally).'

    c.   Gianni$_i$ mi$_j$ ha promesso [di PRO$_i$ farlo].
    c'.   Gianni$_i$ mi$_j$ ha promesso [di farlo **lui**$_i$].
        'G. promised me to do it (personally).'

d. *Gianni$_i$ mi$_j$ ha promesso [di PRO$_j$ farlo].
d'. *Gianni$_i$ mi$_j$ ha promesso [di farlo io$_j$].
   'G. promised me that I would do it.'

e. Gianni$_i$ mi$_j$ ha chiesto [di PRO$_j$ farlo].
e'. Gianni$_i$ mi$_j$ ha chiesto [di farlo io$_j$].
   'G. asked me to do it (personally).'

f. *Gianni$_i$ mi$_j$ ha chiesto [di PRO$_i$ farlo].
f'. *Gianni$_i$ mi$_j$ ha chiesto [di farlo lui$_i$].
   'G. asked me for him to do it (personally).'

g. [PRO$_{arb}$ andarci] sarebbe un errore.
g'. [Andarci **noi**] sarebbe un errore].
   '(For us) to go there would be a mistake.'

If we ignore, for a moment, Burzio's (1986) and Piera's (1987) accounts and assume the structures to be as represented in (48), we see that PRO can always be substituted for by an emphatic subject. Like PRO, it has to be either coindexed or arbitrary, and in the positions where PRO or an emphatic subject appears, no R-expressions are admitted in their place. In the Aux-to-Comp construction in (47b), R-expressions are admitted, so there is obviously a case position available (as is shown in the following chapters). In this respect, the emphatic pronouns also behave like PRO; that is, they cannot appear in this context. The problem of Burzio's and Piera's interpretation is that it is difficult to integrate it into more recent assumptions in generative grammar, that is, that subjects are base-generated in SpecVP, where they are assigned their theta role. In the structures discussed here, PRO is the subject. This would mean that PRO is base-generated in SpecVP. However, movement of PRO to AgrP is not motivated because movement of a subject DP to SpecAgrP will be effected either for case assignment purposes or to establish agreement with the subject. Emphatic pronouns appear postverbally. Why should we not assume that they are located in SpecVP, which would be the most probable assumption if we take into account the results of the preceding sections? If we put all these pieces together, nothing would prevent us from saying that PRO and emphatic subjects are of the same type. Now, consider the traditional typology of DPs:

(49) Typology of DPs (according to Haegeman 1994:453)

Type	overt	nonovert
[+anaphor, –pronominal]	anaphor	DP trace
[–anaphor, +pronominal]	pronoun	*pro*
[–anaphor, –pronominal]	R-expression	*wh* trace
[+anaphor, +pronominal]	– – – – – – – – –	PRO

If emphatic pronouns behave like PRO, they should also be classified as [+anaphor, +pronominal], and the only difference with PRO would then be the fact that they are overt. I therefore claim that the emphatic pronouns under dis-

cussion fill the gap left open in (49); in other words, Romance emphatic pronouns are a kind of overt realizations of PRO.[39] If our assumptions about case
theory are correct and movement to SpecAgrP is an A-movement induced by the
case filter, then emphatic pronouns (which, like PRO, are not subject to the case
filter), will remain in SpecVP. The latter assumption correctly predicts why they
always appear in postverbal position.

Chomsky (1995:119–24) proposes—and this would also be in conformity
with our analysis—that PRO is not caseless but receives a "null case."[40] In English, this null case is assigned in the same configuration as the nominative, with
the difference that the case-assigning functional category Agr° has reduced or no
agreement features in infinitive clauses (i.e., [–Tns,–Agr]).[41] For Romance languages, we should assume that the null case is assigned to PRO and to emphatic
pronouns by governing T°, which will account for the postverbal position.

3.3.3   Determiners and prepositions

A further point that has to be examined before the data are analyzed is the status
of the prepositions and determiners by which Romance infinitive constructions
can be introduced.

The issue of determined infinitive clauses was examined thoroughly by
Bottari. Bottari argues that these constructions have the status of clauses, which
becomes evident from the grammaticality of auxiliaries (indicating that the construction contains an IP; cf. Bottari 1992:72),[42] as well as negation (p. 73), which
implies the existence of NegP from the point of view of our framework:

(50) a. [L' *essere* tradito] è una triste esperienza.   MI
         the to-be betrayed is a   sad   experience
         'To be betrayed is a sad experience.'

     b. [Il suo *non* voler   firmare] ci aveva scocciati.
         the his not to-want to-sign us had   bothered
         'The fact that he did not want to sign had bothered us.'

Bottari assumes a DP structure in which the infinitive clause is a complement of
D°. Note that this claim, which follows logically from the DP hypothesis, makes
it possible to explain why some languages (e.g., French) do not allow this kind of
construction: by assuming that D° in those languages does not subcategorize for
an (infinitive) clause but only for NP.

The issue of prepositions is somewhat more complicated because there are
different types to be distinguished. Consider the following division of Italian
prepositional infinitive constructions taken from Benucci (1992:23–26),[43] which
is based on the observation of the alternation between infinitive constructions and
other constituents:

(51)

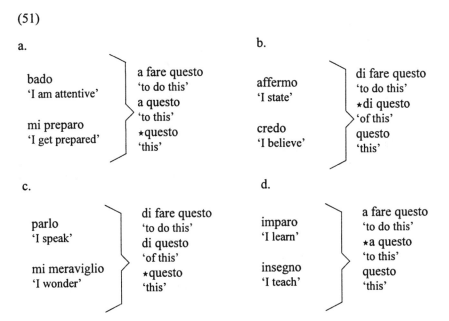

a.

bado
'I am attentive'

mi preparo
'I get prepared'

a fare questo
'to do this'
a questo
'to this'
*questo
'this'

b.

affermo
'I state'

credo
'I believe'

di fare questo
'to do this'
*di questo
'of this'
questo
'this'

c.

parlo
'I speak'

mi meraviglio
'I wonder'

di fare questo
'to do this'
di questo
'of this'
*questo
'this'

d.

imparo
'I learn'

insegno
'I teach'

a fare questo
'to do this'
*a questo
'to this'
questo
'this'

In (51b) and (51d), the preposition appears only when the verbs selects an infinitive clause, and it can therefore be considered a complementizer.[44] In (51a) and (51c), the preposition is present even if the verb selects a DP, so that in this case it is interpreted as a real preposition. Therefore, the following structures can be assumed:

(52)   a.   b.

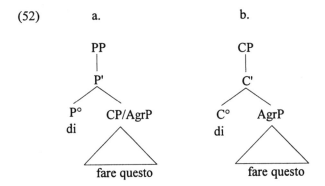

In addition to the verb types mentioned in (51), Benucci observes that some verbs that belong to (51b) behave still differently:

(53)   a. Si vanta [di questo].
            R CL boasts of this

        b. Si vanta [di venire].   Se *ne*   vanta.
            R CL boasts of to-come   R CL thereof boasts

        c. Si vanta [che . . .]   'He boasts of it.'
            R CL boasts that

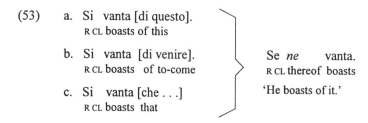

The evidence of the adverbial clitic *ne*, which is used to substitute for PPs, leads
Benucci (1992:30) to the assumption that in (53c) the verb selects a PP, although
its head is phonetically empty.[45] This case is quite interesting for our purposes
because, as was observed in chapter 2, there are infinitive constructions in Old
Romance languages that behave in a similar way (see example 10b of chapter 2),
so that we can assume a parallel interpretation.

Benucci's (1992) way of distinguishing between real prepositions and complementizers, based essentially on the question of whether the infinitive construction preceded by a preposition can be substituted for by DP or PP, can be
applied to nonselected infinitive clauses, too. Consider the following two Spanish
examples, in which the infinitive construction is an adjunct:

(54) a. [Para hacerlo] necesitaría   100.000 Pesetas.   (final)
            for   to-do-it (I) would-need 100,000 P.
            'I would need 100,000 P. for doing it.'

     a'. [Para ello] necesitaría   100.000 Pesetas.
            for   it   (I) would-need 100,000 P.
            'I would need 100,000 P. for it.'

     b. [De hacerlo] necesitaría   100.000 Pesetas.   (conditional)
            if   to-do-it (I) would-need 100,000 P.
            'If I did it, I would need 100,000 P.'

     b'. ⋆[De ello] necesitaría   100.000 Pesetas.
            if   it   (I) would-need 100,000 P.
            'In that case I would need 100,000 P.'

The infinitive construction in (54a) can be substituted for by [PP [P' [P° DP]]],
whereas this is not possible in (54b), which is similar to what happens in selected
constructions like (51b) and (51d). I therefore assume that the Spanish conditional *de* has the status of a complementizer.

Somewhat more difficult to interpret is the Romance temporal construction
selected by the preposition *a* + determiner, as in the following Spanish example,
which should have the structure represented in (51b):

(55) a. al   llegar a casa
            on-the to-arrive at home
            'on the arrival at home'

     b. [PP a [DP l [CP/AgrP llegar a casa]]]

There is, however, some evidence that Spanish *al* and its counterparts in other Romance languages (Portuguese/Galician *ao/ó* and Old French *au* or *à l'*), although originally a preposition followed by a determiner, is a lexicalized element that has the status of C°. First, this construction is also found in languages that usually do not permit D° to select an infinitive clause with a specified subject, as in Old French (cf. section 2.2). Second, in an infinitive construction embedded into DP, D° can also be a demonstrative adjective, although this does not seem to be possible in the *al*-construction:

(56) a. al   llegar tú al   aereopuerto   MS
        on-the to-arrive you at-the airport
        'when you arrived at the airport', 'on your arrival at the airport'

     b. *a este llegar tú al   aereopuerto
        on this to-arrive you at-the airport

Third, their interpretation is always temporal, but when the article is missing, the construction with *a* has other interpretations, for example, final in Old French and Old Italian or conditional in Classical and Modern Spanish.

3.4 Summary

In this chapter I outline some basic assumptions about the analysis of finite and nonfinite constructions in the Romance languages. I argue that both behave in conformity with the Split-Infl hypothesis, where the order of functional categories (from left to right) is Agr(S)P (NegP) TP (AgrOP). I show how verb movement can account for basic cross-linguistic differences in word order, whereas other differences seem to be related to language-specific properties of C°. I also point out that AgrP can be held responsible for a fundamental property of earlier stages of most Romance languages, namely, that any 2-bar constituent could be fronted, usually leading to a V2 effect.

As for case theory, I support Roberts's (1993, 1994) point of view, according to which both T° and Agr° are potentially in a position to assign the nominative case to the subject of a finite verb, although usually the former assigns case under government, whereas the latter needs to be in a Spec-head configuration with the subject. The assumption that in most Romance languages both mechanisms are available predicts that subjects are permitted to remain in their base position, SpecVP. In addition, this assumption offers a quite appropriate explanation for the lack of agreement between verbs and postverbal subjects, which is sometimes found in Old Romance languages.

For infinitive clauses, I suggest that we consider emphatic subject pronouns as overt counterparts of PRO, which seem to be available in all Romance languages. This assumption explains the fact mentioned in the introduction that standard French allows emphatic subject pronouns in infinitive clauses but rejects nonemphatic subjects, to which all kinds of R-expressions belong. Finally, the status of determiners and prepositions used to introduce infinitive clauses is examined. In particular, I present a method for distinguishing infinitive clauses embedded into PPs from another type, in which the preposition has to be considered an infinitival complementizer.

The basic assumptions about the ordering of functional categories in Romance languages; the position of subjects, clitics, and adverbs; and the range of verb movement in the different linguistic varieties are valid both for the traditional generative analysis and for a minimalist approach. The most important difference between what has been assumed here and the minimalist program is the fact that government is a not a valid principle in the latter. The consequences of this claim for the analysis of our data is discussed at length in chapter 7, together with a basic outline of the minimalist approach to Romance syntax.

4

Romance Infinitives with Specified Subjects:
The State of the Art

In this chapter I discuss existing generative accounts of specified subjects in Romance infinitive constructions. After a brief summary, each proposal will be explored in the light of the data presented in chapter 2 and the theoretical framework outlined in chapter 3. It will become evident from this chapter that although there has been a considerable number of attempts to explain some of the relevant data for individual languages, no unified solution applicable to all Romance languages has been given so far, particularly for nominative subjects.

The chapter is organized as follows. In section 4.1, I discuss infinitive subjects in the accusative case, which have been explained by exceptional case marking and in which the infinitive construction is selected by perceptional, causative, and permissive verbs. Section 4.2 is dedicated to an outline of some basic approaches toward infinitive subjects that appear in the main clause, both in raising and in *wh* contexts. These two sections include some additional data that have not yet been introduced.

The main part of this chapter is section 4.3, in which I discuss the most important existing accounts for nominative subjects in infinitive clauses. This section is much more extensive because many different and, in part, contradicting accounts have been given for these phenomena. Basically, we can distinguish three types of approaches, each of which is treated in a different subsection: nominative assignment by agreement (4.3.1), Aux-to-Comp analyses (4.3.2), and nominative assignment by tense (4.3.3).[1]

4.1 Accusative subjects and exceptional case marking

The attempt to explain the so-called A.c.I. constructions can be traced back to the very beginnings of generative grammar.[2] Our discussion here is limited to a brief sketch of those explanations, which follow the line of Chomsky (1981),[3] including some additional ideas related to the Split-Infl hypothesis.

Romance A.c.I. constructions have commonly been explained by the structure shown in (1):

(1) Je vois [$_{IP}$ [$_{DP}$ l' **homme**]$_i$ [$_{I'}$ [$_{I°}$ –*finite*] [$_{VP}$ t_i venir]]]. MF
  I see   the man   to-come.
  'I see the man come.'

The verb of the main clause assigns the accusative to the subject of the subordinate infinitive clause (*exceptional case marking*, abbreviated ECM). Thus ECM functions according to the same principle as accusative assignment to a direct object, that is, to a DP governed by the verb:[4]

(2) a. Case marking of a direct object   b. Exceptional case marking

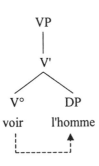
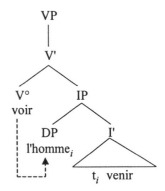

It is assumed that the structure in (2b) is possible because the main verb, in this case *voir*, subcategorizes for an infinitival IP and that IP, in contrast to CP, is transparent for government by a head situated in the main clause (cf. Kayne 1984:ch. 1; Massam 1985:43–44; Chomsky 1986a:71; Haegeman 1994:550, 630). Consider the following example:

(3) *Je crois [$_{CP}$ [$_{C°}$ Ø [**cet homme** être intelligent]]].
       I believe   this man   to-be intelligent   (cf. Rizzi 1990a:59)

According to Chomsky this is due to the fact that CP is a barrier in these cases. In more recent accounts, the ungrammaticality of (3) is interpreted as a violation of the minimality condition (Haegeman 1994:630), which predicts that a government relationship is avoided by an intervening potential governor (see section 3.1.2): in our case C° is a potential governor (according to Rizzi 1990a), so that in (3) the main verb cannot govern the subject situated in IP and is therefore unable to assign case to it.

On the basis of the Split-Infl hypothesis, Guasti (1989) therefore assumes that Romance perception verbs select infinitive constructions with the status of AgrP. Note, however, that auxiliaries are not permitted in these constructions:

(4) a. *Ho   visto [**Gianni** essere venuto].   MI
          (I) have seen   G.   to-be come
          'I have seen that G. has come.'

     b. *J'ai vu [**Jean** être venu].   MF

In view of this property, Belletti (1990) proposed that the infinitive construction subcategorized by perception verbs is an AgrP without a TP.[5] This analysis, which might seem to be an ad hoc solution at first sight, is supported by further arguments in chapter 6 of this book. The structure assumed, then, is as follows:

(5)

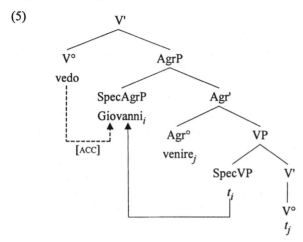

Moreover, it has to be noted that the subject may appear preverbally or post-verbally:[6]

(6) a. Vedo **l' uomo** venire. / Je vois **l'homme** venir.
      (I) see the man to-come

    b. Vedo venire **l' uomo**. / Je vois venir **l'homme**.
      (I) see to-come the man

For (6b), we can assume either that the subject DP remains in its base position[7] or, alternatively, that the main verb permits the incorporation of an infinitive (cf. Belletti 1990:136, fn. 56). The problem is that in some languages infinitive constructions with ECM permit only the postverbal position after certain verbs. This is characteristic of causative verbs, as is illustrated by the following examples with verbs meaning 'to see' in (7a) and 'to make' in (7b):

(7) Romance ECM with perception and causative verbs

	a.	b.
MI	Ho visto [**Gianni** venire].	⋆Ho fatto [**Gianni** venire].
	Ho visto [venire **Gianni**].	Ho fatto [venire **Gianni**].
MF	J'ai vu [**Jean** venir].	⋆J'ai fait [**Jean** venir].
	J'ai vu [venir **Jean**].	J'ai fait [venir **Jean**].
Sard	---	⋆Appo fattu [**Jubanne** benner].
	---	Appo fattu [bennere **Jubanne**].

Kayne (1975), Rouveret and Vergnaud (1980), Burzio (1986), and Jones (1993) assume that in type (7b) the whole VP moves into the main clause:

(8)   Faró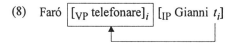

According to Pearce (1990), subjects can generally be generated at the left or the right side of the verb, although in type (7b) they can appear only at the right side. Both proposals are not unproblematic: the hypothesis of VP movement would presuppose that movement processes are lexically selected; Pearce's proposal is not restrictive enough; that is, we have to formulate additional rules to regulate the position to the right or to the left. As an alternative, Belletti (1990:136, note 56) suggests that the infinitive is incorporated into [$_{V^o}$ *fare/faire/facher*] (see Baker 1988 for other languages). This idea was further elaborated by Guasti (1996), and in Mensching (1999) I proposed a similar account for Catalan.[8] Although the incorporation hypothesis has some advantages, I would like to propose an alternative analysis. Consider the following examples, treated as exceptions by nongenerative scholars (e.g., Sandfeld 1943; Skytte 1983), in which a quantifier appears before the infinitive:

(9)   a.   Li   fa   [**tutti** partire].   MI
           them (he) makes all   to-go-away
           'He makes them all go away.' (cf. a similar example in Skytte 1983:70–71)

       b.   Elle fit   [**tout** disparaître].   MF
           she made all   to-disappeear
           'She made everything disappear.' (cf. Sandfeld 1943:167)

We could assume that incorporation is optional, but then there would be no reason for the ungrammaticality of the examples in (7b). How could we then prevent the subject from appearing in the preverbal position, allowing only quantifiers there? Let us investigate a solution within the framework of the Split-Infl hypothesis. In Mensching (1996), I claimed that verbs like French *faire*, Italian *fare*, and Sardinian *facher* subcategorize for an infinitive construction that is a TP (without an AgrP above it).[9] SpecTP is generally considered to be an operator position, a fact that usually prevents it from being a landing site (and a case position) for subjects (cf. Rizzi 1990a; Roberts 1993). In our proposal, this fact explains the ungrammatical examples in (7b). On the other hand, as SpecTP is an operator position, it is, in fact, available for quantifiers. In other words, the grammaticality of the preverbal position of quantifiers is due to the fact that quantifiers are operators (Haegeman 1994:488–94).

Moreover, some other characteristics of the causative construction can be derived directly from my proposal that these constructions are TPs. First, if the construction lacks AgrP, negation should not be possible because Neg° has to be incorporated into Agr°. In fact, we find that this prediction is borne out:

(10) a.   *On a   fait [*ne pas* venir **Jean**]   MF
           one has made not NEG2 to-come J.   (cf. Kayne 1977:222)

     b.   *Hanno   fatto [*non* venire **Giovanni**].   MI
           (they) have made not   to-come G.

c. *An   fattu [*non* benner **Jubanne**].   Sard
  (they) have made not to-come J.

In contrast, negation of the infinitive is possible when the infinitive construction is selected by verbs that subcategorize for AgrP, such as perception verbs in Italian and French, as well as French *laisser*:[10]

(11) a. Je **le** laisse [*ne pas* venir].   MF
    I   him let   not NEG2 to-come
    'I let him not come.'

  b. **Carletto l'** ho   visto [*non* ridere più].   MI
    C.   him (I) have seen not to-laugh anymore
    'I have seen C. not laughing anymore.' (cf. Skytte 1983:248)

  c. Ho   sentito [**i** **bambini** *non* piangere più].
    (I) have heard   the children not to-cry   anymore
    'I heard the children not crying anymore.' (cf. Belletti 1990:81)

Second, for Italian and Sardinian it has been assumed that object clitics move to AgrP (Roberts 1994; Mensching 1996). Similar to what has been said about preverbal subjects and Neg°, the object clitics, too, lack a landing site under our analysis. This explains the following behavior observed by Skytte (1983) and Jones (1993:273–74):

(12) a. ***Mi**   facevano [far*lo*].   MI
    me (CL) (they) made to-do-it (CL)

  a'. **Me**   *lo*   facevano [fare].
    me (CL) it (CL) (they) made to-do
    'They made me do it.'

  b. ***M'**   an   lassadu [*lu*   mandicare].   Sard
    me (CL) they have let   it (CL) to-eat

  b'. **Mi**   *l'*   an   lassadu [mandicare].
    me (CL) it (CL) (they) have let   to-eat.
    'They let me eat it.'

Here, too, the infinitive construction after Italian *lasciare*, which is interpreted as AgrP according to our assumptions, behaves differently:

(13) a. Lasciami [dir*ti*   una cosa].
    Let-me (CL) to-tell-you (CL) a   thing
    'Let me tell you something.'

  a'. Lasciami*ti*   [dire una cosa].
    Let-me (CL)-you (CL) to-tell a   thing

Most of the characteristics just mentioned can also be derived from the incorporation hypothesis (see Guasti 1996), so I do not decide here for either analysis, although it should be pointed out that the advantage of an analysis along the lines of my proposal might be preferable because here the syntactic properties follow in a quite natural way from the subcategorization frame of causative verbs without any additional assumptions.[11]

Before finishing this section, we have to look at ECM constructions after other verbs, the ungrammaticality of which has been repeatedly pointed out in the generative literature (e.g., Kayne 1981, 1984; Rizzi 1982, 1990a):

(14) a. *?Gianni *riteneva* [**Mario** essere una brava persona].   MI
        G.   thought   M.   to-be   a   good person   (Rizzi 1982:89)

   b. *Je *crois* [**cet homme** être intelligent].   MF
      I believe this man   to-be intelligent   (Rizzi 1990a:59)

The ungrammaticality follows, in accordance with the assumptions already mentioned, from the fact that these verbs subcategorize for CP and that CP blocks government of the infinitival subject by the main verb. However, the data presented in chapter 2 show that constructions like (14) were grammatical in earlier stages of French, Italian, Occitan, and Romanian, with the subject appearing in the accusative, so that it has to be examined if they are cases of ECM. If this is the case—and I claim it is in chapter 6—the next question is which characteristics determine the differences in grammaticality between the older and the modern stages of these languages.[12] Sauzet (1989) regards the construction of Modern Languedocian, mentioned in 2.5.2, as an ECM construction. In his explanation, he avoids the problem stated in connection with (14), that is, the nontransparency of CP for government from outside, by postulating that the subject is base-generated in a topic position adjoined to the infinitival CP. This solution is not satisfactory, among other things because Sauzet needs a revision of theta theory for his analysis.[13]

Finally, the Romance constructions mentioned in chapter 2, in which an accusative infinitive subject appears after unaccusative predicates, have hardly received any attention so far in generative grammar. Some considerations about this kind of construction are made by Pearce (1990:181–88) within her analysis of Old and Middle French causative constructions. Her explanation is based on the assumption that unaccusative verbs have changed their subcategorization frames: according to her proposal, these verbs were able to assign the accusative in earlier stages of French but no longer can today. This account is "clearly speculative," as Pearce (p. 188) herself observes. Furthermore, her explanation would mean that the disappearance of ECM after declarative and epistemic predicates, on the one hand, and after unaccusative predicates, on the other, would have had two different causes. This would be possible, of course, but before postulating such an analysis we should look for a unitary explanation. Such an account is presented in chapter 6. The account I give is not of a speculative nature because it is able to explain a whole series of differences among different languages and among diachronic, diastratic, and diatopic varieties of one language.

4.2 Infinitival subjects extracted to the main clause

4.2.1 Raising constructions

Raising constructions are generally well known in generative grammar (see Haegeman 1994:306–9; Müller and Riemer 1998:133–39), so that I limit this section to some brief observations, included above all for the sake of completeness. The first case to be considered here is the construction known as *Nominativus cum Infinitivo* (N.c.I.) in traditional grammar, in which the subject of the subordinate clause appears in the subject position of the passive main clause. Consider (15):

(15) a. Ho visto [$_{AgrP}$ Gianni$_i$ riparare$_j$ [$_{VP}$ t_i t_j la macchina]].
      (I) have seen   G.   to-repair   the car.
      'I saw G. repairing the car.'

    b. ⋆È stato visto [$_{AgrP}$ Gianni$_i$ riparare$_j$ [$_{VP}$ t_i t_j la macchina]].
       is been seen   G.   to-repair   the car

    c. Gianni$_i$ è stato visto [$_{AgrP}$ t_i riparare$_j$ [$_{VP}$ t_i t_j la macchina]].
       G.   is been seen   to-repair   the car.
       'G. was seen repairing the car.'

When V° is in the active voice, as in (15a), the subject DP of the infinitive construction undergoes movement to the position SpecAgrP, where it receives the accusative from the main verb, as described in the preceding section. Note that passive constructions are unaccusative structures. When V° is in the passive voice, as in (15b), accusative assignment is not possible because in Burzio's (1986:184) generalization, an unaccusative verb fails to assign the accusative case, so that ECM is excluded. Since the subject cannot receive case inside the infinitive clause, it moves into the main clause, where it receives the nominative case, as in (15c).

    Raising verbs, like 'to seem' (Spanish *parecer*, Italian *sembrare*, French *sembler*, etc.), behave similarly to passive constructions, as can be seen in the following examples:

(16) a. ⋆Sembra [Giovanni essere arrivato].
      seems   G.   to-be arrived

    b. Giovanni$_i$ sembra [t_i essere arrivato].
      G.   seems   to-be arrived
      'G. seems to have arrived.'

These verbs do not assign a theta role to their subject position either, so that here this position also functions as the landing site for the subject of the subordinate clause. Since raising of the subject is considered to be due to the fact that no case can be assigned to the subject in the infinitive clause, movement does not take place in finite constructions:

(17) a.   Sembra [che Giovanni sia arrivato].
          seems   that G.   is   arrived
          'It seems that G. has arrived.'

     b.   *Giovanni$_i$ sembra [che t_i sia arrivato].
          G.   seems   that   is   arrived

Just as in ECM constructions that are selected, for instance, by French *voir, faire,* and *laisser,* the infinitive constructions subcategorized by raising verbs are traditionally considered to be IPs (Burzio 1986:218–20; Graffi 1994:343), or AgrPs in more recent terminology, since it is assumed that an intervening C° would block the extraction of the subject to the main clause because of the minimality condition. The structure that can be assumed, following these standard assumptions, is thus roughly as follows:

(18)   Giovanni$_i$ sembra [$_{AgrP}$ t_i essere$_j$ [$_{TP}$ t_j [$_{VP}$ t_i arrivato]]].

If these assumptions are correct, in languages that license specified nominative subjects inside the infinitive constructions, we should also observe that raising does not take place, that is, that structures like (15b) and (16a) are grammatical. As for passive predicates, we have already seen in chapter 2 that this assumption is correct. In section 2.4, we have also seen Portuguese examples like (19):

(19) Parece [ter   o   **João** chegado].
       seems   to-have the J.   arrived
       'It seems that J. has arrived.'

This property of Portuguese was observed and analyzed by Raposo (1987). It is not restricted to Portuguese, however. In the course of this book, I adduce and analyze structures that are similar to (19) in other Romance varieties, such as the following example from Italian of the last century:

(20) A lui   pareva, [tale essere la opportunità e   la necessità di **questa**
     to him seemed   such to-be the opportunity and the necessity of this
     alleanza, che . . .]
     alliance   that
     'It seemed to him that the opportunity and the necessity for such an alliance was such that . . .' (Botta, VIII, p. 50; cf. Schwendener 1923:79)

Although the fundamental assumptions about raising are maintained in this book, it has to be explained why some varieties admit structures like (19) and (20) and others do not.

4.2.2   *Wh*-extracted subjects

Another phenomenon observed in the literature is the case in which a *wh*-marked subject of an infinitive clause appears in the main clause. This behavior was studied as a characteristic of Italian and French, for instance by Rizzi (1978, 1982, 1990a) and Kayne (1981, 1984). Consider the following examples:

(21) a. Les deux couples qui habitent dans cette maison sont des   MF
the two couples who live   in   this house   are of-the
personnes **que**$_i$ j'imagine [t_i être gentilles].
persons   that I imagine   to-be friendly
'The two couples who live in this house are persons of whom I imagine that
they are friendly.' (cf. Seelbach 1978:151)

b. Le persone **che**$_i$ suppongo [t_i non essere state messe al   corrente MI
the persons that (I) suppose   not to-be been put   on-the current
delle vostre decisioni] sono molte.
of-the your decisions   are   many
'The persons who I suppose not to be kept abreast of your decisions are numerous.' (cf. Rizzi 1982:78)

c. **[Quante persone]**$_i$ ritieni [t_i poter   pagare un simile riscatto]? MI
how-many persons   (you) believe can (INF) to-pay a   similar ransom
'How many persons do you believe to be able to pay a similar ransom?'

Since *wh*-marked elements move to SpecCP (cf. 3.1.2), the subject of such an
infinitive construction is situated in a configuration in which it can be case-
marked through ECM, according to Rizzi (1982:90–92, 95–97) and Kayne (1984:
ch. 5). This is illustrated in (22):

(22)

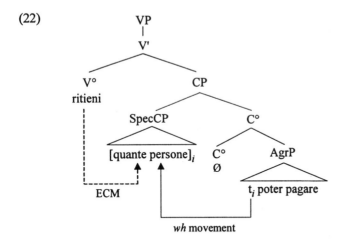

wh movement

Consequently, when C° contains an overt complementizer, the extraction of the
subject is blocked:

(23) *[Quante persone]$_i$ ritieni [$_{CP}$ *di* [$_{AgrP}$ t_i poter pagare un simile riscatto?]]

The ungrammaticality of (23) can be explained by the fact that overt complementizers, in contrast to C° = Ø, are not strict governors. However, as pointed
out by Rizzi (1990a:59), this account leaves the following differences in grammaticality unexplained:[14]

(24) a. Quante   persone credi   essere disposte ad aiutarci?   MI
         how-many persons (you) believe to-be   ready   to to-help-us
         'How many persons do you believe are ready to help us?'

    a'. ⋆Quante   persone vuoi   essere disposte ad aiutarci?
         how-many persons (you) want to-be   ready   to to-help us
         'How many persons do you want to be ready to help us?'

    b. Qui   crois- tu   être intelligent?   MF
         whom believe you to-be intelligent
         'Whom do you believe to be intelligent?'

    b' ⋆Qui   veux- tu   être intelligent?
         whom want   you to-be intelligent
         'Whom do you want to be intelligent?'

The solution proposed by Rizzi (1990a:58–60) follows straightforwardly from
the properties of C° mentioned in 3.1.2. According to Godard (1985), the substi-
tution of the conjunction *que* for *qui* in French (explained here by means of
[+Agr] in C°) is possible after exactly the same verbs as in (21) to (24), that is,
those that allow *wh* extraction of subjects from infinitival complement clauses
(epistemic and declarative verbs but not volitional verbs). Rizzi's (1990a:52)
account, supported by parallels in numerous other languages, is that *wh* extraction is blocked both by empty and by overt C° but not by a C° that contains
[+Agr]: only the latter acts as a governor in the sense of the ECP. The governing
faculty of C°[+Agr] is derived from a general property of agreement and does not
need to be explained by an additional rule. In view of this, the grammaticality
facts shown in (24) are due to lexical properties; that is, declarative and epistemic
verbs select C°[+Agr], whereas volition verbs subcategorize for C° = Ø.

Nevertheless Rizzi has a justified objection against the structure given in (22),
in which the accusative is assigned to the *wh*-marked subject in SpecCP. In Italian and French (and presumably in all Romance languages), SpecCP is usually
not a case position. If we assume that this prohibits accusative assignment in
SpecCP, the only possibility is to hypothesize that case is assigned to the subject
in SpecIP (SpecAgrP). Rizzi therefore assumes, against Kayne (1984), that the
feature [+Agr] is responsible for case assignment:[15] "Case can be assigned under
government by the selected Comp in subject position. . . . (It could still be the
case that the Case feature originates in the main verb and is transmitted under
government to Agr in Comp, which then assigns it to the subject trace . . .)"
(Rizzi 1990a:59). If this is the case, it is unclear why case marking is not possible
when the subject is not *wh*-marked, as in the examples in (14). According to
Rizzi, this is an effect of the following condition: [+Agr] in C° must be licensed
by coindexation with a subject under Spec-head agreement. When an infinitival
subject is extracted, this condition is fulfilled because SpecCP functions as an
intermediate landing site and [+Agr] is coindexed with the trace of the subject:

(25)   Qui$_i$ crois-tu [$_{CP}$ t_i [$_{C°}$ +Agr_i] [$_{AgrP}$ t_i être intelligent]]?

          ⌞_____⌟
          Spec-head agreement

In contrast, when the subject is not *wh*-moved, this coindexation cannot take place, and for this case Rizzi assumes that [+Agr] in C° cannot be selected. It must be observed here that Rizzi's (1990a) account might not be unproblematic in view of more recent assumptions on case assignment. We have seen that agreement is usually associated with nominative case when it is situated in a Spec-head configuration with a subject (3.2.3). In view of this fact, the assumption that an agreement feature coindexed with a subject operates as an assigner or transmitter of the accusative case might not be desirable.[16] In addition, the claim that the presence of [+Agr] is restricted to certain syntactic contexts does not seem very satisfactory from the point of view of lexicon theory. Whereas it is true that lexically selected properties can trigger movement,[17] the reverse case, in which movement would trigger lexical selection, is not very easy to imagine. Although the presence of [+Agr] in C° plays an important part in the rest of this book, Rizzi's theory is somewhat modified. For the discussion in the following chapters, we look at similar phenomena in Italian and French, as well as in other Romance languages. In addition, I take into account cases in which a non-*wh* subject is extracted. Such structures are typically found in older stages of the Romance languages, as in the following examples:

(26) a. **Les nues et nuées**$_i$ / Commanda [t_i estre ensemble usitées].   MF
     the n.   and n.   (he) commanded to-be together   usual
     'He commanded that (the forms) *nues* and *nuées* be indifferently used.'
     (Marot, 510; quoted by E. Stimming 1915:136)

    b. **Aquella proporción**$_i$ . . . [t_i juzgo   incomparablemente ser   OS
     that   proportion   (he) judged incomparably   to-be
     mejor que la   que   Paris juzgó entre   las tres deesas].
     better than that which P.   judged among the three goddesses
     'He judged that that proportion was incomparably better than the one which P.
     judged among the goddesses.' [Celest., I,64 (29)]

In view of these data, Rizzi's theory on [+Agr] in C° is problematic—movement of [–*wh*] constituents is not supposed to pass through SpecCP (Massam 1985: 48)—and must be revised. A further complication arises from the fact that in the Ibero-Romance languages, these subjects do not bear the accusative case, but rather the nominative.

4.3   Nominative subjects

4.3.1   Nominative assignment by agreement

4.3.1.1   Portuguese (Raposo)

As we see in chapter 2, Portuguese allows nominative subjects in infinitive clauses, which usually appear together with infinitive forms inflected for agreement. The starting point of Raposo (1987) is the assumption that [+Agr] belongs to the [+N] categories (cf. Chomsky 1982),[18] which can contain case features in null-subject languages.[19] Moreover, when I° is specified for [+Agr], either [–Tns] or [+Tns] may be selected. In most languages, however, the selection of [+Agr] automatically yields the selection of [+Tns]; that is, usually I° will be specified either as [+Agr, +Tns] or [–Agr, –Tns] (Raposo 1987:93) (but cf. 3.2.2 and 4.3.3.3).

The phenomenon of the inflected infinitive in Portuguese leads Raposo to the logical claim that in this language I°[+Agr] can co-occur with [–Tns].[20] He assumes that usually [+Tns] functions as the nominative assigner.[21] Of course, this cannot be applied to the Portuguese infinitive structures, so only [+Agr] can possibly be the nominative assigner in infinitive constructions. Raposo observes that the inflected infinitive is ungrammatical in main clauses, and he concludes that [+Agr], as a [+N] category, must have case itself in order to be able to assign it to the subject of the clause where it occurs. According to Raposo, the case of [+Agr] is assigned by an element of the matrix clause, a supposition that he tries to demonstrate for different types of infinitive constructions.

The example in (27a) exemplifies an infinitival subject clause selected by impersonal predicates. Raposo (1987) proposes the structure represented in (27b), in which the infinitival IP is in an extraposed position, appearing right-adjoined to the VP, with a coindexed empty category in SpecIP:

(27) a.   Será   difícil [**eles** aprovarem   a proposta].
          will-be difficult they to-approve-3PL the proposal
          'It will be difficult for them to approve the proposal.' (Raposo 1987:95)

b.

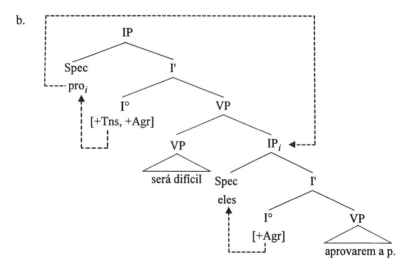

The category I°[+Tns, +Agr] of the main clause governs and case-marks *pro* in SpecIP. Its case is transferred to the coindexed infinitival IP[22] and is passed on to its head I° through percolation.[23] The feature [+Agr] inside the infinitive construction is now case-marked and since it governs the subject of the infinitive clause (*eles*), it assigns case to it.

For infinitive constructions that are complements of factive predicates, Raposo (1987:97) observes that they can occur with or without a determiner:

(28) a. Nós lamentamos [**eles** terem   recibido pouco dinheiro].
       we   regret   they to-have-3PL received little   money
       'We regret that they have received little money.'

     b. Nós lamentamos [o [**eles** terem   recibido pouco dinheiro]].
       we   regret   the they to-have-3PL received little   money
       'We regret the fact that they have received little money.'

Verbs like *lamentar* select a [+N] complement, which is obvious in (28b). Since
I° is also a [+N] category, the subcategorization frame of a verb like *lamentar* is
sufficient to explain the selection of the infinitive construction, without the definite article in (28a) as well, if it is considered to be an IP:

(29) a. Nós lamentamos [$_{IP}$ **eles** terem recibido pouco dinheiro].
     b. Nós lamentamos [$_{NP}$ o [$_{IP}$ **eles** terem recibido pouco dinheiro]].

The subject is then licensed in both structures, according to Raposo's basic assumptions, mentioned above: in (29a) and (29b) the infinitival IP receives its
case from the main verb.
    Finally, Raposo (1987:97) considers prepositional constructions that function
as adverbials:

(30) A Maria entrou en casa [$_{PP}$ sem [$_{IP}$ **os meninos**   ouvirem]].
      the M.   entered in house   without the young-men to-hear-3PL
      'M. entered the house without the young men hearing them.'

Here, he assumes that the preposition case-marks the infinitival IP.
    Raposo's (1987) account has various problems. Apart from the fact that he
examines only a small portion of the construction types documented in chapter 2
for Portuguese, his proposal that [+Agr] must be case-marked by an element of a
matrix clause is based chiefly on the ungrammaticality of cases like (31):

(31) ⋆Sera difícil [*que* **eles** *aprovarem*   a   proposta].
     will-be difficult that they to-approve-3PL the proposal

Note, however, that it is sufficient to say that *que* is a complementizer that c-
selects an IP specified by [+Tns]. This excludes the presence of an infinitive, a
fact that must be assumed for other languages as well (cf. Lenerz 1984:83). In a
similar way, an infinitive can be prevented from occurring in independent clauses
because [+Tns] should be necessary for this (cf. also 4.3.3.3).
    Another critical point is the fact that Raposo (1987) adopts a kind of case-
transferring mechanism. For instance, in the configuration in (27b), the node
I°[+Tns, +Agr] will pass on a feature [+NOM] to the infinitival IP. This feature
will percolate to its head and then be passed on to the subject of the infinitive.
This seems to be straightforward. However, in the other constructions Raposo
discusses, the governors of the infinitival IPs are transitive verbs and prepositions, and both of them usually assign accusative case, so that the percolating
feature will be [+ACC]. It does not seem plausible that this mechanism should be

able to assign the nominative case to the subject of the infinitive clause. In other words, it is difficult to imagine that a node must receive the accusative in order to assign the nominative to another element.

This inconsistency was also noticed recently in Müller and Riemer (1998: 178). The solution given there, according to which only the case-assigning faculty is passed on to the infinitival I°, and that nominative is chosen as a default, is not very convincing either because it does not seem to follow from any independent principles. Moreover, the status of the constructions that are examined as IPs is not sure; but even if this could be demonstrated, it would be doubtful from a more recent point of view if the node I° of the main clause can actually govern the infinitival IP in the assumed configurations because the finite V° intervenes in the sense of the minimality condition, thus blocking the government relationship. In addition, some of the data in section 2.4 suggest that at least the historical varieties of Portuguese allow an overt C° between the main clause and the infinitive clause, according to the analysis of prepositions in section 3.3.3:

(32) que nõ era cousa convinhavil [$_{CP}$ *de* [$_{IP}$ **tu** morreres agora]]
     that not was thing   convenient   C°   you to-die-2SG now
     'that it was not convenient for you to die now' (Barlaão, 45; cf. da Silva Dias
     1954:219; Said Ali 1971:341)

This would definitely lead to a blocking of the government relationship, so those varieties remain unexplained in Raposo's (1987) framework.

4.3.1.2 French (Reuland; Vinet)

Reuland (1983) examines infinitive constructions in modern French of the following type:

(33) [**La France** battre le Brésil], ce serait   inconcevable.
     the F.   to-beat the Brazil this would-be inconceivable
     'France beating Brazil would really be inconceivable.'

He, too, assumes that I° in these constructions is specified by [+Agr, –Tns], although agreement does not show up overtly, and that [+Agr] is responsible for case assignment to the subject. Reuland's analysis is continued by Vinet (1985). In addition to cases like (33), Vinet includes an examination of similar constructions from Canadian French:

(34) [**Jean** sortir   sa vieille Plymouth], là, on aurait   du   fun.
     J.   to-take-out his old   P.   there one would-have of-the fun
     'If J. took out his old P., we would really have some fun.' (Vinet 1985:408)

Since these constructions are neither subject clauses nor complements of verbs or prepositions, and since they always appear sentence-initially, Vinet considers them to be dislocated infinitive constructions. With respect to their position, she postulates TopP, the left daughter of S", which might correspond to SpecCP in today's notation. She argues that the infinitive clause itself lacks a complementizer position because it is not introduced by prepositions, and neither can it contain a *wh*-moved element. Thus, from the present point of view, it has the status of an IP. In accordance with the accounts we have described so far, Vinet also supposes that I° has three possible expansions in French:

(35) a. [+Tns, +Agr] in finite clauses
b. [−Tns, −Agr] in infinite clauses without a specified subject
c. [−Tns, +Agr] in infinite clauses with a specified subject

For the case of (35c), she now claims that [+Agr] possesses an "abstract marker representing 'infinitive'" (G'), which governs and case-marks the infinitival subject,[24] as illustrated in the following:

(36)

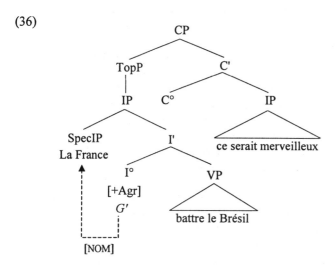

She further proposes the following rule for French in order to exclude the presence of lexical subjects in other types of infinitive constructions:

(37) In a clause where INFL is marked [−Tense +AG], G' is a governor and assigns Nominative Case only if S is dominated by TOP. (Vinet 1985:421)

This rule, formulated to explain the necessity of topicalization of the infinitive construction, is described by the author herself as "a fair approximation of this environment" (Vinet 1985:421). It must be considered an ad hoc assumption because it remains completely unmotivated. Then, why lexical subjects in contemporary French are possible only in these two configurations still has to be explained. Reuland (1983) and Vinet basically assume the same case-assigning mechanism as Raposo (1987) does for Portuguese, that is, nominative assignment to SpecIP through [+Agr]. Why, then, do we find lexical subjects in such a considerable number of infinitive constructions in Portuguese but not in French? An interesting observation made by Vinet is that the infinitive constructions she examines always seem to have a conditional meaning. Unfortunately, she does not include this fact in her explanation. It seems to me that this semantic component indicates that case assignment here has to do with [+Tns] rather than with [+Agr]. I return to this point in 6.4.2.

4.3.1.3 Sardinian (Jones)

Jones (1992, 1993) focuses on the licensing of nominative subjects in Sardinian infinitive constructions that are introduced by prepositions and may or may not present inflected forms of the infinitive. As pointed out in 2.5.1, in the varieties of Logudorese (including Central Sardinian or Nuorese) both the inflected and the uninflected forms of the infinitive are grammatical, whereas in Campidanian only the uninflected forms exist. The position of the subject is always to the right of the infinitive.

Jones assumes that these Sardinian infinitive constructions, too, are specified by [+Agr, −Tns]. To explain the postverbal position of the subject, Jones (1992) proposes that the feature [+Agr] relevant for nominative assignment in infinitives is not situated under I° but under V°, in contrast not only to finite constructions in Sardinian but also to infinitive constructions in Portuguese. In Jones (1993), this theory is slightly modified: the feature [+Agr] is base-generated in I° both in finite and infinitive constructions. When [+Tns] is present, [+Agr] may remain in I°, from where it can license a preverbal subject in SpecIP. On the other hand, when [+Tns] is missing, as in infinitive constructions, [+Agr] must leave the node I° and incorporate into V°. From this position, it governs only the postverbal subject inside of the VP. These assumptions provide a straightforward account for the different subject position in finite and nonfinite clauses.[25]

Jones proposes that the postverbal subject is either adjoined to VP or that it might be situated in some other position inside the VP.[26] It is clear that this assumption is compatible with the current theory on the base position of the subject (cf. 3.1.1), so that the structure needs almost no modifications and can be represented as follows:

(38)

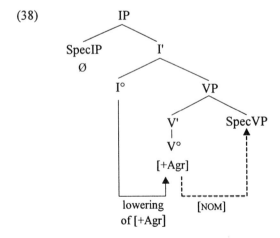

Jones's proposal also accounts for another striking property of Sardinian, which was mentioned in chapter 2: specified subjects are not possible when the infinitive clause is introduced by a determiner:

(39) *su andare s' omine
     the to-go the man

According to Jones (1993:284–85), this is due to the fact that in Sardinian such infinitive constructions are VPs that are immediately embedded into NP, so they lack the node I° that bears the feature [+Agr] relevant for case assignment. This, too, can be easily reformulated in our framework on the basis of the assumptions expounded in 3.3.3: in Spanish, Portuguese, and Italian, as well as in other languages, D° selects either NP or CP/IP, whereas Sardinian D° subcategorizes for NP or VP.

    Jones's (1993) assumptions are, therefore, straightforward. However, some questions remain from a pan-Romance point of view because Sardinian shows striking parallels to other Romance languages, which have never licensed inflected infinitives (even from a historical perspective) but still license an exclusively postverbal subject in infinitive constructions.

4.3.1.4 Middle and Classical French (Junker and Martineau)

Junker and Martineau's (1992) account presents the subjects in Middle and Classical French infinitive constructions as nominatives. This is hardly legitimate, as I have demonstrated in section 2.2. Nevertheless, their article has a certain theoretical relevance to the application of the Split-Infl hypothesis for the phenomena examined here; in addition, their explanation of postverbal subjects in French infinitive constructions is interesting because it relates the existence of infinitival subjects that appear postverbally to pro-drop phenomena.

    Junker and Martineau (1992) examine infinitival subject and complement clauses, which are introduced by some examples that represent constructions selected by impersonal, epistemic, declarative, volitional, and perceptional verbs:

(40) a. Il luy sembloit [**le roy** estre affoibly].
        it him seemed   the king to-be enfeebled
        'It seemed to him that the king was in a feeble condition.' (Commynes, I, 15; cf. Diez 1882:945; E. Stimming 1915:165–66; Meier 1955:284)

     b. On imagine [**l' objet** desiré estre tel . . .]
        one imagines the object desired to-be so
        'One imagines that the desired object is so . . .' (Desc. Pass., 120, p. 151; cf. A. Haase 1965:207)

     c. Affermerent [**cecy** estre vray].
        (they) stated this to-be true
        'They affirmed that this was true.' (Vigneulles, 51, 8; quoted by Martineau 1990:447)

    d. et aucuns . . . eussent voulu [**les Bourguignons** . . . estre dedans Paris]
        and some   had   wanted the B.   to-be inside P.
        'and some . . . had wanted the B. . . . to be inside P.' (Commynes, Mémoires,
        979).

    e. tant   qu'il veit [**son marry** estre à l' ostel]
        so-much as he sees her husband to-be at the lodging
        'as long as he sees that her husband is at the lodging' (Vigneulles, 71, 50; quo-
        ted by Martineau 1990:447).

Junker and Martineau's account is based on the Split-Infl hypothesis and on the assumption that the subject is base-generated inside VP. Moreover, the following additional assumptions are made: (i) infinitive clauses have no TP; (ii) among all the functional categories in one clause there is only one specifier position at the disposal of the subject (cf. Pollock 1989); (iii) in contrast to the earlier stages of the language, AgrP has no specifier position in Modern French, as postulated by Junker (1990:366). Given these assumptions, the authors claim the following structure for the infinitive constructions under discussion:

(41)

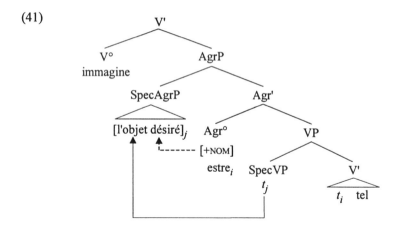

The subject moves to SpecAgrP, following standard assumptions. Given the presuppositions mentioned, the position SpecAgrP is missing in infinitive clauses in Modern French, so that the subject has no landing site and is therefore ungrammatical. In addition, Junker and Martineau assume that specifiers are licensed only in phrases whose heads have functional features (Fukui and Speas 1987), which leads them to the following theory: in Middle and Classical French, Agr° has a feature [+NOM] that is responsible for case assignment to subjects in both finite and nonfinite clauses. As a functional feature, it licenses the specifier of AgrP. For Modern French, in contrast, it is assumed that the nominative-assigning category is T°. However, since one of their basic assumptions is that infinitive clauses have no TP, subjects will be ungrammatical in Modern French.

    As we observe in chapter 2, Middle and Classical French show both preverbal and postverbal subjects. According to (41), case is assigned under Spec-head agreement, so the subject will occur preverbally. The post-verbal position is explained as follows:

> If we assume that nominative Case can be assigned to an empty pro-nominal such as *pro* (recall that Middle French is a language with null subjects) in the Specifier of AGRP and transmitted to the NP in its VP-internal position, sentences such as (37b) [cf. our (16b) in chapter 2] are licit in Middle and Classical French. (Junker and Martineau 1992:146)

This is an interesting point, to which we return in chapter 6.

Apart from the misguided assumption that these subjects bear the nominative case, Junker and Martineau's account needs a large number of additional assumptions. Moreover, various other points are rather problematic. First, as I point out in 4.1, the lack of TP should not be postulated here because these constructions permit auxiliaries. Second, the argumentation on which an ECM analysis is rejected is rather weak. In support of their opinion, the authors try to present some cases in which the infinitive construction is an independent clause, so that there is no main verb that could possibly assign the accusative case. However, consider one of their examples (Junker and Martineau 1992:133), represented here as (42):

(42) Le médicin respondit en son art bien avoir remèdes propres   pour
     the doctor   answered in his art well to-exist remedies appropriate for
     faire   parler les femmes, n' en avoir pour les faire   taire:
     to-make to-speak the women not A CL to-exist for them to-make to-be-silent
     [remède unicque estre surdité du   mary].
     remedy unique   to-be deafness of-the husband
     'The doctor answered that in his art there were remedies appropriate for making
     women speak, but that there were none to keep them quiet, and that the only remedy
     was the deafness of the husband.' (Rabelais, 452; cf. Lorian 1973:200)

This is quite obviously a case of indirect speech (following the Latin pattern), where the infinitive clause "remède unicque estre surdité du mary" is still dependent on the verb *respondit* 'he answered', so ECM is not excluded. As another argument against the ECM analysis, the authors state that in Middle and Classical French it was ungrammatical to put one or more constituents between a verb and its direct object (Junker and Martineau 1992:134), as in (43a), although they did find cases in which this was documented for infinitive constructions; see (43b):

(43) a. ★Les moins experimentez *recognoissoient*, à veüe d' oeil, dit- il,   MidF
       the less   experienced   recognized   at view of eye says he
       les actions humaines.
       the actions human
       'The less experienced recognized the human actions with the naked eye, said
       he.'

b. Les moins experimentez recognoissoient, à veüe d' oeil, dit- il, [**les**
the less   experienced   recognized   at view of eye says he the
actions humaines estre tributaires à la censure du   public].
actions human   to-be tributary   to the censure of-the public
'The less experienced recognized with the naked eye that the human actions are
tributary to public censure.' (Les Caquets de l'accouchée, I, 11; quoted by
Damourette and Pichon 1911–33:III, 572)

As a proof for the adjacency condition between the case-assigning verb and the
direct object, the authors state that they did not find any contradictory examples
in a syntactic analysis of two Middle French texts (a total of 2,000 sentences).
This is, however, still a very small corpus, so their argument should not be considered valid.[27] Furthermore, they mention the following example, in which there
is both an accusative clitic and the pronoun *cela*:

(44) Les gentilhommes *l'* asseuroient [**cela** estre vray].
the gentlemen   him assured   that to be true
'The gentlemen assured him that that was true' (d'Aubigné, V, 372; cf. Junker and
Martineau 1992:135; according to E. Stimming 1915:155)

The authors' argument against ECM here is that the accusative could not possibly
be assigned twice, so *cela* must be nominative. However, this is instead proof *for*
ECM because the older stages of French did know the double accusative construction, as was pointed out by E. Stimming (1915:39–40, 154–55) and, particularly, by Groß (1912:55ff).

Yet, there is one observation in Junker and Martineau's (1992) article that
must be taken seriously, in the sense that it really seems to argue against an ECM
analysis: not all the main verbs preceding the infinitive constructions under discussion are transitive; for example, all impersonal verbs like *sembler* and *falloir*
can appear there. I return to this point in the following chapters.

4.3.2   Aux-to-Comp and related analyses

4.3.2.1 Aux-to-Comp in Modern Italian (Rizzi)

Rizzi (1982) is the first generative linguist who drew attention to the fact that certain Romance infinitive constructions license overt subjects.[28] The third chapter
of his *Issues in Italian Syntax* bears the title "Lexical Subjects in Infinitives:
Government, Case and Binding." Rizzi discusses the Italian configurations already pointed out in section 2.1 of this book, represented here by the examples in
(45).

(45) a.   Questa commissione ritiene [aver   **loro** sempre ottemperato agli
this   commission   believes to-have they always   obeyed   to-the
obbligi   previsti dalla legge].
obligations provided by-the law
'This commission believes that they have always obeyed the obligations provided by the law.'

b. Il giudice è stato sospeso   per [aver   **suo figlio** commesso una
   the judge   is been suspended for to-have his son   committed a
   grave imprudenza].
   serious imprudence
   'The judge was suspended because his son had committed a serious imprudence.'

c. L' [aver   **lui** affermato che ti   vuole aiutare] non implica che
   the to-have he stated   that you wants to-help   not implies that
   sei   fuori dei   guai.
   (you) are outside of-the troubles
   'The fact that he affirmed that he wants to help you does not imply that you are
   out of trouble.'

Rizzi's (1982:77) analysis is based on the D-structure in (46a), parallel to
finite clauses, represented as in (46b) in a more modern notation:

(46) a. $[_{S'}$ COMP $[_S$ NP infinitive VP]]
          [+lex]

b.

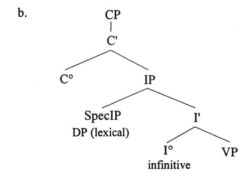

Since it is assumed that nonfinite I° is not a case assigner, the case filter predicts
that the infinitive construction is ungrammatical in the linear order shown in (46).
But, as Rizzi observes, these sentences become grammatical when the subject
occurs after the verb, and the infinitive must always be either an auxiliary or a
copula. Therefore Rizzi (1982:87) assumes a special rule for Italian to account
for his data:

(47) Given the logic of the Case approach, the natural answer is the follo-
     wing: the grammar of Italian has a special Case assignment process, in
     addition to the core rules . . .[29] which assigns nominative Case to an NP
     in post-Aux position:

Assign Nominative Case to NP in the context Aux __.

Hence it seems that the infinitives of Italian *essere* and *avere* are able to govern and case-mark a DP situated to their right. For the derivation of the assumed S-structure, Rizzi (1982:85) postulates movement of the auxiliary to $C°$:

(48) $C°$ NP Aux

In this way, Rizzi's condition (47) is fulfilled. Thus, example (45a) would have the following structure:

(49)

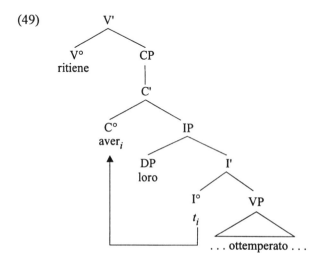

The hypothesis of $C°$ as the S-structural position of the infinitive is based on the observation that the same linear order, that is, Aux + DP, shows up in finite conditional clauses when the conditional complementizer *se* 'if' is omitted. Consider the following grammaticality facts:

(50) a. [*Se* lui avesse capito   al volo], tutto sarebbe andato bene.
         if he had   understood at flight all   would-be gone   well
         'If he had understood at once, all would have gone well.'

   b. [*Avesse* lui capito al volo], tutto sarebbe andato bene.

   c. *[*Se avesse* lui capito al volo], tutto sarebbe andato bene.

Sentence (50c) is ungrammatical according to Rizzi's analysis, because here the overt complementizer (*se*) blocks movement of the auxiliary *avesse* to $C°$.[30]

The grammaticality of lexical postverbal subjects in infinitive constructions by means of Aux-to-Comp movement is related to the subcategorization properties of verbs assumed by Rizzi (1982): volitional verbs do not permit an infinitival complement with a lexical subject because they subcategorize for IP rather than for CP (cf. Chomsky 1981a:ch. 5). For the same reason, the construction

with an overt complementizer (*di* or *a*; cf. 2.1 and 3.3.3) does not permit a specified subject, parallel to the conditional clause in (50c), so the only possible subject is PRO:

(51) Credevo [$_{C°}$ di [PRO aver   vinto]].
     (I) believed   C°   to-have won
     'I believed to have won.'

Summing up, the verbs considered (*affermare, ritenere,* etc.) select either infinitive constructions with a prepositional complementizer or infinitive constructions
with an empty complementizer. The latter permit Aux-to-Comp, thus licensing
overt subjects.[31]

Rizzi's (1982) hypothesis has justly been cited and taken up in numerous
studies because it is able to explain different phenomena connected to the construction under discussion: the limitation of the construction to CP, the ungrammaticality of the structure in case of overt C°, and the limitation of the construction to auxiliary and copulative verbs. Nevertheless, (47) is somewhat problematic because it postulates a mechanism that is restricted to Modern Italian and
does not seem directly explicable by more general principles. In section 4.3.3.2, I
discuss a reinterpretation of the case assignment mechanism in Aux-to-Comp
configurations developed by Roberts (1993, 1994) for gerunds. This approach is
further modified in chapters 5 to 7.

As we have seen, Rizzi's (1982) observations reflect quite well the data ex-
posed in section 2.1, as far as certain style types of contemporary Italian are concerned. In contrast, his analysis is not compatible with the situation that can be
observed in the earlier stages of the language and even in the first half of the
twentieth century. Here I recall just two of the phenomena mentioned in chapter
2: the occurrence of infinitives of transitive verbs, as in (52a), and preverbal
subjects, as in (52b):

(52) a. in [quel primo *offendermi* **la effigie** di colui]
         in   that first   to-offend-me the effigy of him
         'in that first offense done to me by the effigy of him' (Alberti Fam. *B*, 269, 7;
         cf. Dardano 1963:113)

     b. La prima virtù pensò che sia [**l' uomo** costrignere la sua lingua].
         the first virtue (I) think that is the man to-constrain the his tongue
         'The first virtue is, I think, that a man holds his tongue.' (Libro di Cato; quoted
         by Segre 1991:118, according to Nannucci 1858:95)

Both properties, examined in the following chapters, obviously contradict the
Aux-to-Comp analysis.

4.3.2.2 Aux-to-Comp in Portuguese (Raposo)

The starting point of Raposo's assumptions on Aux-to-Comp in Portuguese is the
fact that after some verbs infinitival complement clauses only permit the subject
to appear postverbally, as mentioned in 2.4. Consider the following examples,
given by Raposo (1987:98):

(53) a. *O Manel pensa [os amigos terem   levado   o livro].
       the M.   thinks the friends to-have-3PL taken-away the book
       'M. thinks that the friends had taken away the book.'

    b. O Manel pensa [terem os amigos levado o livro].

As we saw in section 4.3.1.1, Raposo claims that nonfinite I° is specified by [+Agr] in Portuguese and that this feature assigns nominative case to the subject of the infinitive, under the condition that I° itself is governed and case-marked. Similar to Rizzi (1982), Raposo (1987:99) assumes that the sentence in (53b) has a D-structure like that in (54):

(54) [$_{V°}$ pensa [$_{CP}$ C° [$_{IP}$ os amigos [I° +*Agr* [$_{VP}$ ter levado o livro]]]]]

Here [+Agr] in I° is ungoverned because, according to the definition of government assumed by Belletti and Rizzi (1981), government is blocked by the maximal projection CP between V° and IP (Raposo 1987:90). Therefore, this feature must move together with the verb to C° to be governed and case-marked by the main verb. As a result, the feature [+Agr] itself is in a position to assign case to the subject of the infinitive:

(55)

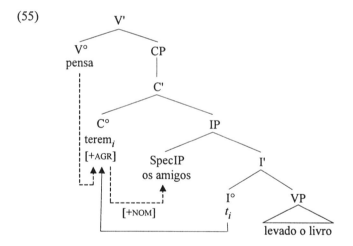

The problem with the case-assigning mechanism assumed by Raposo (1987) has already been pointed out in section 4.3.1.1. The Aux-to-Comp hypothesis illustrated in (55) presents further problems. Although it is true that the linear order of the constituents in the constructions examined by Raposo closely corresponds to the Italian Aux-to-Comp structure, there are also some basic differences, which can be drawn from section 2.4. First, the characteristic complementary distribution of overt complementizers and Aux-to-Comp observed by Rizzi (1982) is not found in Portuguese. Also, as Raposos himself admits, unlike Italian, Portuguese admits specified postverbal subjects with infinitives of nonauxiliary and noncopular verbs, for instance, with intransitive and sometimes even transitive verbs, as in the following literary example:

(56) a moda grega, que consistia [em darem   **os chefes** explicações
     the fashion Greek which consisted in to-give-3PL the chiefs explications
     da   sua conduta aos   soldados]
     of-the their behavior to-the soldiers
     'the Greek fashion which consisted in the fact that the chiefs gave explanations to
     the soldiers about their behavior' (A. Ribeiro Arcanjo, 135; cf. Sten 1952:225)

Moreover, this example shows a postverbal subject in a construction type that does not license any Aux-to-Comp construction at all in Italian. In chapters 5 and 6, I present further arguments against Aux-to-Comp in Portuguese, including Ambar's (1994) criticism, and opt for an alternative solution.

4.3.2.3 Spanish (Fernández Lagunilla)

Although the account of Fernández Lagunilla (1987) is not an Aux-to-Comp analysis, it is in some way similar because the verb is also assumed to move to the left of I°. Fernández Lagunilla almost exclusively deals with Spanish adverbial infinitive clauses introduced by prepositions.[32] She observes that infinitival clauses that function as direct objects do not allow specified subjects,[33] and she concludes that, unlike Italian Aux-to-Comp, a lexical subject in Spanish is licensed only when the infinitive clause is not a complement of the main verb. In fact, this is the case in the constructions she discusses because they are adjuncts. Moreover, she notes that there are two possibilities in word order, the former of which is not possible in Italian Aux-to-Comp constructions (Fernández Lagunilla 1987:131):

(57) a. De   *haberlo sabido* **Juan,** no hubiera   pasado   esto.
         C° (COND) to-have-it known J.   not would-have happened this
         'If J. had known it, this would not have happened.'

    b. De *haberlo* **Juan** *sabido*, no hubiera pasado esto.

Fernández Lagunilla further assumes that the prepositions that introduce adverbial infinitive clauses are complementizers—which can be supported by our analysis in 3.3.3 at least for examples like (57)—and then concludes that the constructions are to be considered as S', that is, CPs in the current terminology. However, as shown in (57), in contrast to the Italian constructions discussed by Rizzi (1982), C° is not a possible landing site for the verb. Fernández Lagunilla nevertheless postulates verb movement to explain the postverbal position of the subject, as illustrated in the following tree diagram:

(58)

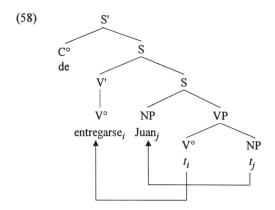

According to this structure, infinitive clauses are not projections of I° but of V°. Fernández Lagunilla then postulates a case-assigning mechanism, according to which the nominative case is assigned to the NP immediately dominated by S.

The main problem of this approach is the lack of compatibility with X-bar theory and the structure-preserving principle. If the infinitival constructions at stake are projections of V°, the node S must be reinterpreted as VP, so that Fernández Lagunilla's (1987) case-assigning mechanism would not work. Moreover, the movement of an X' constituent is usually not accepted today; however, even if this were admitted, the landing site could not be an adjunct to X" because the adjunct, too, must be maximal in this case. Finally, it should be mentioned that the absence of I° in constructions of this type is not compatible with the framework used in this book, as I have already stated concerning some of the other approaches.

4.3.3   Nominative assignment by T°

4.3.3.1   Romanian (Motapanyane; Dobrovie-Sorin)

Motapanyane (1989) and Dobrovie-Sorin (1994) consider Romanian a language in which governing T° functions as a nominative assigner. This assumption does not need a more detailed discussion here because the analysis is essentially parallel to the one presented for finite constructions in section 3.2.3. From this property, Motapanyane and Dobrovie-Sorin derive the characteristic of Romanian to license subjects in infinitive constructions. According to Motapanyane (1989), the second option for case assignment, namely, by Spec-head agreement of the subject and Agr°, is not available in infinitive clauses, so that preverbal subjects will be excluded (cf. the data mentioned in section 2.5.4). In contrast, Dobrovie-Sorin (1994:88) assumes that preverbal subjects in Romanian arise by A'-movement: "(Spec,IP) . . . is an A'-position which in indicatives is accessible to left dislocated elements . . ." In infinitive constructions, this movement is not supported, so preverbal subjects are not licensed. At least for finite constructions, Dobrovie-Sorin's assumptions on SpecIP as an A'-position were rejected by Motapanyane (1994) on the basis of an examination of preverbal constituents.

For infinitive constructions, it must be observed that the behavior of specified subjects in Romanian is similar to that in contemporary Spanish and Sardinian, although SpecIP is not supposed to be a possible A'-position in these languages (see the discussion in Fontana 1993 for Spanish). Moreover, I show in the course of the following chapters that in those Romance varieties in which SpecIP is an A'-position, this property is usually shared by finite and nonfinite constructions. Therefore, in Mensching (1997) and Mensching and Popovici (1997) we supported Motapanyane's point of view. In chapter 6 of this book it is shown that the assumption that T° is the only nominative assigner in infinitive clauses can be extended with a few modifications to account for other Romance languages.

Old Romanian, which permitted preverbal subjects, as shown in 2.5.4, is not treated by the two authors discussed in this section. See Mensching and Popovici (1997) for discussion; the results of this article are summarized and interpreted in section 6.5 in light of similar cases in Italian.

4.3.3.2 Gerunds with specified subjects in Italian and French (Roberts)

This brief analysis of Roberts (1993, 1994) concerns part of his theory, already found in section 3.2.3. He treats Italian gerund constructions of the following type:

(59) avendo Gianni fatto questo
      having G.   done this

Although the analysis of gerunds is beyond the scope of this volume, Roberts's account is relevant for a further understanding of nonfinite Aux-to-Comp constructions according to Rizzi (1982), as presented in section 4.3.2.1. Roberts offers a reinterpretation of the Aux-to-Comp analysis on the basis of more recent assumptions (the Split-Infl hypothesis, relativized minimality, and incorporation). Similar to Motapanyane (1989) and Dobrovie-Sorin (1994), Roberts argues that finite and nonfinite structures are based on the same nominative-assigning mechanisms.

In comparison to nonfinite Aux-to-Comp structures like (59), Roberts (1993: 72–73) emphasizes the ungrammaticality of the same word order pattern in cases with finite auxiliaries, in contrast to other languages, such as English:

(60) a. *Ha Gianni parlato?   MI
          has G.   spoken?

      b. *A Jean parlé?   MF

      c. Has John spoken?   ME

The ungrammaticality in Romance is explained as follows: French and Italian select a parametric option for nominative assignment that is different from Germanic languages. The case-assigning properties of the functional heads Agr° and T° are summarized as follows:

(61) Nominative-assigning heads in English and Romance

Language	Agr° (Spec-head agreement)	Agr° (government)	T° (government)
ME	yes	yes	no
MF/MI	yes	no	yes

Now consider (62), which roughly shows the structure of Aux-to-Comp constructions:

(62)

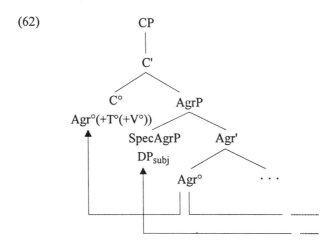

Here the subject position is governed by the complex head Agr°(+T°(+V°)), established through incorporation. Since English allows nominative assignment by governing Agr°, according to (61), this structure is grammatical in English but not in Italian and French. This last step can be understood better by considering the incorporation structure of finite Agr° assumed here, which I illustrate somewhat more explicitly in (63):

(63)

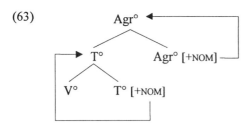

According to the assumptions on complex heads and the percolation of features, made, for instance, in Marantz (1984) and Lieber (1990), the nominative feature of Agr°, but not that of T°, is passed on to the upper Agr° node by percolation. In

Italian and French, the nominative cannot be assigned under government by the nominative feature of Agr°, so the structure in (62) is excluded. Still, the nominative feature of T° is not effective here because it cannot percolate to the uppermost X° projection. However, according to Roberts (1993), the [+NOM] feature can be relevant in other contexts. For Italian and French, this is the case in the configurations illustrated in (64) and (65). First, consider (64):

(64)   a.   b.

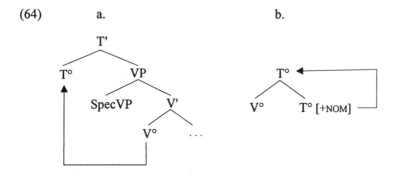

This is the case of T° in its base position, after V° has been incorporated, where T° has the incorporation structure represented in (64b). Second, consider nonfinite Agr° in (65). Similar to what Motapanyane (1989) claims for Romanian (see 4.3.3.1), Roberts assumes that nonfinite Agr° has no [+NOM] feature, in contrast to nonfinite T°, which does contain the feature. Therefore the case feature of T° can percolate to the highest Agr° head in the incorporation structure. Consider (65), in contrast to the finite structure in (63):

(65)

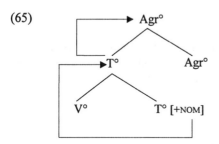

Both in (64) and in (65), the nominative is assigned by T° to a DP that it governs. Roberts generalizes this as follows: "T can assign nominative under government from positions where it has not combined with AGR [+Nom]." However, the possibility of nominative assignment by T° incorporated into Agr°, shown in (65), cannot be used in the base position of Agr°. The reason for this is that SpecVP, the base position of the subject, is not governed by Agr° because of the minimality condition, as the head T° intervenes. To be case-marked, the subject could move to SpecTP, a position that is governed by Agr°, but this possibility is excluded because SpecTP is not an A-position. The only configuration in which case assignment to the subject can be accomplished by the mechanism described is the Aux-to-Comp configuration because here Agr° governs the A-position SpecAgrP.

The attraction of Roberts's (1993) theory stems from the fact that it can explain a whole series of word order facts in numerous languages by a single parameter. Moreover, we can make an extremely interesting prediction that is relevant for our concerns: in languages in which T° assigns the nominative under government we expect the subject to appear postverbally in infinitive constructions. This is a quite satisfactory preliminary result because postverbal subjects are indeed predominant in the Romance data we are examining, as we see in chapter 2 and in this chapter.

Nevertheless, it must be pointed out that Roberts's (1993) theory is not sufficient to explain our data. Roberts developed his theory mainly on the basis of an examination of finite verbs, whereas the analysis of Aux-to-Comp takes into account only gerund constructions. For the infinitive constructions at issue, several important questions are left open. First, if T° has the general property of case-marking the subject in SpecVP under government in Italian and French, that is, if nonfinite T° also has a [+NOM] feature, this mechanism should also be valid for infinitives. In other words, since we find postverbal subjects with a finite verb like (66a), we should also find infinitive constructions like (66b), that is, without Aux-to-Comp:

(66) a. Telefonò Gianni.
         phoned   G.

     b. ★(di/a/per) telefonare Gianni
         of /to/for to-phone   G.

It is not clear in Roberts's account why (66b) should be ungrammatical in Modern Italian. It is interesting, however, that constructions like (66b) were grammatical in earlier stages of Italian, and they still are in other Romance varieties, as shown by the material in chapter 2. Second, according to Roberts's assumptions, French shows a similar situation, from which he derives the following gerund constructions with Aux-to-Comp, parallel to the Italian example in (59):

(67) ayant ce bon homme fait tout son possible
     having this good man   done all   his possible
     'this good man having done all which was possible for him'

The problem here is that French has never had infinitival Aux-to-Comp constructions, as is shown in chapters 5 and 6. As I have repeatedly emphasized—and I still return to this point—subjects in similar French infinitive constructions are accusatives. French examples with the same linear ordering as in Italian Aux-to-Comp structures ("pseudo-Aux-to-Comp") must then find another explanation.

4.3.3.3 Romance "historical infinitives" (Mensching)

In Mensching (1995) I examined absolute infinitive constructions with a narrative function, known in descriptive grammar as "historical infinitives," which exist in almost all Romance languages. As I show in this sec'ion, such infinitival main clauses may be considered examples of a special case of nominative assignment by [+Tns] in infinitive constructions.[34]

Syntactically, the historical infinitive is characterized both by the presence of a preposition and the possibility of a preceding lexical subject. Let us look at the following examples:

(68) a. E **noi tutti** *a* ridere.   MI
     and we all   P° to-laugh
     'And we all laughed.' (Gattopardo, 102; cf. Salvi and Vanelli 1992:III, 53)

    b. Et **tous** *de* rire,   et **la conversation** *de* se mettre . . . sur un   MF
       and all   P° to-laugh and the conversation   P° R CL to-put   on an
       autre sujet.
       other subject
       'And all laughed, and the conversation was directed . . . to another subject.'
       (L'Oeuvre, 11/16/1932, p. 1a; quoted by Lombard 1936:82)

    c. **El marido** *a* ganar dinero y **ella** *a* despilfarrarlo en trapos.   MS
       the husband P° to-earn money and she P° to squander-it on duds
       'The husband earned the money and she threw it down the drain buying duds.'
       (Molho 1975:689)

    d. Estando nestas razões, / **Dom Alberto** *a* chegar.   MP
       being   in-these reasons D. A.   P° to-arrive
       'While he was reasoning like this, D. A. suddenly arrived.' (Rom. Ger., II, 33;
       cf. Prado Coelho 1950:135)

Apart from the use that is determined by pragmatic and stylistic factors ("dans un récit vif"; cf. Lombard 1936:9), from a semantic point of view the historical infinitive corresponds to a historical perfect, describing a completed action that occurred at a certain time.[35] In contrast, there is another absolute infinitive construction, the so-called descriptive infinitive, which usually does not refer to a particular time.[36] Consider the following example of descriptive infinitives in French:

(69) Que *devenir* maintenant? Se *lever*   tous les matins, se *coucher*
    what to-happen now   R CL to-get-up all   the mornings R CL to-go-to-sleep
    tous les soirs.   Ne plus *attendre* Durande, ne plus la *voir* partir, ne
    all   the evenings not more to-await D.,   not more her to-see to-leave not
    plus la *voir* revenir.
    more her to-see to-return
    'What would happen now? To get up each morning, to go to bed each evening. Not to wait for D. anymore, not to see her leave anymore, not to see her return anymore.' (Victor Hugo, passim; quoted in Lombard 1936:178)

This type of construction lacks the syntactic properties of the historical infinitive observed above. The differences between both types are summarized as follows:

(70) Historical versus descriptive infinitive in Romance

Property	Historical infinitive	Descriptive infinitive
Temporal reference	past, punctual	none or depending on context
Preposition	yes	no
Specified subject	yes	no

In Mensching (1995), I claim that this distribution leaves no doubt about an interpretation in the generative framework: in contrast to the descriptive type, the historical infinitive construction is specified for [+Tns]. The mandatory co-occurrence of the preposition with [+Tns] leads us to suspect that the preposition in Romance historical infinitive constructions is a kind of overt realization of the tense feature and that it is responsible for licensing the lexical subject. I therefore assume that the preposition is an infinitival particle specified for [+Tns],[37] and I hypothesize the structure in (71), in which the subject, base-generated in SpecVP, moves to SpecIP, where it receives the nominative through Spec-head agreement by the overt I° specified for [+Tns]:

(71)

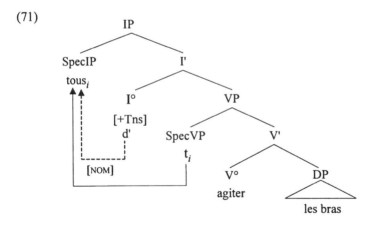

To adapt this structure to the Split-Infl framework, I examine word order facts in historical infinitive constructions with adverbs and negation. They show the linear ordering that is typical in French infinitive clauses when VP-initial adverbs are present (cf. Pollock 1989; Belletti 1990; Schmidt 1992). I also demonstrate that verb movement is optional, just as in any other French infinitive construction, whereas the tense marker is clearly situated outside the VP. In negated sentences, both the preposition and the subject are above NegP. I therefore assume that the prepositional tense marker is situated in Agr° and that the subject position is SpecAgrP.

This result is rather revealing if we consider the assumptions of Roberts (1993, 1994), discussed in sections 3.2.3 and 4.3.3.2. As we saw, Roberts excludes the possibility of nominative assignment by T° through Spec-head agreement because SpecTP is not an A-position. In the present case, however, the Spec-head configuration is established in AgrP.[38] In a finite construction with a [+NOM] feature in Agr°, case assignment by T° is blocked because of the incorporation and percolation properties assumed by Roberts. In the structure we have been discussing here, however, Agr° has no [+NOM] feature; that is, the case feature that belongs to T° is passed on to the highest Agr° head, similar to that which Roberts postulated for Aux-to-Comp structures. Now consider the following Portuguese example:

(72) [**Os santos** a *pregar* pobreza] e segui-la em tudo.
   the saints P° to-preach poverty, and to-follow-it in all
   'The saints began to ask for poverty and they followed this concept in all they did.'
   (Maurer 1968:148)

Here, the noninflected form of the infinitive is used, so this clause must be considered to be specified as [–Agr]. This supports my assumption that the case-marking properties of Agr° are not involved in nominative assignment in the historical infinitive construction. I return to this point with respect to another type of construction in 6.4.2.

4.4   Summary

In this chapter I discuss the most important approaches to specified subjects in infinitive clauses proposed so far. Apart from the fact that there are numerous Romance varieties—for example, all earlier stages, with the exception of French—that have not been considered so far, most of the existing analyses of infinitival nominative subjects represent older stages of generative theory, containing elements that cannot be accepted from a more recent point of view because of our present knowledge of principles like government, Spec-head agreement, relativized minimality, incorporation, and others. For the same reason, most of the accounts are not even compatible among themselves, so they cannot possibly be used for a comparative interpretation of the Romance languages. Furthermore, some of the accounts present serious theoretical inconsistencies, and in general it can be said that the amount of data is usually incomplete and too small.

I also try to show that some of the existing theories, particularly those that are based on the Split-Infl hypothesis, contain some valuable points, which are included in the course of the discussion in the following chapters. Particularly, the theory about infinitival T° as a case assigner seems interesting because it might account for the general tendency of the Romance languages to license postverbal subjects in infinitive constructions. As far as ECM and constructions with extracted subjects are concerned, the general picture of the state of the art is much more homogeneous and almost sufficient. Some minor points are already modified in 4.1 and 4.2, and others form a point of discussion in the rest of the book. Here, too, the main problem seems to be a lack of analysis of the older stages.

In the following chapters I provide a unified account of Romance infinitive constructions with lexical subjects. I proceed in two steps: first, I generalize from the linear word order recognizable in the data to obtain a structural description on the basis of the Split-Infl hypothesis and the assumption of a VP-internal subject (chapter 5). This is accomplished by means of the usual tests, including such facts as the position of negation, adverbs, and clitics. Second, I investigate the principles that license the relevant structures, taking case assignment as a central point (chapter 6). Since both steps are, of course, dependent on each other, some points must be left open in chapter 5 in order to be explained in chapter 6. Nevertheless, the two-step procedure has been chosen for the sake of clarity. Moreover, the results of chapter 5, that is, the structural properties of Romance infinitive constructions, also serve as a basis for the minimalist discussion in chapter 7.

5

The Position of Subjects
in Romance Infinitive Clauses

In this chapter, I analyze the data presented so far to establish the structural position of the constituents in the infinitive constructions under discussion. As suggested by its title, the main aim of this chapter is to identify the different subject positions. Since the analysis of other constituents is involved in determining the location of subjects, I also examine the position of verbs, adverbs, negation, and clitics so that this chapter will contribute to understanding the structure of old and modern Romance infinitive clauses in general. As for the subject positions, I reject some of the proposals presented in chapter 4, whereas others turn out to be compatible with the Split-Infl hypothesis and with the assumption that SpecVP is the base position of subjects.

As I explained in chapter 1, causative and similar constructions are not discussed because the analyses reviewed in section 4.1.1 are sufficient to account for those structures. Moreover, in this chapter, the difference between accusative and nominative subjects is ignored because the issue of case assignment is discussed at length in chapter 6. Thus, I now explore the question of where the subjects are located in the clause, and in the next chapter I examine what licenses these positions and the movements involved.

In section 5.1, I analyze the position of preverbal subjects. The main issue is whether preverbal subjects in infinitive clauses are located in CP or in AgrP. In section 5.2, postverbal subjects are considered, where postverbal is understood in a broader sense; that is, it is not limited to the strict adjacency of the infinitive and the subject. The subject may appear either directly after the (first) infinitive or, in the case of compound tenses (e.g., French *avoir acheté* 'to have bought'; *être acheté* 'to be bought'; *avoir été acheté* 'to have been bought'), after one of the participles involved. It is shown that in the latter case, each language behaves differently. Concerning the position of postverbal subjects, one of the main tasks is to distinguish between Aux-to-Comp constructions and other structures. It is evident that the study of verb movement plays an important role here. For purely expository reasons, I begin with the present stages of the different languages. Finally, in section 5.3, I look briefly at clause-final subjects.

5.1   Preverbal subjects

The position of preverbal subjects is much easier to identify than that of postverbal subjects. On the one hand, preverbal subjects are located higher up in the tree so that there are not so many possibilities, given the structural assumptions presented in chapter 3. On the other hand, cross-linguistic variation is not as strong as in the case of postverbal subjects. For this reason, I do not deal with each language separately.

Let us begin with negated infinitive clauses. Consider the following examples from those varieties that allow preverbal subjects:

(1) a. Seco   avvisò, [lui [*mai non* doversi   far   cristiano]]. OI
         with-himself got-aware him never not must (INF)-R CL to-make Christian
         'He understood that he would never become a Christian.' (Bocc. Dec., I, 2, p. 44)

     b. 'jiu 'biɾːa un nɛ 'katːo 'kju pi [**tu** [*um* 'bivere *'kju* 'biɾːa]]   Sic
         I   beer not A CL buy   more for you not to-drink more beer
         'I don't buy beer anymore, so that you don't drink any more beer.'
         (Corleone, Palermo)

     c. Il   aesment [**lui** [*non* pooir   estre si cort par vẽue, loqueil il   OF
         they think   him not can (INF) to-be so short by sight whom he
         avoit si grant par opinion]].[1]
         had so great by opinion
         'They think that the one of whom he had such a high opinion could not be so
         short-sighted.' (Greg., 27, 9; cf. E. Stimming 1915:117)

     d. N' avoir femme est ne soy   appoiltronner autour d' elle,   MidF
         Not to-have wife is not oneself to-repose   around of her
         pour [**elle** [*ne* contaminer celle unicque et suprême affection que
         for   her not to-pollute that unique and supreme affection that
         doibt l' homme à Dieu]].
         owes the man   to God
         'Not to have a wife means not to rest upon her, so that she cannot disturb that
         unique and supreme affection which man owes to God.' (Rabelais, 456; cf.
         Maurer 1968:72)

     e. pour [**lui** [*ne pas* courir]]   RF
         for   him not NEG2 to-run
         (ALF, 896 and 1075, point 295; cf. Lewent 1925:229, fn. 3)

     f. los quales creerían   [**yo** [*no* haber   leido las reglas]]   OS
         the which   would-believe I   not to-have read the rules
         'those who would believe that I had not read the rules' (Santillana Prov., XXIII;
         cf. Diez 1882:946)

     g. confesando [**yo** [*no* ser   mas santo que mis vccinos]]   CS
         confessing   I   not to-be more saintly than my neighbours
         'confessing that I was not more saintly than my neighbours' (Laz. 1554, 2r,
         14–15)

h. Por [yo [*no* saber *nada* me sorprendieron]].   MS
   for I   not to-know nothing me (they) surprised
   'Since I didn't know anything they surprised me.' (cf. Gili Gaya 1985:189)

i. Temo que inda que concedesse nesse casamento do soldã, GP
   (I) fear that although that (I) consented in-this marriage of-the soldier
   [minha neta Polinarda [*nom* ser contenta]].
   my   niece P.   not to-be contented
   'I fear that, although I consented in this marriage with the soldier, my niece P.
   would not be satisfied.' (Rui de Pina, passim; cf. Maurer 1968:28)

j. Fica a cousa declarada, / **[Meu parecer [*não* ser nada]].** CP
   remains the thing declared   my opinion not to-be nothing
   'I declare that my opinion is of no importance.' (Camões Seleuco, III, 273; cf.
   Otto 1891:380)

k. Incomoda-me a circunstancia de **[estas pessoas [*não* viverem**   MP
   bothers   me the circumstance of these persons not to-live-3PL
   mais na cidade]].
   anymore in-the city
   'The fact these persons do not live any longer in the city bothers me.'

As can be observed, the preverbal subject is located to the left of the negative
marker, so we can clearly localize its position as somewhere above NegP. This is
confirmed by the fact that the linear ordering *Neg + subject* could not be documented for the earlier stages of the languages involved and is ungrammatical today. Compare the following grammaticality facts with examples (1b), (1e), (1h),
and (1k):[2]

(2) a. ⋆ pi [*un* [**tu** 'bivere *'kju* 'biɾ:a]]   Sic
    b. ⋆ pour [*ne* [**lui** *pas* courir]]   RF
    c. ⋆ por [*no* [**yo** saber nada]]   MS
    d. ⋆ a circunstancia de [*não* [**estas pessoas** viverem *mais* na cidade]]   MP

Since SpecNegP is not a possible subject position, and in any case it is assumed
that Neg° is incorporated into Agr°, there are two other phrases in which the
subject could be located, AgrP and CP. The latter can be excluded for various
reasons. First, it can be observed that the subject always follows the complementizer:[3]

(3) a. Si dícinu [*di* [**tu** mangiarimi]], mi mangi.   Sic
    if (they) say C° you to-eat-me me (you) eat
    'If they told you to eat me, then eat me!' (Pitrè, 4, 165; cf. Rohlfs 1949:539, fn.;
    Maurer 1968:71)

b. Pour quel raison fu establi / [*De* [**deus homes** combatre ainsi /   OF
For   which reason was established C° two   men   to-fight   so
Encontre un seul]]?
against   one alone
'For what reason was it established that two men should fight like this against
only one person?' (Cleom., 9746: cf. Tobler 1921:93; E. Stimming 1915:123).

c. No era marauilla [*de* **tan grand mortandat** seer mostrada por   OS
not was wonder   C° so great   mortality   to-be shown   by
tantas   sennales]].
so-many signs
'It was no wonder that such a great death was announced by so many signs.'
(Cron. 236b34; cf. Beardsley 1921:261)

d. Nõ era cousa convinhavil [*de* **tu**   morreres agora]].   GP
not was thing convenient   C° you to-die-2SG now
'It was not convenient for you to die now.' (Barlaão, 45; cf. Silva Dias 1954:219;
Said Ali 1971:341)

e. Nem   temas tu   [*d*' **os meus alegres** serem].   CP
Neither fear   you C° the mine cheerful to-be-3-SG
'And do not fear my people to be cheerful.' (Camões, Eclogues 14, II B. 283;
cf. Otto 1991:382)

f. Era a   própria Idalina quem lhe pedia, agora, [*para* **ele** sair].   MP
was the very   I.   who him asked now   for he to-go-out
'It was I. herself who now asked him to go out.' (Ferreira de Castro, 386; cf.
Sten 1952:232)

Second, in several old Romance linguistic varieties, *wh* extraction of a constituent was possible:

(4) a. un servigio [*il* *quale*]$_i$ ella pensò [**niuno** doverglielo   fare t_i]   OI
a service   the which she thought no-one must (INF)-her-it to-do
'a service of which she thought that nobody should do it to her' (Bocc. Dec., IX,
1, p. 474)

b. s' il y a science   ou ignorance, ce *que*$_i$ Metrodorus Chius   MidF
if there is knowledge or ignorance, that which M.   C.
nioit [**l'** **homme** pouvoir dire t_i]
denied the man   can (INF) to-say
'if there is knowledge or ignorance, a fact of which M. C. denied that anybody
could say so' (Montaigne *A*, II, 12, vol. 4, p. 28, note 5; Montaigne *B*, vol. 2, p.
277; cf. Junker and Martineau 1992:137; see Damourette and Pichon 1911–
13:III, 571)

c. los oídos de aquella [*a quien*]$_i$ [yo segunda vez hablar t_i] tengo   OS
the ears of that-one to whom I second time to-speak (I) hold
por impossible
as impossible
'the ears of the one to whom I think it is impossible to speak a second time'
(Celest., II, 17, p. 59)

In these examples, the constituents in italics have moved into the main clause as a result of *wh* movement. It is therefore necessary to assume that the CP specifier of the infinitive construction functions as an intermediate landing site so that SpecCP is excluded as the subject position. This is illustrated in the following structure for example (4a):

(5)   [[il quale]$_i$ ella pensò [$_{CP}$ t_i [$_{AgrP}$ **niuno** dovergliele fare t_i]]]

Third, the subject can be preceded by adverbials and, in some languages (e.g., Old Spanish), by other fronted constituents:

(6)   a.   ragguardato . . . [*così* l' **ira   et il furore** essere di gran noja   OI
            considered   so   the wrath and the furore to-be of great anger
            e   di pericolo]
            and of danger
            'considered . . . that thus wrath and furor were a great annoyance and a danger'
            (Bocc. Dec., Intr.; cf. Schwendener 1923:72)

      b.   que je souhaitte [*parmy eulx* . . . **Juppiter** se promener].   MidF
            that I wish   among them   J.   R P to-promenade
            'that I wish that J. would promenade among them.' (Rabelais, 786; cf. E. Stimming 1915:138)

      c.   Non serié   buen derecho / [*a bassallo ageno* yo buscar tal   OS
            not would-be good right   to vassal   foreign I to-seek such
            provecho]. /
            profit
            'It would not be lawful for me to try and get such a profit out of another person's vassal.' (Berceo, Mil. N.S., 784 (739); cf. Beardsley 1921:258)

      d.   Él tenía la costumbre de ensuciarlo   todo [para *luego* yo   MS
            he had the habit   of to-make-dirty-it all   for then   I
            limpiarlo].
            to-clean-it
            'He had the habit of making everything dirty, for me to clean it afterward.'

      e.   Esta frase   originou-se   de [*na   épcoa romana* **todas as**   MP (E)
            this sentence originated-R.CL from in-the epoch roman   all   the
            vias militares irem ter   ao   forum da   capital do   orbis]
            ways military to-lead-3PL to-the forum of-the capital of-the o.
            Romanus.
            R.
            'This sentence originated from the fact that in Roman times all ways led to the forum of the capital of the Orbis Romanus.' (Leite de Vasc., Op., I, 225; cf. Sten 1952:206)

    f. não poder ver   ninguém, sem [*logo* a **outra pessoa** lhe   MP (B)
       not can (INF) to-see nobody   without then the other person him
       lembrar aquilo]
       to-remind that
       'not to be able to see anybody without the other person reminding him of it
       afterward' (Ferreira de Castro, 266)

    g. O mariñeiro ten un delejado para levá -la contabilidade, ou os MG
       the sailor   has an employee for to-carry the bookkeeping   or the
       caixóns, que . . . venden para [*despós* **eles** faseren   o changüí].
       boxes   that   (they) sell for   later   they to-make-3PL the ration
       'The sailor has an employee for doing the bookkeeping, or for keeping a record
       of the boxes, in order for them to distribute the shares later on.' (ALGa 1990
       seqq.; quoted by Gondar 1978:64)

On the basis of the current assumption that sentence-initial adverbs are situated in a position left-adjoined to AgrP (cf. Duarte 1989; Belletti 1990), the facts shown in (6) also exclude the location of the subject inside or above the CP.

    It is therefore evident that the phrase containing the preverbal subject can be identified cross-linguistically as AgrP. Nevertheless, we still do not know the preverbal subject's exact position inside AgrP. As we see in chapter 3, SpecAgrP is a typical subject position, so it seems to be the most probable candidate. We cannot, however, completety exclude a position left-adjoined to AgrP, and with adjunction being defined by a recursive rule, this would still be compatible with the data presented in (6). Since AgrP plays an important role in case assignment, I leave this point open for the moment and return to it in the next chapter. There it is shown that SpecAgrP should, in fact, be considered the preverbal subject position in most of the languages examined here, whereas I postulate adjunction for Modern Spanish and Catalan.

5.2   Postverbal subjects

5.2.1   Italian

5.2.1.1 Contemporary Italian

For contemporary Italian, it is usually assumed without discussion that the postverbal position of the subject in infinitive clauses is due to Aux-to-Comp movement (cf. chapter 4).[4] Of course, this assumption, which dates back to a rather old stage of generative grammar, has to be reconfirmed against the background of the Split-Infl hypothesis. As a starting point, I assume, with Belletti (1990:71; cf. chapter 3), that in Italian both finite verbs and infinitives move to Agr°, where they are incorporated together with Neg° (*non*). Consider the following examples of negated infinitive clauses with specified subjects:

(7) a. Tra   queste distinzioni una delle principali è [il *non* essersi **egli**
       Among these   distinctions one of-the main   is the not to-be-R CL he
       più   accontato con i fuorusciti].
       anymore mixed   with the runaways
       'Among these distinctions, one of the main ones is the fact that he did no longer
       get associated with the runaways.' (cf. Körner 1983:84)

b. ? Il ministro afferma [*non* essere **il presidente** *più* disposto ad
   the minister states   not to-be the president more disposed to
   aiutarci].
   to-help-us
   'The minister states that the president would no longer be willing to help us.'

c. *Il ministro afferma [essere *non più* **il presidente** disposto ad aiutarci].

d. *Il ministro afferma [*non più* essere **il presidente** disposto ad aiutarci].

According to the assumptions made on negation, the word order in (7a) and (7b) can, in fact, only be explained if we admit that [$_{Agr°}$ [*non essere*]] is located in C°, whereas the subject is situated in the specifier of AgrP, so that Rizzi's (1982) Aux-to-Comp analysis can be confirmed. The Aux-to-Comp structure revised on the basis of the Split-Infl hypothesis is illustrated in (8):[5]

(8)

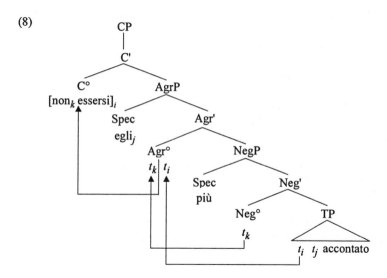

I put forward another argument in the following section in connection with the position of adverbs, which is examined on the basis of the earlier stages of Italian.

5.2.1.2 Stages of Italian up to the nineteenth century

As shown in section 2.1, one of the basic differences between Modern Italian and the earlier stages of the language is the fact that today postverbal subjects in infinitive constructions are restricted to infinitives of copulative and auxiliary verbs, whereas this restriction did not hold in Old Italian, where this construction can also be found with transitive and intransitive verbs, among others. This Old Italian situation can still be documented in literary texts up to the nineteenth century.

A simple explanation for these facts could be that movement to C° was not restricted to special verb types in the earlier stages. However, before such an assumption is made, we must see whether $V°$-to-$C°$ movement really obtains. Remember that one of the basic arguments by which the Aux-to-Comp analysis was initiated was the observation that an overt subject is excluded when a prepositional element appears in $C°$. The problem with Old Italian is that there are cases of infinitive constructions in which a prepositional complementizer actually does co-occur with an overt subject (cf. the data in 2.1 and the analysis of prepositions in 3.3.3):[6]

(9) È una grande fatica [$_{CP}$ a [$_{AgrP}$ conservare l' uomo la pecunia]].
     is a   great   fatigue   C°   to-preserve the man   the money
     'It is a great effort for a man to preserve his money.' (Giord. Riv., 225; cf. Segre 1991:119)

Aux-to-Comp movement is therefore excluded in cases like (9). If the infinitive in these structures is not situated in $C°$ and the subject is not in SpecAgrP, it is obvious that these Old Italian cases have a totally different structure, which I examine now.

A first hint is provided by the dative clitic *gli* in the following example:

(10) Non gli sarà   egli gravissimo all'   animo . . . [non *gli* essere lecito
     not him will-be it very-hard for-the spirit   not him to-be licit
     quanto vorrebbe   et gioverebbe a dirizzare il figliuolo ad una o
     all-that would-want and would-help to direct   the little-son to one or
     un'altra virtude o lode].
     another virtue or fame
     'It would not be very hard for his spirit . . . that he would not be allowed to do all which is necessary and helpful for directing his little son towards virtue or fame of one kind or another.' (Alberti Fam. *A.*, I, p. 73; cf. Schwendener 1923:80)

The preinfinitival position of the clitic that is seen in (10) can still be found in the written language of the nineteenth century, as the following example with the adverbial clitic *ci* ('there') shows:

(11) Ma egli . . . può negar con la bocca, [non *ci*   esser **giusta superiorità** d'
     but he   can deny with the mouth   not there to-be just   superiority of
     uomo sopra gli uomini].
     man over the men
     'But he . . . can deny with his mouth that there is not a legitimate superiority of one man over the others.' (Promessi Sposi, ch. 22, p. 318; cf. Schwendener 1923:57)

According to Kayne (1991), the position of a clitic before the infinitive (which is regular, e.g., in Modern French) may indicate that the verb has not moved so far to the left as would be the case with the enclitic position, in which the verb has moved past the clitic (cf. 3.1.3). Thus, whereas infinitives move to Agr° in Modern Italian, it may be argued that they stayed below AgrP in earlier times. Nevertheless, the modern structure seems to be more frequent,[7] so I assume that movement of the infinitive to Agr° and (maybe further up to $C°$) was optional in those stages of the language.

A possible hypothesis to account for examples (10) and (11) would then be that V° is under T° and that the subject stays in SpecVP. A strong argument for this hypothesis is provided by the position of adverbs. Belletti (1990:49, 55) observes the ungrammaticality of the linear order V-Adv-DP$_{subj}$ in present Aux-to-Comp structures. Compare (12a) with the grammatical example (12b):

(12) a. *Ritenevano [aver   probabilmente **lui** sbagliato troppe   volte].
         (they) believed to-have probably   he erred   too-many times
         'They believed that he had probably committed errors too many times.'

     b. Ritenevano [aver **lui** *probabilmente* sbagliato troppe volte].

If we accept that *probabilmente* is situated in a position left-adjoined to VP, the ungrammaticality of (12a) is obviously due to the fact that the subject has not moved to SpecAgrP so that the Aux-to-Comp configuration is not established. On the other hand, (12b) is grammatical:

(13) Ritenevano [aver$_j$ **lui**$_i$ t_j [$_{VP}$ probabilmente [$_{VP}$ t_i sbagliato troppe volte]]].

It is interesting that the word order in (12a), ungrammatical today, can in fact be documented for earlier stages:

(14) Rispondevasi . . . [esser *veramente* **Venezia** infelice]
     (it) answered-R CL   to-be really   Venice   unlucky
     'It was answered . . . that Venice was really unlucky.' (Botta, VIII, p. 57; cf.
     Schwendener 1923:63)

My assumption that the subject remains in SpecVP correctly predicts that (14) is wellformed, which can then be analyzed roughly as follows:

(15) esser [$_{VP}$ veramente [$_{VP}$ Venezia infelice]]

According to Cinque (1999:86–87, 106), epistemic adverbs are situated in a rather high position in the tree, more precisely in his Mood$_{epistemic}$ phrase, which is somewhere between CP and the T$_{past}$ phrase, with other mood phrases above it. Note that the analysis I am proposing is compatible with the structures assumed by Cinque. Within his framework, the subject in (12b) could be argued to be in the highest mood phrase immediately below C°, which contains the auxiliary, whereas the subject in (14) is in its base position, in conformity with my assumption.

Further support for my analysis comes from compound infinitives of the type *infinitive + participle*. In contrast to Modern Italian, the subject still frequently appeared after the participle in the nineteenth century:

(16) a. da   questo [*essere abbandonati* **gli infermi** da'   vicini]   14th c.
         from this   to-be abandoned   the ill   by-the neighbors
         'from this fact, namely that the ill were abandoned by their neighbors' (Bocc.
         Dec., Intr., 29; cf. Dardano 1963:113, fn. 46)

b. Orarono,   [*essere venuti* **gli uomini Lombardi** a   19th c.
    (they) announced to-be   come   the men   Lombards   to
    congratularsi . . .].
    congratulate-R CL
    'They announced that the Lombards had come in order to congratulate . . .'
    (Botta, IX, p. 78; cf. Schwendener 1923:58)

Typically, in Aux-to-Comp constructions only the auxiliary moves to C°. This
strongly suggests that another structure must be postulated here, although the C°
position is not filled by an overt complementizer. Let us return to my hypothesis
that the infinitive was located in T° in earlier Italian, whereas the subject remained in its base position.[8] In fact, the word order in (16) is compatible with
such an analysis, if we assume that the participle moves out of the VP. The illus-
tration in (17) shows how this could be done, following Roberts's (1993:118)
analysis for similar finite constructions in Old French:[9]

(17) $[_{TP} [_{T°}$ essere venuti$_i$] $[_{VP}$ gli uomini t_i]]

Finally, the structure I assume is supported by the following example with
complex negation:

(18) Un suo edito . . . bandiva . . . [*non più* avere **il regno** fazioni o parti].
      a   his edict   proclaimed   not more to-have the kingdom sections or parts
      'One of his edicts . . . proclaimed . . . that the kingdom was no longer made up of
      sections or parts.' (Colletta, IV, 3, p. 244; cf. Schwendener 1923:50)

The infinitive *avere* follows both negative markers (*non più*). According to the
assumptions concerning negation discussed in chapter 3, we can postulate the
following structure:

(19)

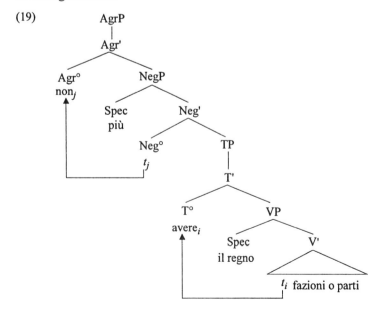

To sum up, the results achieved in this section show two configurations in which postverbal infinitival subjects can be found in the history of Italian:

(20) a. $[_{CP} V°_j [_{AgrP} DP_{subj\ i} \cdots t_i\ t_j \cdots]]$
     b. $[_{TP} V°_i [_{VP} DP_{subj}\ t_i \cdots]]$ (until the nineteenth century)

For those stages of the language that admitted the configuration (20b), it is furthermore to be expected that overt postverbal subjects were also possible in infinitival AgrPs not embedded into CPs. This can actually be shown for some constructions. Let us consider infinitive constructions selected by raising verbs, which are usually considered to be AgrPs (IPs in the earlier terminology; cf. Burzio 1986:218–20; Graffi 1994:343). Since CP is missing in these constructions, the Aux-to-Comp construction (20a) is excluded, as Rizzi (1982:129, 140–41) has shown for Modern Italian:[10]

(21) ⋆Sembra / pare [esser **loro** arrivati in ritardo].
        seems   to-be they arrived in delay
        'It seems that they have arrived late.'

Yet, in earlier stages of Italian overt subjects are possible in such cases, as expected:

(22) A lui pareva, [tale essere **la opportunità e la necessità di questa**
        to him seemed such to-be the opportunity and the necessity of this
        alleanza . . .]
        alliance
        'It seemed to him that the opportunity and the necessity of this alliance was such
        . . .' (Botta, VIII, p. 50; see Schwendener 1923:79)

In a similar fashion we could possibly explain why overt subjects are ungrammatical today (but not in the earlier stages) in other construction types, for example, those in which the infinitive clause works as a subject,[11] a predicate nominal, or a prepositional object. Several facts make these constructions appear to be AgrPs rather than CPs. First, note that none permits an overt complementizer:

(23) a. [⋆Di/⋆a parlare cosí] vuole dire ignorare i fatti.
           C°   to-speak so   wants to-say to-ignore the facts
           'To speak like this means to ignore the facts.'

     b. Bisogna   [⋆di/⋆a farlo].
        (it) is-necessary C° to-do-it
        'It is necessary to do it.'

     c. Non andarci   sarebbe [⋆di /⋆a essere stupido].
        not to-go-there would-be   C° to-be stupid
        'Not to go there would mean to be stupid.'

     d. Mi hanno   forzato a [⋆di / ⋆a farlo].
        me (they) have forced   C°   to-do-it
        'They forced me to do it.'

Second, they do not permit *wh* elements:

(24) a. *[Cosa dire]   significa ignorare i   fatti?
         what to-say means   to-ignore the facts
         'To say what would mean to ignore the facts?'

     b. *Bisogna   [cosa fare]?
         is-necessary what to-do
         'What is necessary to do?'

     c. *Non andarci   sarebbe [cosa essere]?
         not to-go-there would-be what to-be
         'Not to go there would mean to be what?'

     d. *Ti   hanno   forzato a [cosa fare]?
         you (they) have forced   to what to-do
         'They forced you to do what?'

If these constructions lack a CP projection, then, Aux-to-Comp is excluded but not the configuration (20b), a fact that correctly predicts the possibility of lexical subjects in earlier stages of the language.

5.2.2   Spanish

5.2.2.1 Modern Spanish

Modern Spanish behaves very similarly to Old Italian in the verbs permitted as infinitives and the presence of complementizers.[12] Example (25a) shows a post-verbal lexical subject (*Juan*) with the infinitive of a transitive verb (*tener*). The C° is occupied by *de* here (cf. 3.3.3 and 4.3.2.3), so verb movement to C° can be excluded. The position of the adverb in (25b) shows the subject in its base position:

(25) a. $[_{CP}$ De $[_{AgrP}$ [no tener **Juan** mucho dinero]]], María no se habría
                 C° (COND) not to-have J.   much   money M.   not R CL would-have
         casado con él.
         married with him
         'If J. had not had much money, M. would not have married him.' (Fernández
         Lagunilla 1987:132)

     b. $[_{CP}$ De $[_{AgrP}$ estar$_i$ $[_{TP}$ t_i $[_{VP}$ verdaderamente $[_{VP}$ **Juan** t_i en casa]]]]], él
                 C° (COND) to-be   really   J.   at home   he
         nos habría   salvado.
         us   would-have saved
         'If J. had really been at home he would have saved us.'

In contrast to earlier Italian, the infinitive is situated between both negative markers in Modern Spanish:[13]

(26) a. a pesar de [*no* restar *ya* **más que seis varones en el coro**]
in spite of not to-remain anymore more than six men in the choir
'in spite of there not remaining more than six men in the choir' (Camino, 178; cf. Skydsgaard 1977:707)

b. ?El hecho de [*no* volver *más* **Juan** a casa es algo que me preocupa].
the fact of not to-return more J. to home is s.th. that me worries
'The fact that J. won't come back home anymore is something that worries me.'

c. ★El hecho de [*no más* volver **Juan** a casa es algo que me preocupa].

According to our assumptions on negation, movement of T°(+V°) to Agr° is mandatory. The structure can be described as follows:

(27)

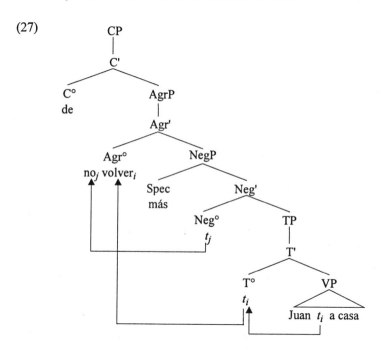

We still might ask if Spanish has Aux-to-Comp structures with the subject in SpecAgrP. Concerning this issue, the following example seems to be rather surprising (cf. also Fernández Lagunilla 1987):[14]

(28) a. [De *haberse* **Juan** *ido*], no habría andado lejos.
C° (COND) to-have-R CL J. gone not (he) would-have walked far
'If J. had gone away, he would not have walked far away.'

b. [De *haberse ido* **Juan**], no habría andado lejos.

The linear ordering of the constituents in (28a) is identical to the one we find in Italian Aux-to-Comp structures, though the latter should be excluded here because of the presence of the complementizer *de*. In fact, this can be confirmed if we look at complex negation in comparison to the Italian example (7):

(29) ??[De   *no* haberse   **Juan** *nunca* ido], no me habría   pasado esto.
       C° (COND) not to-have-R CL J.   never gone not me would-have happened this
       'If J. had never gone away, this would not have happened to me.'

To interpret examples like (28), I therefore assume that V° (i.e., a participle or a gerund) stays in situ in (28a), whereas it is incorporated into T° (which then moves to Agr°) in (28b). This is a difference in the behavior of a participle in finite clauses, as is demonstrated by the following examples:

(30) a. ⋆[Se ha Juan ido].
          R CL has J.   gone
          'J. has left.'

    b. ⋆[Si se   hubiera Juan ido], no habría   andado lejos.
          If R CL had   J.   gone not (he) would-have walked far
          'If J. had left, he would not have walked far away.'

This obviously means that incorporation into T° is obligatory when it is [+finite] but not when T° is [−finite], in conformity with the assumptions made by Pollock (1989).

5.2.2.2   Old and Classical Spanish

The facts in Old and Classical Spanish are very similar to the data for Modern Spanish. As in the earlier stages of Italian and in Modern Spanish, postverbal subjects were possible even when there was an overt C°:

(31) casas, que, [CP *a* [AgrP   estar **ellas** en pié y   bien labradas]] . . . valdrían
       houses which   C° (COND) to-be they   on foot and well built   would-cost
       más de   doscientas veces mil   maravedís
       more than two hundred times thousand m.
       'houses which, if they were erected and built well, would cost more than two hundred thousand maravedís' (Laz. 1554, 46v)

The idea that in the earlier stages of Spanish, too, the subject of the infinitive remained in SpecVP is supported by examples like the following, in which a complement appears before the infinitive:

(32) [*Profession* fazer **el frayre**], es renunçiar el mundo.   OS
       profession to-do the monk   is to-renounce the world
       'For a monk to practice his profession means to renounce all worldly things.'
       (Cron., 692a3; cf. Beardsley 1921:259)

In section 3.1.2, I argue that the preverbal position of the direct object in similar finite structures can be interpreted as A'-movement to SpecAgrP. If we accept this for infinitive clauses as well—and I argue in chapter 6 that this must be assumed—we must also accept that SpecAgrP is blocked as a landing site for the subject, so it must have remained in its base position.

A basic difference from Modern Spanish is the position of clitics. Clitics could have the same position as in Modern Spanish, that is, immediately following the infinitive (and thus before the subject), as in (33a).[15] However, in contrast to Modern Spanish, we also find the clitic to the left of the infinitive, as in (33b):[16]

(33) a. Fue abraham en esta edad derechero [de fablar *le* **nuestro sennor**
 was A. at this age authorized C° to-speak him our Lord
 dios].
 God
 'At that age Abraham was authorized to be spoken to by God our Lord.' (Gen. Est., 47r)

 b. Es asaz conplimiento [para *se* guardar **omne** . . . de los
 is enough convenience for R CL to-beware man of the
 mezcladores].
 agitators
 'It is most convenient for man to beware of the agitators.' (Cal. e D. *A*, 178)

At first sight, the proclitic position in (33b) might be regarded as an effect of verb movement to T° rather than to Agr°, similar to what has been shown in 5.2.1.2 for the earlier stages of Italian. This is ruled out, however, by the following examples:

(34) a. Et non es maravilla [en *me* *non* anparar **yo** de la ventura].
 and not is wonder in myself not to-protect I from the fate
 'And it is no wonder that I do not protect myself from fate.' (Cal. e D. *A*, 204)

 b. & dixol alli luego [por *se* *non* tardar *mas*] & yr se ayna
 & said-him there then for R CL not to-retard more & go R CL away
 'and then he said to him, in order not to lose more time and to go away' (Gen. Est., 148r)

Unlike the Italian examples (10) and (11), the clitic precedes Neg° in (34a). In (34b), the infinitive is situated between both parts of the negation. If we assume that *mas* occupies SpecNegP, it is clear that the infinitive must have moved to Agr°, where it is incorporated with Neg°, just as in Modern Spanish.

Now, compare the following case in which the clitic appears before the preverbal subject:

(35) Et fío por vuestro saber [en *vos* **yo** *consejar* et vos amar].
 and (I) trust for your knowledge in you I to-counsel and you to-love
 'And, for the sake of your knowledge, I have confidence in my counseling and loving you.' (Cal. e D. *A*, 148)

All these facts show that the differences in word order between Old Spanish and the later stages are not due to any difference of subject placement or verb movement but rather to clitic movement. Although I do not discuss clitics in greater detail here, I would like to suggest that the clitic has moved to CP:

(36) a. Et fío por vuestro saber [$_{PP}$ en [$_{CP}$ vos$_k$ [$_{AgrP}$ yo$_i$ consejar$_j$ [$_{TP}$ t_i t_j t_k . . .]]]]

     b. Et non es maravilla [$_{PP}$ en [$_{CP}$ me$_j$ [$_{AgrP}$ non$_k$ anparar$_i$ [$_{NegP}$ t_k [$_{TP}$ · · · yo t_i t_j . . .]]]]]

It might be argued that the clitic is incorporated into C°,[17] which is Kaiser's (1992) suggestion for Galician-Portuguese. In the case of negation, we more often observe the following order, with the clitic appearing between Neg° and the verb:

(37) por *non te* querer **Dios** ayudar
     for not you to-want God to-help
     'because God does not want to help you' (Cron., 40b47; cf. Beardsley 1921:260)

In a framework like that of Kaiser, this could be explained by assuming that the clitic can alternatively be incorporated into Neg° (or rather tends to do so).[18] One might generalize from both cases by saying that in Old Spanish clitics could be incorporated into all functional heads above TP.

I therefore assume that the positions of the infinitive and of the subject have remained unchanged from the Old Spanish time up to now, whereas the observed differences of word order are due to a change in the behavior of clitics. The clitic phenomena that we have observed began to fade away in the transition period from Old to Classical Spanish. In the texts I have examined, the last examples can be found in the sixteenth century,[19] after which we usually observe the Modern Spanish word order.[20]

The question of whether Old and Classical Spanish had infinitival Aux-to-Comp constructions is rather difficult to answer. It is, however, a fact that the Aux-to-Comp like word order shown in (28a) for Modern Spanish is the only word order that could be documented for Old Spanish in our corpus.[21] Consider (37) above and (38):

(38) a. que se   doliessen ellas . . . [por el miedo de *seer* **ellas** *penadas* . . .]
     that R CL suffered they   for the fear of to-be they punished
     'that they suffered for the fear of being punished' (Gen. Est., 8r)

     b. Jamás noche á faltado   [sin   *ser* **nuestro uerto** *escalado*
     never night has been-missing without to-be our   orchard ascended
     como fortaleza].
     like fortress
     'No night has passed without our orchard being conquered like a fortress.'
     (Celest., XVI, 17, p. 243)

   c. Bien afirmaremos [*ser* **todas las cosas** *crïadas* a manera de contienda].
      well (we) will-state to-be all   the things created in fashion of struggle
      'We will surely state that all things are created by means of struggle.' (Celest.,
      Prefacio, 18, p. 11)

Since no examples with overt C°, complex negation, or adverbs were found in the
texts I examined, this issue cannot be resolved here and will be left for future research (see also 6.2.1). However, as has been shown, verb movement properties
have not changed from Old Spanish up to now, so Aux-to-Comp should be considered the less probable solution. It should rather be assumed that the data in
(38) are the result of a restriction on the movement of participles, in the sense
that the Modern Spanish option of a nonfinite V° incorporating into T° together
with an auxiliary was not yet available.

5.2.3   Portuguese

5.2.3.1 Modern Portuguese and Galician

As pointed out in 4.3.2.2, Raposo (1987) assumes that postverbal subjects in Portuguese infinitive constructions are due to Aux-to-Comp movement. His assumption is based on the following observation: the (generally more frequent) preverbal subject position is ungrammatical in some constructions, one of which corresponds to exactly the same configuration in which Aux-to-Comp is observed in
Italian, namely, an infinitive clause as a complement of declarative and epistemic
verbs. It must be pointed out, however, that the attempt to apply the Aux-to-
Comp solution to Portuguese was basically motivated on the basis of the older
assumption that subjects are base-generated in SpecIP, so that V°-to-C° movement was the simplest explanation for the linear ordering verb + subject.

    Ambar (1994)[22] rejects Raposo's (1987) Aux-to-Comp hypothesis by exam-
ining the position of sentential adverbials, as is shown in (39):

(39) a. Penso *só* *ontem* terem   eles recebido a notícia.
       (I) think only yesterday to-have-3PL they received   the news
       'I think that they received the news not before yesterday.'

    b. ★Penso terem *só ontem* eles recibido a notícia.

Adverbials of this type are usually situated in a position that is left-adjoined to
AgrP. If these structures were really cases of Aux-to-Comp movement, (39b)
should be grammatical, whereas (39a) should be ungrammatical, in contradiction
to the facts.

    In addition to Ambar's objection against Aux-to-Comp, more arguments can
be found to refute Raposo's assumption. Remember that for Modern Italian the
Aux-to-Comp analysis is justified, as is shown in 4.3.2.1 and 5.2.1.1, because it
can explain several phenomena, such as the limitation of the construction to CP,
the ungrammaticality of the structure when C° is overt, and the limitation of the
construction to auxiliary and copulative verbs. However, in contrast to Italian,
none of these properties can be observed in Portuguese. First, both in Modern
Portuguese and in Galician the construction is not limited to infinitival comple-

ment clauses but can also be found in infinitive constructions selected by raising verbs, which lack a CP projection (cf. the examples given in section 2.4).[23] Second, postverbal subjects can co-occur with overt complementizers, as in the following example from Galician:

(40) O rapáz ordeou de ir el soio a   feira, pois, [*de*   iren   **os**
     the boy ordered to go he alone to-the fair because C° (COND) to-go-3PL the
     dous] non mercarían   nunca].
     two   not (they) would-trade never
     'The boy ordered him to go alone to the fair, because, if both of them went, they would never do any trading.' (Contos da Galiza, 94, p. 209; cf. Gondar 1978:91)

A third argument, which was already mentioned in section 4.3.2.2, is the following: in contrast to Modern Italian, the Portuguese infinitive can have a postverbal subject even if the main verb is neither an auxiliary nor a copulative verb. In addition to (56) from chapter 4, the following examples can be given:

(41) a. à vista dos   quais pareceu conveniente [*começarem* **os respectivos**
        at sight of-the which seemed convenient   to-begin-3PL the respective
        trabalhos]
        works
        'to whose point of view it seemed convenient that their respective works should begin' (Revista, XIV, 140; cf. Sten 1952:97)

    b. Soares considerava deselegante [*pagarem* **outros** o que seria   gasto].
        S.   considered   inelegant   to-pay-3PL others what would-be spent.
        'S. considered it inelegant that others should pay what would be spent.' (Costa, Solar, 32; cf. Sten 1952:119)

Moreover, the data presented in chapter 2 show that this construction is possible in a far larger number of configurations than in Modern Italian; it can be found in almost all kinds of infinitive constructions. This is similar to our findings in Old Italian and Spanish, that is, in Romance varieties that license postverbal infinitival subjects without Aux-to-Comp movement.

Furthermore, the fact that the phenomena mentioned are not due to Aux-to-Comp can be supported by an examination of negation:

(42) a. O presidente afirmou [terem   **estas pessoas** vivido na   cidade].
        the president affirmed to-have-3PL these persons lived in-the city
        'The president affirmed that these persons had lived in the city.'

    b. ? O presidente afirmou [*não mais* terem   vivido **estas pessoas**
        the president affirmed not more to-have-3PL lived   these persons
        na   cidade].
        in-the city
        'The president affirmed that these persons had not lived in the city any longer.'

    c. *O presidente afirmou [*não* terem **estas pessoas** *mais* vivido na cidade].

Although negation generally seems to cause a loss of grammaticality when the infinitival subject occurs in a postverbal position, there are various degrees of grammaticality according to speakers' judgments. The most widely accepted order is the one in (42b), in which both elements of negation precede the infinitive, as well as the subject. [24] This can be analyzed just like the parallel Old Italian and Spanish data:

(43) $[_{TP} [_{T^o}$ terem vivido$_i]$ $[_{VP}$ estas pessoas t_i]]

In contrast, the linear ordering in (42c), which would be yielded by Aux-to-Comp (cf. the Italian example 7a), is, in fact, ungrammatical.[25]

In summary, it can be concluded that in Modern Portuguese and Galician postverbal subjects in infinitive constructions are situated in their base position and the infinitive moves to T°, with a further movement to Agr° accepted by some speakers.

5.2.3.2 Galician-Portuguese / Classical Portuguese

For the earlier stages, too, Aux-to-Comp can be excluded by the presence of overt complementizers:

(44) Non é guisado / $[_{CP}$ de me forçaredes **vos**]].   GP
       not is appropriate   C° me to-force-2PL you
       'It is not appropriate for you to force me.' (Cantigas, no. 135, v. 91-92; cf. Gondar 1978:94)

In addition, C° can be excluded as a verb position on the evidence of clitics. The behavior of clitics in Galician-Portuguese and, in part, in Classical Portuguese, is similar to that in Old Spanish (see 5.2.2.2; cf. Kaiser 1992). The fact that the clitic is in CP is demonstrated in (45a), which has a parallel structure to the Old Spanish example in (36a), where the preverbal subject (presumably situated in AgrP) is located between the clitic and the verb. A similar case is (45b), which shows an adverb between the clitic and the infinitive:

(45) a. Pedya . . . que se non entrometese   de coller . . . mays o dito
         (he) asked that R CL not (he) should-insist in to-take   more the mentioned
         portalgo et que lles lo leixasse   liure . . . [pera o **elles** colleren
         toll   and that them it should-leave free   for it they to-take-3PL
         e   recabdaren . . .]
         and to-collect-3PL
         'He asked . . . [him] not to try any longer to collect . . . the toll that was mentioned and that he should leave it at their disposal . . . in order for them to collect it.' (Devanceiros, t. II, doc. 407, p. 414; cf. Gondar 1978:65)

b. Os (morauedis) que me el deue pagueos   logo [pera *me logo*
    the m.   which me he owes (he) shall-pay later   for me later
    acorreren pera   alma].
    to-help-3PL for-the soul
    '[As to] the morauedis that he owes me, he shall pay them to you later, so that
    they may then be of help for my soul.' (Devanceiros, t. 1, doc. 42, p. 64; cf.
    Gondar 1978:66)

Example (44), where we find both a postverbal subject and a complementizer
immediately followed by the clitic, may then be assigned the structure in (46):

(46) Non é guisado / [$_{CP}$ de me [$_{AgrP}$ forçaredes **vos**]].

All that we have seen so far is perfectly compatible with the following example,
in which the subject is located below NegP:

(47) cõ   medo de [o   *nõ* matarẽ   **os mouros**]
     with fear of him not to-kill-3PL the Moors
     'fearing that the Moors would kill him' (Miragres, p. 147, 1. 2–3; cf. Gondar
     1978:127)

Concerning the position of the subject and the infinitive, we can therefore conclude that the structure has remained unchanged from the Middle Ages to today.

5.2.4   Old and Middle French

As in all Romance varieties discussed so far (with the exception of Modern Italian), Old French shows postverbal subjects co-occurring with overt prepositional
complementizers:

(48) Quel joie a cascun   Est [$_{CP}$ *d'* [$_{AgrP}$ habiteir **freres** en un]].
     what joy to everybody is   C°   to-live brothers in one
     'What a joy it is for everybody that brothers live in unity.' (Brandan, 156; quoted by
     Lachmund 1878:25; Lewent 1925:223; Lerch 1929:154–55)

In addition, in Old French we find inversion structures typical for languages in
which SpecAgrP can function both as an A-position and as an A'-position (cf.
3.1.3 for finite clauses in Old French and example 32 in this chapter for Old
Spanish):

(49) a. car   [*miracle* estre **ce**] savoit
         because miracle to-be this (he) knew
         'because he knew that this was a miracle' (N. D. Chartr., 117, 6; cf. E.
         Stimming 1915:115; Tobler 1921:91; Meier 1955:284)

b. Mes a   anvis ou volenters / Convient   [*au   sene* aler **le**
    but against will   or voluntarily   is-convenient to-the synod to-go the
    prestre].
    priest
    'But it is convenient that the priest go to the synod either against his will or
    voluntarily.' (Ren. Montaub., I, 741; cf. E. Stimming 1915:105)

As has been pointed out in 5.2.2.2 for Old Spanish, it is usually assumed that the
subject remains in its base position (SpecVP) when another constituent has
moved to SpecAgrP. This assumption is supported in the next chapter in the
course of the discussion of case assignment. Since no examples with negation or
adverbs could be found in our material, it is not possible at this point to further
elaborate on the structure of Old French infinitive clauses.

We can, however, be more precise for Middle French. As has been shown in
chapter 4, Junker and Martineau (1992) suggest on purely theoretical grounds
(partly based on wrong assumptions about case; cf. 4.3.1.4) that a postverbal
subject in infinitive constructions of Middle and Classical French remains in
SpecVP. Their assumption about the subject position can in fact be confirmed by
means of the usual criteria (position of adverbs and negation). Consider the following example:

(50) pour [en tel   lieu *n' estre point* **les François** *subjects* au   gouvernement
     for   at such place not to-be NEG2 the French   subject to-the government
     d' Angleterre]
     of England
     'because at such a place the French were not subject to the government of England'
     (d'Aubigné, Hist., IV, 133; cf. Lewent 1925:231–32, according to Palmgren
     1905:115–16)

With respect to negation, the example shows the word order *ne + infinitive +
point/plus/pas*, which is characteristic for the earlier stages of French, and has
been explained by verb movement to Agr° (cf. Roberts 1993 and Rohrbacher
1994:223–24, among others). I therefore conclude that the subject in (50) is situated beneath NegP, as illustrated in (51):

(51)

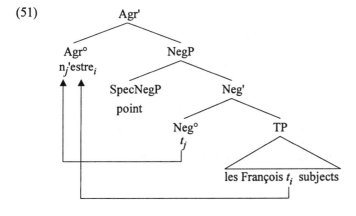

The following examples in (52) show that the subject is located even further down in the tree. According to Cinque (1999:106), the two adverbs involved are aspectual adverbs, which are located in one of the aspect phrases in the lower part of the tree structure to the left of VP. In the framework adopted here, I assume that the adverbs are located beneath TP, under Pollock's (1989) assumption that adverbs like *souvent* and *toujours* are situated in a position left-adjoined to VP:

(52) a. pour [*avoir toujours* **ceste isle** *esté subjecte* à recevoir rudes
       for   to-have always   this   island been subject to to-receive rude
       traictements]
       treatments
       'because this island had always been subject to rude treatment' (d'Aubigné, IV, 135; cf. Palmgren 1905:115–16; Lewent 1925:232)

   b. jusques à [en *estre souvent* l' **âme** *désemparée* du   corps]
       until   to ACL to-be often   the soul abandoned   by-the body
       'until the soul was frequently abandoned by the body' (Rabelais, 549; cf. Saenger 1888:33–34; Lewent 1925:230)

I therefore conclude that the infinitive clause in (52b) has the structure shown in (53):[26]

(53)

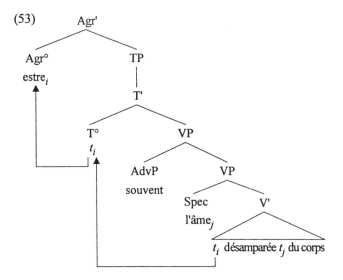

In our corpus no evidence could be found for subjects that appear after *estre* + *participle* (cf. chapter 2). This can possibly be interpreted by assuming that participles did not undergo movement and obligatorily remained inside the VP (cf. 51), which is similar to what I have said about Old Spanish.

5.2.5   Other linguistic varieties

In Sicilian, as observed in 5.2.1.2 for the earlier stages of Italian, postverbal lexical subjects are not restricted to infinitives of copulative and auxiliary verbs (cf. the data in 2.5.1). As in almost all other varieties discussed so far, postverbal subjects are licensed in infinitive constructions with overt complementizers, so that the following structures can be assumed:

(54) a.   l   i'nitsju   ra   sa'luti ɛ [$_{CP}$ ri [$_{AgrP}$ ka'nuʃiri l 'omo a s:ɔ
           the beginning of-the health is   C°   to-know the man the his
           mala't:ia]]
           illness
           'The beginning of health is when one recognizes one's illness.'

   b.   [$_{CP}$ ri [$_{AgrP}$ 'ʈi:ri **mi 'paʈɾi** a 'k:j:ɛza]] um mi 'pjatʃi
        C°   to-go my father to church   not me pleases
        'I don't like it that my father goes to church.'

The fact that the postverbal subject is located beneath AgrP in Sicilian can also be confirmed by the following negated sentences, according to the judgment of various speakers:[27]

(55) a.   um pɔ 'ɛs:iri ['ʈi:ri *kju* '**jiu** a 'k:jɛza]
           not can to-be to-go more I to church
           'It is impossible for me not to go to church anymore' (Corleone, Palermo)

   b.   ★um pɔ 'ɛs:iri [*kju* 'ʈi:ri '**jiu** a 'k:jɛza]

Unlike the earlier stages of Italian, here the verb must move to a position higher than NegP, as is demonstrated by the ungrammaticality of (55b).[28] We can therefore assume a structure that is essentially the same as the Spanish one in (27).

   The structure is the same in Sardinian as in Spanish and Sicilian. First, consider the following examples from Logudorese:

(56) a.   Sa cosa menzus diat   esser [$_{CP}$ a [bennere **babbu** cun mecus]].
           the thing best   would to-be   C° to-come Daddy with me
           'The best thing would be if Daddy came with me.'

   b.   At   segadu sos pratos [pro [*non manigare pius* **tue**]].
        (he) has broken the plates for not to-eat   more you
        'He broke the plates so that you could not eat any more.'

   c.   ★At segadu sos pratos [pro [*non pius* manigare **tue**]].

   d.   ★At segadu sos pratos [pro [*non* manigare **tue** *pius*]].

We can therefore confirm Jones's (1992,1993) assumption that the subject is located inside the VP (cf. 4.3.1.3). Concerning the infinitive itself, I do not follow Jones's proposal, according to which it remains inside the VP, but I rather assume that it moves to $T°$ and then further up to $Agr°$. In our framework, this follows from the evidence of the adverb in (57): [29]

(57) Babbu meu m' at nadu [de andare$_i$ [$_{VP}$ *ispissu* [$_{VP}$ PRO t_i a su dottore]]].
father my me has told $C°$ to-go   frequently   to the doctor
'My father told me to go frequently to the doctor.'

Moreover, Jones assumes a VP-final subject position, which seems to be plausible on the basis of the following examples (cf. Jones 1992:308, fn. 4):

(58) a. Non credo [de *ésseret giratu* **Juanne**].
          not (I) believe $C°$ to-be-3SG returned J.
          'I don't believe that J. has returned.'

    b. *Non credo [de *ésseret* **Juanne** *giratu*].

However, the following speakers' judgments show the subject either VP-initially or VP-finally (the final position is discussed in 5.3):

(59) a. At   segadu sos pratos [pro [no manigare [$_{VP}$ **tue** su pane]]].
          (he) has broken the plates for not to-eat   you the bread
          'He broke the plates so that you could not eat the bread.'

    b. At segadu sos pratos [pro [no manigare [$_{VP}$ su pane **tue**]]].

I therefore conclude that the subject is base-generated in SpecVP, situated at the left-hand side of the VP, as has been suggested for the other languages. I would like to propose that in Sardinian, the participle in (58) must move out of the VP to the left both in finite and in nonfinite clauses. This differs from other languages, in which this incorporation is mandatory only in finite clauses (e.g., in Spanish; cf. 5.2.2.1).

    For the remaining varieties, we can also stipulate that the postverbal subject is VP-internal. For Gascon, this can be shown by some of the data from 2.5:

(60) a. [$_{PP}$ sense [. . . *l'* . . . [$_{TP}$ aué [$_{VP}$ **digun** bist]]]]
              without him   to-have nobody seen
          'without anybody having seen him'

    b. [$_{PP}$ en [. . . [$_{TP}$ dura [$_{VP}$ *toustems* [$_{VP}$ **era guerro**]]]]]
              in   to-last still   the war
          'the war still lasting'

Here, the clitic position in (60a) has been interpreted, following Kayne (1991), by assuming that the infinitive does not move as high as $Agr°$, and we might fix $T°$ as its position (cf. my analysis of Old Italian in 5.2.1.2); the incorporation of the participle into $T°$ is optional in nonfinite clauses, as in most Romance languages.

Finally, for Romanian, a VP-internal position of the subject has already been postulated by both Motapanyane (1988) and Dobrovie-Sorin (1994) (see 4.3.3.1). This assumption has recently been confirmed and extended to Old Romanian by Mensching and Popovici (1997). It must be remembered that in Romanian the verb remains in T° both in finite and in nonfinite structures (cf. 3.3.1):

(61) Pentru [a nu-mi mai înțelege   **Petrică** cuvintele], am   vorbit
    for   to not me more understand (INF) P.   words-the (I) have spoken
    încet.
    loud.
    'Since P. did not understand my words anymore, I spoke loud.'

In this example, the subject appears between the verb and the direct object, so the following analysis can be postulated:

(62) pentru a nu-mi mai [$_{TP}$ înțelege [$_{VP}$ [$_{Spec}$ Petrică [$_{V'}$ cuvintele]]]

For Catalan, see Mensching (1999).

5.3   Clause-final subjects

The data presented in chapter 3 have many examples in which the subject occurs after the infinitive, although it is not adjacent to it. Some of these cases have been explained in section 5.2 by taking into account the idea of participle movement. However, we still have to explain those cases in which the subject is situated at the right periphery of the infinitive clause. Consider the following examples:

(63) a. Venne definitivamente riconosciuto [spettare al   ramo   MI
        became definitely   recognized   to-be-due to-the branch
        Barberino Colonna di Sciarra **il diritto** . . .].
        B.   C.   di S.   the right
        'It was definitely recognized that the branch B. C. di S. was entitled to the right
        . . .' (*La Nazione*, 12 marzo 1921, passim; quoted by Schwendener 1923:62)

    b. Aristote dit [appartenir aux beaux **le droict de commander**]. MidF
        A.   says to-belong to-the beautiful the right of to-command
        'A. says that the right of commanding belongs to the beautiful persons.'
        (Montaigne *A*, III, 12, vol. 6, p. 303, note 6; cf. Nyrop 1930:219)

    c. [Ganar las elecciones suecas **el partido conservador**]   MS
        to-win the elections Swedish the party   conservative
        significa que disminuirán los impuestos.
        means   that will-decrease the taxes
        'The fact that the conservative party will win the Swedish elections means that
        the taxes will decrease.' (Hernanz Carbó 1982:355)

d. Liga   contra o costume [de amostraren as ligas **as**   MG
(he) fights against the habit   of to-show-3PL the garters the
señoritas].
young-ladies.
'He fights against the habit that the young ladies show their garters.' (O porco,
124; cf. Gondar 1978:127)

In generative grammar we can distinguish between basically two approaches. Traditionally (e.g., in Burzio 1986), such cases have been regarded as extraposition, that is, adjunction to the right of the VP. This implies that the subject will not always show up clause-finally because other constituents can be right-adjoined either to the VP or to some functional category. Consider the following Spanish example:

(64) a. Y   trabajo así [de hacer un circuito **vosotros** para fuerza.
and (I) work so   C° to-do one circle   you   by   force
'And I work like this, [I mean] that you will be obliged to run one circle.'
(Corpus Oral, CCON018b)

b. de [hacer$_i$ [$_{VP}$ [$_{VP}$ t_i t_j un circuito] vosotros$_j$] para fuerza]

Another point of view is that the base position of the subject, SpecVP, is generated at the right side of the VP in some languages. Roberts (1993) believes that this is the case, for instance, in Modern Italian and French. Since no infinitival subjects are licensed in this position in these two languages, I do not consider this possibility here. Furthermore, I show in section 5.2 that the data from most of the Romance varieties can be accounted for, if we assume that SpecVP is located at the left-hand side of VP.[30] I therefore prefer the traditional account; that is, I will consider examples like (63) and (64) to be cases of extraposition. As an alternative, it might be argued that some Romance languages allow for SpecVP to be generated on either side of the VP. Note, however, that this is not desirable if we follow Kayne. For the right-dislocation assumed here, see Kayne (1994:ch. 7), where these constructions (in finite clauses) are reinterpreted according to the rules of Kayne's theory that entirely prohibits any type of rightward movement.[31] Since finite constructions are not the focus of this book, I will leave this point for future research.

5.4   Summary

In this chapter, I examine the preverbal, postverbal, and sentence-final positions of lexical subjects in Romance infinitive clauses. It can be shown that the preverbal subjects are located in AgrP, presumably in its specifier position. For postverbal subjects, Rizzi's (1982) Aux-to-Comp analysis is confirmed for Modern Italian, but I put forward ample evidence for rejecting such an analysis in all the other varieties, including Portuguese (against Raposo 1987). I show that except for Modern Italian, the subject always remains in its VP-internal base position, the linear ordering *infinitive* + *subject* being a result of verb movement to T° and, in most varieties, further up to Agr°. This is also true for Old Italian and the written Italian language up to the nineteenth century. Note that the assumption that postverbal subjects are usually located in SpecVP is in conformity with Cinque's (1999:111) conclusion that the subject either remains in SpecVP or, whenever it is outside the VP, it necessarily comes to precede the verb. Other differences in word order can be explained by language-dependent conditions on the movement of clitics and other elements, such as participles. Note that for participles, the view assumed here has recently been confirmed by Cinque (1999: 44–49, 146–48). In contrast to Aux-to-Comp constructions, the assumption of this structure, which is shared by almost all Romance languages and their dia-chronic and diatopic varieties, correctly predicts, among other things, that post-verbal lexical subjects are not restricted to infinitives of auxiliary and copulative verbs and that they co-occur with overt prepositional complementizers. Finally, I discuss sentence-final subjects, arguing that they should be considered extra-posed subjects.

6

Case Assignment to the Subject of Infinitive Clauses

The aim of this chapter is the investigation of the case assignment mechanisms by which subjects in Romance infinitive clauses are licensed. First, let us repeat the basic case properties we observed in the data described in chapter 2:

1. The nominative is general in all Ibero-Romance languages, in Gascon, in Sardinian, in present-day Italian, and in Romanian.
2. The accusative is general in the Gallo-Romance languages examined, except for Gascon.
3. In Old Italian, postverbal subjects generally appear in the nominative case, whereas preverbal subjects bear the accusative, with some exceptions found in texts written before the fifteenth century. This situation can be observed in the written language until the nineteenth century (inclusively). A similar situation is found in Old Romanian, whereas in present-day Italian and Romanian preverbal subjects are excluded.

In this chapter, I interpret these and other facts in the light of the results concerning subject positions of chapter 5, taking into account the basic assumptions made in chapter 3 and the earlier accounts summarized in chapter 4. The order in which I examine the different major languages is the same as in chapter 5. I begin with Italian in section 6.1, where we find two main case assignment mechanisms, which can then be extended to the other Romance languages. I then turn to Ibero-Romance (Spanish in 6.2 and Portuguese in 6.3). Afterward, I discuss French, where, among other things, one of the mechanisms I assume for Portuguese is rediscovered (6.4). Finally, in section 6.5 I consider the other linguistic varieties.

I focus on preverbal and postverbal subjects. The clause-final position is usually not considered. In section 5.3, I argued that clause-final subjects are the result of extraposition; they therefore have to be considered as subjects derived through A'-movement from one of the case positions that are discussed. On the other hand, A'-movement must be considered for preverbal subjects. In this context I discuss some additional data in which the subject is extracted to the main clause.

6.1   Italian

6.1.1   Nominative case

6.1.1.1   Postverbal subjects (thirteenth–nineteenth centuries)

As shown in section 2.1, postverbal subjects have always had nominative case in Italian. In the preceding chapter I establish the following two configurations in which we can find postverbal subjects in infinitive constructions up to and including the nineteenth century:

(1)   a.

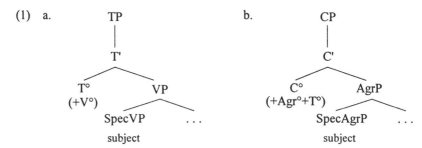

Both configurations are expected on the basis of Roberts's (1993, 1994) assumptions about the property of $T°$ that assigns nominative case under government (cf. 4.3.3.2), either from its base position or from the incorporated position inside $C°$. In this section, I claim that, in fact, configuration (1a) can be explained if we generalize from Roberts's assumptions by including nonfinite $T°$, whereas the explanation for (1b) should be revised.

Let us first consider the configuration in (1a), in which the subject receives the nominative case from the governing $T°$. This assumption is compatible with the properties of perception verbs pointed out in section 4.1, according to which these verbs select an AgrP without TP. This means that in the infinitive construction selected by perception verbs, the head $T°$, responsible for nominative assignment is nonexistent. Consequently, nominative subjects have never been licensed, as shown by the documentary evidence (see Schwendener 1923:16–25).[1] Under the view that causative verbs select a VP (cf., e.g., Guasti 1996), our assumption is not a problem either since in this case the TP is also missing. On the other hand, it seems to be problematic if we follow the alternative solution presented in section 4.1, according to which *fare* ('to make') selects a TP, which would not exclude nominative subjects according to the analysis just offered and contrary to the facts. There is, however, a simple solution for this problem if we look at the infinitive constructions selected by *fare* in earlier stages of Italian:

(2)   a.   *Fa'* [**li tuoi savj** venire].
            make the your wise to-come
            'Make your wise men come.' (Conti d'ant. Cav., 10; cf. Schwendener 1923:17)

    b.   Dionisio fero / chc *fe'* [**Cicilia** aver   dolorosi anni]
            D.   wild that made Sicily to-have painful years
            'the wild D. who caused Sicily to have painful years' (Dante Div. Com., Inf. XII, 107–8, p. 144; cf. Schwendener 1923:23)

c. *Fecero*   [**tutto il luogo** . . . risplendere . . .].
(they) made all   the place   to-shine
'They made the whole place shine . . .' (Gozzi, Oss., 46; cf Schwendener 1923:17)

On the evidence of the preverbal subjects in these examples, the ECM construction selected by *fare* can be assumed to have been identical to the one selected by perception verbs, in contrast to Modern Italian. We can therefore say that here, too, the TP is missing so that the ungrammaticality of nominative subjects is correctly predicted. To summarize, we can say that the Old Italian example in (3a) has the structure represented in (3b):[2]

(3) a. È una grande fatica [a conservare **l' uomo** la pecunia].
is a   great   fatigue to preserve   the man   the money
'It is very hard for a man to preserve his money.' (Giord. Riv., 225; cf. Segre 1991:119)

b.

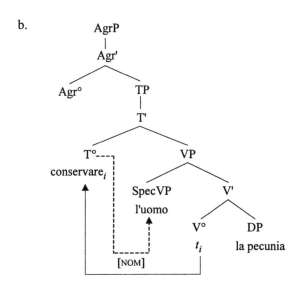

Let us now turn to the second option, the Aux-to-Comp configuration in (1b), which is still grammatical in Modern literary Italian. Roberts (1993, 1994) claimed that here the governing T° is responsible for nominative assignment, although in this case it has moved to C° along with the auxiliary. This is interpreted as a difference in a language like English, where it is assumed that it is Agr° in C° that licenses finite Aux-to-Comp structures. As I point out in 4.3.3.2, Roberts comes to this rather surprising conclusion because, contrary to English, Aux-to-Comp is excluded in Italian when the auxiliary is finite (see example 60a of chapter 4). Although this can be accepted for Modern Italian, it is not true for earlier Italian, where the typical Aux-to-Comp word order was grammatical in finite clauses:

(4) a. Perciò *fue* esso *accusato* di quella morte.   13th c.
         therefore was he   accused   of that   death
         'Therefore he was accused of that murder.' (Brunetto Lat., 80, 18; cf. Segre
         1991:195)

     b. Che dicitura vi *abbiam* noi *sostituita*?   19th c.
         what style   there have   we substituted
         'What kind of writing style have we substituted there?' (Promessi Sposi, Intr.)

If we follow Roberts's argumentation, these data show that nominative assignment by the governing Agr° was actually possible in the earlier stages of Italian,
and consequently we should claim that Aux-to-Comp in finite constructions was
licensed by Agr° and not by T°. I assume this for now, so the diachronic contrast
can be summarized as follows:

(5) Nominative case assignment in Italian (preliminary version)

Variety	(A) Agr° (Spec-head agreement)	(B) Agr° (government)	(C) T° (government)
until the 19th c.	yes (if V° = finite)	yes (if V° = finite)	yes
today	" " " " "	no	"

Thus, the parallel situation in finite Aux-to-Comp structures in English and
other Germanic languages is not a coincidence but can be reduced to the same
principle, namely, nominative assignment by Agr° under government. In contrast,
it seems to be impossible to extend column (B) of (5) to include nonfinite verbs
because, as I argue above, nominative subjects were not licensed in the infinitive
construction selected by perception and causative verbs: still assuming that they
select an AgrP without TP, Agr° would govern the subject in SpecVP, so the
nominative could be assigned. A further generalization, which would reduce
finite and nonfinite Aux-to-Comp constructions to the same mechanism, might be
desirable, however. In this issue the question arises of whether we could argue
that in the earlier stages of Italian discussed here, agreement could assign the
nominative under government only if movement to C° applies (i.e., in an Aux-to-
Comp structure), which would exclude nominative assignment to the infinitival
subject after perception verbs.

This is where the option of the feature [+Agr] in C°, as discussed in chapters
3 and 4, becomes relevant. In Rizzi and Roberts (1989), it is claimed that this
feature is responsible for Aux-to-Comp movement in infinitive constructions.[3]
Given the assumptions just made about agreement in the earlier stages of Italian,
it seems natural to extend this point of view by saying that the feature [+Agr] in
C° not only motivates the movement of the auxiliary but also functions as the
nominative assigner. Note that this does not contradict the results summarized in
(5): we can argue that the functional head Agr° in nonfinite structures has no (or
at least no sufficient) agreement properties—to simplify we can say that it is
[–Agr]—so that it cannot license Aux-to-Comp. However, infinitival C° may
contain [+Agr]. When this option applies, Aux-to-Comp with a specified subject
is licensed. We must keep in mind that Rizzi (1990a) has shown that the feature

[+Agr] in C° is cognate to the agreement properties of finite constructions. In this way, we can still maintain the parallelism between nonfinite Aux-to-Comp constructions and finite ones like those in (4). On this basis, I would like to alter (5) in the following way, which accounts for both finite and nonfinite Aux-to-Comp constructions:

(6) Nominative case assignment in Italian (revision 1)

Variety	(A) Agr (Spec-head agreement)	(B) Agr (government)	(C) T (government)
until the 19th c.	yes, in case of [+Agr]		yes
today	yes, in case of [+Agr]	no	"

In accordance with my considerations about agreement, [+Agr] is used here to integrate both the agreement feature in C° and the functional head Agr° in finite clauses. The fact that the nominative cannot be assigned by C°[+Agr] to the subject in SpecCP under Spec-head agreement (which would predict preverbal nominative subjects in infinitive clauses, contrary to the facts) is sufficiently explained by the common assumption that SpecCP is not an A-position. I return to this discussion later in this chapter.

The generalization just made concerning the nominative-assigning function of agreement is not only more economical but also relevant for the diachronic development that is examined in the following sections. I discuss further properties of Aux-to-Comp within the context of contemporary Italian in section 6.1.1.3. For the possible consequences for ECM phenomena, see 6.1.2.2.

6.1.1.2 Preverbal Subjects (thirteenth–fourteenth centuries)

According to the results of the preceding section, preverbal subjects in the nominative case should not be expected in Italian because none of the functional categories in infinitive clauses assigns case under Spec-head agreement. Nevertheless, there is at least one example in Old Italian that shows a preverbal nominative subject:

(7) perchè io dissi [io aver   trovato iscritto . . .]   13th c.
     because I said   I to-have found   written
     'because I said that I had found that it was written . . .' (Malispini, ch. 42; cf. Diez 1882:946)

In addition, the data in (8) are rather strange. Although the case cannot be identified here on morphological grounds, the infinitive constructions are used in the function of adverbial clauses in (8a) and (8b) and as a predicate nominal in (8c). In these construction types, the documentary evidence shows no accusative subjects whatsoever:

(8) a. Se madonna m' à   fatto sof[e]rire / [per **gioia d'amore** avere
         If my-lady me has made to-sufffer [for joy   of love   to-have
         compimento] . . .
         accomplishment
         'If my lady has made me suffer in order to render the joy of love possible . . .'
         (Guido delle Colonne: *La mia gran pena e lo gravoso affanno*, V. 28–30, in
         Rime Scuola Sic., 76.; cf. Wiese 1928:147, §84)[4]

     b. Allora rimane questa ne' loro pensieri; [per **questa** . . . tanto   essere
         then   remains this (F) in their thoughts for this (F)   so-much to-be
         perfetta quanto . . . essere puote l' umana essenza].
         perfect as-much   to-be can the human essence
         'Then this (woman) remains in their minds, for her being so perfect as the
         human essence can be.' (Dante Conv., III, VI, 8, p. 90; cf. Segre 1991:255)

     c. La prima virtù pensò   che sia [**l' uomo** costrignere la sua lingua].
         the first   virtue (I) think that is the man   to-constrain the his tongue
         'The first virtue is, I think, that a man holds his tongue.' (Libro di Cato, quoted
         by Segre 1991:118, according to Nannucci 1858:95)

These data are from the thirteenth and fourteenth centuries. A possible account
would be that infinitival Agr° was able to assign the nominative under Spec-head
agreement in the Old Italian of these centuries. However, note that this is not a
very probable solution because in finite clauses (where Spec-head agreement is
usually assumed) this is the most frequent order; that is, the subject occurs preverbally in most cases. We might therefore argue that case assignment by Spec-
head agreement is usually the unmarked option. In sections 6.3.1.1 and 6.5.1 we
see that this point of view can be extended to infinitive constructions; that is, in
languages that allow case marking under Spec-head agreement in nonfinite constructions, SV(O) word order is also the unmarked option. This clearly contradicts our data because cases such as (7) and (8) seem to be marked constructions,
considering their extremely low frequency.

   In view of these considerations I opt for another solution, which accounts for
the data in (7) and (8) and, at the same time, explains the marked character of this
construction. In 3.1.2 we saw that, at least in finite clauses, SpecAgrP could function as an A'-position in Old Italian, in accordance with the characteristics of
most of the Old Romance languages. In other words, SpecAgrP could function as
a landing site for DPs that are already case-marked. In the preceding chapter, I
show that this can also be claimed for infinitive constructions in some Old Romance varieties. Old Italian is not an exception, as is strongly suggested by the
following data with a preposed complement (cf. Segre 1991:167, who gives more
examples):

(9) a. [*Visio* operare] è sempre inn oni etate vietato.
         vice to-apply is always in each age forbidden
         'At every age it is forbidden to make use of vices.' (Guitt., 306, 204; cf. Segre
         1991:167)

b. invitare regi, principi e signori [a[l *decto passaggio* fare]]
to invite kings princes and gentlemen to-the mentioned voyage to-do
'to invite kings, princes, and gentlemen to do the mentioned voyage (Cron.
Fior., in Schiaffini, 109,23; cf. Segre 1991:167)

c. [per *lo tosone* conquistare]
for the fleece to-conquer
'in order to conquer the fleece' (Distr. Troia, in Schiaffini, 152, 23; cf Segre
1991:167)

If the preverbal position of the fronted complement is to be interpreted as A'-movement to SpecAgrP, as I suppose, we should assume the same for preverbal subjects: if SpecAgrP is free (i.e., not filled by another constituent), the subject, case-marked in SpecVP by governing T° and thus licensed, can move to SpecAgrP, as illustrated in (10):

(10)

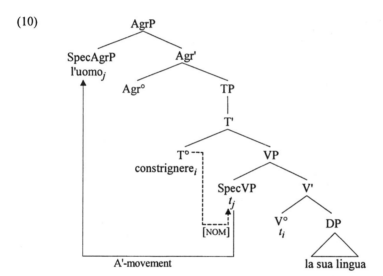

According to Durante (1981:ch. 16), the disappearance of the word order shown in (9) above and in (18) of chapter 3 are among the characteristics that mark the transition from Old to Modern Italian during the sixteenth century. Given my interpretation, this change was due to the fact that SpecAgrP was losing its ability to function as an A'-position. This assumption not only explains the disappearance of preposed nonsubject constituents but also, and what is important here, predicts that preverbal infinitival subjects in the nominative case were limited to Old Italian, so they cannot be found after this period.

6.1.1.3 Postverbal subjects in contemporary Italian

It has to be noted that Roberts's (1993,1994) assumption about the case-marking properties of T°, which I have modified and adapted to earlier stages of Italian, is not compatible with the data from contemporary Italian infinitive constructions. As I claim, the earlier stages of Italian licensed the configuration in (1a), in which the nominative is assigned to SpecVP by T°. If we follow Belletti (1990) and assume that the infinitive obligatorily moves to Agr° in present-day Italian, the relevant configuration would be as follows:

(11) $[_{AgrP}$ arrivare$_j$ $[_{TP}$ t_j $[_{VP}$ Giannii $t_j]]]$

This is roughly the structure that Roberts assumes for a finite clause with a post-verbal subject (cf. 3.2.3).[5] However, as we have already seen in 4.3.3.2, this structure is ungrammatical if the verb is an infinitive, so that we get the following contrast:

(12) a. perchè arriva Gianni
        because arrives G.

     b. *per arrivare Gianni
        for to-arrive G.

As we see in the preceding chapters, the only grammatical solution is the Aux-to-Comp configuration, which is excluded in (12b) because there is no auxiliary. If, however, nonfinite T° in the configuration shown in (11) is not able to assign the nominative, why should it have this ability after incorporation into C°, as is suggested by Roberts?

In view of these considerations, let us now return to the assumptions made about earlier Italian in 6.1.1.1. There, I reinterpret infinitival Aux-to-Comp as nominative assignment by governing agreement or, more precisely, by the feature [+Agr] contained in C°. If this could be assumed for present-day Italian, too, the difference from the earlier stages would just be due to a restriction of the case properties of the functional heads Agr° and T°, a claim that is tempting, of course.[6] However, we have to remember the following problem, which led Roberts (1993:25, 72) to object to nominative assignment by governing agreement in contemporary Italian, namely, that finite Aux-to-Comp structures like (13) are ungrammatical:

(13) a. *Ha Gianni preso il libro?
        has G.   taken the book

     b. *Che film ha Gianni visto?
        which film has G.   seen

It is interesting that Roberts (1994:229) notes that "these examples are more acceptable at a very high stylistic level, but many native speakers reject them." He does not go into this observation any further, and, in addition, he does not mention one essential point that is crucial for our discussion: nonfinite Aux-to-Comp structures, too, belong to a high stylistic level. This is true not only for the gerund constructions discussed by Roberts but even more so for the infinitive constructions at stake.[7] Generalizing from these facts, I conclude that contemporary literary Italian has preserved the characteristics of Old Italian, in the sense that governing agreement is, in fact, able to assign the nominative. Together with the results of section 6.1.1.1, we obtain the following distribution from a diachronic and diastratic point of view:

(14) Nominative case assignment in Italian (revision 2)

Variety	(A) Agr (Spec-head agreement)	(B) Agr (government)	(C) T (government)
until the 19th c.	yes, in case of [+Agr]		yes
today (literary)	" " " " "		yes in case of [+Tns]
today (standard)	yes, in case of [+Agr]	no	" " " " "

Summarizing, we can say that the case assignment properties of governing T° are limited to finite constructions in present-day Italian,[8] so nominative assignment to the subject in situ is impossible in nonfinite clauses. Another diachronic difference is that in modern standard Italian, agreement is no longer able to assign the nominative in a government configuration, whereas this option is still possible in literary style, a fact that can thus be interpreted as a syntactic archaism.

Let us reconsider, based on this background, the configurations in which infinitival Aux-to-Comp is still grammatical as a stylistically marked option. First, I would like to return to the infinitive construction selected by declarative and epistemic verbs, as discussed within the context of earlier Italian. These two classes of verbs are the same as those that, according to Rizzi (1990a), select a C° with [+Agr] (cf. 3.1.2). This is a clear contrast with respect to volitional verbs, as Rizzi pointed out, and also with respect to factive verbs. Now, it is interesting that Rizzi and Roberts (1989) suggested the following explanation for Aux-to-Comp structures:[9]

> As this option is lexically selected (e.g. epistemic verbs allow it, but volition verbs do not), a natural way to express this restriction is to say that epistemic verbs but not volition verbs select an embedded C° with an agreement morpheme, which in turn morphologically subcategorizes an I° slot.

Note that this hypothesis follows the assumptions on case assignment presented in section 6.1.1.1, in the sense that we can actually argue that the selected [+Agr] feature in C° not only yields Aux-to-Comp movement but also functions as a nominative assigner. Both properties correctly predict the grammaticality facts known since Rizzi (1982; cf. 4.3.2.1), which are repeated here as (15):

(15) a. Il ministro *afferma* [essere **il presidente** disposto ad aiutarci].
         the minister states   to-be the president   ready   to to-help-us
         'The minister states that the president is ready to help us.'

     b. *Il ministro *preferisce* [essere **il presidente** disposto ad aiutarci].
         the minister prefers   to-be the president   ready   to to-help-us
         'The minister prefers that the president be ready to help us.'

Our explanation will also account for the situation of infinitive constructions selected by unaccusative predicates. For instance, in Modern Italian, nonemphatic specified subjects are not grammatical in infinitival complements of impersonal verbs like *conviene* 'it is convenient' or *succede* 'it happens', and neither can they occur when the infinitive construction is the D-structural subject of a SC (see 3.3.1). These two groups do not belong to either of the classes of predicates for which [+Agr] in C° is assumed. However, when the infinitive construction is selected by passive forms of declarative or epistemic verbs, Aux-to-Comp constructions with overt subjects can occur, according to the documentary evidence put forward by Skytte (1983:494). Note that this is a direct consequence of the assumption that [+Agr] in C° is lexically selected[10] since the selection of this feature is general and does not depend on whether the verb is in the active or passive voice.

There are still two syntactic configurations that have to be explained: first, the infinitive construction selected by D° in (16a) and, second, the one that follows the preposition *per* in (16b):

(16) a. [$_{DP}$ *l'* [$_{CP}$ essere **il presidente** disposto ad aiutarci]]
　　　　the   to-be the president   ready   to to-help-us
　　　'the fact that the president is ready to help us'

　　 b. [$_{PP}$ *per* [$_{CP}$ essere **il   presidente** disposto ad aiutarci]]
　　　　for   to-be   the president   ready   to to-help-us
　　　'in order for the president to be ready to help us'

To explain these data, it has to be kept in mind that, as Rizzi (1990a:59) points out, the selection of C°[+Agr] is a property that varies cross-linguistically. Up to now, C°[+Agr] has usually been observed in CPs that are complements of certain verbs. This is due to the fact that, so far, the existence of the feature [+Agr] in C° has been examined mainly in connection with the extraction of constituents from CP, not as related to a possible property of this feature as a nominative case assigner. Now, for the examples in (16), I would like to suggest a solution along the following lines: if [+Agr] in C° in (15a) is responsible for case assignment, as I have assumed, it seems a reasonable assumption to postulate this feature also for the examples given in (16), which also show Aux-to-Comp. Further on, I show that the possibility of D° selecting a CP with C°[+Agr] can be supported by further arguments from Brazilian Portuguese (in section 6.3.1.3). In addition, this assumption is not out of place in view of the DP analysis. According to Abney (1987:17–21), D° actually contains a feature [+Agr], which is responsible for agreement and, in some languages, for case assignment inside the NP. Note that it has been claimed that the agreement features of D° are not always realized in D° itself, but that they may appear in the complement of D° (see Vater 1990:26; Olsen 1991),[11] as is the case here. Finally, the preposition *per*, as we have already seen, is the only preposition that allows the selection of a CP with Aux-to-Comp and a specified subject, so we have to consider this as a lexical property of this preposition. I do not pursue this point any further, but it seems plausible that *per* also selects a CP with C°[+Agr].

At the end of section 5.2.1.2, I make some conjectures about the differences between the earlier stages of Italian and the present-day language concerning the types of infinitive clauses that allow specified subjects. Given the results of this section, we can now make the following generalization: in present-day Italian, specified subjects in infinitive clauses are licensed only by case assignment through governing agreement (and no longer through governing tense). Consequently, the (nonemphatic) subject of an infinitive clause can only be overt in infinitive clauses that are CPs whose head contains the feature [+Agr]. In section 4.2.2, I observe some problems with the condition on the licensing of [+Agr] in C° formulated by Rizzi (1990a). Remember that Rizzi postulated a Spec-head relationship between [+Agr] and the subject as a condition for the feature to be selected. The properties of [+Agr] elaborated in this section confirm this point, showing that such a condition should not be assumed, at least for present-day Italian. We see further arguments and a modification of Rizzi's theory in the course of our discussion in section 6.1.2.2. of the relationship between *wh* extraction of subjects and C°[+Agr].

6.1.2   Accusative case

6.1.2.1   Motivation and operation of ECM

According to the data in section 2.1 and the assumptions in 6.1.1, preverbal subjects in Italian infinitive constructions generally bear the accusative, at least from the fifteenth century onward. According to the documentary evidence, preverbal accusative subjects are found in the configurations illustrated in the following examples:

(17) a.   Intese   [**me** essere più savio di   lei].
          (she) understood me to-be   more wise than her
          'She understood that I was wiser than her.' (Alberti Fam. *B.*, 240, 15; cf. Dardano 1963:108)

     b.   S' accorse   [**lui** del tutto esser morto].
          R CL (she) got-aware him of whole to-be dead
          'She became aware of the fact that he was totally dead.' (Bocc. Dec., IV, 6, p. 248)

     c.   Non m' è . . . uscito   di mente [**me** avere   questo mio affanno   offerto
          not me is   gone-out of mind   me to-have this   my sufferings offered
          alle oziose . . .]
          to-the otious (F PL)
          'I could not get the idea out of my mind that I had offered my suffering to the otious women . . .' (Bocc. Dec., Concl., p. 579; cf. Schwendener 1923:85)

In all these examples, the infinitive clauses are complements of verbs: in (17a) of the transitive verb *intendere* 'to understand', in (17b) of *accorgersi (di)* 'to become aware (of)', and in (17c) of the unaccusative verb *uscire (di mente)* 'to go out (of one's mind)'. As shown in chapter 2, we also find preverbal subjects in infinitive constructions that are complements to passive verbs and in those that take the place of subjects in small clauses; both are structurally similar to (17c), as seen in section 3.3.1.

Traditionally, these constructions are interpreted as cases of A.c.I. It is therefore self-evident that we should see if they can be interpreted as ECM constructions in our framework. We can actually find a classical ECM structure in cases like (17a): here the infinitive clauses are complements of verbs that also allow for DP complements, to which they assign the accusative. The ECM analysis is also confirmed by the behavior of reflexive and nonreflexive pronouns:

(18) a. **[Tutti insieme]**$_i$ apertamente confessarono [sé$_i$ essere stati . . .]
      all   together openly   confessed   themselves to-be been
      'All openly confessed together that they had been . . .' (Bocc. Dec., III, 7; cf. Schwendener 1923:51)

   b. Grabino$_j$, **che**$_j$ ode **[lui**$_k$ essere Cionello$_k$] . . . se$_j$ li$_k$ gittò a'
      G.   who hears him to-be C.   himself him threw to-the
      piedi.
      feet
      'G., who heard that he was C. . . . threw himself at his feet.' (Sercambi, Nov. 15; cf. Schwendener 1923:76)

Following binding theory, the coindexation facts show that the governor of the infinitival subject is situated in the main clause.

Let us now turn to the case of (17b): verbs like *accorgersi* 'to become aware' never select a DP in Modern Italian, rather a PP, and this property can be found in Old Italian. In section 3.3.3, I argue that the infinitive construction can also be embedded into a PP, as a complement of a phonetically empty prepositional head.[12] The first question to be answered to account for (17b) is how ECM is possible with a verb that does not subcategorize for a direct object. I think this is not too difficult to imagine if we consider case theory: in contrast to cases like genitive or dative, the accusative case is a structural case, at least in the languages we are discussing.[13] This means that the capability of V° to assign the accusative is not a lexical property: the lexical entry of a transitive verb (e.g., *intendere* in 17a) contains no information whatsoever about its case assignment properties. So, what I would like to suggest is that ECM can be explained in all three constructions in (17) by a traditional definition of structural case, such as the following one adapted from Rizzi (1982:86):

(19) Assign accusative case to DP if governed by V.

In view of these considerations, let us now consider the structure of (17b). To simplify matters, I here assume that all infinitive constructions in (17) are AgrPs. I reconsider this assumption in the next section.

(20)

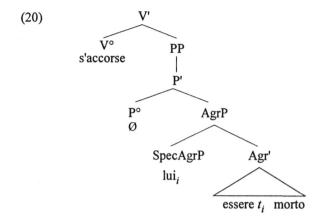

Here, V° c-commands the subject *lui* in SpecAgrP. Since the accusative is assigned, let us assume that the verb *s'accorse* actually governs the infinitival subject. It will then follow from relativized minimality that [p Ø] is not a potential governor, at least in the earlier stages of Italian, which allowed for this construction. Note that there are no examples of preverbal accusative subjects preceded by an overt P°. We could thus say that only empty P° is not an intervening head (a potential governor in Rizzi's terminology), whereas overt P° is, so that it will block the government relationship. In other words, the rather striking fact that the preposition disappears in infinitive clauses like (17b) is easily explained by our assumptions on case assignment. Further evidence comes from the fact that, in contrast, a postverbal subject could co-occur with overt P° (see section 2.1). Reconsider the following example, noted in chapter 2 (10a):

(21) . . . si   dolga . . . il   core / [pp *d'* [AgrP esser tradito sotto fede **Amore**]].
  R CL hurts   the heart   of   to-be betrayed under trust Love.
'. . . the heart grieves about the fact that Love has been betrayed under trust.' (Bocc. Dec., IV, Concl., p. 268)

Here it can be assumed that T° assigns the nominative and that the subject is then extraposed (cf. section 5.3), so a nonovert preposition would not be motivated.

Finally, the condition that V° governs the subject of the infinitive construction is also true in (17c). Since this is an unaccusative structure, the infinitive clause is also a complement of the verb (the term "unaccusative" is, of course, not appropriate in this context). An infinitive construction such as the one in (22a) can be represented by the structure in (22b), where the infinitival AgrP is also governed by V°:

(22) a. Spesso avviene, [**coloro** . . . da amore essere incapestrati].
       often   happens   those   by love to-be   entangled
       'It often happens that those . . . are entangled by love.' (Bocc. Dec., VIII, 7; cf. Schwendener 1923:78)

b.

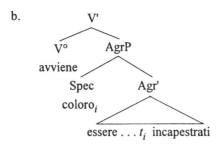

How can we explain the paradoxical phenomenon in which an unaccusative verb may assign structural accusative to a constituent inside the complement but not to the complement itself? Remember that a finite clause without a subject is ungrammatical. Thus, in an unaccusative structure, the complement must move either to a position where it can receive the nominative case, that is, to SpecVP, or to SpecAgrP. If it stays in place, it can be assumed that the nominative will be assigned to an empty expletive element and passed to the complement through the chain. However, if the complement were assigned to the accusative by V°, there would be a case conflict: the complement could not move to a nominative position, and neither could it receive the nominative by forming a chain with an empty element, so the sentence would be ungrammatical. Let us now return to our construction. Here, the complement is the infinitive clause. If we assume that clauses need not be case-marked, there is no reason for structural accusative assignment to be suppressed. Note, however, that we can even assume that the infinitive clause receives the nominative case. The accusative-assigning force of V° can be satisfied without any problem because there is another candidate available, namely, the subject of the infinitive clause.[14] Summarizing, I would like to suggest that potentially every V° can assign the accusative to a DP that it governs, unless there is some other principle by which this is avoided. We could postulate this as a property of the earlier stages of Italian, no longer valid for Modern Italian, to account for the present ungrammaticality of the constructions discussed here, but we see in the next section that this is not necessary.

Finally, I turn to raising contexts. Consider the following grammaticality facts from modern Italian:

(23) a. ⋆Sembra [**Gianni** riparare la macchina].
       seems   G.   to-repair the car

   b. ⋆È stato visto [**Gianni** riparare la macchina].
      is been seen   G.   to-repair the car

As we see in chapter 4, raising verbs cause the subject of the infinitive to move into the subject position of the main clause because the subject cannot be assigned case inside the infinitival complement clause. However, this is not to be expected if our assumptions about structural accusative assignment and ECM are correct. I assume that unaccusative verbs block the assignment of structural case to their complement, but not to a constituent inside the complement (i.e., the infinitive construction). Why should (23a) and (23b) be ungrammatical then?

One possibility would be to exclude raising predicates as accusative assigners. The reason could be that if the verb has no subject of its own, the subject position of the main clause tends to be filled by the infinitival subject rather than by an expletive element. It has to be observed that cases like (23a) seem to have been impossible, too, in the older stages of the language. It is interesting, though, that there are similar cases:

(24) a. A lui pareva, [tale essere **la opportunità e la necessità di**   19th c.
          to him seemed   such to-be   the opportunity and the necessity of
          questa alleanza, che . . .]
          this   alliance   that
          'It seemed to him that the opportunity and the necessity for such an alliance was
          such that . . . .' (Botta, VIII, p. 50; cf. Schwendener 1923:79)

    b. Gli fu rivelato da Dio, [**la sua morte** dover   esser in breve].   14th c.
        him was revealed by God the his death   must (INF) to-be in short
        'It was revealed to him by God that his death would be necessary to take place
        soon.' (Cavalca, 131; cf. Schwendener 1923:63)

In (24a), there is a nominative subject licensed by T°. The example illustrates that raising was not obligatory. Example (24b) is a similar case, but here the subject is most probably accusative, so ECM seems to have taken place. Note, however, that the infinitive construction in (24b) is selected by a declarative verb, and declarative verbs were claimed to select CP, at least when Aux-to-Comp appears in the infinitive clause. Since I have not found any examples like (24b) with perception verbs, we might claim that a CP boundary is actually necessary to account for ECM in raising contexts. This question should be dealt with in further studies on raising and unaccusative verbs, so I do not investigate it here any further. However, in the next section I show that most of the cases I tentatively consider AgrPs in this section should instead be interpreted as CPs.

6.1.2.2 C° and ECM

At least a number of the main verbs involved in the ECM phenomena just discussed usually subcategorize for CP (cf. 3.3, 4.3.2.1, and 5.2.1). But, as mentioned in sections 4.1 and 4.2.2, it is generally assumed that the specifier of AgrP cannot be governed by the main verb if the clause is embedded into CP, so it cannot be case-marked by ECM. According to Rizzi (1990a), an empty C° is an intervening potential governor in the sense of his relativized minimality. On the other hand, as we have seen, Rizzi assumes that C°[+Agr], which can be selected only in the case of *wh* movement, is capable of transmitting the structural case of V° to SpecAgrP; as a result the *wh*-marked subject is licensed and can be extracted from the infinitive clause.[15] We can therefore observe the following contrast in Modern Italian:

(25) a. *Credo [$_{CP}$ [$_{C°}$Ø [$_{AgrP}$ queste persone essere disposte ad aiutarci]]].
          (I) believe   these   persons to-be ready   to to-help-us
          'I believe these persons are ready to help us.'

b. Quante   persone$_i$ credi [$_{CP}$ t_i [$_{C°}$ +Agr_i [t_i essere disposte ad
    How-many persons   (you) believe   to-be   ready   to
    aiutarci]]]?
    to-help-us
    'How many persons do you believe are ready to help us?'

As we have seen, sentences like (25a) were grammatical in earlier stages of Italian; that is, even nonextracted subjects could be licensed by means of ECM. Another difference of those stages of the language is that a subject could be extracted even if it was not marked as [+*wh*]. The extracted subject also displays accusative case:

(26) E **mme**$_i$ conoscesti [$_{CP}$ t_i essere figliuolo di pistore]?
     and me (you) knew   to-be son   of baker
     'and you knew me to be the son of a baker?' (Novellino; quoted by Wiese 1928:215, 53; cf. 141, §61)

Here, movement is not supposed to take place by using the *wh* position SpecCP as an intermediate landing site, so something like the structure in (27) has to be assumed:

(27)   E mme$_i$ conoscesti [$_{CP}$ [$_{AgrP}$ t_i [$_{TP}$ essere$_j$ [$_{VP}$ t_i . . . t_j . . .]]]]?

                                              [ACC]

Note that Rizzi's (1990a) assumptions about [+Agr] in C° (cf. section 4.2.2) are problematic in view of this structure. Since SpecCP is not filled by a subject or by its trace, [+Agr] would not be selected, and in Rizzi's system the structure would be ungrammatical for at least two reasons: first, a C° that lacks the feature [+Agr] would block structural case assignment; second, an empty C° is not a governor, although it is a potential governor, so that it would block the extraction of the subject. Even if case had been assigned by some other mechanism, the subject could not move into the main clause. Therefore, cases like (26) confirm my suspicion, formulated in sections 4.2.2 and 6.1.1.3, that Rizzi's proposal (namely, that the selection of [+Agr] depends on the coindexation of this feature with a subject in SpecCP) is not valid. As I have claimed for Aux-to-Comp, verbs like *conoscere* generally select a CP complement that contains the feature [+Agr]. This also explains why Romance ECM constructions of the type in (17a) or in (26) are usually selected by the same verbs that permit Aux-to-Comp. The question is how these considerations can be made consistent with Rizzi's theory about ECM. Since we have detected independent problems with Rizzi's proposal that [+Agr] operates as a transmitter of the structural case of the verb to SpecIP (see section 4.2.2), the mechanisms claimed by Rizzi should be modified in any case.

Let us proceed on the following assumption: as a general property of Italian, certain verbs select a CP of the type [$_{CP}$[$_{C°}$ +Agr] . . .]. The different syntactic possibilities follow from relativized minimality and the properties of C°, as is illustrated in the following:

(28) C° as an intervening head in Italian in the sense of minimality

Variety	C° = Ø	C° = [+Agr]	C° = lexical
until the 19th c.	no	no	yes
today	yes	yes (except when co-indexed with a subject under Spec-head agreement)	"

Note that in the earlier stages of Italian, a phonetically nonrealized C° is not an intervening head, regardless of whether or not it contains an agreement feature. This assumption accounts for the fact that ECM in the earlier stages of the language was also possible in CPs that did not select [+Agr], for example, volitional verbs, as in the following Old Italian example:

(29) Non *vorrai*   **[umanitate alcuna** essere da   te   lontana].
     not (you) will-want humanity   any   to-be from you far
     'You will not want any humanity to be far away from you.' (Alberti, Fam. *A*, I, p. 42; cf. Schwendener 1923:78)

Moreover, we can now also consider the ECM construction selected by unaccusative predicates like (17c) as CPs (where C° = Ø). To sum up, together with the results of the preceding sections, (28) will correctly predict the following facts about volitional and unaccusative predicates: first, in the earlier stages of Italian, overt subjects in accusative were licensed through ECM. As another option, following the results of 6.1.1.1, the subject could remain in its base, where it was assigned the nominative by T° (totally independent from the properties of C°). In addition, it has to be noted that Aux-to-Comp cannot apply because C° lacks the feature [+Agr]. According to (28), in contemporary Italian, ECM is generally blocked by a phonetically empty C°, so preverbal subjects of infinitive clauses are excluded. Postverbal subjects can be licensed by Aux-to-Comp if C° has the feature [+Agr]. This is not the case when the CP is selected by volitional or unaccusative predicates, so under no condition is any nonemphatic specified subject licensed here. In contemporary Italian, the status of C°[+Agr] as a potential governor can be canceled only when a subject is coindexed with the agreement feature in a Spec-head configuration. Under the assumption that SpecCP is accessible only for *wh*-marked constituents, the contrast shown in (25) follows.

Let us briefly return to the verbs that select [+Agr] in C° in the earlier varieties of Italian. When the Aux-to-Comp construction is selected, the infinitival auxiliary is in C° so that it is no longer empty:

(30) Non posso . . . dissimulare [$_{CP}$ [$_{C°}$ aver$_j$ +Agr [$_{AgrP}$ io$_i$ [. . . t_j t_i inteso . . .]]]]
not (I) can   pretend   to-have   I   understood
'I . . . cannot pretend that I have understood . . . ' (Gold., L'avv. on., II, 16; cf.
Schwendener 1923:54)

Relativized minimality, then, predicts (on the basis of 28) that ECM is blocked.
The subject can receive nominative case only, as described here. Finally, (28)
predicts that the infinitive construction cannot have a preverbal subject in the
accusative when the complementizer is overt; in fact, such a construction could
not be documented (see section 2.1).

To sum up, in this section I have argued that the infinitive constructions in
examples like (17) are CPs, the main difference between the earlier stages of
Italian and contemporary Italian being that in the former varieties, phonetically
empty C° was not an intervening head in the sense of relativized minimality.

6.2   Spanish

6.2.1   Postverbal subjects from Old Spanish to Modern Spanish

In Spanish, as in the earlier stages of Italian, the postverbal subject of the infinitive bears nominative case and is located in SpecVP. It seems that the best way to
account for this similarity is to assume the same case-assigning mechanism as for
the earlier stages of Italian, namely, nominative assignment by governing T°.
However, in contrast to Italian, throughout the history of Spanish, movement of
T°(+V°) to Agr° is obligatory (cf. section 5.2.2). The following summarizes the
properties of both languages just mentioned:

(31) Language	Obligatory movement of T°(+V°) to Agr°	Postverbal subject allowed in SpecVP
earlier stages of Italian	no	yes
contemporary Italian	yes	no
Spanish	yes	yes

Although the contrast between earlier and contemporary Italian might suggest
that the case-assigning capability of T° is related to the fact that movement of T°
is not obligatory, the Spanish situation shows that both properties are not related
universally. Note that this is in conformity with the government transparency
corollary (GTC), according to which T° governs SpecVP even after T° has
moved to Agr°, so we can assume that in Spanish, too, T° assigns the nominative
under government. I therefore claim that the structure of a Spanish infinitive
clause such as that in (32a) can be represented as shown in (32b):

(32) a. al   castigar **el juez** a   los culpables
on-the to-punish the judge ACC PART the guilty
'when the judge punished the guilty' (Fernández Lagunilla 1987:130)

b.

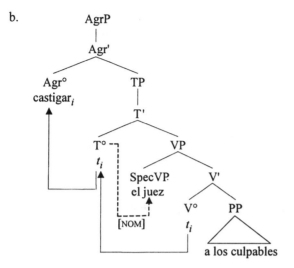

Another question is whether governing agreement may function as a nominative assigner.[16] In chapter 4 I reject the possibility that Modern Spanish licenses Aux-to-Comp constructions. If Aux-to-Comp works as I have suggested for Italian, we should then exclude [+Agr] as a possible nominative assigner under government in Spanish. Note that this is compatible with the fact that finite Aux-to-Comp is not possible, either:

(33) a. ⋆Ha **Juan** comprado el libro?
　　　　has J.　 bought　 the book

　　 b. ⋆Qué　película ha　**Juan** visto?
　　　　which film　　has J.　 seen

In contrast to this behavior, this word order was possible in Old and Classical Spanish:

(34) a. ¿Hauiale **yo** de ignorar?
　　　　had-him I　 to to-ignore
　　　　'Did I have to ignore him?' (Celest. 161)

　　 b. ¿Has **tú**　visto más valeroso caballero?
　　　　have you seen more valiant　 knight
　　　　'Have you seen a more valiant knight?' (Quij. 1, 10, p. 37; cf. Gessner 1893:32)

　　 c. ¿No han **vuestras mercedes** leido?
　　　　not have your　　 grace-PL　 read
　　　　'Has Your Grace not read?' (Quij. 1, 13, p. 49; cf. Gessner 1893:33)

This would suggest that in Old Spanish and in Classical Spanish, finite Agr° could assign the nominative case under government, similar to what has been assumed for the older stages of Italian and for stylistically marked constructions in present-day Italian, as well as for English and German. According to our corpus, the issue of whether this was also the case for nonfinite agreement cannot be decided, as shown in chapter 5. Let us leave this point open and establish our results in the following:

(35) Nominative assignment in Spanish

Variety	(A) Agr° (Spec-head agreement)	(B) Agr° (government)	(C) T° (government)
OS and CS	yes, if Agr° is [+Agr]		yes
MS	yes, if Agr° is [+Agr]	no	"

As in the earlier stages of Italian, postverbal nominative subjects in infinitive constructions selected by perception verbs and causative verbs cannot receive the nominative because these constructions lack TP (see section 6.1.1.1).[17]

6.2.2.   Preverbal subjects

6.2.2.1   Old Spanish and Classical Spanish

Although the preverbal position of the subject in the nominative case is much more frequent in Old and Classical Spanish than in Old Italian, it is still a fact that postverbal subjects clearly prevailed in infinitive clauses. The situation is thus comparable to Old Italian, in the sense that the preverbal subject was a rather marked option in Old and Classical Spanish, too. I therefore claim that in Old and Classical Spanish the same explanation given in 6.1.1.2 for Old Italian holds, namely, A'-movement of the subject to SpecAgrP. As I suggest in chapter 5, in Old and Classical Spanish infinitive clauses, the position SpecAgrP could also function as an A'-position. Thus, example (32) of chapter 5 has the following structure:

(36) [$_{AgrP}$ profesión$_j$ [$_{Agr'}$ fazer$_i$ [$_{TP}$ [$_{T°}$ t_i [$_{VP}$ [el   frayre] t_i t_j]]]]]
profession   to-do   the monk
'for a monk to practice his profession'

Here, the complement *profession* appears in SpecAgrP, whereas the subject *el frayre* remains in SpecVP. As I claimed for Old Italian, example (37a) can be assigned the structure in (37b):

(37) a.   commo a mí acaesció en [yo perder a   Calila].
as   to me happened in I   to-lose ACC PART C.
'as it happened to me on my losing C.' (Cal. e D. *A*, 196)

 b.   [$_{AgrP}$ yo$_j$ [$_{Agr'}$ perder$_i$ [$_{TP}$ t_j [$_{T°}$ t_i [$_{VP}$ t_j t_i a Calila]]]]]

In the constructions that are under discussion here, no subjects in the accusative case can be found during the whole history of Spanish. Thus, A'-movement of the nominative subject licensed in SpecVP by governing T° was the only way to yield a word order which is comparable to the ECM construction in Italian (and, as we see later in this chapter, in French until the eighteenth century). Compare the following examples, in which the infinitive clause is selected by *creer/credere* 'to believe' and *confesar/confessare* 'to confess'.

(38) a. los quales *creerían*   [yo no haber   leido las reglas . . .]   OS
          the which would-believe I   not to-have read the rules
          'who would believe that I had not read the rules . . .' (Santillana Prov., XXIII;
          cf. Diez 1882:946)

     a'. *credendo* [**lui** esser tornato dal   bosco]   OI
          believing   him to-be returned from-the wood
          'believing that he had returned from the wood' (Bocc. Dec., I, 4, p. 50)

     b. *confesando* [**yo** no ser mas santo que mis vecinos]   CS
          confessing   I not to-be more saintly than my neighbors
          'confessing that I was not more saintly than my neighbors' (Laz. 1554, 2r, 14–15)

     b'. che *confessi*   [**me** solo esser felice]   OI
          that (you) confess me alone to-be lucky
          'that you confess that I am the onlyone to be lucky' (Orl. Fur., V, 36; cf.
          Schwendener 1923:51)

The similarity in word order—which caused some traditional accounts to propose that it is the same construction, probably copied from Latin—is only superficial and, as we have seen, is produced by two different mechanisms in both languages. Taking into account our assumptions about Italian, the fact that the accusative case has never been possible in these configurations suggests that CP in Spanish has never been transparent for outside government so that the mechanism of structural accusative assignment is blocked.[18] Against this background, it may be somewhat surprising that the older stages of Spanish allowed for a non–*wh*-marked subject to appear in the main clause:

(39) a. [**El obispo** . . .]$_i$ / non conviene [. . . t_i sin   sangne quel   OS
          the bishop   not is-convenient without blood   that
          rancon entrar].
          corner to-enter
          'For the bishop it is not convenient to enter into that corner without blood.'
          (Berceo, Sac., 91; cf. Beardsley 1921:258)

     b. [**Aquella proporción** . . .]$_i$ juzgo [t_i . . . ser mejor . . .]   OS
          that   proportion   (he) judged   to-be better
          'He judged that that proportion was better . . . ' (Celest., I, 64, p. 29)

     c. [**Cualquier gusano de la madera**]$_i$ . . . pensaba [t_i ser la   CS
          any   worm   of the wood   (he) thought to-be the
          culebra].
          serpent
          'Of every worm in the wood he thought that it was the serpent.' (Laz. 1554,
          20v–21r)

The following shows the structure of example (39b):

(40)   [Aquella proporcion]$_i$ [juzgo CP]

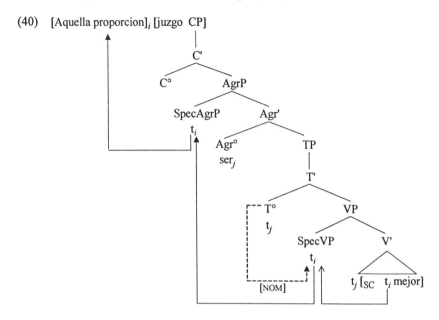

The subject of the adjectival small clause A-moves to the only possible case position inside the infinitive clause (SpecVP), where it is licensed by nominative assignment through governing T°. Since SpecAgrP is an A'-position in Old Spanish, the subject can reach this position by A'-movement. Note that this step is necessary to explain the extraction of the subject into the main clause, just as in the earlier stages of Italian. An important point to keep in mind here is the case of the extracted subject: in Italian the movement of the DP to SpecAgrP is an A-movement; that is, the subject receives its case in this position through ECM; consequently, after movement into some position of the main clause, the ex-tracted subject will surface as the accusative (cf. 6.1.2.2, example 27). In con-trast, as expected, in Old and Classical Spanish the extracted subject surfaces in the nominative case. Note that the fact that ECM is not possible, although the subject can be extracted by passing the CP boundary, means that C° is a proper head governor in these varieties.

6.2.2.2 Present-day Spanish

In present-day varieties of Spanish, SpecAgrP is not an A'-position, and as I claim, it also has to be assumed that nonfinite Agr° cannot assign the nominative through Spec-head agreement. From this we can conclude that SpecAgrP is not accessible at all to the subject of an infinitive clause. The fact that SpecAgrP lacks A'-properties not only explains the ungrammaticality of a fronted com-plement[19] but also accounts for the impossibility of a preverbal subject in infinitive constructions. At the same time, this property rules out the extraction of the subject into the main clause because SpecAgrP is needed as an intermediate landing site. In this context, let us examine the following examples:

(41) a. Encontramos [ser **el poema austríaco** del   siglo   XIII, Kudrun,
         (we) find   to-be the poem   Austrian   from-the century 13th K.
         fuente de baladas . . .]
         source of ballads
         'We find that the Austrian poem from the thirteenth century, K., is the source of ballads . . .' (Pidal Romancero, 185; cf. Skydsgaard 1977:273)

     b. ⋆[**El poema austríaco** . . .] encontramos ser   fuente de baladas . . .]
         the poem   Austrian   (we) find   to-be source of ballads

     c. El poema austríaco **que**   encontramos [ser   fuente de baladas . . .]
         the poem   Austrian which (we) find   to-be source of ballads

     d. ¿**Qué poema** encontramos [ser   fuente de baladas . . .]?
         which poem   (we) find   to-be source of ballads

As the examples show, only a DP that is marked [+wh] can be moved out of the infinitive clause. The situation in (41) is similar to present-day Italian, but, according to the results of the previous sections, we have to interpret the underlying mechanisms as totally different, as summarized in (42):

(42)

Phenomenon	Explanation (Spanish)	Explanation (Italian)
postverbal subject	nominative assignment by T° in SpecVP	nominative assignment by [+Agr] in SpecCP (Aux-to Comp)
extraction of a wh-marked subject	wh movement of case-marked subjects (nominative) to SpecCP, then further movement up to the main clause	accusative assignment by the main verb to the subject in SpecAgrP via ECM, then further movement up to the main clause

The wh-marked subjects in Spanish bear the nominative, which is shown by the fact that the accusative particle *a* is ungrammatical:

(43) ⋆[¿A   qué   individuos] sabíamos ser   caníbales?
        ACC PART which individuals (we) knew to-be cannibals
        'Which individuals did we know to be cannibals?'

This interpretation, according to which SpecAgrP is excluded as a case position in infinitive clauses, can explain the different grammatical and ungrammatical word order facts. At the same time, it accounts for the differences in the diachronic level. On the other hand, the analysis proposed still does not completely exclude the possibility of preverbal subjects because it only predicts that a preverbal nominative subject must be motivated by A'-movement. A'-movement of the subject will succeed only if there is an appropriate A'-position inside the infinitive clause.

As we see in chapter 2, preverbal specified subjects in Modern Spanish infinitive clauses are possible only in a small set of constructions, namely, infinitival PPs that are adjuncts, as in the following example (cf. 25b of chapter 2):

(44) cosas que pasaron [antes de [yo nacer]]
     things that happened before of I to-be-born
     'things that happened before I was born' (Muchachos, 18; cf. Skydsgaard 1977:655)

It is striking that this type of infinitive construction also regularly admits other constituents at the left of the infinitive, for example, adverbs:

(45) a. No lo hagas [sin   *antes* avisarme].
         not it (you) do without before to-warn me
         'Don't do it without warning me before.'

     b. Sal   al   claro   de luna [para *bien* verte].
         go-out to-the brightness of moon for well to-see-you
         'Go out into the moonlight in order (for me) to see you well.' (Retablo, 18; cf. Skydsgaard 1977:853)

     c. [para *luego* llegar   a casa y   meterme en la cama]
         for then to-arrive at home and to-put-R CL in the bed
         'in order to arrive at home then and to go to bed' (Corpus Oral, CCON034a)

In other types of infinitive clauses, for example, in impersonal constructions, clause-initial adverbs, as well as preverbal subjects, are ungrammatical:[20]

(46) a. *[*Bien* trabajar] requiere mucha paciencia.
          well to-work requires much patience

     b. *[*Yo* trabajar] requiere mucha paciencia.
          I to-work requires much   patience

In Mensching (1998, 1999) I have shown that this holds for other constructions as well, both in Spanish and in Catalan. The correlation between the licensing of clause-initial adverbs and preverbal subjects suggests that both occupy the same position—not SpecAgrP, but a position adjoined either to AgrP or to CP. Since clause-initial adverbs are usually assumed to be adjunctions to AgrP, we can postulate the following structure for example (44):

(47)

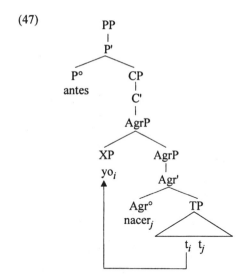

The question is why the relevant adjoined position to AgrP is available only in infinitive constructions that are complements of P°. In Mensching (1999), I tentatively assume for Catalan that the position of the subject and of the adverbs in examples with the word order in (44) and (45) is SpecCP. This accounts for various aspects, for example, the fact that neither adverbs nor subjects can be fronted in the conditional *de* construction or the temporal *al* construction (recall that *de* and *al* are complementizers).[21]

An interesting alternative is suggested by taking into account the results of Cinque. Within his theory of multiple functional categories, he argues that in Italian and Spanish, infinitives usually move to the uppermost functional head beneath CP so that no adverbs are allowed to the left of the infinitive (Cinque 1999:143–47, 226), as in example (46). However, at least for Italian, he notes that in some types of infinitive constructions the infinitive is allowed to stay lower. One of the constructions he mentions is similar to the cases shown in (45): "It was noted in Cinque (1983) that . . . some 'higher' adverbs can intervene between an infinitive and a real preposition taking it as a complement, differently from the case of prepositional complementizers" (Cinque 1999:146). The problem is that an adverb like *bien* in (46a) is usually considered to be a lower adverb. This would probably mean that the infinitive is allowed to remain inside the VP in these cases. It could therefore be argued that the subject has not moved in examples like (44) either, so that no additional rules on subject movement would be necessary. I do not discuss this point any further because it should be examined within the context of a thorough study of adverb positions in Spanish. I briefly return to this construction in chapter 7.

6.3   Portuguese and Galician

6.3.1   Nominative subjects

6.3.1.1   SpecVP and SpecAgrP as case positions

According to the results of chapter 5, postverbal subjects in Portuguese and Galician are located in SpecVP and preverbal subjects are located in SpecAgrP, as in most of the linguistic varieties examined so far. In both cases the verb moves to T° and optionally further on to Agr°.[22] For the postverbal position, I assume here that in Portuguese, too, the infinitival T° is a nominative assigner so that, up to now, this can be argued to be an almost pan-Romance property.

Concerning the preverbal subject, grammatical in many more configurations than in Modern Spanish, we could argue that movement of the subject to SpecAgrP in Portuguese and Galician is an A'-movement, similar to the situation in the historical varieties of Italian and Spanish. Since Portuguese is generally considered to be more conservative than Spanish, this would not be surprising. There are at least three arguments against such a hypothesis, however. First, whereas SpecAgrP was a possible A'-position in Old Portuguese (cf. 3.1.2), this is not the case in Modern Portuguese.[23] Second, most frequently the subject appears preverbally—note that this is in clear contrast to Old Spanish and Old Italian—a behavior that is not different from finite constructions. In contrast, the construction with the postverbal subject is usually the marked option.[24] Third, the postverbal position is not always acceptable, at least in the modern spoken varieties of Portuguese, as shown in section 2.4. Further on I assume that the postverbal subject is ungrammatical for most speakers in certain configurations because case assignment by T°(+V°) to SpecVP is blocked (see 6.3.1.2). As we will see, this is also a parallel to finite constructions.

Taking into account these considerations, we can conclude that the movement of the subject to SpecAgrP should instead be interpreted as A-movement. According to our assumptions on nominative assignment, A-movement of the subject to SpecAgrP, with the verb staying below, is a typical case of nominative assignment through Spec-head agreement. Summarizing this discussion, I therefore claim that the following properties of the functional categories T and Agr have been valid for all diachronic stages of Portuguese and Galician:

(48)   Nominative case assignment in Portuguese and Galician

(A) Agr° (Spec-head agreement)	(B) Agr° (government)	(C) T° (government)
yes	no	yes

The fact that infinitival Agr° in Portuguese assigns the nominative by Spec-head agreement suggests to us that there may be some relationship with the agreement features in nonfinite Agr°, which show up overtly in the shape of the inflected infinitive. This assumption becomes even more plausible against the background of a quite interesting property of Modern Galician:[25] when the subject is preverbal, the infinitive always appears in the inflected form. The agreement morphol-

ogy is, however, not obligatory when the subject occurs in the postverbal position (Álvarez et al. 1989:395), as in the following examples, where the forms
durmiren and *darmos* would be expected:[26]

(49) a. Deben de se consideraren coma cubículos [pra *durmir*   **os homes**].
     (they) must R CL to-consider-3PL as   niches   for to-sleep-Ø the men
     'They must be considered as niches used by the men to sleep.' (Prosas galegas,
     148; cf. Gondar 1978:64)

    b. Xa   estabamos aqui [para lles   *dar*   **nós mesmos** aquel encargo].
     already (we) were   here   for   them to-give-Ø we ourselves that   order
     'We were already here, so we could give them the order personally.' (Álvarez et
     al. 1989:395)

This phenomenon can be regarded as a further example of the lack of agreement
between the subject and the verb, described in 3.2.3 as a characteristic property
of VS(O) structures; this can be explained by the fact that T° is responsible for
case assignment, without the intervention of Agr°, to which agreement phenomena usually belong.[27] In Old and Classical Portuguese, we sometimes find infinitives without inflection, although the subject is preverbal. This may be explained
quite easily through the properties of SpecAgrP as an A'-position. Cases in
which a Portuguese or Galician infinitive lacks agreement morphology even
though there is an overt subject are therefore not an exception, or even a "cu-
rioso desvio da sintaxe normal portuguêsa" (Maurer 1968:152), but a property
that is perfectly compatible with or even predicted by general syntactic principles.[28]

6.3.1.2 *Restrictions on the postverbal position of subjects*

As we see in section 2.4, postverbal subjects are usually less acceptable or sometimes even ungrammatical in contemporary Portuguese. To illustrate this point
again, let us repeat some examples from chapter 2:

(50) a. *Penso comprarem **eles** o   livro.
     (I) think to-buy-3PL   they the book
     'I think that they will buy the book.'

    b. ?Aconteceu interromperem **eles** as comunicações.
     happened   to-interrupt-3PL they the communications
     'It happened that they interrupted the communications.'

The lower degree of acceptability of the postverbal subject position with infinitives of transitive verbs is a property of spoken Portuguese, which is not limited
to infinitive constructions. In literary Portuguese, all these sentences are grammatical. This complies with the difference between written and spoken language
for finite clauses, as observed by Schellert (1958:93–96). Moreover, it has to be
observed that a configuration that yields a VS(O) word order with transitive
verbs is possible in various Romance varieties in finite and nonfinite construc-

tions.[29] This was also possible in earlier stages of Portuguese and is still used in literary texts.[30] Generally, however, real VSO order is an option that is not very frequently chosen by subject-prominent languages (cf. Sasse 1987:537). The issue under discussion should therefore be treated in a more general study of the syntax of verbs, and consequently is not resolved here. Nevertheless I do venture some remarks on the subject.

In a case-oriented approach to the licensing and linear ordering of DPs, such as the one I am considering in this chapter, a solution that rather intuitively might have some plausibility would be to assume that in the configuration $[_{T^\circ}V^\circ_i$ $[_{VP}$ DP_{subj} t_i $DP_{obj}]]$ there is a kind of minimality violation, where minimality is understood in a slightly modified sense: the intervention of a potentially case-assigning element, in this case the transitive verb. On a more or less semantic level, blocking case assignment to the postverbal subject in this configuration would avoid ambiguity, as does the minimality condition: "Minimality reduces potential ambiguity with respect to government relations" (Haegeman 1994:630). The problem of this solution is that the transitive verb is not located in a separate head position but rather in a head position adjoined to T° by incorporation. In other words, V° does not really intervene between the subject and the nomina-tive-assigning head T° but is part of it:

(51)

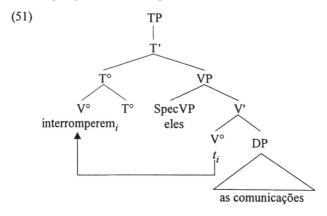

However, it could be argued that the incorporated head c-commands the subject in SpecVP and thus causes the minimality effect.[31] Dobrovie-Sorin (1987, 1994:147, fn. 22) argues the other way around: she hypothesizes a condition according to which accusative assignment to a direct object is blocked by an intervening subject.[32] However, these assumptions are rather problematic: either the accusative is assigned on D-structure, so that there will be no blocking effect, or the accusative assignment is performed on S-structure, but in this case the GTC ensures that this case can still be assigned from the target position of the transitive verb. According to G. Müller (1995), in an X° chain, only the last member can assign case under government. A trace inherits the case-assigning capacity from the head of the chain. Nevertheless, Müller claims that not all categories are capable of transferring their case-assigning properties to traces.[33] We might assume that something like this holds for T° in languages that do not support the configuration in (51), in the sense that T° blocks case assignment to the direct object when it contains a [+NOM] feature.

The problem discussed here did not escape the attention of Roberts. The future discussion of this problem should take into account the following brief comment:

> What prevents [V+I] from assigning Accusative to the subject and Nominative to the object? . . . Such a configuration of Case assignment would give rise to a morphologically ergative system. Tentatively, then, we leave this possibility open at the level of UG: some parameter, whose precise nature is unclear, determines the distribution of cases here. (Roberts 1993:76, note 8)

A solution that comprises both the issue brought up by Roberts and the problem under discussion in this section may probably be found if we take into account the percolation properties of case features. The question relevant here is whether the accusative feature of V° percolates to the uppermost head after the incorporation of V° into T°. We could imagine various configurations, for instance:

(52)   a.   b.

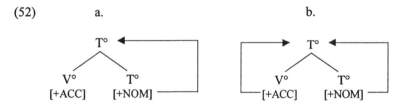

In configuration (52a), only the feature [+NOM] arrives at the upper T°; this means that the subject DP governed by T° receives the nominative case, whereas the accusative is assigned by means of the GTC to the complement. This is the case in the languages discussed so far, in which the governing T° assigns the nominative even if the [+ACC] feature is present, to which the earlier stages of Portuguese and Galician, as well as the modern literary language, belong. In the configuration in (52b), both features arrive at the uppermost head T°. We can assume that this is the case of contemporary spoken Portuguese, but in contrast to those systems that are "morphologically ergative" in Roberts's terminology, Portuguese has no mechanism that could cope with both features in order to assign case correctly, so the structure is avoided.

Another account (Ambar 1994) is discussed in connection with the minimalist program in chapter 7.

6.3.1.3 Restrictions on the preverbal position of the subject in Modern Portuguese

Before discussing the restrictions on the preverbal position of the subject, let us summarize some of the results of the preceding sections. I claim that in infinitive clauses in Portuguese, two case-assigning mechanisms are available: (i) under Spec-head agreement by Agr° and (ii) under government by T°. In spoken Portuguese, mechanism (ii) is usually blocked when T° contains a transitive verb, so only mechanism (i) comes into play in this case. We now have to examine why mechanism (i) cannot be applied in some configurations.

According to our presentation of the data in 2.4, preverbal subjects are un-grammatical in the following configurations: first, in infinitival clauses that are complements of declarative and epistemic verbs (53a); second, in infinitive clauses that are complements of *parece* ('seems') when no raising occurs (53b); third, only in Brazilian Portuguese, in infinitive constructions that are comple-ments of D° (53c):

(53) a.   O presidente afirmou [*serem*   **essas actividades** úteis para o país].
         the president   stated   to-be-3PL these activities   useful for   the country
         'The president stated that these activities were useful for the country.'

  a'.★O presidente afirmou [**essas actividades** *serem* úteis para o país].

   b.   Parece [*serem*   **essas actividades** úteis para o país].
        seems   to-be-3PL these activities   useful for   the country
        'It seems that these activities are useful for the country.'

  b.'★Parece [**essas actividades** *serem* úteis para o país].

   c.(★)[O [**ele** *ganhar* as eleições]] significa uma mudança radical.
        the he to-win   the elections   means   a   change   radical
        'The fact the he wins the election means a radical change.' (ungrammatical in
        Brazilian Portuguese).

Why should these restrictions hold? Let us start with the construction in (53a). The verbs that cause the ungrammaticality here are the same ones that select an infinitival Aux-to-Comp construction in Italian. As I claim in 6.1.1.3, in Italian these verbs subcategorize for an infinitival CP with the feature [+Agr] in C°. Let us assume that this is the case in Portuguese, too. We would then get the follow-ing structure:

(54)

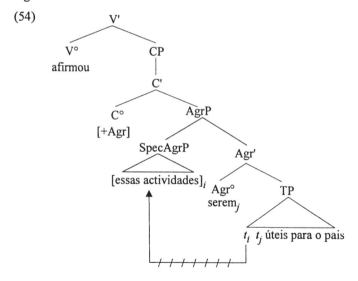

Why should movement to SpecAgrP be forbidden, as illustrated in (54)? I would like to argue that it is the very feature [+Agr] governing the position SpecAgrP that makes it impossible for the subject to move there. It is important to remember that in Portuguese the preverbal subject in SpecAgrP receives the nominative case through Spec-head agreement. The configuration illustrated in (54) strongly reminds us of the following regularity, formulated by Roberts (1993:26): "In a language where Agr° assigns Nominative Case only under [spec-head] agreement, then Agr to C movement . . . destroys the context in which Agr° can assign nominative to SpecAgrP."

As I show in connection with Italian Aux-to-Comp in 6.1.1.1, the agreement features of finite Agr° and the lexically selected feature [+Agr] in C° are very similar in nature. It is therefore not surprising that [+Agr] in C° should behave just like an Agr° that has moved to C° with respect to the suppression of case assignment through Spec-head agreement,[34] so Roberts's generalization correctly predicts the facts about Portuguese infinitive clauses. We can now also understand why preverbal subjects are not suppressed in the case of factive verbs like *lamentar*,[35] which do not select [+Agr] in C°:

(55) Lamentou [**essas actividades** serem   úteis para o   país].
     (he) deplored these   activities   to-be-3PL useful for   the country
     'He deplored the fact that these activities were useful for the country.'

The question is whether this explanation can be applied to the other constructions mentioned. As for Brazilian examples such as (53c), in which the infinitive is a complement of D°, such an assumption does not to seem implausible. After all, the same structure licenses Aux-to-Comp in Italian, and I hypothesize in 6.1.1.3 that this is because Italian D° elements select infinitival CPs with [+Agr]. Since this should be considered a language-specific property, we can easily explain the difference in grammaticality in Brazilian, on the one hand, and Portuguese and Galician, on the other, by assuming different lexical properties of determiners.

Examples like (53b), where the construction is selected by the verb *parecer* 'to seem', are more difficult to interpret. Apart from the syntactic option discussed here, with the subject remaining inside the infinitive clause, *parecer* also allows for the raising construction. This would be an argument against CP but in favor of AgrP (see 4.2 and 6.1.2.1). In contrast, Raposo and Uriagereka (1990: 534) assumed that *parecer* subcategorizes for CP in Portuguese, although they did so chiefly because they interpreted this construction as Aux-to-Comp. As a further argument, they point out that *parecer* also permits a finite CP complement, but this might not be sufficient. There is, however, one property that is characteristic for the Portuguese verb *parecer* in contrast to similar verbs in other Romance languages. Consider the following example from the nineteenth century, which is still accepted as grammatical by some speakers today:

(56) a multidão dos   infieis, [os **quaes**]$_i$ lhes pareceu [t_i dirigirem-se
　　 the multitude of-the infidels the which (PL) them seemed (SG) to-direct-R CL
　　 para o lado   do   celebre mosteiro
　　 toward the lateral-part of-the famous monastery
　　 'the multitude of the infidels, who seemed to move toward the lateral part of the
　　 famous monastery' (Herculano Eur., 169; quoted by Said Ali 1971:346)

The *wh* extraction cannot be explained by raising: the relative pronoun *os quaes*
is plural, whereas the verb *pareceu* '(it) seemed' is singular. Moreover, Portuguese admits the same structure even with a finite CP complement, as in the
following examples (taken from Sten 1952:100):

(57) a. **Vocês**$_i$ parece [que t_i vêm   a dormir]?!
　　　　 you   seems that (you) come for to sleep
　　　　 'It seems that you come here for sleeping?!' (T. Coelho, Amores, 189)

　　 b. **As foices**$_i$ parece [que t_i les   caem].
　　　　 the sickles seems that them fall
　　　　 'It seems that the sickles are falling off their hands.' (Redol, Gaibéus, 26)

Here we have a classic example of a violation of the so-called *that-trace* filter
(Chomsky and Lasnik 1977).[36] An important point is that similar constructions
are interpreted by Rizzi (1990a:52–54) as licensed through [+Agr] in C°. It thus
seems to be perfectly justified to assume that *parecer* selects a CP that contains
this feature, even more so if we take into account the fact that the latter phenomenon (i.e., extraction of a non–*wh* subject from a clausal complement selected by *parecer*) can also be found in infinitive constructions:[37]

(58) **Os pés**$_i$ parecía [t_i terem   criado raízes no   chão].
　　 the feet seemed (SG) to-have-3PL produced roots on-the floor
　　 'The feet seemed to have produced roots on the floor.' (Duarte Vencidos, 28; cf.
　　 Sten 1952:100)

We can thus conclude that *parecer* in Portuguese generally subcategorizes for a
CP with [+Agr] in C°, so that the nonavailability of SpecAgrP for the subject in
all three configurations mentioned at the beginning of this section can be explained in a uniform way.
　　 In view of the results achieved so far, consider now the following examples:

(59) a. Aconteceu [**eles** interromperem as comunicações].
　　　　 happened   they to-interrupt-3PL the communications.
　　　　 'It happened that they interrupted the communications.'

　　 b. É um axioma literario [**as frases famosas** repetirem-se   em muitas
　　　　 is an axiom literary   the famous sentences to-repeat -3SG-R CL in many
　　　　 obras].
　　　　 works
　　　　 'It is a literary axiom that famous sentences are repeated in many works.'

c. ??Foi declarado [o **presidente** não ter   razão].
    was declared   the president   not to-have reason
    'It was declared that the president was not right.'

d. ?Foi lamentado [o **presidente** não ter   razão].
    was deplored   the president   not to-have reason
    'It was deplored that the president was not right.'

When the infinitive construction is a complement of impersonal verbs or appears within a SC, the preverbal position of the subject is grammatical, as is shown in (59a) and (59b). Although these constructions should be considered CPs, [+Agr] in C° is not to be expected here (cf. section 6.1.1.3), so it is not surprising that this word order is not suppressed. In contrast, if the infinitive construction is a complement of passive predicates, as in (59c) and (59d), there is a clear difference in grammaticality depending on the main verb (i.e., whether it is declarative or factive), which is similar to what is observed when these verbs are in the active voice. This turns out to be compatible with our assumptions. As I have repeatedly emphasized, the property of a verb like *declarar* to select [+Agr] in C° is determined by its lexical entry, and this is, of course, maintained in the passive voice.

I finally turn to the situation of the earlier stages of the language. Although this cannot be judged for the constructions after a determiner and the verb *parecer* because of the small number of examples that could be found, the preverbal position was possible in complements of epistemic verbs, as shown in example (30) of chapter 2. Although we cannot completely rule out the possibility that this might have been due to imitation of Latin models, there is some evidence that the option of a preverbal subject was really grammatical: in contrast to the present varieties, Classical Portuguese allowed for the extraction of non–*wh*-marked subjects:

(60) E s' **isto**$_i$ conhecesseis / [t_i Ser   verdade . . .]
    and if this (you) recognized   to-be truth
    'And if you recognized this to be true . . .' (Camões, Canç., 9, II, 326; cf. Otto 1891:378).

This construction is not grammatical today since the subject cannot move to the infinitival SpecAgrP because of the restriction we have discussed. The example in (60) shows again that such a restriction does not seem to have been valid in earlier stages of the language. Several possible explications could be found for this phenomenon. One possibility is to simply assume that the subcategorization frame of the respective verbs did not include the feature [+Agr] for the subcategorized infinitive construction. Note that the preverbal subject is somewhat more acceptable in Modern Brazilian Portuguese with some verbs (see chapter 2), which might be regarded as a continuation of their earlier lexical properties. Another quite interesting solution, which might be examined in future work with a focus on Portuguese, is that the historical varieties of the language did not yet allow case marking of the subject by Agr° in a Spec-head configuration. This would probably mean that the preverbal position of subjects in infinitive clauses

was the result of A'-movement, just as in Old Spanish. Note that [+Agr] in C°
would not have any influence in this case because it only interferes in A-movement.[38]

6.3.2   Accusative subjects in Brazilian Portuguese

In chapter 2, I mention a construction that seems to be limited to some varieties
of Brazilian Portuguese and in which the subject appears in the accusative case:

(61) a.   Êle trouxe um sanduíche [para **mim** comer].
          he brought a   sandwich for   me   to-eat   (Thomas 1969:185)

     b.   Toque qualquer coisa [para **mim/ti** [39] dançar   com ela].
          play   any   thing for   me/you   to-dance with her
          (Information provided by a speaker from Porto Alegre)

In contrast to the Italian constructions with an accusative subject, discussed in
section 6.1.2, this cannot be considered to be an ECM construction. Note that in
(61) the verb of the main clause has a complement to which it assigns the accusative (*um sanduíche/qualquer coisa*), and in any case, these prepositional infinitive clauses are adjuncts. Finally, a preposition intervenes between the main
clause and the infinitive. We can assume that an overt P° between the main
clause and the subject of the infinitive blocks ECM, as in Italian. On the other
hand, there is a striking similarity between this construction and the following
well-known structure in English (cf., e.g., Haegeman 1994:167):

(62) a.   I prefer very much [*for* **him** to go now].

     b.   [*For* **him** to attack Bill] would be illegal.

It is generally assumed that the preposition *for* in these examples is an infinitival
complementizer, which assigns the accusative to the infinitival subject in the
specifier of AgrP, as illustrated in the following:

(63)

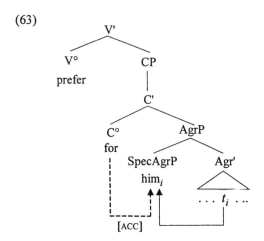

Apart from the case phenomenon, another property that the Brazilian construction has in common with the one in English is that the preposition and the subject of the infinitive clause are adjacent. All this makes us assume that the mechanism involved in both constructions is similar, that is, that *para* assigns the accusative to the subject:

(64)

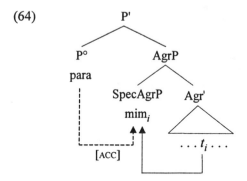

Accusative marking is possible here because, on the evidence that the overt agreement morphology is missing (i.e., the infinitive is not inflected), it can be argued that Agr° has no appropriate agreement features so that nominative assignment by Agr° is not supported. As (64) shows, the difference from the English construction is that we have to consider *para* as a P° (cf. the analysis in section 3.3.3).

The licensing of the structure in (64) can be interpreted as a lexical property of the preposition *para*, which is limited to some varieties of Portuguese. Note, however, that this assumption is not very elegant because *para* assigns the accusative case to DP in all varieties of Portuguese; in addition, and strictly speaking, this is not a lexical property but a general characteristic of all prepositions in Portuguese and most of the other Romance languages. An additional lexical entry that would determine that *para* may assign the accusative to the subject of an infinitive clause is not very elegant either. We could avoid the latter assumption by claiming that *para* is a complementizer in Brazilian Portuguese, the subcategorization of which is therefore different from the homonymous preposition.[40] A simpler and more general solution would be to assume that *para* subcategorizes for AgrP in the linguistic varieties under discussion but that it selects CP in the other varieties of Portuguese, just as all other prepositions. This would predict the ungrammaticality of this construction in most of the Portuguese varieties because it has to be assumed that empty C° blocks outside government in the sense of the minimality condition (in contrast to the earlier stages of Italian). This is not an additional assumption because it is needed in any case to account for the ungrammaticality of ECM in infinitival CPs in all Ibero-Romance languages.[41]

6.4   French

In this section I assume, as discussed in 2.2 and 4.3.1.4, that specified subjects in infinitive clauses in French are generally assigned the accusative case, with the exception of two marginal configurations studied by Reuland (1983) and Vinet (1985). As shown in 2.2, the accusative case is morphologically visible in Old French, and later the use of reflexive pronouns suggests that it is still there.

The fact that French generally licenses only accusative subjects can also be concluded on theoretical grounds. The nonprepositional infinitive constructions in which overt subjects can be found during the history of French are exactly the same ones in which ECM is documented in Italian, that is, infinitival complement clauses. On the other hand, in chapter 2 I observe that specified subjects in the following configurations do not seem to have existed in French, in contrast to the other Romance languages, where they are frequently found: (i) infinitive constructions that are subjects of nonimpersonal predicates, (ii) infinitive constructions that are predicate nominals, and (iii) infinitive clauses embedded into DP. The last point is rather striking because at least until the sixteenth century, infinitive constructions without an overt subject were perfectly possible in this context. For the three configurations mentioned, ECM should be excluded, according to the results of section 6.1.2, and in the other languages discussed these configurations permit specified subjects only because they allow for nominative subjects.[42]

Apart from the configurations mentioned, we can also find specified subjects in infinitive clauses that are complements of prepositions and of overt complementizers. I argue in 6.4.1.2 that these cases can be explained by assuming a similar mechanism as that in Brazilian Portuguese (see 6.3.2). The rather striking constructions examined by Reuland (1983) and Vinet (1985) are discussed in 6.4.2. I put forth some reasons according to which the subjects that appear in those constructions are the only ones that receive nominative case.

6.4.1   Subjects in the accusative case

6.4.1.1   Exceptional case marking

To explain specified subjects in complement clauses, we can adapt the results achieved for ECM in Italian. It can be assumed that CP was transparent for case assignment by the main verb from Old French until the Classical period. The situation seems to be exactly the same as in Italian, in that a nonovert C° did not block case assignment from outside. Hence, I claim that the table in (28) for Italian is also valid for the earlier stages of French. Examples (65a) and (65b) can thus be represented as shown in (65c) and (65d), where the dotted lines indicate ECM:

(65) a. Or covient   [**chascun** estre hardi comme sangler].
        now is-convenient everyone to-be daring like   wild-boar
        'Now it is convenient that everyone be daring like a wild boar.' (Ren.
        Montaub., 231, v. 37; cf. E. Stimming 1915:105)

b. Pour ce vueil   et si le desir / **[Vous touz** a un seul obëir].
   for   this (I) want and so it (I) wish you   all   to one only to-obey
   'Therefore I wish and desire that all of you obey to one alone.' (Perceval, 3241;
   cf. Tobler 1921:91; E. Stimming 1915:114)

c. covient [$_{CP}$ [$_{AgrP}$ **chascun**$_i$ [$_{TP}$ t_i [$_{VP}$ t_i estre hardi comme sangler]]]]
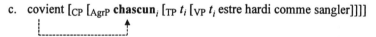

d. desir [$_{CP}$ [$_{AgrP}$ **[Vous touz**]$_i$ [$_{TP}$ t_i [$_{VP}$ t_i a un seul obëir]]]]
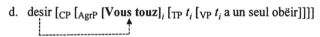

It is not necessary to discuss every configuration in detail because the relevant data from sections 2.2 and 4.3.1.4 can be explained by an analysis that is virtually identical to our account for Italian, presented in 6.1.2.

I thus assume that in the earlier stages of French, too, there is a relationship between the option of licensing a subject in SpecAgrP through ECM and the possibility of extracting a non–*wh*-marked subject, to be explained by specific properties of C°. In fact, this assumption correctly predicts examples like (66), with a structure that is identical to the Italian one in (27):

(66) a. **Mahomet** t_i cuident [t_i remanoir].[43]   OF
       M.   (they) believe to-stay
       'They believed M. would stay.' (Mahom., 1582; cf. E. Stimming 1915:114)

   b. **Bethleem**$_i$ avons   lu [t_i estre le lieu de son enfance].   MF
      B.   (we) have read to-be the place of his childhood
      'We have read that B. was the place of his childhood.' (Marg. de Nav., II, 108;
      cf. E. Stimming 1915:160)

   c. **La vertu**$_i$ se pourra dire [t_i avoir   la cause précédente de   CF
      the virtue R CL can (FUT) to-say to-have the cause preceding   of
      l' envie].
      the envy
      'We can say that virtue has the preceding cause of envy.' (Malh. Épîtres, II, 683;
      cf. A. Haase 1965:207)

In contrast, the issue of postverbal subjects in French infinitive clauses needs some further discussion. The difference from Italian is that French postverbal subjects take the accusative case, just like preverbal subjects. As we see in chapter 5, it must be assumed that postverbal subjects are located in SpecVP, as in most Romance languages. Consider example (67a), from Middle French, with the corresponding simplified tree diagram in (67b):

(67) a. Vos philosophes nyent [estre par vertuz de figures **mouvement** faict].
       your philosophers negate to-be by virtue of figures movement   made
       'Your philosophers deny that movement is performed by virtue of the figures.'
       (Rabelais, 877; cf. E. Stimming 1915:162)

b.

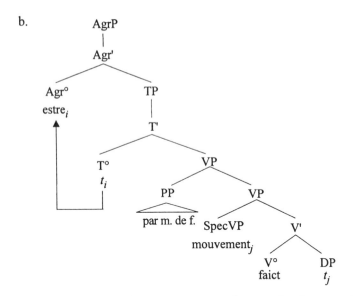

The difficulty here is that there are too many elements that intervene between the main verb and the subject of the infinitive, so it is not very probable that the accusative could be assigned through ECM from the main verb directly to the position SpecVP. I therefore assume, with Junker and Martineau (1992), that case is assigned to an empty category in SpecAgrP and that it is then transmitted through the chain to the coindexed overt subject in SpecVP (see 4.3.1.4):[44]

(68)   nient [$_{CP}$ [$_{AgrP}$ *pro*$_i$ estre$_j$ [$_{TP}$ t_j [$_{VP}$ mouvement$_i$ fait t_i]]]]

        ECM   case transmision

Null subjects are well documented for the Old and Middle French period. According to Brunot (1905:III, 477–81), null subjects can still be observed in the sixteenth century, whereas they are virtually unattested to in the seventeenth century (cf. also Roberts 1993:214–16).[45] This fits our data quite well: as seen in section 2.2, our material does not show postverbal subjects in any of the relevant constructions from roughly about that time onward.

The properties of C° that make Modern French different from the earlier stages can also be held to be the same as in Italian. In present-day French, CP generally blocks ECM. This blocking mechanism can be neutralized only by a feature [+Agr] in C°. Consider the following examples:

(69) a.   Les étudiants **que** t_i je croyais [$_{CP}$ t_i +*Agr*$_i$ [$_{AgrP}$ t_i travailler à la
           the students   that   I believed   to-work at the
           bibliothèque]], étaient partis   faire du   ski.
           library   were   gone-away to-do of-the ski
           'The students that I believed to be working at the library had left to go skiing.'
           (Seelbach 1978:151)

b. ⋆Je croyais [$_{CP}$ +*Agr* [**les étudiants** travailler à la bibliothèque]].
   I   believed   the students   to-work   at the library

c. ⋆les étudiants **que** t_i je voulais [$_{CP}$ Ø [$_{AgrP}$ t_i travailler à la
   the students   which I wanted   to-work   at the
   bibliothèque]]
   library

d. ⋆Il convient [$_{CP}$ Ø [**les étudiants** travailler à la bibliothèque]].
   it is-convenient   the students   to-work   at the library

Our assumption correctly predicts these data. The subject of the infinitive clause
can show up overtly only if it is *wh*-marked and extracted to the main clause, as
in infinitival complements of epistemic and declarative verbs in Italian (cf.
6.1.2.2).[46]

The last point to be discussed in this section concerns clitics. In contrast to
Modern Italian, in Modern French the subject of the infinitive can surface as an
object clitic in the main clause (cf. A. Haase 1965:207), which is a stylistically
marked option today:

(70) On **l'**$_i$ estime [$_{CP}$ t_i être sage].
     One him (CL) thinks   to-be wise
     'People think that he is wise.'

This kind of construction is quite usual with perception and causative and permissive verbs, which lack a CP projection, as we see in chapter 4. Nevertheless,
the fact that this is possible, too, in a CP of the type under discussion is not surprising given the results of this section. Since the clitic has to pass through various functional categories by incorporation, it will finally be incorporated into C°
before it is extracted. We might assume that its incorporation into C° [+Agr] has
a similar effect as the coindexation assumed above so that case assignment by the
main verb and subsequent clitic climbing succeed. Note that the assumptions
about C° made above predict that in earlier stages of French, clitic climbing of
the infinitival subject was possible even with main verbs that do not select [+Agr]
in C°, which is in fact the case:

(71) Miez **lo**$_i$ vient [t_i returner].
     better him comes   to-return
     'It is better that he returns.' (P. mor., 266d; cf. Tobler 1921:91)

The reason is that C° was transparent for ECM even without [+Agr], as we claim.
Moreover, the contrast with Italian is interesting. The observation that Italian
does not allow the construction shown in (70) might be explained by the fact that
[+Agr] in C° is a potential nominative assigner in Italian, which may cause a
conflict within the complex head C°, so that the clitic cannot receive the accusative case from the main verb.[47]

6.4.1.2 Accusative subjects in prepositional contexts

As has been mentioned, the major difference from the other Romance varieties is that in the varieties of French we are considering here the subject of the infinitive regularly bears the accusative case, even in those infinitive constructions that are preceded by a prepositional element. This fact—which was morphologically visible in Old French—attracted the attention of scholars in historical grammar. Meyer-Lübke (1899:546) explained the accusative by assuming that in an early stage the subject was always located preverbally, immediately following the preposition, so that the subject appeared in the same morphological form (i.e., the same case) as the one that is usually found after prepositions. Later in the development of French, the subject could also appear in other positions, but it preserved the case properties of the original position. Lewent (1925) rejected Meyer-Lübke's claim and interpreted the construction as an "organical development of pre-existing modes of expression," that is, an extension of the A.c.I. construction, in which the infinitive clause has the function of a direct object, as in (72a), to infinitive clauses that fulfill the function of prepositional objects, as in (72b):

(72) a. Il voloit *laissier* [arriver les Engles].
     he wanted to-let   to-arrive the English
     'He wanted to let the English arrive.'

    b. Il voloit *consentir a* [arriver les Engles].
     he wanted to-consent to to-arrive the English
     'He wanted to consent to the arrival of the English.'

Lewent conjectures that as a further development, this construction was then extended by analogy to independent infinitive clauses (i.e., adjuncts). In contrast, Lerch (1929:152–69) argues that the origin of the construction in which the preposition *de* takes the position of an overt complementizer in our framework is a mere imitation of the Latin A.c.I. construction. As a main piece of evidence, Lerch quotes an Old French example, which we see in chapter 5 (ex. 48). I repeat it here as (73a). Lerch correctly identifies this sentence as a translation of Psalm 133, which I quote as (73b):

(73) a. Quel joie a cascun   est [$_{CP}$ *d'* [$_{AgrP}$ habiteir **freres** en un]].
     what joy to everybody is   C°   to-live brothers in one
     'What a joy it is for everybody that brothers live in unity.'

    b. Ecce quam bonum, et quam iucundum [habitare **fratres** in unum].
     behold how good and how pleasant to-live brothers in one
     'Behold, how good and how pleasant it is for brothers to live in unity.'

It has to be objected, however, that if the translator had wanted to imitate the Latin construction, hc could have used another syntactic option of Old French that is identical to the Latin construction, namely, leaving out the preposition. Old French supported this option, and in chapter 2 (ex. 15a) I actually quote another translation of the same verse along these lines. The example brought forward by Lerch proves the contrary, namely, that the construction chosen by the translator already existed in Old French.[48]

The accounts just mentioned are related to the two mechanisms pointed out in this chapter to explain accusative subjects: (i) case assignment through ECM (cf. 6.1.2 and 6.4.1.1) and (ii) case assignment through a preposition (cf. 6.3.2). For the analysis within the present framework, I start by looking at the different configurations in which this kind of structure is found. First, the preposition is in reality a complementizer, used in infinitival complements, as in (73a) and in the following example:

(74) Or ne pensés [$_{CP}$ de [$_{AgrP}$ ce plus avenir]].
     now not (you) think C°   this more to-happen
     'Now do not think that this will happen anymore.' (Auberi, 55, 21; cf. Tobler 1921:92)

Second, in the following examples the prepositional element is a P°, used in various configurations:

(75) a. s' il voloit consentir [$_{PP}$ a [arriver **les Englés** en ses fortereces
       if he wanted to-consent   to to-arrive the English in their fortresses
       'if he wanted to consent to the arrival of the English at their fortresses'
       (Froissart, Chron. VI, 311; quoted by E. Stimming 1915:123 and Lewent 1925:229)

    b. Vous donneriez occasion [$_{PP}$ de [s' esmouvoir **grans tumultes** sans
       you   would-give occasion   of R CL to-rise   great tumults without
       profit]].
       use
       'You would give people the opportunity to arise great tumults without need.'
       (Calvin Lettres, II, 380; cf. A. Haase 1890:214; Lewent 1925:231)

    c. et quant vint li termines [$_{PP}$ de [naistre   **l' enfançon**]
       and when came the date   of to-be-born the child
       'and when came the time for the child to be born' (Cygne, 25; cf. A. Haase 1890:214; E. Stimming 1915:123)

    d. Vinrent [$_{PP}$ [a **cest conte** mouvoir]].
       (they) came to this count to-move
       'They came to the count's departure.' (Esc., 157, p. 5; cf. Tobler 1921:94)

    e. J'ocit ma char [$_{PP}$ por [**l' ame** vivre]].
       I kill my flesh   for the soul to-live
       'I kill my flesh, so that my soul can live.' (Bal., 4024, p. 120; cf. E. Stimming 1915:123; Lombard 1936:223)

In most of these examples, ECM must be excluded because the infinitive constructions are either adjuncts or complements of categories other than V°. On the other hand, ECM might be assumed in (74), and perhaps in (75a). Nevertheless, I avoid this in order to arrive at a more unified account. I assume that a lexical P° or C°, intervening between the main verb and the preverbal subject position

SpecAgrP, blocks government and, consequently, case assignment, as we see for Italian in section 6.1.2.[49] Given the results achieved so far, it seems much more probable that the prepositional element under C° or under P° is the case assigner we are looking for. The configurations will thus be similar to the comparable English construction with *for* in the case of (74) and to the situation in Brazilian Portuguese (cf. 6.3.2) in the other examples:

(76) a.   b.

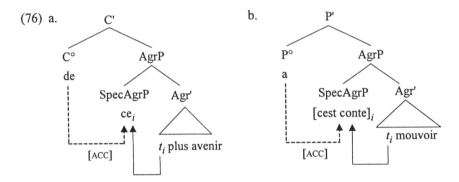

Meyer-Lübke's (1899:546) proposal that postverbal accusative subjects are a later stage in the development of this construction, is not necessary (nor can it be proved by the data). Given the mechanism described in section 6.4.1.1, it has to be assumed that both positions were possible right from the beginning, according to the null subject properties of Old French. The configuration in (76a) is attested to only in Old French, and it seems that later complementizers lost their potential of case assignment.

I now turn to the configuration in (76b), which is somewhat more problematic. For Brazilian Portuguese, I suggested that the infinitive construction embedded into PP is an AgrP, and not a CP, so that there is no blocking effect on the government relationship between the case assigning preposition and the case-receiving position SpecAgrP. As pointed out in section 6.3.2, the advantage of this explanation is that the relevant structure could be explained quite easily by assuming that the preposition *para* subcategorizes for AgrP in the Brazilian varieties at stake, whereas in all other varieties CP is selected. We could now use a similar argumentation for French to explain why prepositions could assign the accusative to an infinitival subject in past centuries but not in Modern, standard French. But note that this is not necessary at all. On the assumption that prepositional infinitive clauses have always subcategorized for CP infinitive clauses, the grammaticality of the constructions in the older stages clearly follows from the property of empty C° of not blocking case assignment in those diachronic varieties (cf. 6.4.1.1). As soon as this transparency vanished, not only did ECM constructions disappear but so did accusative subjects in prepositional infinitive clauses. To sum up, the older structures under discussion are not the result of lexical properties of certain prepositions but are simply an effect of a specific property of C°. This claim is also in conformity with the data in section 2.2, according to which Old and Middle French allowed specified subjects following a considerable number of prepositions.

From the seventeenth century onward, the use of specified subjects in prepositional infinitive clauses is restricted in two respects: first, a specified infinitival subject is licensed only by the preposition *pour* and, second, the subject always appears before the infinitive. With the same restrictions, this construction is still possible in some regional varieties of French (cf. 2.2).[50] The ungrammaticality of the postverbal subject follows from the same assumptions made about ECM in 6.4.1.1, namely, the loss of null subjects during the seventeenth century. The limitation of this construction to the preposition *pour* is somewhat enigmatic, however. Recall that this limitation is exactly the same as in Brazilian Portuguese, so we suspect that a similar explanation will hold. I therefore claim that in the diachronic and diatopic varieties in which this limitation is observed, the preposition *pour* subcategorizes for AgrP. The reason for this can be found in the high frequency of specified subjects in infinitive clauses introduced by *pour* since the time of Old French (see section 2.2). It is very probable that at the time in which C° began to block case assignment, this preposition in some way kept its ability to license a specified subject in the infinitive clause because of the high frequency of this construction. The only way in which the system of the language could achieve this was to change the subcategorization frame of *pour* in the way we discuss.

6.4.2   Nominative subjects

Given the preceding account, there is one type of construction that is rather surprising and which seems to be restricted to French. The relevant data have been given in 2.2 and, in connection with Reuland's (1983) and Vinet's (1985) accounts, in 4.3.1.2. I repeat them here for the reader's convenience:

(77) a.   [**Le frigidaire** tomber en panne], on aurait   vraiment   MF
            the fridge   to-fall in failure one would-have really
            l' air   fin.
            the aspect fine
            'If the fridge broke down we would really have bad luck.'

b.   [**La France** battre le Brésil], ce serait   inconcevable.   MF
            the F.   to-beat the Brazil that would-be inconceivable
            'The fact that France beats Brazil would be inconceivable.'

c.   [Et **lui** estre venu], envoya la charette en son hostel.   MidF
            and he to-be come (he) sent the coach   to his lodging
            'And after he had come, he sent the coach to his lodging'.

Alhough the infinitive construction has a different function in each of the examples, there are at least two things they all have in common. First, the infinitive clause always precedes the main clause, and, second, the subject always precedes the infinitive. What is striking about this construction is that neither are they in an ECM configuration nor is there any preposition that could possibly function as a case assigner. I therefore assume that these subjects bear the nominative case.

But how is the nominative case assigned? Taking into account the two main mechanisms I postulate for the other languages, I can say that nominative assignment to SpecVP through governing $T°$ is to be excluded because it would predict postverbal subjects. If we assumed that case is assigned by $Agr°$ in a Spec-head configuration—which would predict the preverbal subject—we would run into a further problem: it would be difficult to explain why the construction is found exclusively in the configuration described here and why nominative subjects are impossible in any other type of infinitive construction.

We therefore have to look for another explanation. Let us start with the most striking property of the examples from contemporary French. As Vinet (1987: 412) observed, infinitive constructions like (77a) and (77b) are restricted to contexts where the main clause has conditional tense. The use of other tenses in the main clause leads to ungrammaticality, as could be confirmed by the speakers consulted:

(78) ⋆[Le frigidaire tomber en panne], on *a   eu* l' air   fin.
     the fridge   to-fall in failure   one has had the aspect fine

This construction seems to be restricted to hypothetical contexts, comparable to *if* clauses in English. Now, for finite *if* clauses, the parallel French *si* clauses follow the same rules as in English; that is, if there is a conditional tense in the main clause, the *si/if* clause will have past tense:

(79) Si le frigidaire *tombait* en panne, on *aurait*   vraiment l' air   fin.
     if the fridge   fell   in failure, one would-have really   the aspect fine

In some way in a hypothetical sentence, the choice of conditional tense in the main clause imposes the conditional clause to become marked as [+past]. Now, if we apply this rule to our conditional infinitive clauses, we conclude that the infinitive clause also gets marked [+past], although this feature is not realized overtly. The important point here is that this kind of infinitive clause is marked [+Tns], just like a finite clause. The combination of an infinitive marked [−Agr, +Tns] and a preverbal lexical subject strongly resembles the construction of the so-called historical infinitive I discuss in section 4.3.3.3. As I point out there, following Mensching (1995), the historical infinitive can be considered to be a case of nominative assignment through tense under Spec-head agreement. The difference in the construction here is that in the historical infinitive there is an overt $T°$ realized as a prepositional tense marker, whereas in our case we have to assume nonovert tense. Hence, it has to be claimed that French possesses a lexical element with the properties discussed. Since this element comes from the lexicon, it can explain why the construction is limited to French. For clause structure, we have to assume that $T°$ raises to $Agr°$ to establish the Spec-head configuration with the subject.[51]

It is important to understand the difference between this construction and the licensing of overt nominative subjects in the other languages discussed in this chapter. For the other languages, it has been claimed that $T°$ can case-mark a subject even when it is [−Tns]. This explains why specified subjects can appear in such a large number of infinitive constructions. In French, the only possibility of marking the subject of an infinitive as a nominative is in a [+Tns] context. This property of French is rather old, as demonstrated by the Middle French construction represented in (77c). In contrast to Modern French, this infinitive construction is not a conditional but a temporal clause, in which the action expressed by the infinitve occurs before that of the main clause (hence the use of the past infinitive), so is is easy to see that for this construction, too, [+Tns] has to be claimed.[52]

6.5   Other varieties

I have already discussed two other Romance languages in previous articles. In Mensching (1999) I showed that Catalan essentially behaves like Spanish, so that the assumptions made in section 6.2 can also account for the Old and Modern Catalan data in 2.5. Romanian has been discussed in Mensching and Popovici (1997). As we see in sections 2.5 and 5.2.5, Modern Romanian admits only the postverbal position of the subject, which always appears in the nominative case. In Mensching and Popovici (1997), the claim made by Motapanyane (1988) and Dobrovie-Sorin (1994), according to which the subject of an infinitive is licensed by governing T° (section 4.3.3.1), was confirmed, and it can be said that this view receives further support from the results of this chapter since this mechanism seems to be available in most Romance languages, with the exception of French.[53] In addition, we show that examples like (45) from chapter 2 might be explained by ECM, assuming that the same conditions on empty C° as in the earlier stages of Italian and French were valid in Old Romanian although in contrast to Italian and French, the available examples are somewhat marginal, restricted to a few highly learned texts, and do not seem to have been generalized.

There are still some other Romance varieties to be discussed. In the rest of this section, I first deal with Italo-Romance dialects and languages other than Italian and then turn to Occitan.

6.5.1   Non-Tuscan Italo-Romance varieties

Although in the northern Italian varieties no comparable phenomena could be detected, some medieval texts quoted in 2.5.1 were produced in regions geographically adjacent to Tuscany (the southern part of Romagna and Umbria) that show phenomena similar to Old Italian (recall that Old Italian is essentially based on a Tuscan dialect). These data suggest that the mechanisms of nominative assignment claimed for Old Italian were not restricted to Tuscany but obtained in a broader zone of central Italy. It seems probable that this situation extended much further to the south. Consider the following data from nineteenth-century Calabrian, mentioned by Rohlfs and Wagner, in which we can assume case assignment by governing T° and, probably, Aux-to-Comp:

(80) a. [ppi no 'ru vidi$_i$ [$_{VP}$ **lu pappà** t_i]]
   for not it to-see   the father
   'so that the father would not see it' (Caravelli, Canti pop. calabresi, quoted by
   Wagner 1980:381)

   b. Me vasta   sulu dire [$_{CP}$ essere$_j$ [$_{AgrP}$ **Micu**$_i$[$_{TP}$ t$_j$ [$_{VP}$ t_i natu a la casa]]]].
   me suffices only to-say   to-be   M.   born at the house
   'It is enough for me to say that M. was born in the house.' (Gallucci, 10; cf.
   Rohlfs (1949:528)

Because of the small number of examples, we cannot tell if this variety has other
case assignment mechanisms in infinitive clauses.

It can be observed, however, that other southern Italo-Romance varieties are
clearly deviant from the central Italian facts. In Old Neapolitan, we find both
preverbal and postverbal subjects, and the infinitive shows overt agreement morphology. Examples (37a) and (37b) from chapter 2 might be analyzed roughly as
follows:

(81) a. [$_{CP}$ [$_{AgrP}$ [**tanta   copia de cavalieri** . . .]$_i$ . . . [esser*no* [$_{VP}$ t_i venuti . . .]]]]]
      so-much crowd of knights   to-be-3PL   come

   b. [$_{PP}$ de [$_{AgrP}$ [essere*nno* licenciati$_i$ . . . [$_{VP}$ **li Greci** t$_i$]]]]]
      of   to-be-3PL dismissed   the Greek

These data strongly resemble the situation in Portuguese, so it seems very probable that the Old Neapolitan varieties, too, admitted nominative assignment either
by Agr° under Spec-head agreement or by T° under government.[54] A similar
situation can be found in Sicilian until today. The difference from Old Neapolitan
is that Sicilian has no inflected infinitive, and diachronically, there is no documentary evidence that might prove its existence in earlier periods. Since the relevant constructions are still alive and very frequent in Modern Sicilian varieties,
we have a much clearer idea of their nature. In section 5.2.5, I point out that the
postverbal subject is located in SpecVP, and I identify the preverbal position
with SpecAgrP, in accordance with the Portuguese and Galician facts. A further
parallel to Portuguese is the fact that preverbal subjects are preferred. As I argued in section 6.3.1.1, this can be taken as evidence for case assignment by
Spec-head agreement through Agr°. Just as in spoken Portuguese, Sicilian—or at
least the variety of Corleone that I mostly consider in this book—also avoids the
postverbal position of the subject when V° is the infinitive of a transitive verb
(cf. 6.3.1.2):

(82) a. 'jiu rispar'mjavu i   mi 'soɾdi [pi [**mi 'paʈɾi** ka't:arisi   a 'mak:ina]]
      I   saved   the my money for my   father to-buy-R CL the car
      'I saved my money in order for my father to buy the car.'

   b. ??'jiu rispar'mjavu i   mi 'soɾdi ⌊pi [ka't:arisi **mi 'paʈɾi** a 'mak:ina]]

I therefore claim that Sicilian behaves like Portuguese and that the following structures can be assumed for examples (36d) of chapter 2 and (55a) of chapter 5:

(83) a. [$_{AgrP}$ ['jiu$_i$ [$_{Agr°}$ 'ʃːri$_j$ [$_{NegP}$ 'kju [$_{TP}$ t$_j$ [$_{VP}$ t$_i$ t$_j$ a 'kːjɛza]]]]]]

  b. [$_{AgrP}$ ['ʃːri$_j$ [$_{NegP}$ 'kju [$_{TP}$ [$_{T°}$t$_j$] [$_{VP}$ 'jiu t$_j$ a 'kːjɛza]]]]]

I now turn to Sardinian, in which preverbal subjects have never been documented and an Aux-to-Comp construction does not seem to exist. The results of 5.2.5 suggest that only T° can assign nominative, so Sardinian essentially behaves like Spanish. There might be a problem, however, if we take into account the fact that some Sardinian varieties have inflected infinitive forms, a fact that led Jones (1992, 1993) to the plausible assumption that agreement is involved in the licensing of subjects. However, in the framework adopted here, this assumption is not necessary. The only regularity that seems to hold in this framework is that agreement morphology is often optional when case assignment is performed by governing T° (see 3.2.3). In section 6.3.1.1 I claim that this behavior can be confirmed by infinitives in modern Galician. Recall that the same holds for Sardinian: in the varieties that allow the infinitive to show up with agreement morphology, it is optional (cf. 2.5.1 and 4.3.1.3), as is illustrated here by the following Nuorese example taken from Mensching (1994:91):

(84) Isetta [fintzas de [*andàrepo* / *andare* **deo**].
     wait   until   of to-go-1SG / to-go-∅ I
     'Wait until I go.'

My claim that agreement is not involved in nominative assignment can be supported by the observation that in the Old Sardinian examples I present in chapter 2, there is no agreement morphology, and perhaps the development of infinitival agreement morphology is to be interpreted as a later phenomenon. The issue of how overt agreement morphology in Sardinian can be explained from a historical point of view is very interesting. We can probably assume, with Jones, that the inflectional endings of the Sardinian infinitive are directly generated under V° (cf. section 4.3.1.3). In other words, what we have here is lexical and not functional agreement, so it can be argued that Agr° is marked [–Agr] and is thus unable to function as a nominative assigner, in accordance with our assumptions. For the history of the inflected infinitive forms, it has to be noted that they are homonymous with those of the imperfect subjunctive inherited from Latin. Consider Jones's account of the origin of the inflected infinitive in Sardinian:

> Because of their morphological properties, the imperfect subjunctive forms came to be reanalyzed as inflected infinitives, containing AGR . . . but not Tense. However, in order to maintain consistency with the unmarked composition of INFL . . . these features were construed as part of the verb rather than of INFL. (Jones 1992:304)

Note that according to my theory, infinitival T° was already a nominative assigner in Old Sardinian, even with the noninflected infinitive. The similarity of this construction with finite constructions might then have favored the process described by Jones.[55]

6.5.2   Occitan

The Old Occitan data in 2.5, with the subject appearing in the accusative case—infinitival subjects in the nominative case could not be proved by documentary evidence—can be explained by assuming the same two accusative-assigning mechanisms as in Old and Middle French: ECM, and case marking by a preposition (see section 6.4.1). Both can be explained by the same specific properties. Just as Old French, Old Occitan does not seem to have admitted subjects in the nominative case in nontensed infinitival environments. These facts are not really surprising if we take into consideration that both languages are closely related both genealogically and geographically. As we have seen, French has lost the relevant characteristics of C°, so none of the constructions at issue are grammatical today.

What has happened to Occitan in this respect? In the data we have seen in section 2.5 we find a rather large number of infinitive constructions that admit a specified subject. As I observe in chapter 2, in Modern Limousin and Languedocian, the morphological case of the subject cannot be recognized because personal pronouns have the same form in the accusative and in the nominative. The subject is always in a preverbal position, which corresponds to a tendency already visible in Old Occitan. Although all this might indicate that the modern constructions continue the old Gallo-Romance situation, we first have to check the other possibility of explaining preverbal subjects, that is, nominative assignment through Agr° in a Spec-head agreement configuration. Note that this would mean a radical change in the parameters of a Gallo-Romance variety, although we cannot exclude this possibility.

However, a closer examination shows some problems. First, Limousin and Languedocian would be the only Romance varieties that would license nominative subjects in infinitive constructions only by Spec-head agreement with Agr°. Although this possibility cannot be excluded a priori, it would be rather odd because finite constructions in Occitan show typical Romance VS(O) structures (Alibèrt 1976:351-53), which should be explained by nominative assignment through governing T° in the present framework. Second, and more important, the configurations in which specified subjects are grammatical are exactly the same as those that license accusative subjects in the other Romance languages, that is, ECM (after declarative, epistemic, and impersonal predicates) and prepositional configurations (cf. section 2.5.2). I therefore reject the nominative proposal and claim that Limousin and Languedocian are the only modern Romance varieties that still allow ECM in infinitival CP; that is, they continue the Old Gallo-Romance properties of C° in such a way that case assignment is also possible through prepositions. According to 6.1.2.2, this will also explain why volitional predicates still allow this construction (cf. Camproux 1958:279 and 282–83):

(85) Bouge [**toutos las auchos** s'   en   ana al   riu].
    (I) want all   the geese   R CL A CL to-go to-the river
    'I want that all the geese go to the river.'

Postverbal subjects in Gascon, however, should be considered nominative subjects licensed by governing T°, according to the results of section 5.2.5. This relates Gascon to Ibero-Romance, a fact that is supported by other linguistic phenomena as well, as is generally known.

6.6   Summary

In this chapter I analyze how case is assigned to the subject of infinitive clauses. It has been shown that nominative case can be explained by assuming that the case properties of functional categories are parametrized, as suggested by Roberts (1993). I argue that in most Romance languages it can be assumed that T° assigns the nominative to a DP it governs, independently of finiteness criteria. This assumption correctly predicts that nominative subjects in Romance infinitive constructions usually appear in the postverbal position. The basic difference from finite clauses is that normally finite Agr° is the preferred nominative assigner, whereas infinitival Agr° lacks case-assigning properties. Given the fact that Agr° assigns the nominative chiefly under Spec-head agreement in the Romance languages, it can thus be predicted that finite clauses license preverbal subjects, in contrast to infinitive clauses. On the other hand, in Portuguese and Galician, as well as in Sicilian (and probably in Old Neapolitan), infinitival Agr° behaves just like finite Agr°, so preverbal subjects are allowed and even preferred. For Modern Italian, I interpret Rizzi's (1982) Aux-to-Comp analysis by means of a [+Agr] feature in C°, which attracts auxiliary movement and assigns the nominative to the subject. The earlier stages of Italian, as well as almost all the Gallo-Romance varieties discussed, allow the infinitival subject to appear in the accusative case, assigned by ECM, depending-on language specific properties of C°. In Gallo-Romance (with the exception of Gascon), ECM and a similar mechanism in which prepositions can function as case assigners are usually the only ways in which specified subjects are licensed in infinitive clauses because the parameter mentioned above is fixed in a way that neither T°[–Tns] nor Agr°[–Agr°] can assign the nominative case.

7

A Minimalist Interpretation

In this chapter I reinterpret some of the principles and parameters suggested in the last chapter on the basis of the assumptions of the minimalist program. I mostly follow Chomsky (1992), with some additions proposed in Chomsky (1995) and other minimalist literature. As Chomsky has repeatedly emphasized, for example in "Categories and Transformations" (Chomsky 1995: ch. 4), many of the minimalist assumptions have to be checked on the basis of empirical analyses. The topic of this book is extremely appropriate for this purpose because it addresses some central points, such as case assignment, verb movement, and DP movement. In the preceding chapter I also assume some features contained in functional categories that are involved in the licensing of subjects, which may trigger or prevent movement. These kinds of properties are, in principle, compatible with the minimalist program, although here the features are of a different nature than those assumed so far, so that it is quite interesting to see if we can maintain the view expressed in chapter 6, particularly about [+Agr] in C°.

In section 7.1, I present some basic assumptions of the minimalist program that are necessary for our purposes, complementing and in part revising the framework outlined in chapter 3. In section 7.2, I discuss Ambar's (1994) minimalist analysis of some of the Portuguese data. Her account serves as a starting point for our discussion. In section 7.3, I interpret the data, adapting the analysis of Romance infinitive clauses presented in the preceding chapters. Finally, in section 7.4 I briefly evaluate the adequacy of the minimalist program for describing and analyzing phenomena related to Romance languages, providing some additional ideas that should be taken into account in future research within minimalism.

7.1. The minimalist framework

The minimalist program, introduced by Chomsky (1992), picks up the threads of the principles and parameters model, especially with regard to some of the assumptions made in the late 1980s, which are outlined in chapter 3 and applied to the data in chapters 5 and 6. Basically, the clause structure assumed corresponds to the Split-Infl hypothesis, including the functional category AgrOP proposed by Chomsky (1989). Similarly to what is supposed for AgrP (which I call AgrSP from now on, where S stands for subject), one of its functions is to be responsible for agreement phenomena, in this case for direct objects. The clause structure assumed in the minimalist program is thus as follows:[1]

(1)

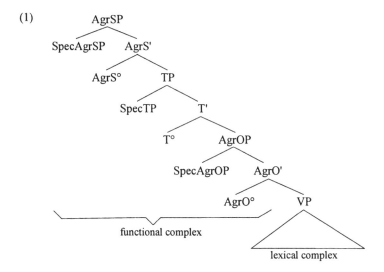

We can distinguish between a lexical complex (VP) and a functional complex with the categories above VP—that is, AgrOP; TP; AgrSP; and if present, CP. It has to be observed that this division is not completely appropriate because functional heads are also part of the lexicon (cf. Chomsky 1995:240; Kim et al. 1995:56), as we see below for complementizers.

Lexical items are projected from the lexicon, and from the lexical heads tree structures are built up inside the lexical complex, following the X-bar scheme. The partial trees that result from this process are assembled by means of a mechanism called *generalized transformation* (GT).[2] The functional complex is then built up, fulfilling the task of licensing the lexical material. In the traditional P&P model, features and/or morphemes for case, agreement, and tense, among others, have generally been assumed to be generated within the functional heads. From a minimalist perspective, the lexical component of grammar supplies fully specified terminal nodes; that is, the lexical heads are generated together with both their inflectional endings and features assigned to them. Thus, a verbal head V° not only contains the concrete inflectional morphology but also includes abstract features (cf. Kim et al. 1995:10).[3] An inflected form like Spanish *trabajabas* 'you worked' can therefore be assumed to have roughly the following structure:

(2)   [[trabaja] [ba] [s]]; [Tns, V, φV]

The functional categories also have features, which are parallel to those of the lexical complex. For my analysis, I assume the following types of features (cf. Chomsky 1995:230–41):[4]

(3) Categorial features: [D], [V], [N], etc.
     Agreement or ϕ-features   [ϕD], [ϕV],[5] etc.
     Tense features   [Tns]
     Case features   [NOM], [ACC], etc.

Features of lexical categories must match with corresponding features of functional categories; if not, the structure is ungrammatical; that is, the derivation of
the sentence fails. It is important to keep in mind that matching features trigger
movement; that is, a node X of the lexical complex with the features [α_L] will
move into a node Y of the functional complex with the matching features [α_F].
This process, known as feature checking (where the features of the functional
categories check the corresponding lexical features), licenses a structure (Chomsky 1993:12–14). As we see in chapter 3, in most Romance languages a verb
moves to T° and then up to AgrS°. In the minimalist program we can assume the
following distribution of features:

(4) Basic features assumed for verb movement in Romance

AgrS°	T°	V°
[V]	[Tns]	[V] [Tns]

The verb with the features [Tns, V] is first moved to T° for [Tns] to be checked
and then to AgrS° to check [V]. According to the same mechanism, subjects and
objects are moved to the corresponding functional positions in SpecAgrSP and
SpecAgrOP because the features of lexical maximal projections are checked in
the specifier position of a corresponding functional category, whereas the features of lexical heads are checked through incorporation into a position adjoined
to an appropriate functional head (cf. Wilder 1995:130). A very important tenet
of the minimalist theory is that the feature-checking mechanism leads to the dele-
tion of both features involved.

   Instead of assuming various levels of representation like D-structure and S-
structure, the minimalist theory of syntax assumes only one level, which is seen
as a dynamic process of building up a sentence structure (derivation). The derivation begins with the insertion of lexical items from the lexical component and
ends "visibly" with spell-out, which forms the input for the phonetic form (PF),
and "invisibly" (or rather "inaudibly") with the logical form (LF). An important
aspect of the minimalist program is the visibility at spell-out. Crucially, a difference is made between strong and weak features. Strong features must not be
present at spell-out, which means that they have to be deleted before through
feature checking, which is achieved by overt movement. Weak features do not
"disturb" at spell-out, and they are assumed to be deleted afterward on LF. A
derivation converges on either level (PF or LF) if it contains only objects that are
legitimate for the respective level. For a sentence to be grammatical, then, its
derivation must converge on both levels. It must be noted that, on PF, only items
that can be realized phonetically and weak features are legitimate objects.

The strength or weakness of features is language-specific. In English, for example, finite nonauxiliary verbs remain inside the VP and auxiliaries are moved to AgrSP. In contrast, both types of verbs are moved in French:

(5) a. [John$_i$ [$_{VP}$ probably [$_{VP}$ t_i comes]]].   ME

     b. *[Jean$_i$ [$_{VP}$ probablement [$_{VP}$ t_i vient]]].   MF

     c. *[John$_i$ comes$_j$ [$_{VP}$ probably [$_{VP}$ t_i t_j]]].   ME

     d. [Jean$_i$ vient$_j$ [$_{VP}$ probablement [$_{VP}$ t_i t_j]]].   MF

     e. *[John$_i$ [$_{VP}$ probably has [$_{VP}$ t_i come]]].   ME

     f. *[Jean$_i$ [$_{VP}$ probablement est [$_{VP}$ t_i venu]]].   MF

     g. [John$_i$ has$_j$ [$_{VP}$ probably [$_{VP}$ t_i t_j come]]].   ME

     h. [Jean$_i$ est$_j$ [$_{VP}$ probablement [$_{VP}$ t_i t_j venu]]].   MF

These data can be explained by assuming that in English only auxiliaries have strong features, whereas in French this is a property of all finite verbs, or more precisely, the [V]-features of AgrS are strong in French and weak in English. Remember that only strong features trigger overt movement. Thus, cross-linguistic variation in word order can be reduced essentially to properties of features of functional categories.

On the basis of the features assumed, their properties, and clause structure (determined by the X-bar scheme and GT), the minimalist program assumes that syntactic facts can be reduced to very general principles, such as *procrastinate* and *self-interest* (cf. Kim et al. 1995:9, 63). According to procrastinate, invisible movement (on LF after spell-out) is preferred to visible movement.[6] For the principle of self-interest, I here use the so-called enlightened self-interest, which says that an element α can be moved to a position β only if a morphological property of α cannot be fulfilled otherwise or if there is no other way to avoid the failure of the derivation.[7] An interesting linguistic property that follows from procrastinate is the fact that the checking of two corresponding weak features will not be performed until LF. In that case, no movement occurs before LF, which means that there is no visible movement at all.

For the discussion of the Romance phenomena discussed in this book, it is very important to reexamine case theory. In the minimalist program, case theory, too, is reinterpreted by means of feature checking. In nominative languages, the case features that belong to nominative subjects [NOM] and direct objects [ACC] are checked in the corresponding agreement phrases AgrSP and AgrOP. It is crucial for our discussion that Spec-head agreement is considered to be the standard configuration for the checking of case features. The functional [NOM] feature is in T°, but the Spec-head configuration is usually reached when T° is moved to AgrS°. Following this line of reasoning, Chomsky (1995:174) describes the assignment of nominative and accusative as follows:

(6) Minimalist case assignment

We now regard both agreement and structural case as manifestations of the Spec-head relation (NP, Agr). But case properties depend on characteristics of T and the V head of VP. We therefore assume that T raises to AGR_S forming (3a) and V raises to AGR_O forming (3b); the complex includes the ϕ-features of Agr and the case feature provided by T, V.

(3) a. $[_{Agr}$ T Agr]
    b. $[_{Agr}$ V Agr]

Therefore, the cross-linguistic syntactic differences described in the preceding chapters for the position of verbs and subjects are usually not interpreted as a consequence of case assignment mechanisms but as a result of the strength or weakness of (noncase) features. We return to this issue later.

Let us now turn to infinitive clauses with specified subjects. Before proposing my own interpretation, I first discuss the approach of Ambar (1994) toward some of the Portuguese data.

7.2 A minimalist analysis of Portuguese infinitive clauses (Ambar)

Ambar (1994) examines one type of Portuguese infinitive clause that we have already seen in sections 2.4, 4.3.2.2, and 6.3.1.3:

(7) Ele disse [existirem **muitos candidatos** nesta eleição].
    he said to-exist-3PL many candidates in-this election
    'He says that many candidates take part in this election.'

As Ambar shows in her article, and in conformity with our results in chapter 5, this construction is not Aux-to-Comp but simply a structure in which the subject remains in its base position inside VP while the verb moves to T° and, optionally, to AgrS°. The reader will remember that the main problem concerning this construction (for which I have presented a nonminimalist solution in section 6.3.1.3) is that it does not permit a preverbal subject, in contrast to most of the other infinitive constructions of Portuguese. How can these facts be accounted for within the minimalist framework? Ambar straightforwardly applies the minimalist principles outlined above and assumes that AgrS° has strong [V]-features, so movement of the verb to AgrS° must occur. She also supposes that the [D]-features of the subject DP are weak, as well as the corresponding [D]-features of AgrS°, so that the subject remains in its base position:

(8)

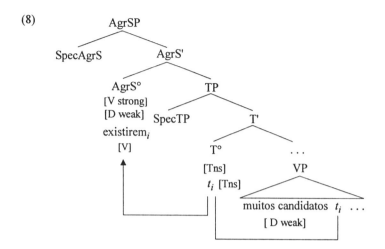

Concerning the issue why the preverbal position is unavailable only with declarative and epistemic matrix verbs, Ambar (1994:19) assumes that these verbs select an infinitival C°, which contains a [+Tns] feature,[8] a situation that leads to a configuration in which AgrS is governed by [+Tns] in C°. She then makes the conjecture that through this relation the [V]-feature of AgrS is strong, while its [D]-feature becomes weak.[9]

As we see on various occasions throughout this book, the postverbal subject position in Portuguese infinitive clauses is generally less acceptable in the case of transitive verbs (see 6.3.1.2). Ambar observes the following contrast:[10]

(9)   a. ★Penso comprarem **eles** o livro.
          (I) think to-buy-3PL   they the book
          'I think that they buy the book.'

      b. ?Penso comprarem **eles** muitos livros.
          (I) think to-buy-3PL   they many   books
          'I think that they buy many books.'

      c. ?Penso comerem **algumas crianças** demasiados chocolates.
          (I) think to-eat-3PL some   children too-many   chocolates
          'I think that some children eat too many chocolates.'

      d. ?O João afirmou comprarem **eles** o jornal todas as sextas-feiras.
          the J.   stated   to-buy-3PL they the journal all   the Fridays
          'J. affirmed that they buy the journal each Friday.'

According to Ambar (1994:5), the difference between the ungrammatical example in (9a) and the acceptable ones is that in the latter the object DP is indefinite (D° ≠ definite article; examples 9b and 9c) or the infinitive construction contains an adverbial, as in (9d). Ambar's starting point is a semantically motivated generalization, according to which the ungrammatical sentences have a definite reference to a single event, with *comprar* ('to buy') showing its intrinsic properties of an eventive verb; on the other hand, in the well-formed sentences, a habitual/ generic reading is available, so instead of a single event reading, we get a stative one. These differences are, however, irrelevant when the infinitive appears with the auxiliary *ter* (the infinitive of perfect tense):

(10) Penso *terem* **eles** comprado o livro.
(I) think to-have-3PL they bought the book
'I think that they have bought the book.'

Because, according to Ambar's generalization, the difference in grammaticality has something to do with tense and/or aspect, she supposes that it is due to the strength or weakness of [Tns] features, assuming the following distribution:

(11) a. [Tns] of T° is weak in infinitive constructions.
    b. [Tns] of *ter* and of stative verbs is weak.
    c. [Tns] of eventive verbs is strong.

Crucially for Ambar's analysis, she claims that strong [Tns] of V° is incompatible with weak [Tns] in T°. Thus, if an eventive verb is used in the construction, the derivation will fail. In the case of stative verbs, however, the features are compatible. Ambar argues that in sentences as in example (9), the verbs originally have strong tense. How is the grammaticality to be explained, then? The solution she offers is a mechanism by which strong tense is weakened by an indefinite DP (see examples 9b and 9c):

> V raises to Agr° and the NP (DP) object to the Specifier position of Agr°. Assume that the NP (DP) object is somehow marked [+generic]. Assume further that by Spec-head agreement the [+generic] feature of the NP (DP) is transmitted to the complex V_Agr°. The Verb ends up with a feature [+generic], compatible with the weak functional Tense, instead of the strong Tense feature with which the verb was selected from the lexicon. . . . Verb raising is then permitted. (Ambar 1994:16)

Something similar is assumed for the adverbial phrase in (9d).

Ambar's article is an interesting starting point for our discussion because it shows how a minimalist approach might explain some nontrivial word order facts in Romance infinitive clauses with specified subjects. As we see in the next section, the general assumptions illustrated in (8) can be supported and extended to other Romance varieties. Ambar also tries to explain why the postverbal subject is obligatory in the construction discussed in this section. It has to be kept in mind that this restriction is related to the selectional properties of certain verbs. The answer given is very similar to my proposal in 6.3.1.3, that is, that some feature in C° has to be assumed. The problem is, however, that Ambar's explanation is not very satisfactory from a minimalist point of view. First, the observation that "the Tense feature in Comp is in a governing position with respect to Agr" (Ambar 1994:19) is not valid in the minimalist program because government is not recognized anymore. The conjecture that the [V]-feature of AgrS becomes strong through some relation with C°, whereas its [D]-feature becomes weak, is interesting, but the problem is how such a relation can be described in a minimalist fashion. I return to this point in section 7.4.

The second problem in Ambar's (1994) approach is the fact that the minimalist principles do not predict that a weak functional feature and a strong lexical feature are incompatible. If there is any incompatibility, it would be the other way around, on the basis of the principle of greed postulated by Chomsky (1992), according to which an element can move only if movement serves its own interest (cf. Chomsky 1995:201). For Ambar's account to work, we might postulate a kind of semantic incompatibility of both [Tns] features. If [Tns] is considered a mnemotechnic term, which in reality represents bundles of more concrete features, such an assumption would be legitimate. Just as a lexical [ϕD] feature specified for third person cannot match a functional feature specified for second person, [Tns] features like [present]-[past] or [punctual]-[durative] will probably not match.

Third, the main problem in Ambar's analysis is that it contradicts the "spirit" of the minimalist program because minimalism admits only those principles and operations that are independently motivated or that are indispensable from a conceptual point of view (Kim et al. 1995:1). For instance, her classification of verbs according to semantical criteria is driven mostly by the data she wants to analyze. She assumes "that the class of 'stative verbs' includes not only traditional statives but also auxiliary *have, be* and modals" (Ambar 1994:14), and for other verbs she offers a rather vague statement, which seems to be motivated only by her data from infinitival clauses: verbs like "*acontecer* ('to happen') and *surgir* ('to crop up') behave more like eventive verbs in some environments." In addition to the partially, somewhat arbitrary assumption of features and their strength or weakness, it has to said that Ambar's proposal that the strength of features may change in the course of the derivation and that the features of one node may modify those of another is not very desirable, especially since the minimalist program does not provide any mechanisms for this. Finally, Ambar uses principles like government and transfer of features, which are not valid in the minimalist program: the fact is that the minimalist program claims that it is possible to renounce all principles of this kind.[11] An approach that uses them is, at best, a modification of the traditional P&P framework, which includes some minimalist assumptions.[12]

7.3   Features and movement in Romance infinitive clauses

In the two preceding chapters, the following structures of infinitival clauses with specified subjects have been described:

1. V° is located in AgrS° and DP$_{subj}$ in SpecVP.[13]
2. V° is located in T° and DP$_{subj}$ in SpecVP.
3. V° (or rather T°)[14] is located in C°[+Agr] and DP$_{subj}$ in SpecAgrSP.
4. V° is located in AgrS° and DP$_{subj}$ in SpecAgrSP.

Following is a rough distribution in the languages and varieties we have examined (A'-movement and accusative subjects have not yet been considered):

(12)	Language	1.	2.	3.	4.
	Romanian		x		
	Sardinian	x			
	Sicilian	x			x
	Earlier Italian	x	x	x	
	Modern Italian			x	
	Gascon	x			
	Catalan	x			
	Spanish	x			
	Portuguese	x	x		x

As we see earlier in this chapter, the minimalist program claims that visible movement is usually induced by strong features. In section 7.3.1, I examine how the location of subjects observed in this table can be interpreted by a feature-based approach. Before this, let us first consider verb movement.

Verb movement can be explained either by strong [Tns] features or strong [V]-features.[15] In the former case, the verb will move at least up to T°, and perhaps further up to AgrS°, to check strong [V]-features. In the latter case, it cannot be decided if the [Tns] features are strong or weak. The distribution in (12) can be interpreted by assuming, for infinitive constructions, that [V] is weak in Romanian and strong in the other languages and varieties. [Tns] is strong in Romanian, whereas in the other languages we cannot decide because verbs always move up to AgrS°. For those languages in which V° moves to T° and further movement to AgrS° is optional (Portuguese in general and the earlier stages of Italian), it can be assumed that [Tns] is strong and that the optional movement to AgrS° is due to a variable strength of [V]-features. The simplest solution would be to tentatively assume that functional [V]-features in AgrS° are weak and that verbs can have either strong or weak lexical features.

An important issue is the Aux-to-Comp construction in Italian, which I explain in chapter 6 by postulating a feature [+Agr] in C°. This account is not unproblematic from a minimalist perspective because [+Agr] is not a legitimate feature in the minimalist program. If agreement is really involved in these constructions, we have to say that C° has ϕ-features. Now we have to explain why the verb moves up to C°. I would like to suggest that this can be done by reinterpreting [+Agr] as strong [ϕV]-features. Let us assume that Italian auxiliaries and copulative verbs possess weak [ϕV]. We could then predict the following behavior, which is in accordance with the Italian facts: first, C° with [ϕV] can be selected only if the derivation includes an auxiliary or a copulative verb;[16] second, when a complementizer with [ϕV] is selected, the verb must move overtly to C°.

7.3.1   Nominative subjects

The issue of licensing and movement of specified subjects in Romance infinitive constructions is much more complex than the problem of verb movement. In the analysis in chapter 6, I claim that the nominative can be assigned by two different mechanisms, Spec-head agreement and government, with the condition that in the Romance languages, AgrS° assigns the nominative case by the former and T° by the latter mechanism. Given these properties of the two functional categories, both the licensing and the word order of subjects in infinitive clauses is derived in a quite straightforward fashion. Recall, however, that in the minimalist program the principle of government is no longer supported and that the Spec-head relationship is considered the standard means of case assignment. The phenomena previously explained by government are partially reinterpreted by the minimalist head-complement relation (Chomsky 1995:172), but this cannot be applied to the government relation we assumed for nominative case assignment because SpecVP is not a complement of T°. All this follows from the assumption that only local relations are possible, "hence no relation between X and a phrase included within YP or ZP" (Chomsky 1995:172–73) plays any role. How can we then reinterpret our results within such a framework? It is usually assumed that [D]-features, and not case features, are responsible for this movement, and as shown in the preceding section, T° is considered the only functional head that has a [NOM] feature. I briefly return to the case approach in section 7.4. Here I try to resolve our problem within the standard minimalist approach.

The extended projection principle (EPP) of the earlier framework, which demanded that the SpecIP position be generated (Haegeman 1994:339–40; Chomsky 1995:55, 123), is replaced by Chomsky (1995:232) by the assumption that AgrS° possesses strong [D]-features, which will necessarily lead to a projection of SpecAgrSP to where the subject must move for checking. It is usually assumed that the subject moves to SpecAgrSP because of strong [D]–features, whereas the checking of the [NOM] feature (generated inside TP and picked up on the way of the subject to SpecAgrSP) is more or less incidental. However, in most of the Romance varieties examined, the subject of the infinitive remains inside its base position, SpecVP. Within the minimalist program, this can be explained only by the assumption that all the features related to the subject DP are weak so that no visible movement operation is applied.[17] Note that this "weakness" of subjects in infinitive clauses might be understood in the sense of the concept of "desubjectivation" (Sasse 1982); in other words, the weak features make the subject appear to be a semisubject (cf. section 1.4).

To sum up these considerations, the most common situation in the Romance languages is as follows:

1. Infinitival T° has weak [NOM]-features.
2. Infinitival AgrS° has weak nominal features [D] and [ϕD].[18]
3. The subject DP in infinitive clauses has weak nominal features.

In languages that permit only the postverbal subject position in infinitive constructions (in contrast to finite constructions, where the preverbal position is possible and usually preferred), the only property in which nonfinite and finite constructions differ is that AgrS° of the former has weak nominal features. In Portuguese, Galician, and Sicilian, infinitive constructions permit both the preverbal and the postverbal position of the subject, behaving essentially like finite constructions. This can be explained by hypothesizing that the nominal features of AgrS° in infinitive constructions are strong. The mechanism which yields both the preverbal and the postverbal position in these languages is then essentially the same as in finite constructions. Chomsky (1995:272–76) alludes to how this works by saying that the expletive *pro* in Romance languages has the same properties as the expletive *there* in English. We could thus say that AgrSP in most Romance languages has the following two options: either it is generated empty—in this case it has strong nominal features—or it is generated as an expletive *pro*, which inherently has weak nominal features. The corresponding features of the subject are always weak. From this, both subject positions follow.[19] On the one hand, if *pro* is selected in a derivation, there is no overt movement of the subject DP. On the other hand, if *pro* is not selected, the subject DP must move to AgrSP to save the derivation by deleting the strong features of AgrS°.

Whereas the basic facts about specified subjects in Romance infinitives thus seem easy to explain within the minimalist program, the issue of licensing overt subjects in Italian Aux-to-Comp constructions is rather more complicated. In present-day Italian, Aux-to-Comp is the only configuration in which specified subjects with nominative case are allowed in infinitive constructions, and Aux-to-Comp depends on the properties of C°. We should therefore assume that infinitival T° has no [NOM] features in present-day Italian, whereas C° with [φV] (i.e., [+Agr] in C°) has a [NOM] feature. This case feature must be weak because otherwise it would have to be checked overtly by movement of the subject to CP. The subject's movement to SpecAgrSP, however, must be motivated independently from the case feature, for example, by strong [D] in AgrS°. For an Italian Aux-to-Comp construction, we thus get the following structure, in which I represent only the relevant categories, features, and movements:

(13)

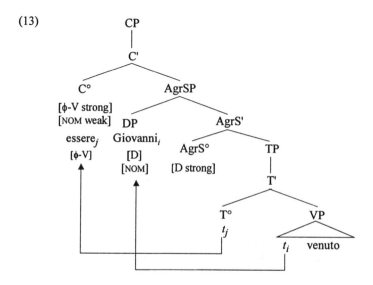

I return to Aux-to-Comp in the final section of this chapter.

Movement that is triggered by one of the features discussed so far is called L-driven movement (L = lexically) in the minimalist program. This type of movement roughly corresponds to A-movement, although overt movement of a DP, as shown, is not performed for reasons of case but for the checking of strong [D]-features. Although the A'-movement of the traditional P&P model is not L-driven, movement in the minimalist program is in principle triggered by features. One type of non–L-driven movement is topicalization, for which a strong feature is assumed (cf. Chomsky 1995:199); the feature is [TOP], according to Wilder (1995:133): "TOP is an m-feature, which may be checked by any phrase with 'topic properties'"). In German, C° bears this feature, according to Wilder, and it is checked by moving a DP to SpecCP (cf. the data in example 14 of chapter 3). For the earlier stages of most Romance languages, I assume in 3.1.2 that AgrSP is a possible A'-position for fronted categories, as the Old Spanish example (17c) in chapter 3 shows, in which the complement *esto* has been fronted:

(14) $[_{CP}$ Quando $[_{AgrSP}$ esto$_j$ entendio$_i$ $[_{TP}$ t_i $[_{AgrOP}$ t_j $[_{VP}$ pharaon t_i t_j]]]]]
      when   this heard   Pharaoh

Consequently, in a minimalist interpretation it should be assumed that AgrSP in Old Romance contained a strong [TOP] feature. The V2 phenomenon—the subject remains in situ—might be explained by assuming that the upper agreement phrase[20] has strong [TOP] instead of [D]-features for checking the subject; the subject has weak [D]-features, which do not need to be checked, according to Chomsky (1995:279–89), because they are interpretable on LF.

In a similar fashion, we can explain the infinitive constructions with a preverbal nominative subject in Old Spanish and Old Italian (6.1.1.2 and 6.2.2.1). The difference between Portuguese, Galician, and Sicilian on the one hand and Old Spanish and Old Italian, on the other is that the movement of the infinitival subject to AgrSP is triggered by strong [D]-features in the former languages and by strong [TOP] in the latter.

7.3.2   Accusative subjects

In chapter 6, I claim that in some varieties of French and Portuguese, prepositions or infinitival complementizers license infinitival subjects by assigning accusative case. This is similar to nominative assignment by C° in Italian Aux-to-Comp, as illustrated in example (13), if we assume that the relevant complementizers and prepositions have a weak accusative case feature, which covertly checks the lexical case feature of the subject located in AgrSP. For further discussion, especially on how AgrOP might be involved in such structures, see Radford (1997a:449–54).

Let us now turn to ECM. In the minimalist program ECM is explained by the aid of the functional category AgrOP: "Exceptional case marking by V is now interpreted as raising of NP to the Spec of the AgrP dominating V. It is raising to [Spec, Agr$_O$], the analogue of the familiar raising to [Spec, Agr$_S$]" (Chomsky

1995:174). The Romance ECM construction selected by perception verbs, treated in 4.1, can thus be assigned the following structure:

(15)   Pietro$_j$ vede$_i$ AgrOP

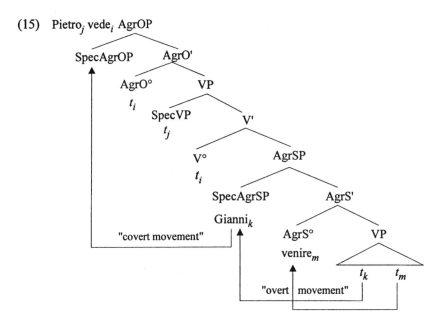

Here the question arises of how movement of the infinitival subject to the specifier of AgrSP can be overt, whereas further movement up to SpecAgrOP is covert. The solution is that the functional [ACC] features, as well as the nominal features, of both the direct object and AgrOP are weak, whereas the overt movement of the subject to SpecAgrSP is triggered by strong [D]-features in AgrS° (cf. Chomsky 1995:345–46). The postverbal position of the subject in *Vedo venire Gianni* can be explained by the expletive *pro*, similar to my proposal for postverbal nominative subjects. For the causative construction with an obligatory postverbal subject, for example, in Italian (*Faccio venire Gianni/*Faccio Gianni venire*), we can maintain the hypothesis formulated in section 4.1, namely, that this construction lacks AgrSP. If AgrSP is missing, the [D]-features of the subject cannot be checked, so any kind of movement is excluded. Note that the [D]-features of the subject must be considered weak, again following Chomsky's (1995:279–89) assumption that weak categorial features need not be checked because they are interpretable on LF.

At this point, various questions arise about the construction in which ECM appears in infinitival CPs, as in the earlier stages of Italian, French, and Romanian, as well as in Old and Modern Occitan. In the nonminimalist interpretation above (cf. especially 6.1.2.2), I explain this by assuming that in those varieties C° is transparent for government from outside the infinitive clause. Of course, in the minimalist program this explanation is not possible because the principle of government is not valid in this framework. Let us look again at some of the relevant data from Modern Italian:

(16) a. *pro$_i$* credo [$_{CP}$ di [essere PRO$_i$ arrivato puntualmente]].
     (I)   believe   C° to-be   arrived punctually
     'I believe to have arrived punctually.'

    b. *⋆pro$_i$* credo [$_{CP}$ [essere PRO$_i$ arrivato puntualmente]].
     (I)   believe   to-be   arrived punctually

    c. *⋆pro* credo [$_{CP}$ [l' amico essere arrivato puntualmente]].
     (I)   believe   the friend to-be arrived punctually

    d. ⋆L' amico$_i$ *pro* credo [$_{CP}$ [t_i essere t_i arrivato puntualmente]].
     the friend (I)   believe   to-be   arrived punctually

    e. L' amico$_i$ che$_i$ *pro* credo [$_{CP}$ t_i [essere t_i arrivato puntualmente]]
     the friend that (I) believe   to-be   arrived punctually

    f. Chi$_i$ credi *pro* [$_{CP}$ t_i [essere t_i arrivato puntualmente]]?
     who believe (you)   to-be   arrived punctually

The three ungrammatical examples were grammatical in earlier stages of the language (cf. 6.1.2.2). How could the present ungrammaticality of (16b), (16c), and (16d) be explained with the aid of properties of C° in a minimalist approach? The simplest solution is the assumption that present-day Italian possesses a special C°, which contains a strong [*wh*] feature (in addition to the C° that I assume to account for Aux-to-Comp). Recall that phonetically empty complementizers are considered to be lexical items in the minimalist program, so we can assume that the lexicon of present-day Italian includes the following complementizers:

(17) a. Ø, C°, <[NOM weak], [φV strong]>   (for Aux-to-Comp)
    b. Ø, C°, <[*wh* strong]>   (for ECM)
    c. *di*, C°   (for control structures)

As a result, we can correctly predict the grammaticality facts in (16):

1. Since PRO has neither [NOM] features nor [*wh*] features, the two Ø-complementizers in (17a) and (17b) cannot be selected if the subject is PRO, as in (16a) and (16b), and the only possibility for the clause is the selection of the overt complementizer *di* in (17c).
2. If the subject of the infinitive clause has the case feature [NOM], the derivation will converge only by selecting the complementizer in (17a); this C° element will trigger Aux-to-Comp because of the strong [φV] feature. If the overt complementizer *di* or the phonetically empty C° in (17b) were selected, [NOM] could not be deleted and the derivation would not converge.
3. If the subject of the infinitive clause has the features [NOM] and [*wh*], the derivation will not converge at all. On selecting the complementizer (17a) the [*wh*] feature cannot be checked, and if (17b) is selected, the case feature cannot be checked. Finally, if (17c), the overt complementizer *di*, is chosen, neither feature can be checked.

4. If the subject of the infinitive construction has the case feature [ACC], the complementizer (17a) is excluded because the features [ACC] of the subject and [NOM] of C° cannot be deleted. The only possibility is the Ø-complementizer (17b). However, two other conditions have to be fulfilled for the derivation to converge: first, there must be an AgrOP above the infinitive clause (i.e., in the main clause) so that [ACC] can be checked and deleted, and second, the subject itself must have a [*wh*] feature.

For point 4., we have not considered one possibility: the selection of the overt complementizer (17c), *di*, would be possible also, contrary to the facts. In the traditional P&P framework, this case is avoided by relativized minimality: the overt complementizer is a potential governor and thus interferes in the government relationship between V° (which assigns the accusative here) and AgrSP, as shown in chapter 6. This is not possible from a minimalist view because the accusative is assigned by LF movement of the case feature [ACC] to AgrOP. The LF-movement is not strictly cyclic (Chomsky 1995:233; Kim et al. 1995:43); that is, a potential landing site may be skipped on LF. A possible explanation could be found by assuming that *di* checks the null case (already introduced in section 3.3.2), similar to the analysis of the English infinitive marker [$_{I^\circ}$ *to*], as proposed by Chomsky and Lasnik (Chomsky 1995:119–20) and further elaborated on by Radford (1997a:191–98), and it would therefore exclude a subject with [ACC] features. Alternatively, the fact that the overt complementizer in (17c) exclusively appears with PRO or with emphatic pronouns (see 3.3.2) suggests that it might have something to do with the properties of control constructions. Proceeding on the features assumed in the minimalist program, I would like to suggest that a control structure like (16a) is characterized by the fact that the agreement features [φD] of the controller (in this case the subject of the main clause) agree with the φ-features of PRO. How could we then exclude the selection of the complementizer *di* in the case of a non-PRO subject of the infinitive clause? Let us assume that the complementizer in some way or another participates in the control relationship. One way in which this could be accomplished would be to suppose that the infinitival complementizer *di* has weak [φD] features coindexed with the [φD] features of the controller, which are checked on LF by [φD] features that come from the infinitive clause itself:

(18)   a. Giovanni$_i$ dice [di$_i$ essere arrivato PRO$_i$ / lui$_i$ puntualmente]
         [φD$_i$]   [φD$_i$]   [φD$_i$]

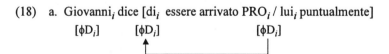

   b. Giovanni$_i$ dice [di$_i$ essere arrivato pro$_j$ / lei$_j$ puntualmente]
         [φD$_i$]   [φD$_i$]   [φD$_j$]

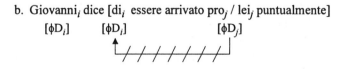

As shown in (18), this will work only with PRO and with emphatic subjects, as in (18a); however, the derivation in (18b) crashes because the features to be checked do not share the same index. Aside from any case issues, *di* is therefore excluded in (18b) because its ϕ-feature cannot be deleted on LF.

The situation in the earlier stages of Italian can be explained on purely lexical grounds by assuming the existence in the lexicon of a phonetically empty complementizer without [*wh*] features instead of (17b):

(19) $\emptyset$, C°

This correctly predicts the grammaticality of (16b) in addition to (16a).[21] It also predicts the grammaticality of ECM without *wh* movement in (16c), as well as the extraction of the non–*wh*-marked accusative subject to the main clause in (16d). The properties of C°, that is, the lexical entries for the earlier stages of French and Romanian and for Occitan, can be supposed to be similar. For those varieties that do not have ECM in CPs, like the Ibero-Romance languages, we could assume that T° is always projected with a [NOM] feature so that accusative subjects are excluded.

7.4   Further perspectives

A minimalist approach, such as the one sketched in the preceding sections, is appropriate for explaining the data I examine in this book. For the language-specific properties, the number of characteristics to be assumed is not considerably smaller than what we had to assume in the traditional P&P model, applied in chapter 6, where we also explained our data with a quite small set of language-specific parameters (case assignment by government or Spec-head agreement, A/A' properties of SpecAgrP, [+Agr] in C°, etc.). What makes the minimalist program seem attractive is that the framework itself needs only very few principles, or, in other words, that the component of universal grammar is smaller. However, whether the minimalist program is really preferable can only be decided if this model is empirically proved by the examination of an equally large number of languages and phenomena as for the preceding model, to which the results of this chapter may perhaps contribute.

We have also seen that minimalism tends to decrease the number of principles and parameters assumed but, nevertheless, to considerably increase the number of features that are necessary to account for syntactic phenomena; it sometimes seems that we have to be careful not to assume the same or even a higher number of features than the number of syntactic facts to be explained. A problem that I overlooked in the preceding sections, but which the reader may have noticed, is that the correlation of certain features is not sufficiently explained. I illustrate this point by reconsidering the proposal concerning a minimalist interpretation of Aux-to-Comp in Italian.

In the P&P version presented in chapter 6, there are at least two syntactic phenomena (case assignment to a subject in SpecAgrSP and movement of the auxiliary to C°) that could be reduced to only one property, a lexically selected feature [+Agr] in C°. In our minimalist interpretation, we find separate explanations for each of the two properties: the licensing of the infinitival subject is determined lexically by the selection of a phonetically empty complementizer with a weak [NOM] feature. This C° element also has a strong verbal feature that triggers the movement of the auxiliary. However, the fact that the [NOM] feature is weak only predicts that the subject cannot surface in SpecCP because it is checked covertly. This feature does not, however, trigger the movement of the subject to SpecAgrSP, for which I postulate an independent, strong nominal feature in AgrS°. Against the background of the older stages of Italian, this is rather enigmatic because here the subject remains in situ, when the nominative feature is situated in T, from which we must conclude that in this case all features of the subject DP are weak. The problem of the minimalist account is that at first sight there is no direct possibility to express an interaction between two different phrases (here CP and AgrSP). Similarly, as discussed in section 7.2, it is still not clear how a property of C° can be made responsible for the weakness of [D]-features in Portuguese. As we note with respect to Ambar's (1994) analysis, a principle like government, by which this could be achieved, is not available.

To illustrate, consider the following two configurations:

(20) a.

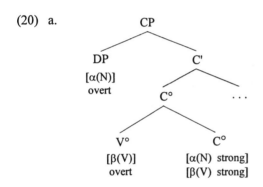

      b.

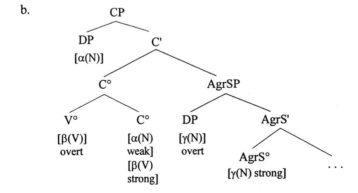

The configuration in (20a) roughly corresponds to the structure proposed by Wilder (1995) to account for the verb-second position in the German main clause. This configuration is easily explainable from a minimalist view if we follow Wilder in assuming a phonetically empty complementizer that possesses the two respective strong features. The configuration in (20b) corresponds to our Aux-to-Comp construction, where α(N) is [NOM] and β(V) in C° is the strong verbal feature that triggers auxiliary movement. What we are seeking is a possible explanation that predicts [γ(N) strong] and excludes [γ(N) weak] in AgrS°.

It is interesting that the minimalist program seems to provide exactly what we are looking for. Consider agreement features (ϕ-features): the ϕ-features of V and DP must be identical in one derivation, according to Chomsky (1995:282); and I tentatively assume that either both are weak or both are strong. The reason for this claim is that both features are needed for one and the same property (subject-verb agreement). This means that the checking of both features must apply at the same time, either before spell-out or on.LF. For the problem related to the Aux-to-Comp construction, the following solution comes to mind, by which the assumption on [+Agr] in C°, and its minimalist reinterpretation of a C° with [ϕV] features receive further support. The special complementizer I claim for Italian is repeated here as (21):

(21) $\emptyset$, C°, <[NOM] weak / [ϕV] strong>.

Note that the strong [ϕV] features will yield overt movement of the auxiliary or the copulative verb to C°, as we have seen. Moreover, strong [ϕV] in C° also predicts that the subject [ϕD] features involved are necessarily strong. Since C° does not contain any [ϕD] features, these are generated in their regular position in AgrSP, so the subject overtly moves to its specifier position, yielding the structure represented in (13) above.

We can now also reinterpret the Portuguese data and the solution offered by Ambar (1994) for prohibiting the subject to appear in SpecAgrSP. Remember that for Portuguese, too, I claim the existence of [+Agr] in C° (see section 6.3.1.3), although its effect is rather the contrary of that which occurs in Italian. We can now assume that the infinitive clause in Portuguese constructions, such as the one in example (50a) in chapter 6, has a C° with weak [ϕV] features, so the verb will not move to C° and the subject will not move to SpecAgrSP.

Note that there might still be some problems. For instance, the relevance of ϕ-features just outlined—which I think receives further support from my analysis of word order in Italian and Portuguese infinitive clauses—were questioned by Chomsky (1995:ch. 4). Although Chomsky (1992) claimed verb movement to be essentially motivated by [ϕV] features, this view was abandoned in Chomsky (1995:349ff.) in favor of the categorial [V]-features. Apart from Chomsky's complex theoretical assumption, which cannot be discussed here, this might seem desirable also for Romance languages because we find configurations in which the subject remains in situ; that is, we have to assume weak [ϕD], although the verb moves to AgrS°, which cannot be triggered by weak [ϕV] features. I leave this point open for further research within Chomsky's (1995: ch. 4) theory about the interpretability of features.

I have some final remarks about case assignment. In the analysis in chapter 6, I claim that, in the spirit of the earlier P&P model, the licensing and the most important word order facts can be directly derived from case theory. However, in this chapter I choose to follow two standard minimalist assumptions formulated in (6): first, that case is usually checked by Spec-head agreement and, second, that T°, but not AgrS°, is the bearer of the nominative feature. It has to be kept in mind, however, that feature checking can be achieved either in a Spec-head configuration or through adjunction of one head to another. With the exception of clitics, I consider subjects to be maximal projections, so only the first mechanism is valid for overt checking. Radford (1997a:329–32) suggests that English auxiliary contraction structures involve head movement, assuming that English subject pronouns (by virtue of being heads) may check their nominative case by adjoining directly to T°. In view of this, reconsider the following Spanish examples from section 2.3:

(22) a. Envió el informe sin   **yo / ??Juan** leerlo.
          (he) sent the report   without I /   J.   to-read-it

    b. Envió el informe sin leerlo **yo / Juan**.

In contrast to postverbal subjects, the preverbal position is usually grammatical only when the subject is a pronoun. As seen in section 6.2.2.2, this construction is possible only in infinitive constructions that are complements of a preposition. We might therefore assume that P° allows for a [NOM] feature that is checked by right adjunction of the pronominal D° head.

The idea that the [NOM] feature usually originates under T° closes a circle in the history of case theory as described in section 3.2: whereas in the early generative literature tense was claimed to be the nominative assigner, tense was replaced by agreement in the course of the 1980s. Now, with the minimalist program, the original idea has returned. Of course, the compromise with the agreement-based nominative approach is that usually tense has to move to AgrSP for the Spec-head relationship with the subject to be established. However, in 3.2.1 and 3.2.2 I pointed out that there are cases in which only one of the two functional heads seems to be involved in nominative assignment, a point supported by some further data in chapter 6. It would be worthwhile to reconsider the minimalist case approach in the light of these results. A way in which this could be carried out would be to claim, for instance, that both AgrS° and T° may have a nominative feature, thus maintaining the idea of a parametric choice formulated by Roberts (1993). We could then say that the [NOM] feature of AgrS° is strong and so must be checked overtly, yielding preverbal subjects, whereas the [NOM] feature of T° is weak and leads to postverbal subjects by covert checking. Actually, Chomsky (1995:232) does not exclude the possibility that case features might be responsible for triggering movement of a subject to SpecAgrSP. This has some explanatory power for our data. Given the fact that the most usual Romance pattern is the word order $V_{inf} + DP_{subj}$, we could hypothesize that infinitival [NOM] features are weak by nature, thus being related with tense rather than with agreement. Of course, this would lead to a change in the usual assumptions of features and their impact on movement processes, and it cannot be decided here what this would mean for the overall theory.

7.5   Summary

In this chapter I show that most of the assumptions in the previous framework can be reformulated straightforwardly in a feature-based minimalist account. If we accept the basic assumptions of the minimalist program, the cross-linguistic differences can be derived from the strength of features. In an approach such as the one originally offered by Chomsky (1992), it is sufficient to say that most Romance languages allow infinitival T° to have a weak [NOM] feature, licensing postverbal subjects by covert checking. Moreover, it must be assumed that a basic property of most Romance languages is that the nominal features related to infinitival subjects are also weak. In Portuguese, Galician, and Sicilian, however, infinitival AgrS° allows for strong nominal features that trigger overt movement of the subject to SpecAgrSP. In the original Chomskyan interpretation, these are either [D] or [φD] features, whereas in the outlook in section 7.4 I suggest that they might also be regarded as strong [NOM] features, in accordance with the results in the previous chapters of this book. In addition, a not uncommon property of Romance languages is that prepositions and complementizers can be argued to have case features, either [NOM], as in the Italian Aux-to-Comp structure and perhaps in certain Spanish constructions, or [ACC], as in the prepositional infinitive constructions in historical and dialectal varieties of French and in sociolectal varieties of Brazilian Portuguese. Finally, an interesting result of this chapter is that our previous assumptions about the involvement of an agreement feature in C° in the word order facts of contemporary Italian and Portuguese could be reinterpreted by means of φ-features.

8

Summary and Outlook

In this chapter I first summarize the results of this book and then discuss some topics related to the history of the Romance languages.

The data described in chapter 2 show that most Romance languages permit specified subjects in infinitive constructions. However, the facts concerning the linear ordering of constituents and case properties show considerable cross-linguistic variation. In contrast to the infinitive constructions selected by perceptional and causative verbs, the subject of the infinitive clause can be either in the nominative or in the accusative case in other constructions. The subject can surface pre- or postverbally. Although some languages admit both positions, in others only one is allowed. Moreover, the syntactic configurations in which specified subjects are licensed also vary considerably. In the varieties that allow both preverbal and postverbal subjects in infinitive constructions, the choice of either position is usually not arbitrary but rather depends on syntactic properties. This is a fundamental difference compared to finite constructions, where the position of subjects is largely dependent on semantic and pragmatic factors. Some examples may be recalled here: in earlier phases of Italian, and presumably also of Romanian, preverbal subjects are licensed only in the accusative case, whereas postverbal subjects bear the nominative case; in Portuguese, where subjects of infinitives usually behave similarly to those in finite clauses, preverbal subjects are suppressed in certain configurations, for example, when the infinitive clause is selected by an epistemic or a declarative verb. It is striking that after this same group of verbs, Italian allows the subject of an infinitive to become overt, also in the postverbal position. Finally, in Modern Spanish, preverbal infinitival subjects are basically limited to infinitive constructions that occur after certain prepositions. Something similar can be found in some diatopic varieties of French and in substandard Brazilian Portuguese, although here I argue that the case is the accusative and, in further contrast to Spanish, postverbal subjects are not allowed.

The review of existing accounts for constructions of this type in chapter 4 shows that many of the phenomena just mentioned were not taken into account up to now, and in addition, the frameworks used mostly corresponded to earlier phases of syntactic theory; thus a revision was necessary. In chapters 5 to 7, I apply two different frameworks to provide a unified description and analysis of specified subjects in Romance infinitive clauses. It could be shown that both the similarities and the differences just mentioned largely follow from a few universal principles, given some specific parameters, and from some lexical properties of Romance languages, which are also needed on independent grounds to explain other phenomena of the languages involved. I now briefly summarize the results.

First, the functional categories Agr, T, and C are seen as crucial, in accordance with current trends in generative grammar. Basically, nominative subjects of infinitives are licensed in most Romance languages because T° has a nominative feature that is not restricted to finite contexts. This is characteristic of most Romance languages, with the exception of the northern and central Romance area comprising Gallo- and Rhaeto-Romance, as well as the northern Italo-Romance varieties. Central Italian, which is also represented by the Italian literary language and the modern national language of Italy, lost this property at some moment in its history, although it survived, at least in literary texts, until the nineteenth century. From a traditional P&P perspective, T° assigns the nominative to a DP that it governs, a property that correctly predicts subjects to occur postverbally, located in their base position SpecVP, as could be confirmed by an analysis of facts about negation and adverbs. From a minimalist view, the fact that the subject of the infinitive remains in its base position follows from the weakness of the features involved, which can be related to the [−Tns] property of infinitival T°, which is similar to Chomsky's (1995:120) claim about the licensing of PRO. Usually, infinitives have no agreement morphology, which follows from the assumption that AgrS is not or is only partially involved in the licensing of subjects that remain in SpecVP. The lack of overt agreement thus relates Romance infinitive constructions to those VS(O) languages that are characterized by the lack of overt agreement even in finite environments. For the Romance varieties that allow inflected infinitives, the properties mentioned are reflected by the fact that infinitival inflection is generally optional with postverbal subjects, as in Galician and Sardinian. It has to be noted that the VS structures found in Romance infinitive constructions are usually licensed with both intransitive and transitive verbs. This makes them different from similar structures found with unaccusative verbs, in which the subject might be argued to bear partitive case, according to Belletti (1987, 1988). Most older varieties of the languages under discussion (basically the medieval stages of the Romance languages) also allowed for the nominative subject to appear in the preverbal position. I claim that this is usually not due to any parametric change of case assignment but that it follows from a general verb-second tendency, which is due to A'-properties of AgrSP. This is a marked option of Old Romance, which should not be confused with other cases in which subjects appear to be preverbal, as discussed in the following paragraph.

Second, some marginal areas of Romance (Portuguese and Galician in the west and Sicilian and perhaps other Italo-Romance varieties in the south) allow for another option, which is essentially identical to the canonical nominative case-marking mechanism assumed for finite structures in Romance and many non-Romance languages: here, the nominative is licensed in a Spec-head configuration between a nominative feature in AgrS° and the subject, which is moved to SpecAgrSP. This obviously yields the unmarked linear order $DP_{subj} + V_{inf}$. In a minimalist interpretation, this option is due either to some strong nominal feature of AgrS° or to the strength of the case feature itself. In Portuguese and Galician, this correlates with obligatory overt agreement on the infinitive.

A third functional category involved in the licensing of nominative case in infinitive constructions is C°. This property seems to be restricted to Italian, where it is still alive as a stylistically marked option that yields the infinitival Aux-to-Comp structure originally proposed by Rizzi (1982). I provide ample evidence for the assumption that this structure is licensed by an agreement feature in C°, which is independently motivated on the evidence of other languages and not restricted to infinitival contexts (cf. Rizzi 1990a). In chapter 6, I argue that this feature, which I call [+Agr] to capture its affinity to finite agreement, serves as a nominative assigner in the Aux-to-Comp structure, realizing the parametric option "nominative case assignment by Agr° through government." In chapter 7, I show that in a minimalist approach, these assumptions can be interpreted by postulating a nonovert complementizer that contains both strong φ-features and a weak [NOM] feature. This complementizer is subcategorized by declarative and epistemic verbs, determiners, and the preposition *per*, a lexical property by which the configurations licensing infinitival Aux-to-Comp are determined. Concerning the similarity with certain Portuguese structures observed by Raposo (1987), I show that the same φ-features in C° (though weak in Portuguese) are involved, without leading to Aux-to-Comp, where these features block DP movement of the subject.

Apart from infinitival subjects in the nominative case, perhaps the most striking fact about Romance, I also reconsider ECM constructions. Up to now, the lack of the CP projection in the infinitive clause has usually been considered to be a presupposition for ECM to apply, with the exception of *wh* environments. I show that this assumption cannot be maintained for earlier stages of eastern and central Romance languages (Romanian, Italian, French, and Occitan), where ECM was generally licensed in spite of the presence of a phonetically empty complementizer. I assume that the governing properties of C° in connection with relativized minimality vary cross-linguistically. From a minimalist perspective, I postulate the existence of special complementizers in the lexicon of the languages involved. Whereas most of the languages mentioned lost this property, it is still found in present-day varieties of Occitan. Moreover, the fact that accusative case was assigned to infinitival subjects by prepositions and prepositional complementizers can be considered a typical Old Gallo-Romance phenomenon. This characteristic, too, is still alive in Occitan, as well as in Lorraine and Walloon varieties of French. Some substandard varieties of Brazilian Portuguese independently developed a similar mechanism.

In chapter 1 I briefly outlined some issues that have been discussed within Romance philology since the last century. The results summarized above allow us to clarify some important points related to the historical development and diversification of the Romance languages.

First, no direct genealogical connection between A.c.I. constructions (ECM) and infinitives with a nominative subject can be found. However, both options are partially related in the sense that they reflect different lexical and parametric properties of functional categories. With respect to ECM, Latin can be characterized as a language in which nonovert C° did not block case assignment to the subject from outside the infinitive clause, a property that is also found in the eastern and central Romance varieties mentioned, and it seems not improbable that these Romance languages continue the Latin situation. A point in which ECM and nominative assignment to the subjects of infinitives seem to be related is the agreement feature in C°, which is responsible both for Aux-to-Comp phenomena and for the licensing of ECM in *wh* contexts, along the lines of Rizzi (1990a). This observation might deserve some future research for Latin, perhaps also including the fact that in Old Gallo-Romance, the infinitival overt C° and P° could assign the accusative to the subject of the infinitive clause. Latin gerundive constructions (in which prepositions function as case assigners) should be included in the investigation of the latter. In any case, it seems that the properties of C° played an important role in the differentiation and the further development of the Romance languages.

Second is the question of which of the constructions mentioned were inherited from Latin and which were later adaptations of Latin models. The Romance languages can be divided into two groups according to the properties of the functional category tense: Gallo-Romance (including northern Italian) and Rhaeto-Romance, on the one hand, where T° never had the ability to function as a nominative case assigner in nontensed contexts, and the rest of the Romance varieties on the other hand, in which T° does have this property. The Italian language (derived from a central Italian dialect) originally belonged to the latter group, whereas it is a part of the former group today. The broad diffusion of the case-assigning properties of infinitival T° and its presence in languages that are considered archaic, such as Sardinian and Romanian, suggest a common Vulgar Latin origin. It has to be kept in mind that in Latin many of the constructions examined in this book involved a gerund or gerundive (recall that it can be argued, following traditional grammar, that these are cases of infinitives with nominal declension). In this respect, consider the following example, with a specified subject, given by Kaulen (1904:299):

(1) [In convertendo **Dominus** captivitatem Sion] facti sumus sicut consolati.
      in undoing   Lord (NOM) captivity (ACC) Zion made (we) are like dreaming.
      'When the Lord lets the prisoners of Zion go, we become like dreamers.' (Vulg., Ps. 125, 1)

In most of the Vulgate manuscripts, the subject is in the accusative case, which seems to have been the usual option in constructions of this kind and is similar to Greek. The structure we find here, however, strongly resembles the standard Romance configuration, with a postverbal nominative subject. I will not analyze the structure of (1), but we can argue that Vulgar Latin already allowed for non-finite T° or some other functional category to assign the nominative case to a subject situated to its right.

Third is the question whether the existence of inflected infinitives and that of specified subjects are related. This question has often been affirmed on rather intuitive grounds by saying that a specified subject in an infinitive clause and overt agreement morphology on infinitives are almost the same (cf., e.g., Meier 1955; Togeby 1955; Maurer 1964). Note that we can now closely examine this issue against the background of the underlying syntactic properties. Some Romance varieties allow nominative assignment by means of Spec-head agreement between the subject of an infinitive clause and infinitival AgrS°. In Portuguese, this goes along with the fact that the infinitive shows overt agreement morphology. However, this corollary is not generalized in the Romance languages. Whereas Sicilian has the same nominative-assigning mechanism as Portuguese, it does not support inflection of the infinitive. In contrast, Sardinian has infinitives inflected for agreement but does not allow for case marking through infinitival AgrS°. At the end of section 6.5.1 (note 55), I tentatively assumed that Portuguese may have behaved like Sardinian in a nonattested phase, in the sense that only T° was a nominative assigner. In these two languages, the similarity in finite clauses may have caused the infinitive to become inflected (probably by adapting the similar past subjunctive forms). It is important to keep in mind Jones's (1992) theory, according to which the infinitival inflection in Sardinian is base-generated within V°, and I reinterpret this by postulating that AgrS° is not involved here. We might extend this to the early Portuguese situation. Recall that the Old Romance languages allowed the postverbal infinitival subject, case marked by T°, to be A'-moved to SpecAgrSP, as a marked option. In Portuguese the output of the S-structure of such infinitive clauses was almost identical to a standard finite clause, with a preverbal subject and an inflected verb. We can now argue that the speakers reanalyzed this as case assignment by AgrS° to the subject in SpecAgrSP, in an analogy to finite contexts. Thus, lexical agreement as postulated by Jones was reanalyzed as a property of the functional category AgrS°. Note that by making such an assumption, we can derive the facts about nominative subjects in infinitives from one basic property of T° that may be traced back to Vulgar Latin.

Finally, I return to the question of syntactic borrowing. This is relevant for the A.c.I. construction, which I have regarded as exceptional case marking to an infinitival subject inside a CP. It has almost been a standard claim of historical grammar that this construction was a learned imitation and/or borrowing from Latin texts during the Middle Ages. Note that this should not be assumed for Occitan, since in this language this kind of ECM construction has been a phenomenon of popular language until today in some varieties, so future research might reveal that it was inherited from Latin. Such a view may be generalized for Gallo-Romance, considering the fact that that the accusative case can still be assigned to the subject of an infinitive clause in some French varieties, namely, by prepositions. For Old Italian (and probably for Old Romanian), however, the borrowing hypothesis can be supported. Note that Old Italian behaved essentially like the other non–Gallo-Romance languages, in the sense that infinitival subjects bore nominative case licensed by T°. As a result of A'-movement, we find structures with preverbal nominative subjects, identical to the Ibero-Romance data. Reconsider the following examples from Old Italian and Classical Spanish, respectively (cf. examples 7 and 38c of chapter 6):

(2) a. perchè io dissi [$_{CP}$ [$_{AgrSP}$ io aver trovato iscritto . . .]]
   because I said   I to-have found   written
   'because I said that I had found that it was written . . .'

   b. confesando [$_{CP}$ [$_{AgrSP}$ yo no ser mas santo que mis vecinos]]
   confessing   I not to-be more saintly than my neighbors
   'confessing that I was not more saintly than my neighbors'.

Recall that the C° blocks ECM in all diachronic varieties of Spanish, and we can assume the same for the original situation in Italian. Notably, the Italian example (2a) is from the thirteenth century, whereas the borrowing of the Latin A.c.I. construction is usually assumed to have occurred afterward, within the humanist period. Consequently, from the fourteenth century onward we find exclusively accusative subjects in configurations like (2). The borrowing hypothesis implies that although originally this construction was an imitation of Latin, ECM became grammatical, by means of a change in the properties of C°, for speakers who used the stylistic varieties involved. At the same time, these speakers would consider preverbal subjects in the nominative case, as in (2a), to be ungrammatical. These assumptions predict the regular complementary distribution of preverbal accusative subjects and postverbal nominative subjects in Italian. Note that this regularity presupposes that the mechanisms involved belonged to the linguistic competence of the speakers. In contrast, in the early phase, in which the borrowing originally occurred through a conscious imitation of Latin models, we may expect divergences from this general rule. In fact, the data I analyze show one such example, and significantly it is a quite early piece of evidence, dating from the first half of the fourteenth century, in which the borrowing, we can argue, was in process:

(3)   Chiamo per testimonio Dio . . . [avere **me** veduto e   trovato in quelle
       (I) call   for testimony God   to-have me seen   and found in those
       parti dell' eremo . . . due Monaci].
       parts of-the hermitage   two monks
       'I call God to witness . . . that I saw two monks in those parts of the hermitage . . .'
       (Cavalca, 20; cf. Schwendener 1923:65)

The postverbal accusative subject may indicate that the author of these lines consciously applied a rule such as "Subjects in Latin infinitive clauses have an accusative after verbs of saying." However, the author left the subject in the standard Italian position for nominative subjects, that is, after the infinitive. The result is a structure that I would argue has never been grammatical in Italian. A further discussion of these kinds of problems, which are related to the origin of the properties of Romance infinitive clauses, lies outside the aims of this work, principally because this can be achieved only through a detailed analysis of Latin and thus would deserve a book of its own.

Returning to the theoretical results of this book, I show that the data analyzed here generally confirm the case-assigning mechanisms assumed in works like Koopman and Sportiche (1991) and Roberts (1993, 1994), as well as the minimalist view on case assignment. The case properties of functional categories are parametrized with respect to finiteness. Moreover, the constructions I analyze provide further support for the fact that the Split-Infl hypothesis is appropriate for explaining the syntactic structure of Romance languages. Finally, it can be said that specified subjects in infinitive clauses can be added to those constituents that are indicators for verb movement in infinitive clauses.

In a recent article, Chomsky (1998) picks up and elaborates on the minimalist assumptions made in Chomsky (1995:ch. 4). Some of these assumption have not been discussed here. For example, Chomsky (1998) states that C and T are among the core functional categories (CFCs), "constituting the core of the systems of (structural) Case-agreement and 'dislocation' (Move)." For subject case assignment in infinitive clauses, the results presented in this book are highly compatible with Chomsky's view, in the sense that C and T are crucial for explaining the data analyzed here. In contrast, case assignment by infinitival Agr is a marginal phenomenon, restricted only to a few peripheral Romance varieties; Chomsky claims that Agr might not even exist as a functional category. Chomsky's view obviously aims at reducing the categories assumed within generative grammar. But there is also the inverse tendency, represented, for example, by Cinque (1999). Perhaps this book can be considered to be between these two currents and, I hope, will give rise to further studies in either direction within the investigation of the structure of Romance languages.

Notes

Chapter 1

1. See the discussion in sections 4.1 and 4.3.3.3.

2. See the detailed review in Mensching (1997:section 1.3), Mensching and Popovici (1997), and Mensching (1998, 1999).

3. Generalizations of this kind, which have to be revised on the basis of the results achieved in this book, can be frequently found in Romance philology. Consider Lausberg (1972:§822), who states that the subject occurs before the infinitive in Old Spanish and Portuguese, whereas it is placed after the infinitive in Modern Spanish.

4. The following points he makes to support this idea are quite interesting, although most of them are clear overgeneralizations, as will become evident further on in this book: (i) the existence in earlier stages of Romanian and Italian of infinitival clauses with subjects that are complements of declarative and volitional verbs; (ii) the inflected infinitive in Portuguese, which Meier regards as a continuation of the Latin A.c.I. ("'É melhor *vires*' = Latin 'te venire'"); (iii) the frequency and the vitality of prepositional infinitives with specified subjects; and (iv) the widespread use of nominalized infinitives with the definite article in the same environments that triggered A.c.I. constructions in Latin.

5. I am referring to §21, entitled "*A pessoalidade do infinitivo: inovação românica comum.*" Here we find examples from various Romance languages that correspond to quite different configurations but which nevertheless are claimed to be parallel or even identical. Consider the following Italian example from the thirteenth century:

(i)   Comprese la   reina [**ella** essere la   sua figliuola].
        understood the queen she to-be the her little-daughter
        'The queen understood that she was her little daughter.' (Malispini, ch. 18)

Maurer claims that this construction survived over the centuries and is still found dialectally today, indicating as parallels the examples that I discuss later on in chapter 2, example (36a), and note 3. As I show, these are three different constructions, which have to be considered the result of different mechanisms of grammar (see chapter 6).

6. For instance (see the bibliography at the end of this book for the abbreviations used): Bocc. Dec., Dante Div. Com., Testi non tosc. Qu. (Italian); Celest., Cond. Luc., Gen. Est., Laz. 1554 (Spanish).

7. For example, the *Corpus oral de referencia de la lengua española contemporánea* for Spanish; the works of Meyer-Hermann (1973), Gondar (1978) and Lemos Monteiro (1994) for Portuguese and Galician; and the material offered by Franz (1915, 1920) and Frei (1929) for dialectal data of French.

8. Although strictly speaking the minimalist program is a continuation of the P&P model (cf. Chomsky 1995:170), I use this designation for a nonminimalist framework, if not mentioned otherwise.

9. For example, the verb derived from the Latin *timere* 'to fear' selects an infinitive construction with a specified subject in Old Italian and in earlier varieties of French, whereas it was usually constructed with a finite subjunctive clause in Latin. See Schwendener (1923:4, 75) and E. Stimming (1915:145, 177) for examples and further discussion and, for Latin, Draeger (1881:II, 394).

10. See chapter 4, note 31, and chapter 6, note 7.

Chapter 2

1. E. Stimming's (1915:119–20) syntactic criteria to distinguish this type of construction from the infinitive construction represented by (2b) deserve to be mentioned here because they can serve as a starting point: (i) the subject of the infinitive has no relationship with the governing verb but is only the subject of the infinitive; (ii) the specified subject of the infinitive can even occur when it is identical to the subject of the governing verb; and (iii) the infinitive is often an auxiliary verb followed by a participle, including the passive, which Stimming also considers to be the imitation of Latin models.

2. Rizzi (1982:112) also mentions *dovere* 'must', with a slightly doubtful acceptability. An example can be found in the twentieth-century literary texts:

(i)   Il Croce sottolinea [doversi   intendere   **questo fare** «nel   senso
      the C.   emphasizes must (INF)-R CL to-understand this   to-do in-the sense
      più ampio . . .»].
      most wide
      'C. emphasized that this doing must be understood «in the broadest sense . . . .»'
      (Garin Cronache, 253; cf. Skytte 1983:311)

Note that the word order is different from the usual construction mentioned by Rizzi. This construction seems to be an example of the older type (see example 12).

3. Cf. the documentary evidence in Schwendener (1923:44–45, 56, 61, 65–66, 70, 77) concerning the verbs *lamentarsi, querelarsi, vantarsi, accorgersi, avvedersi, dubitare, imaginarsi, essere memore,* and *rallegrarsi.* Note that this construction has usually been avoided by using a determiner:

(i)   Io mi rallegro veramente assai [de*llo* aver   **voi** preso moglie].
      I me delight really   much of-the to-have you taken wife
      'I am really very pleased about the fact that you got married.' (Mach. Istorie II, 3,
      p. 70, line 10; cf. Vockeradt 1878:241; Rohlfs 1949:519; Maurer 1968:71)

4. Examples from the twentieth century like the following one are extremely rare and considered archaic:

(i)   Si sentiva un sussurrio . . . che disse a Johnny [**nulla** essere assolutamente
      R CL heard   a murmuring that said to J.   nothing to-be absolutely
      accaduto al   paese].
      happened at-the village
      'There were rumors which told J. that absolutely nothing had happened at the
      village.' (Fenoglio: Il part., 136; cf. Skytte 1983:307)

5. Only two counterexamples to this generalization could be found, both from before the fifteenth century. See chapter 6, example (7), and chapter 8, example (3).

6. The personal pronouns *lui* 'him' and *lei* 'her', although originally accusatives, could be used for the nominative as well in Old Italian (cf. Rohlfs 1949:158–60, 163–64, 242–44). However, in contrast to Dante (cf. Rohlfs 1949:159), Boccaccio, at least in the Decameron, from which this example is taken, strictly distinguishes between *lui/lei* (accusative) and *egli/ella* (nominative).

7. Usually constructions with both cases have been designated as A.c.I. in the traditional literature (e.g., Schwendener 1923; Rohlfs 1949; Segre 1991). Meier (1955:280–81) refers to the Italian examples as "nominativo con infinitivo (= a.c.i.)" without further explanation. Only Skytte (1983:293) points out that the term *accusativo con l'infinitivo* is inappropriate for contemporary Italian (cf. also his comments in Renzi and Salvi 1991:528). It has to be noted, however, that Skytte treats preverbal subjects in examples such as the one mentioned in note 4 also as nominatives, which is problematic in view of the results presented here, particularly in chapter 6.

8. Cf. Meyer-Lübke (1899:§502); Gougenheim (1951:138); A. Haase (1965:179); Harris (1978:197).

9. Cf. 6.4.1.2 for further discussion of this example.

10. La Fontaine seems to be the only author who still used this construction in the seventeenth century. This is usually considered to be an archaism (E. Stimming 1915:109; Meier 1955:284). Consider the following example:

(i) Il faut   [**tous** prendre patience].
     it is-necessary all   to-take patience
     'It is necessary for all to be patient.' (Laf., *Je vous prends sans vost*, ed. Siegert, XIII, 350; quoted by Stimming (1915:109)

11. For instance:

(i) Il jugeait [**cette recréation** lui devoir   être profitable].
     he judged   this recreation   him must (INF.) to-be profitable
     'He judged that this recreation would be profitable for him.' (Bovary, 243; cf. E. Stimming 1915:179)

12. The type represented by the Italian example in (10b), in which the infinitive construction is a prepositional complement of a verb, can still be found in the sixteenth century. Consider the following example, with the verb *se doubter de*:

(i) se   doubtant [**cecy** estre faict a   la main]
     R CL supposing this to-be made by the hand
     'supposing that this was handmade' (Larivey Morf., II, 4; cf. E. Stimming 1915: 147)

13. These cases are usually considered archaisms. Cf. E. Stimming (1915:124), Tobler (1921:95), Nyrop (1930:219–20), Lombard (1936:224), and A. Haase (1965:§85, p. 201, Rem. II).

14. The judicial language of nineteenth-century French itself has not been studied in this respect. The authors usually list a few examples taken from literary texts, for instance:

(i) Nous avons dressé   le présent constat [pour **la requerante** en faire
     We   have drawn-up the present record   for the complainant (F) A CL to-make
     tel usage . . .]
     such use
     'We drew up these minutes in order for the complainant to use it in such a way . . .'
     (Courteline, Théâtre II, 1922:266; quoted by Lombard 1936:224)

See Nyrop (1930:220) and Lerch (1929:158–59) for further examples.

15. The phenomenon is known as belonging to Walloon and (northern) Lorraine. Cf., among others, Franz (1915:118–19, 1920:36ff.), Lerch (1929:37), Prein (1921), Lewent (1923), Frei (1929), Brunot (1934:302, fn. 2).

16. I have adapted the phonetic transcription used by Franz according to the IPA standard.

17. The main difference with the earlier stages of Spanish is the fact that the use of specified subjects in nonprepositional infinitival complement clauses is characteristic of literary and academic style. An example is given in chapter 6, no. (41a). Moreover, when the infinitive clause is used as a subject of impersonal constructions, it shows a strong tendency to occur at the beginning of the sentence, as is shown by the following example, taken from Hernanz Carbó (1982:356–57):

(i)   [Negarlo **tú**] no basta.   (ii) ⋆No basta [negarlo **tú**].
      to-deny-it you not suffices
      'It is not sufficient for you to deny it.'

However, the speakers consulted by me did not usually reject (ii) as ungrammatical, although all agreed that it sounded somewhat strange. We might consider it as a very marked option in Modern Spanish.

18. This is usually not found in the type represented by (2a). It has to be noted that this has nothing to do with the fact that specified subjects are present but, rather, that it is a general tendency of Spanish.

19. With nonpronominal NPs, the grammaticality of the preverbal subject decreases considerably (cf. Fernández Lagunilla 1987:127, fn. 3):

(i)   ??Envió   el informe [sin   **Juan** leerlo].
      (he) sent the report   without J.   to-read-it
      'He sent the report without J. reading it.'

20. It has to be noted, however, that this regularity is not always followed, especially in earlier stages. Consider the following example from Galician-Portuguese:

(i)   Era costume . . . [de **cavaleiros andantes** *seer*   recebidos em lugares estranhos].
      was custom   *de* knights   errant   to-be received in places foreign
      'It was a custom . . . that knights-errant were received at foreign places.' (A Demanda do Santo Graal, §423, quoted by Maurer 1968:152)

21. We might even consider Modern Portuguese as more conservative since some of the restrictions mentioned for present-day Spanish do not hold in Portuguese and Galician. First, unlike Modern Spanish, the use of a specified subject in infinitival complement clauses is not restricted to literary or formal stylistic levels (see note 17). Second, in impersonal constructions, the ordering main clause + infinitive clause appears regularly (cf. the examples in 59 of chapter 6, in contrast to the Modern Spanish example in note 17), a property that it shares with Old and Classical Spanish, as well as with earlier stages of the other languages mentioned. Third, some impersonal verbs, which do not license our construction in Modern Spanish, are still allowed in Portuguese and Galician, for example, *acontecer/suceder* 'to happen' and *convir* 'to be convenient'.

22. The infinitive has no overt inflection for the first- and the third-person singular. Although the infinitive can usually be argued to have a zero morpheme in these cases, I do not represent this information in the translation.

23. For Calabrian, see section 6.5.1.

24. Examples (36b), (36c), and (36d), as well as all other examples throughout the book that are marked as belonging to the variety of Corleone, are taken from an inquiry carried out by Mensching (1997).

25. For this type, consider the following example from the last century, offered by Rohlfs (1949:528):

(i)   Comu mai è possibuli, [**voscienza** piagghiari a mè figghia]?
      why ever is possible   you   to-beat to my daughter
      'How can it be possible that you beat my daughter?' (Pitré 4, 230)

He interprets this as the imitation of a "solenne stile academico." This is not in accordance with our data because the Italian literary language of the nineteenth century did not license preverbal subjects in infinitival subject clauses. As example (36d) shows, this construction is popular even today in Sicilian.

26. This is an old phenomenon, as is shown by the following example from the fifteenth century:

(i) Vinni qa   unu don Nicola Furmica, dichendu [eu aviri   una sua cona].
    came here a d. N.   F.   saying   I to-have a his icon
    'A certain N. F. came here, saying that I had an icon of his.' (Testi non Tosc. Qu., 38, 3, p. 47; text from Salemi, A.D. 1439)

27. Note that this sentence is a translation from Latin (Matt. 19:24/Mark 10:25/Luke 18:25). In the Occitan version, a postverbal subject was used against the Latin model: "Facilius est camelum per foramen acus transire, quam divitem intrare in regnum caelorum."

28. "Ce que Ronjat avait senti néanmoins, c'est que cette tournure a une valeur, ne disons pas, littéraire, mais artistique, stylistique, si l'on veut. En tout cas, elle est spontanée sur les lèvres des montagnards du Gévaudan, extrêmement fréquente chaque fois qu'il s'agit d'exprimer la nuance que nous avons déterminée plus haut" (Camproux 1958:282).

29. See also Alibèrt (1976:305), who offers the following literary example from Languedocian:

(i) Se plorava dempuèi tres jorns, [sens degun lo poder   consola].
    R CL cried   during three days   without no-one him can (INF) to-comfort
    'He cried for three days without anybody being able to comfort him.' Besson (passim)

Chapter 3

1. Concerning the question of further categories in addition to AgrO, see, among others, Schmidt (1994), Webelhuth (1995), Rowlett (1998), and Cinque (1999).

2. See note 1 of chapter 7 for the different Agr categories and their labels.

3. This follows from Kayne's linear correspondence axiom (LCA). Although the present book was not written within this framework, some important points in chapters 5 to 7 are compatible with Kayne's assumptions.

4. An example of the incorporation of an object clitic in Neg° is *n-o* in the Romanian sentence in example (3a); see sections 5.2.2.2 and 5.2.3.2 for a similar phenomenon in Old Spanish and Galician-Portuguese. For an explanation of the common assumption that V° (or more precisely, T° with incorporated V°) moves to Agr° without landing in Neg° (which is a violation of the ECP; see note 5), cf. Belletti (1990:31–32), in particular her reference to Moritz (1989). It has to be noted that the assumption that both Neg° and the verb are cliticized to Agr° also contradicts Kayne's (1994) LCA, according to which multiple adjunction to a head is not allowed. However, I usually admit multiple adjunction to heads, although this might be considered to be a simplified structure that could be reinterpreted by assuming a larger number of functional heads.

5. Cf. Rizzi (1990a:32):

A nonpronominal empty category must be
(i) properly head-governed (Formal Licensing)
(ii) antecedent-governed or Theta-governed (Identification)

It must be observed that theta government in clause (ii) is probably not necessary (cf. 76–85). For the possibility of also eliminating the condition on antecedent government, cf.

85–104 and Haegeman (1994:654–660). I therefore consider clause (i) of Rizzi's ECP to be essential.

6. For government, I assume that a strict c-command relationship (instead of an m-command one) will usually be sufficient. The question of whether m-command is necessary in contemporary syntactic theory is discussed in Rizzi (1990a:111–112, note 4) and Roberts (1993, 1994); see also section 3.2.1, especially note 19. For barriers, it has to be pointed out that the original definition of Chomsky (1986a)—according to which all maximal projections that are not L-marked (with the exception of IP) are barriers, where L-marking is essentially reduced to theta government—is controversial (cf. Rizzi 1990a:112–113, note 6). According to Cinque (1990), an "XP is L-marked iff XP is directly selected by an $X° \neq [-V]$." Since functional categories are generally not specified for [±V], VP and IP are not barriers, a fact that is of certain importance for the case assignment mechanisms discussed in section 3.2 (cf. also Roberts 1993:21–22). For another definition that also predicts that neither IP nor VP are barriers, see Baker (1988:64).

7. That is, "a base generated position that could bear the relevant . . . government relation to Y" (Rizzi 1990a:7), where Y is the element that is supposed to be governed (here t_i under SpecAgrP). In practice, this means that in a configuration [α X° Y° β], movement from β to α is possible only if X and Y belong to the class of governors.

8. Cf. the summaries in Rizzi (1990a) and Bondre-Beil (1994). For similar phenomena in Bantu languages, cf. Carstens and Kinyalolo (1989). According to Chung and McCloskey (1987), Irish has a special complementizer (*aL*), which is only used in cases of *wh* movement. For West Flemish, see Haegeman (1992).

9. Note that with a *wh*-moved complement, *qui* is ungrammatical:

(i) *l' homme que je pense qui Jean connaît
    the man   that I think that J. knows   (Rizzi 1990a:56)

10. See Mensching (1996), but consider the extensive discussion in Jones (1993:332–351). For similar constructions in Portuguese, cf. Duarte (1989).

11. For example, a finiteness operator [+F], according to Platzack and Holmberg (1989), or obligatory movement of Agr° to C° (cf. Roberts 1993).

12. The examples in (18) are taken from Segre (1991:162) and the one in (19) from Schellert (1958). For V2 effects in Galician-Portuguese, see note 23 of chapter 6.

13. This contrasts with the noninverted word order in Cid, 321: *ca el plazo viene açerca*.

14. Consider the following explanation by Rohrbacher (1994:244): "In Italian infinitives, the verb first raises to TNS (and then further to AGRS); up to this point, AgrOP with the clitic on AGRO are not yet present. . . . When AgrOP with the clitic on AGRO is interpolated towards the end of the s-structure derivation . . . the verb is already higher up in the tree and to the left of the clitic which therefore encliticizes to it. In French infinitives, the verb does not raise to TNS, i.e. it stays in situ until AgrOP with the clitic on AGRO is interpolated. . . . When this happens, the verb presumably substitutes into AGRO (but does not move higher) and proclisis follows."

15. Incorporation presupposes that clitics are heads, so that clitic movement is taken to be head movement and clitics are assumed to be X° elements that do not subcategorize any complement. Clitics are thus different from nonclitic pronominals, which must be considered 2-bar elements. This point is sometimes understated in the literature. Consider, for example, the assumption mentioned in Roberts (1994) that clitics are base-generated as maximal projections and are changed into heads by movement.

16. The structure represented in (22) and the considerations concerning Italian and Spanish were preliminary results of a project in computational linguistics ("Verb Movement in the Romance Languages"), directed by Jürgen Rolshoven and supported by the

central public funding organization for academic research in Germany (DFG). For a complete account and the modified version we finally adopted (because of problems with parsing and generating incorporation structures, a fact that may be relevant for human language processing, too), see Rolshoven et al. (1998).

17. I use the more traditional term *accusative* instead of *objective* case. The distinction between accusative assigned by V° and oblique case assigned by P° (cf., e.g., Chomsky 1995:110) is not relevant here.

18. Without any additional stipulation, this accounts for the fact that in a language like English, in which the verb stays in V°, VS(O) structures of the Romance type are excluded.

19. Note that m-command may be necessary, however, for other structural relations, for example, theta relations. Tobias Schoofs (personal communication) objected to restricting case assignment to strict c-command because this will be problematic for case assignment to indirect objects, which are often assumed to be adjuncts to V'. One might argue, however, that the strict c-command condition holds only for structural case assignment. For the discussion of alternative approaches to indirect objects, see Chomsky (1995:62–64). For m-command, cf. also the following remark by Chomsky (213, note 9): "In Chomsky 1981a and other work, structural Case is unified under government, understood as m-command to include the Spec-head relation (a move that was not without problems); in the framework considered here, m-command plays no role." Concerning the minimalist program, we see in chapter 7 that government is not considered there.

20. Contreras (1991) argues in another way: he claims that I° in Spanish is a lexical and not a functional category. As a lexical category, I° L-marks VP, following Chomsky (1986a), so that VP is not a barrier, which will permit I° to govern and case-mark the subject inside VP. I do not think that it is desirable to assume that IP is a lexical category in Romance languages, and, anyway, it has to be noted that the status of VP as a barrier is controversial (see note 6 and McCloskey 1991:290–91, note 25).

21. It should be noted, however, that focalization is only one function of postverbal subjects. Another function, pointed out by Sasse, is based on the distinction between thetic and categorical expressions. Categorical expressions consist of two independent parts, namely, the predication base and the predication, in the sense that an assertion (the predication) is made about an individual person or object (the predication base). In contrast, thetic expressions consist of the assertion only: "The logical relations between the various parts of the communicated state of affairs remain unanalyzed" (Sasse 1987:554). According to Sasse (531–35), the VS(O) word order in Romance is an option to establish thetic expressions, which is accomplished by the fact that the subject is not located in the position that is typical for a predication base, that is, the preverbal position. Within our framework, this means that the subject remains in its base position. Moreover, as Cecilia Poletto (personal communication) pointed out, it must be observed that postverbal subjects can be of two types; for instance, in standard Italian they can be focalized or nonfocalized (in so-called presentational sentences). The two types should not be confused because they behave differently concerning the possibility to insert an object that yields a VOS structure. For the discussion of clause-final subjects, see section 5.3 and chapter 6, notes 8 and 51.

22. See section 4.3.2.1.

23. Chomsky (1981:209–22) also needs the coindexation of agreement with the subject for binding theory, cf. the summary in Haegeman (1994:216–22).

24. Her argument is based not only on the fact that Vata has no agreement morphemes (Koopman 1984:72–76) but also on the analysis of how binding theory works in this language (76–81).

25. A similar account is found in Platzack (1986:189), who claims that I°[+Tns] is a case assigner when the tense feature is supported by a lexical item.

26. The nonavailability of the option "T° assigns case under Spec-head agreement" is due to the common assumption that SpecTP is not an A-position. Note, however, that this does not necessarily exclude the option missing in (31) because a Spec-head configuration could be established by movement of T°. Theoretically, it should be possible that a T° incorporated into a head X°, that is, X°(+T°), is in Spec-head agreement with SpecXP. In sections 4.3.3.3 and 6.4.2, I argue that such a configuration can, in fact, be found in the Romance languages.

27. Such phenomena were noted before in linguistics; see, for example, Greenberg (1966a:138) and Sasse (1982,1987). As Sasse (1987) shows, the function of the different options of word order varies cross-linguistically. For instance, SV(O) word order yields a thetic expression in Classical Arabic, in contrast to several Modern Arabic dialects, which behave similarly to Romance languages (cf. note 21).

28. Consider the following Italian examples:

(i)   Ha telefonato Maria.
      has phoned   M.
      'M. phoned.'

(ii) *Ha Maria telefonato.

Given the linear ordering of constituents, Roberts (1993:24) assumes that SpecVP is located on the right-hand side of VP (cf. also Rizzi 1990a and Giorgi and Longobardi 1991). I return to the issue of the position of SpecVP in section 5.3. As for participles, I present a different account in chapter 5.

29. Movement of T°(+V°) to Agr°, which is supposed to apply in Italian, is not represented in this structure for reasons of simplification. This will not be a problem for the case-assigning mechanism because it can be assumed that SpecVP is still governed by T°'s trace. Roberts himself uses Baker's (1988) government transparency corollary (GTC): "An X° which has an item Y° incorporated into it governs everything which Y° governed in its original structural position" (Roberts 1993:27). The GTC ensures that SpecVP is governed by T°(+V°) even after it has moved to Agr°. Some further details concerning the incorporation structure of functional categories are discussed in 4.3.3.2.

30. Similar phenomena can be found in Italian dialects; cf. Brandi and Cordin (1989). See also, outside generative grammar, Tobler (1921:234), Wandruszka (1981), and Sasse (1982,1987), as well as the literature mentioned in the following note. It should be observed that in Modern French, postverbal subjects are limited to unaccusative verbs. It has to be assumed that "real" subjects are not allowed to remain in SpecVP, but I do not discuss this issue here; see also the discussion that follows in the text.

31. The French example (36a) is taken from Tobler (1921:233), who mentions some further data for the lack of agreement (also for gender). For Spanish, see Hanssen (1910: 142–43) and García de Diego (1951:274), among others. The Italian example (36b) comes from Durante (1981:124). Dardano points out that this has been a phenomenon of popular language throughout the history of Italian—learned texts, particularly strongly latinizing ones, avoid this construction (cf. Dardano 1963:111)—and that it can still be found in various modern Italian varieties (cf. Alisova 1967; Stefanini 1969; Brandi and Cordin 1989). For Portuguese, see Huber (1933:251), from which example (36e) was taken.

32. And also in Classical Spanish, as demonstrated by the following example (with a clause-final subject, however):

(i)   no causó   poca admiración a Sireno *las palabras del*   *pastor* *Syluano*
      not caused (SG) few admiration to S.   the words of-the shepherd S.
      'The words of the shepherd S. caused great admiration to S.' (Diana, 17r, 3; cf. Keniston 1937:488)

33. Some considerations about the fact that many languages try to avoid VS(O) structures with transitive verbs are offered in section 6.3.1.2.

34. I do not consider the "short movement" of the French verb here; see Rowlett (1998) for discussion.

35. For clitics, see 3.1.3, as well as Pollock (1989), Kayne (1991), and Dobrovie-Sorin (1994).

36. See also Strozer (1976:ch. 5) and Hernanz Carbó (1982:344).

37. That is, they can be used in finite clauses:

(i) Julia telefoneó *ella.*
    J.   phoned   she
    'J. phoned personally.'

38. "In the framework of LGB 6, in which Case requirements are a reflex of θ-role assignment, this follows naturally from the fact that ep's have no θ-role, that is, they are non-arguments . . . The fact that ep's are formally nominative (i.e. identical to nominative argument pronouns), forces us to assume that nominative is the unmarked form in Italian" (Burzio 1986:114).

39. It has to be noted that emphatic pronouns share properties not only with PRO. As Burzio (1986:111–14) observes, they can also occupy the position of DP traces. This might be achieved in the account given above by characterizing emphatic pronouns as [+anaphor, ±pronominal]. It is interesting that here, too, they usually occupy the trace that is left behind in SpecVP, in conformity to what has been proposed for infinitive clauses.

40. It is usually assumed that PRO may not appear in case positions. This is accounted for by the PRO theorem, which, strictly speaking, states that PRO must be ungoverned. The analysis just proposed presents the problem that PRO and its overt counterparts are located here in a governed position (SpecVP). However, in the light of the more recent assumption that (preverbal) subjects are not case-marked under government, but by means of Spec-head agreement, the PRO theorem cannot be maintained in this form.

41. "Recall that nominative Case is standardly checked in [Spec,IP] where I involves the features of tense and agreement (T, Agr). It is thus a realization of a Spec-head relation . . . It is natural, then, to take null Case to be a realization of the same relation where I lacks tense and agreement features: the minimal I checks null Case, and the minimal NP alone can bear it" (Chomsky 1995:120). See chapter 7 for further explanations of minimalist case theory. Note that for agreement, this point of view is compatible with our claim that PRO in Romance languages is located in SpecVP, in the light of the results of 3.2.3: SpecVP is a position that is only to a small extent related to agreement, up to the point that when subjects remain there, the verb can even lack overt agreement.

42. Other properties mentioned by Bottari (pp. 70–74) cannot be taken as evidence for the clausal status of the infinitive construction because they are valid also for VPs, such as the presence of a direct object (*il mangiare la carne* 'the to-eat the meat' and the presence of clitics (*il ricordarmene* 'the to-remind-me-of-it'). For our data, only the clausal type is relevant. There is another type analyzed by Bottari, which lacks clausal properties:

(i) il (*voler) chiacchierare delle due donne
    the to-want to-chat   of-the two woman

Here, the infinitive is purely nominal, as can be seen by the fact that the agent of *chiacchierare* shows up in the genitive. Hence, auxiliaries are not allowed, as shown in the example, and neither are adverbs or negation.

43. Cf. also Rizzi (1982). Part of Benucci's views are adapted from Acquaviva (1989), a publication that I could not obtain.

44. Benucci proposes, following Kayne (1990, fn. 26), that the preposition in (52b) is not in C° but in SpecCP. Although this proposal has some interesting consequences, I do not use it because it has no crucial bearing on our data.

45. This is not the case in all Romance languages. In Spanish, the preposition does not disappear in the same configuration:

(i)   Se jacta de que . . .
       R CL boasts of that
       'He boasts of the fact that . . .'

Chapter 4

1. The minimalist analysis of Ambar (1994) for Portuguese is not discussed here, because I treat it within the minimalist program in chapter 7.

2. I do not discuss older generative approaches like that of Postal (1974), where it was assumed that the subject of the infinitive construction is moved to the complement position of the main verb (see the discussion in Massam 1985:17–18). For Romance languages, cf. Bordelois (1974), Hernánz Carbó (1982), and Seelbach (1978) and the literature cited there. Note, however, that in the minimalist approach outlined in chapter 7 we return to the idea that the subject might leave the infinitive clause in ECM contexts.

3. Cf. also Massam (1985:34–35) and Haegeman (1994:169–171).

4. Cf. also Massam's (1985:35–36) criticism of the designation exceptional case marking: "Although we retain the title 'ECM'", it is considered to be a misnomer, in that there is nothing in the Case marking itself which is exceptional, although the effect of this Case marking might be so considered in that Case is assigned to a non-sister which does not receive a theta-role from this verb. . . . The second claim made here, a consequence of the non-exceptionality of Case marking in ECM structures, is that the cross-linguistic characterization of ECM . . . is not a unitary syntactic process, but rather an effect . . . achieved by general principles of grammar such as government and Case assignment . . . in conjunction with language-specific subcategorization or selection properties of certain verbs."

5. "A possible interpretation of this fact could be that an aspectual auxiliary must necessarily combine with Tense, and that perception verb complements lack an independent T projection" (Belletti 1990:139, note 74).

6. In the earlier phases of most Romance languages, this type was also possible after verbs of permission and causative verbs. In Modern French, *laisser* 'to let' still belongs to this group, and in Modern Italian *lasciare* does, although this is not generalized in all varieties (cf. Skytte 1983:49–75; Sandfeld 1943:165ff).

7. The movement of V° to Agr°, motivated on independent grounds (cf. Belletti 1990), yields the linear order V + DP$_{subj}$. This would presuppose that the main verb governs SpecVP. It would seem that transitive verbs block the government relationship. I do not discuss this point further, but a possible explanation could be that transitive verbs (but not intransitive ones) are potential governors in the sense of minimality. In this way, we could explain the ungrammaticality of sentences like the following:

(i)   ★Je vois manger [l' enfant une pomme].
       I see to-eat the child an apple

See note 9 for the issue of barriers. I briefly discuss the influence of transitive verbs on subject case assignment in 6.3.1.2. For alternative solutions, see Guasti (1989, 1996) and Mensching (1999).

8. Note that for this assumption we have to admit adjunction to the right, which is not generally accepted. I usually permit right-adjunction, at least to heads, in this book; see my ideas about participles in chapter 5. Concerning this option, cf., among others, Chomsky (1995:340) and Wilder and Cavar (1994). For further discussion see Siebert (1999).

9. If TP and/or VP are considered to be barriers, the barrier status can be unblocked by the incorporation of the infinitive into the main verb (following Belletti's suggestion); according to Baker (1988), the heads which are involved are nondistinct. Cf. also chapter 3, notes 6 and 20.

10. Other examples of this type can be found in Kayne (1977:222).

11. Obviously, a problem in this account is that, just as in the construction selected by perception verbs, no auxiliaries are allowed in this structure (cf. note 5). This might be solved by assuming that auxiliaries need both AgrP and TP to be licensed.

12. A simple solution would be to assume that the subcategorization properties of these verbs have changed (e.g., IP in the older stages, CP in the modern varieties). In any case, one cannot simply assume that this construction is the same as the one selected by perception verbs and causative verbs since there are clear syntactic differences. At this point I mention just two phenomena, described by E. Stimming (1915:119–20), by which we can distinguish the construction that follows declarative and epistemic predicates from the one selected by perception and causative verbs: (i) in the latter construction, the infinitive is never accompanied by a reflexive pronoun, even if it is the infinitive of a reflexive verb, and (ii) the accusative can be turned into a dative, particularly when the infinitive has a direct object. More criteria are mentioned in Schwendner (1923) and Skytte (1983).

13. Sauzet treats this construction together with finite constructions like the following, in which the subject of the subordinate clause appears before the complementizer *que*:

(i) Pensava   las vacas [que manjavan son sadol].
     (he) thought the cows   that (they) ate their feed
     'He thought that the cows had eaten their feed.'

Both for this case and for the infinitive construction with a preverbal subject he proposes the following parallel structures:

(ii) Pensava [$_{CP}$ [las vacas]$_i$ [$_{CP}$ [$_{IP}$ PRO$_i$ manjar son sadol]]].
(iii) Pensava [$_{CP}$ [las vacas]$_i$ [$_{CP}$ que [$_{IP}$ *pro$_i$* manjavan son sadol]]].

In both cases Sauzet regards the constituents *[las vacas]* as base-generated topic elements, which lack a theta role, according to Millner (1980), but are licensed because of their status as a predication base. Sauzet, following Chomsky (1986b:116), calls this a κ-role (from the Greek κατεγορει ν). Case marking is effected by the main verb (*pensava*).

14. Rizzi (1990a) discusses only the French examples. I have added the Italian ones from Rizzi (1982) because they can be explained with the same mechanism. The examples from Old Italian listed here, as well as the results later in this book (6.1.2.2), suggest that *wh*-extracted subjects should be analyzed as accusatives in Modern Italian, too, in contrast to what I show for languages like Spanish and Portuguese. Rizzi possibly interpreted *quante persone* in (24a) as a nominative (in the context of Aux-to-Comp-constructions; cf. 4.3.2.1).

15. A similar proposal can already be found in Massam (1985:79–87).

16. Unless we interpret it as AgrOP; cf. chapter 7.

17. For example, the assumption of [+F], a special feature for finiteness in C°, which triggers the movement of the verb to C° in German; cf. note 11 in chapter 3.

18. Concerning the assumption that Agr is a [+N] element with nominal φ-features, see Chomsky (1981:52) and also Rouveret (1980), Zubizarreta (1980), and Reuland (1983).

19. This follows from the null-subject parameter: "In null-subject languages verbal Agr is a set of specifications for number, person, and, optionally, Case. In non-null-subject languages Agr is not specified for Case" (Raposo 1987:93).

20. Raposo (1987:92–93) assumes a separate parameter for this (the Infl-parameter).

21. "The presence of [+Tense] in Infl is sufficient to allow nominative Case marking by Infl (or Agr in Infl)" (Raposo 1987:93).

22. Since $I°$ [+Agr] is a [+N] category, it projects an IP that is also a [+N] category ("it is nondistinct from NP") and will be case-marked.

23. Cf. Belletti and Rizzi (1981) on this point.

24. When these constructions appear without a lexical subject, we have to assume that the subject is PRO_{arb} or controlled PRO (depending on the construction type):

(i) [PRO_i Avoir plus d' instruction], je$_i$ pourrais parler mieux.
   to-have more of training I could to-speak better
   'If I had more training I could speak better.' (Vinet 1985:411)

(ii) [PRO_{arb} Pouvoir partir en vacances], ce serait merveilleux.
   can (INF) to-go on vacation-PL. this would-be marvelous
   'To go on vacation would be marvellous.' (p. 411)

According to the author, arbitrary PRO is confirmed by the fact that the construction is possible with meteorological verbs (p. 112).

25. For an explanation of the alternation between inflected and noninflected forms of the infinitive based on the notion of markedness (as a part of the theory of language acquisition), cf. Jones (1992:304–6), where it is assumed that the inflected forms, derived by reanalysis from the forms of the past subjunctive, were obligatory in an earlier phase. See section 6.5.1 and chapter 8 for further discussion.

26. For a discussion of the proposal that the subject is situated to the right of the VP, see section 5.3. Moreover, it has to be noted that lowering should rather be avoided in the framework adopted in this book.

27. Moreover, the authors state that such a construction is not possible in Modern French either. This was contradicted by my informants, who accepted examples like (43a).

28. A first generative account of the construction mentioned can be found in Rizzi (1981).

29. Cf. case theory following Vergnaud (1979) and Chomsky (1980). The most important rules, quoted from Rizzi, are these:

(i) Assign Nominative Case to NP in the context ___ TENSE.
(ii) Assign Objective Case to NP if governed by V_x.
(iii) Assign Oblique Case to NP if governed by P.

Cf. also section 3.2 in this book.

30. Another syntactic context for which Aux-to-Comp movement is assumed can be found in gerund constructions of the following type:

(i) [Avendo **Mario** accettato di aiutarci], potremo risolvere il problema.
   having M. accepted C° to-help-us (we) can (FUT) to-resolve the problem
   'M. having accepted to help us, we will be able to resolve the problem.'

Here, too, C° is empty, so it can serve as a landing site for the auxiliary. Cf. also the account given by Roberts (1993, 1994), summarized in section 4.3.3.2.

31. This is the marked option; the unmarked case is the construction with a prepositional C° or a Comp-less construction, that is, IP. Cf. Rizzi's comments about the stylistically marked character of this construction: "The *ritenere* construction would be theoretically characterized by the choice of a marked option. It would then be reasonable to expect that the construction be part of the productive knowledge of Italian only for those speakers who have abundant direct evidence of its existence (i.e. evidence requiring departure from the unmarked case), and that such speakers will restrict the marked option to the "grammar(s)" of the stylistic level(s) which the direct evidence belongs to (. . .), this being a consequence of a rather natural assumption on the non-generalizability of marked options beyond the domains which directly enforce their choice" (Rizzi 1982:92).

32. She also mentions infinitival subject clauses. Infinitive constructions introduced by determiners are not considered separately. For instance, the following two sentences are used to illustrate subject clauses:

(i) [El decirlo **tú**] me sorprende mucho.
     the to-say-it you me surprises much
     'The fact that you say it surprises me a lot.'

(ii) [Ir **yo** a la facultad mañana] va a ser imposible.
     to-go I to the faculty tomorrow will to to-be impossible
     'It will be impossible for me to go to the faculty tomorrow.'

33. This is not exactly true since lexical subjects are grammatical at least as a stylistically marked option; cf. 2.3, note 17.

34. Another approach was presented by Barbaud (1988), who considers the subject of the historical infinitive to be topicalized, bound with PRO, and thus caseless (cf. 3.3.2 and 4.1). Benucci (1992:40–41) pays some attention to this construction, and although he accepts Barbaud's theory for the contemporary varieties, he proposes that the older stages of Romance generally knew "personal infinitives"; thus these constructions were licensed similarly to Portuguese, although their inflectional endings were invisible (cf. in 4.3.1 the other accounts for [+Agr] in nonfinite I°). The assumption that one and the same construction has different explanations in different stages of a language does not seem very convincing. Neither Barbaud nor Benucci takes into account the semantic and syntactic properties of the construction.

35. "Une action considérée non pas dans son développement, mais aoristique, rapportée à un point déterminé, en général à celui de son apparition, et situé dans le passé" (Lombard 1936:9–10).

36. "Diversamente dall'infinito narrativo, l'infinito descrittivo non ha un riferimento temporale definito, potendosi riferire al passato . . . al presente . . . o avere un riferimento temporale puramente virtuale" (Salvi and Vanelli 1992:III, 55).

37. The inflectional ending of an infinitive (*-are,-ere*, etc.) can be interpreted as a default agreement marker for [–Agr]; cf. Rohrbacher (1994:269, fn. 3).

38. This goes in the same direction as Chomsky's (1992, 1995) assumptions within the minimalist program, according to which the nominative is assigned in the configuration $[_{AgrS} T \ Agr]$. Cf. chapter 7 for details.

Chapter 5

1. According to E. Stimming, this is a translation from Latin ("et aestimabat tam brevem per visionem non esse **quem**"), but note that the syntactic divergence shows that it is not a simple imitation of the Latin model.

2. These examples might be acceptable if the negation has scope over the subject ("not I"), but they are ungrammatical as cases of sentential negation.

3. Another characteristic of Old Spanish as well as of Galician-Portuguese is that CP is a possible position for clitics; see sections 5.2.2.2 and 5.2.3.2, especially example (35), which might be roughly analyzed as follows:

(i)   [$_{PP}$ en [$_{CP}$ vos [$_{AgrP}$ yo consejar]]]
       in   you (CL) I to-counsel
       'by my counseling you'

4. Aux-to-Comp is a case of I°-to-C° movement. I continue to use the term *Aux-to-Comp* because this movement is characteristic for auxiliaries; in other words, Aux is not used here as an old-fashioned name for I°.

5. Clitic movement is not relevant here and is not taken into account.

6. For another example, see chapter 2, example (11a).

7. Consider the following examples:

(i)   esser*gli* ciò avvenuto
       to-be-CL that happened
       'this to have happened to him' (Varchi, book 8, ch. 25, p. 153; cf Schwendener 1923:47)

(ii)   non esser*vi*   alcuna scelleratezza in loro
       not to-be-A CL any   criminality   in them
       'not to be any criminality in them' (Mie prigioni, Cap. LVI; cf. Schwendener 1923:51)

8. Analytic passive forms and structures of the type modal auxiliary + infinitive are analyzed in a similar fashion by Baker (1988). It is then to be expected that we will find analogous structures with modal auxiliaries in earlier stages of Italian. This is, in fact, the case:

(i)   E   ciascuno   affermava [*dovere   essere   stata* la paura d' Anichino
       and everybody stated   must (INF) be (INF) been the fear   of A
       grandissima].
       very-great
       'And everybody affirmed that A.'s fear must have been very great' (Bocc. Dec., VII, 8, p. 387)

(ii)   Egli giudicava [dovere   essere   gli uomini . . . meno facili a gittare
       he judged   must (INF) be (INF) the men   less easy to throw-away
       la vita.
       the life
       'he judged that for men it must be less easy to throw away their lives' (Leop., Stor. gen. um. 12; quoted by Schwendener 1923:54)

On the other hand, nonmodal, and nonpassive complex verbs generally also show Aux-to-Comp movement in the earlier stages of Italian:

(iii) senza   avere   ella in cosa alcuna peccato
       without to-have she in thing any   sinned
       'without her having sinned in anything' (Bocc. Dec., VII, 5, p. 379)

9. I assume with Baker (1988) that here the participle *venuti* is incorporated into T°. Consider also the following example:

(i)   che io rammenti [*essere stato* [a 10 di agosto di quell'anno 1792 [**il re**
     that I remind   to-be   been on 10 of August of that year 1792 the king
     assalito nella reggia]]]
     assaulted in-the palace
     'that I remind you of the fact that the king was assaulted in the palace on August
     10th of that year, 1792' (Colletta, III, 1, p. 136; cf. Schwendener 1923:61)

Here the participle *assalito* remains inside the VP below the subject. For the structure represented in (17), rightward adjunction can be avoided either by assuming that the participle is adjoined to AgrO° (or to some other functional head, see Cinque 1999:44–49) or by claiming that the auxiliary is base-generated somewhere inside the VP.

    10. One might also consider the following argument: according to Rizzi (1982:91) volitional verbs in Modern Italian select IP, not CP, so that Aux-to-Comp is impossible and, as a consequence, lexical subjects are ungrammatical. However, things are different in Old Italian:

(i)   E non era niuno . . . che non *bramasse* [a lui venire **ogni male**].
     and not was no-one who not wished   to him to-come every evil
     'And there was no one who did not wish that all evil should fall upon him.'
     (Sacch. Nov., 117; cf. Schwendener 1923:77)

A possible conclusion would be that the construction was possible because in Old Italian Aux-to-Comp movement was not necessary for licensing the overt subject. But this would be a valid argument only if these verbs selected IP in Old Italian, too. This does not seem to be the case, however: In Old Italian, infinitive clauses that depend on volitional verbs could be introduced by prepositions that must be considered complementizers in our framework (see Dardano 1963:99–107).
    11. For the IP status of subject clauses, cf. also Raposo (1987:95).
    12. I do not discuss Catalan since I have already done so in Mensching (1999). Both Old and Modern Catalan behave almost exactly like Old and Modern Spanish, respectively.
    13. In addition to (26b) the following word order is also possible:

(i)   El hecho de [*no* volver **Juan** *más* a casa es algo que me preocupa].

This order could be explained by assuming Aux-to-Comp, but we must exclude this on the basis of the preceding arguments. *Más* is an adverb and thus can also be generated outside of NegP. In this case SpecNegP is filled by a coindexed empty operator, according to Haegeman (1995). It might even be supposed that this is the base position of *más* (for an interpretation of this kind of element, cf. Belletti 1990:36–39, 59 and Cinque 1999). The word order in (i) is identical to one of the options for adverbs and adverbial expressions, which can be observed in the following examples:

(ii)   ?[De estar **Juan** *verdaderamente* en casa], él nos habría salvado. (cf. 25b)

(iii)   por [ser **el teatro** *en muchas ocasiones* una finanza]
      for to-be the theatre on many occasions a finance
      'since the theatre is, on many occasions, a commercial matter' (Lorca 819, cf. Skydsgaard 1977:804).

    14. Consider the following further examples that illustrate the strict postverbal position after an auxiliary:

(i)   al [*estar* **Juan** *haciendo* la tesis]
     at to-be J. making the thesis
     'on J.'s writing his thesis' (Fernández Lagunilla 1987:128)

(ii)   antes de [*haber* **yo** *cumplido* los seis años]
        before   to-have I completed the six years
        'before I became six years old' (Unamuno, 9; cf. Maurer 1968:74)

(iii)   por [*haber* **yo** *conocido* en aquel estudio a . . .   Don Antonio de Trueba]
        for   to-have I known   in that studio ACC PART Don A.   de T.
        'because in that studio I got to know Don A. de T.' (Unamuno, 125; cf. Maurer
        1968:74)

15. The facts about clitic positions in infinitive clauses are identical to those in Old
Spanish finite constructions, as described by Gessner (1893).

16. This is the so-called Wackernagel position, which is not restricted to Romance
languages. Cf., for example, Lenerz (1984:87) for German.

17. This suggestion is based on the observation made in various studies that this word
order is characteristic of subordinate clauses (see, e.g., Gessner 1893; Menéndez Pidal
1964). For instance:

(i)   por que *las* *vos* dexastes
        because them you left
        'because you left them' (Cid, 3368)

(ii)   assi como *uos*   *lo nos* contamos
        so   like you (DAT.) it we told
        'just like we told it to you' (Gen. Est., 218r)

(iii)   Respusol   heliab que*lo* non farie.
        answered-him H.   that-it not (he) would-do
        'H. answered him that he would not do it.' (Gen. Est., 281v)

In these cases, it may be argued that the clitic is incorporated into $C°$. The contracted
forms like *quelo*, from *que* + *lo* in (iii), might be adduced in support of such an analysis.
The analysis of the finite constructions shows that this position of the clitic usually occurs
either when $C°$ is overt or when SpecCP is filled with a *wh*-marked element. (Note that
this might mean, with respect to the infinitive constructions, that all the prepositions
found in the examples are situated inside the CP.) The properties of Old Spanish clitics
have been thoroughly analyzed by Fontana (1993). Since he regards Old Spanish clitics as
maximal projections, he assumes for cases like ours that the clitics are left-adjoined to
AgrP. This, too, would conform to my assumption that the word order facts about clitics
are not due to verb movement or subject placement. Regularities of this kind seem to be
quite common in Old Romance languages (cf. MidF *de le non croire*, Cent N.N. 240;
quoted in Pearce 1990:284).

18. The assumption of a possible incorporation into $Neg°$ corresponds to the fact that
the proclitic position is favored by the presence of a negative marker. Consider the observation of Gessner (1893:37), who stated that negation that accompanies the finite verb
almost always attracts the clitic. Here, too, we might adduce contracted forms like *nol*,
from *non* + *le*, in support of such an analysis.

19. Cf. the following example:

(i)   De que vió   [no *le* aprovechar nada   su remedio], dijo: ". . ."
        when (he) saw not him to-be-of-use nothing his remedy (he) said
        'When he saw that nothing was of any use at all for him he said: ". . ."' (Laz.
        1554, 20r, 13–14)

20. Cf. also Valdés, Dial., 234–35: "Se deve usar esta composición de la manera que
digo, y no andar por las ramas como algunos, que por no hablar como los otros dizen por
ponerlos, los poner, y por *traerlas, las traer*, etc. [One must use this construction in the

way that I say, and keep to the point, unlike some people, who, in order not to speak like the others, say instead of *ponerlos, los poner*, and for *traerlas, las traer*, etc.]"

21. An early example of the word order favored today is the following one from the sixteenth century:

(i) Alguna   tiene   [no *estar fundado* **el monesterio** en mucha perfeción].
    Some (F) claims not to-be founded the monastery   on much   perfection
    'Some women claim that the monastery is not founded on great perfection.' (Santa Teresa, Vida, ch. V, p. 141)

22. Cf. my discussion of her article in the course of the minimalist analysis in section 7.2.

23. Nevertheless, Raposo and Uriagereka (1990:534) claim that *parecer* is followed by an Aux-to-Comp construction, assuming that *parecer* subcategorizes for CP in this case (just like a finite subordinate clause). For the CP status of this construction, see also the discussion in 6.3.1.3.

24. At best, some speakers still accept the construction with the participle remaining inside VP as shown in (i); in addition, the auxiliary can move up to Agr° as in (ii):

(i) ?? O presidente afirmou [*não mais* terem **estas pessoas** vivido na cidade].
(ii) ?? O presidente afirmou [*não* terem *mais* **estas pessoas** vivido na cidade].

The auxiliary itself can either be supposed to be base-generated in T° or, at least, to have obligatory movement to T°.

25. Further evidence for the assumption that the subject may remain in situ is provided by passive structures; for example, (i) below shows a word order that is parallel to the earlier stages of Italian and can be assigned the structure in (ii). In contrast, the example in (iii) shows the participle (*sido*) remaining inside VP, as illustrated in (iv):

(i)   Fazem   supor [*ter*   sido **a Serra** ... coberta de arvoredo].
      (they) make suppose to-have been the Sierra   covered by bushes
      'They make us think that the Sierra had once been covered by bushes.' (Revista, IV, 96, cf. Sten 1952:112)

(ii) [$_{CP}$ [$_{AgrP}$ [$_{TP}$ [$_{T°}$ ter sido$_i$] [$_{VP}$ a Serra t_i coberta de arvoredo]]]].

(iii) Dir- se- ia   [*haverem* **estas linhas** *sido ecritas* propositadamente ...].
      say R.CL. would to-have-3PL. these lines   been written deliberately
      'One would say that these lines have been written ...' (Costa, Solar, 28; cf. Sten 1952:110)

(iv) [$_{CP}$ [$_{AgrP}$ [$_{TP}$ [$_{T°}$ haverem [$_{VP}$ estas linhas sido escritas ...]]]]].

26. The fact that this is a passive sentence is irrelevant here.

27. Here the head of the infinitival NegP is empty.

28. Of course, the speakers accept the following variant: "um pɔ 'ɛs:iri 'kju ['ɟi:ri 'jiu a 'k:jeza."

29. In contrast, the following structure is ungrammatical since in Sardinian, too, infinitives move up to Agr°: "*Babbu meu m'at nadu [de *ispissu* andare a su dottore]."

30. For further discussion, also for case assignment, see chapter 6, notes 8 and 51.

31. Cinque (1999:111) assumes that the sentence-final position coincides with SpecVP generated to the left of the VP (Kayne 1994; Ordóñez 1994). See note 8 in chapter 6 for further discussion.

Chapter 6

1. When verbs of perception are used in a figurative sense, describing a mental activity (e.g., Italian *vedere* meaning 'to recognize, to understand'), they behave like epistemic verbs and select another construction, which is discussed below. Consider the following example:

(i)   Videno, [**Joannni** *essere* stato principio di tutti questi mali].   OI
    (they) see J.   to-be been beginning of all these evils
    'They recognize that J. was the beginning of all this evil.' (Sercambi, Nov., 4; cf.
    Schwendener 1923:76)

Here, the auxiliary indicates that the infinitive clause contains a TP. In the example, the subject is presumably accusative (see 6.1.2.1 for discussion), but it could also bear the nominative case placed postverbally (cf. Skytte 1983 for Modern Italian). See also E. Stimming (1915) for the parallel phenomenon in French A.c.I. constructions.

2. Optional movement of the infinitive to Agr° cannot be excluded, according to the results of the last chapter, but this is not relevant for the assumptions made here because of the GTC introduced in note 29 of chapter 3. For further discussion, see section 6.2.1.

3. Rizzi and Roberts point this out for the Aux-to-Comp movement in Portuguese infinitive constructions postulated by Raposo (1987; see 4.3.2.2), but there is also a reference to Rizzi's (1982) Italian examples (see 4.3.2.1). In 5.2.3.1, I argue against the Aux-to-Comp analysis of Portuguese, although I demonstrate below that the existence of C° with [+Agr] in these constructions has to be maintained on independent grounds (cf. 6.3.1.3).

4. However, this may be an influence of Sicilian (see 6.5) because the author was born in Messina.

5. Roberts assumes that the subject is on the right-hand side of the VP. This is not relevant here because the VP-final position of the infinitival subject is excluded, too, in present-day Italian. See note 2 about the fact that T° can govern the base-generated subject even after movement to Agr°.

6. This assumption will make the correct predictions if we follow Roberts (1993:21–22) in assuming that Agr° cannot govern SpecVP. This would predict that Aux-to-Comp is the only possibility of licensing the subject. In Roberts's system, which is based on Cinque's (1990) definition of L-marking (see chapter 3, note 6, and Roberts 1993:21), no barrier is supposed to intervene between Agr° and SpecVP. However, government is suppressed by the minimality condition.

7. Cf. Rizzi's remarks about to the relevance of stylistic markedness in the theory of grammar (1982:ch. 5, note 31). For the concept of markedness in generative grammar and its relationship to language change, see Lenerz (1984). For another Aux-to-Comp construction that is also classified as literary according to Rizzi (1982:84–85), see section 4.3.2.1, example (50b). This example, too, has clear parallels in English and German.

8. Probably this is not the case either. Roberts assumes that SpecVP is at the right-hand side of VP in the Romance languages (cf. 5.3). In the older stages of the language, in addition to the linear ordering $V° + DP_{obj} + DP_{subj}$, we can also find the word order $V° + DP_{subj} + DP_{obj}$ (cf. Segre 1991:173). For example:

(i)   Mandò il re li soi messi.
    sent   the king the his messengers (Sette Savi, 21; cf. Segre 1991:173)

This word order is possible in Spanish and in Romanian even today. Probably it should be assumed, in contrast to Roberts, that in Old Italian (as well as in Spanish and Romanian until the present) T° could assign the nominative case under government but that present-day Italian does not allow it. Such an assumption would be much more plausible than the hypothesis of a change in the position of SpecVP. The postverbal subjects mentioned by Roberts would then be extraposed subjects (cf. 5.3). The assumption I have just made would lead to a further generalization about case-assigning mechanisms. As an alternative we might follow Cinque (1999:111–12), according to whom the sentence-final position coincides with SpecVP, all higher positions involving the specifier of a functional projection. Concerning the ungrammaticality of (i) in present-day Italian, Cinque assumes that today the subject cannot remain in SpecVP unless it bears narrow (contrastive) focus. Note, however, that this point of view presents the same problem as Robert's account— that is, that we could not reduce the diachronic difference to a change in the nominative case assignment.

9. Note, however, that this explanation was chiefly intended for Portuguese; see note 3.

10. Probably we have to assume instead that the selection is driven by semantic properties. This is suggested by the fact that the verbs that select this feature belong to certain semantically, relatively fixed verb classes, which subcategorize for this feature in numerous languages (see Rizzi 1990a). This also explains the occurrence of Aux-to-Comp in infinitive constructions as complements to nouns that are semantically related to declarative and epistemic verbs; cf. Skytte (1983:406) and Renzi and Salvi (1991:546–47), from whom the following example was taken:

(i) *l' asserzione recisa* [essere **la donna gentile** la filosofia aristotelica . . .]
    the assertion definite to-be the D.   G.   the philosophy Aristotelian
    'the definite assertion that the donna gentile represents Aritotelian philosophy . . .'
    (Garin Storia, 189).

Further evidence for such an assumption is the behavior of perception verbs mentioned in note 1, which select [+Agr] or not, depending on their exact meaning.

11. However, this assumption holds for empty D°.

12. The verb *accorgersi* already belonged to Benucci's (1992) *vantarsi* class (cf. section 3.3.3 here) in Old Italian, as the following examples show:

(i) S' accorsero [*d'* una dilettevol bellezza].
    R CL (they) got-aware of a delightful beauty
    (Bocc. Dec., III, Introd., p. 150)

(ii) Lo scolare cattivello . . . accorgendosi [*d'* esser beffato . . .]
    the teacher bad   getting-aware-R CL of to-be cheated
    (Bocc. Dec., VIII, 7, p. 436)

(iii) questi accorto non se *ne* fosse [che egli fosse stato da lui veduto]
    he aware not R CL A CL was that he was been by him sold
    (Bocc. Dec., I, 4, p. 133)

13. With the exception of the double accusative construction, for example, in Middle French (see 4.3.1.4), where the accusative case is assigned to one complement structurally and to the other one lexically.

14. For further discussion, cf. Haegeman (1994:57, fn. 14, and 183, fn. 13) and the literature mentioned there.

15. The mechanism proposed by Rizzi (1990a:62–71), according to which subjects can directly be extracted from VP, without using SpecIP as an intermediate landing site, is not available in contemporary Italian because the subject of an infinitive cannot receive case inside of SpecVP, according to the results of section 6.1.1.3.

16. The issue of whether infinitival Agr° can assign nominative case under Spec-head agreement is discussed in 6.2.2.

17. The infinitival subject can appear preverbally after causative verbs:

(i) Juan hizo [a **Pedro** abrir la puerta].
    J.   made ACC PART P.   to-open the door
    'J. made P. open the door.'

This word order is grammatical in Spain and in most of the Latin American varieties, with the exception of Rioplatense, according to Treviño (1992:310, fn. 2).

18. For the occurrence of the subject of the infinitive clause as an object clitic in the main clause, see note 47.

19. For indefinite DPs, which are still allowed in this position, see Contreras (1991).

20. Piera (1987:151–53) mentions similar cases in another context.

21. (i) de/ al trabajar **yo**   (ii) $\star$de/$\star$al **yo** trabajar
    $C°/C°$ to-work I
    'in case of / on my working'

22. For structures with postverbal subjects, this has been shown in section 5.2.3.1. That verb movement to $Agr°$ is not obligatory when the subject is preverbal either, is demonstrated by the fact that (ii) is accepted by many speakers in addition to (i):

(i) a circunstancia [de **estas pessoas** *não viverem*   *mais* na   cidade]
    the circumstance of these persons not to-live-3PL more in-the city
    'the fact that these persons do not live anymore in the city'

(ii) a circunstancia [de **estas pessoas** *não mais viverem* na cidade]

23. Schellert (1958:41–47) examined word order in Galician-Portuguese. In his corpus, the linear order $XP + V + DP_{subj}$, where XP is a direct or a prepositional object, can be seen in about 95.5 percent of the cases (cf. the table in 1958:44); when a predicate nominal appears sentence-initially, it is even 100 percent. In the sixteenth century the situation still seems to be similar (1958:53–85). In Modern Portuguese—Schellert examines the written language of the nineteenth and twentieth centuries—no such correlation could be detected. For a generative approach to V2 phenomena in Galician-Portuguese, see Ribeiro (1993).

24. In Classical Portuguese, however, postverbal subjects in infinitive constructions were extremely frequent. In Mensching (1998), I interpret this as an influence of Spanish, as part of a general tendency of the literary texts produced in that epoch.

25. For Portuguese, cf. Silva Dias (1954:98), who considers the use of the noninflected forms as "afeitação de arcaísmo," or, in the popular poetry, caused by metrical reasons.

26. The subject in (49b) is an emphatic pronoun, but as (49a) shows, this is not the reason for the lack of the inflectional endings.

27. The fact that the infinitive is usually inflected even when the case is assigned by $T°$ has a parallel in finite structures, with the exception of the cases mentioned in section 3.2.3. Roberts notes that this is in clear contrast to languages like Welsh, where subjects always receive the nominative by governing $T°$ and there is no agreement between the subject and the verb (except with pronouns). According to Roberts, the difference is that in Welsh $Agr°$ is never relevant for nominative assignment, whereas in the Romance languages $Agr°$ can assign the nominative under Spec-head agreement: "and so it is not entirely divorced from the assignment of Nominative. To capture the fact that postverbal subjects . . . always agree, we provisionally stipulate a cosuperscripting relation between $Agr°$ and $T°$" (Roberts 1993:25).

28. The fact that these properties were not observed in the present varieties of Portuguese may be due to the normative influence, which was absent for Galician until

relatively recently. For further discussion from a historical point of view, as well as with respect to the origin of the inflected infinitive, see 6.5.1, especially note 55.

29. See, among others, note 9 in this chapter.

30. Schellert observes that the VS(O) word order in finite clauses was already relatively rare in Galician-Portuguese when the verb was transitive. He also observes (1958: 93 ff.) a general aversion of spoken nineteenth- and twentieth-century Portuguese against VS structures, which are almost exclusively found with intransitive verbs. Exceptions are declarative verbs. Cf. also his final diachronic comparison, which is quite interesting. In all, Schellert notes a regression of VS word order from about 40 percent in the Middle Ages to about 23 percent in nineteenth- and twentieth-century texts.

31. Here, c-command would instead be i-command (cf. Sportiche 1988a), according to which α c-commands β iff α does not dominate β, and the first X' projection dominating α dominates β (see also Roberts 1993:19).

32. Cf. her considerations about Italian, which in contrast to Romanian does not allow this word order: "The impossibility of this word order may be due to a locality condition on the assignment of Objective Case, which could be blocked by an intervening subject. . . . In those configurations in which Objective Case is not assigned, in particular in passives (see also active constructions with intransitives and unaccusatives) nothing would block a structure where the subject NP is under [Spec, VP] and the NP-trace under [NP, VP]."

33. G. Müller assumes that functional heads allow this but lexical heads do not.

34. The suppression of Spec-head agreement does not seem to occur in the case of *wh* movement. The fact that the coindexation of [+Agr] with the trace of a *wh*-marked subject is able to change the properties of this feature or the behavior of C° is discussed here with respect to Italian; see section 6.1.

35. Cf. Raposo (1988), but with another argument.

36. "The sequence of an overt complementizer followed by a trace is ungrammatical." Cf. also Haegeman (1994:399). As I point out in 3.1.2, this property can be explained through the ECP.

37. Portuguese allows *wh* extraction in structures like (54), as is illustrated by the following example:

(i)   **que**$_i$ ele se   propunha demonstrar [t_i haverem   sido . . . roubados t_i . . .]
      which he R.CL. endeavours to-demonstrate to-have-3PL been   stolen
      'of which he endeavours to demonstrate that they were . . . stolen . . .' (Revista, III, 75; cf. Sten 1952:110)

Here it is not to be assumed, however, that this is an effect of [+Agr] in C° because factive and volitional verbs allow extraction also (see the examples in Raposo 1988:363). For the analysis, see the interpretation of Spanish in 6.2.2.2.

38. See note 55 for some further discussion.

39. The use of *tu/ti* instead of the usual Brazilian form *você* is characteristic for Porto Alegre; cf. Lemos Monteiro (1994:158–59).

40. In fact, in another configuration, we must consider *para* to be a complementizer. Verbs meaning 'to ask (for something)', both in contemporary European and Brazilian Portuguese, can select an infinitive clause introduced by *para* (cf. Maurer 1968:56). This phenomenon is of popular origin but has been accepted in other registers. Consider example (3f) in chapter 5 and the following:

(i)   E o tenente   disse [*para* **nós** não sairmos   mais de   casa].
      and the lieutenant said   for   we not to-go-out more from home
      'And the lieutenant said that we should not leave home anymore.' (M.J. Dupré, *Éramos seis*, 114; quoted by Maurer 1968:146)

Since the preposition is missing when the infinitive construction is substituted by a DP, *para* should be considered to be a C° here, according to 3.3.3. Note, however, that in this construction the subject is in the nominative.

41. However, the subject can surface as an object clitic in the main clause. See note 47 for a brief discussion.

42. For those constructions that are complements of D°, it has to be said that D° should be assumed to block case assignment from outside the infinitive clause.

43. Translated from the Latin *credebant Mahomen . . . superesse,* according to E. Stimming (1915:114). Note that the subject is not extracted in the original.

44. In the earlier stages of Italian, this configuration is excluded because the subject receives the nominative in SpecVP and it cannot be coindexed with a *pro* in the accusative. In the case of Aux-to-Comp, the auxiliary in C°[+Agr] blocks ECM by minimality.

45. According to Brunot (III, 481), in the seventeenth century they were only possible in fixed expressions, that is, fossilized.

46. As predicted by the preceding assumptions, the earlier stages of French also permitted *wh* extraction with main verbs that are not declarative or epistemic, that is, without [+Agr] in the infinitival C°, as in the following Middle and Classical French examples with unaccusative verbs:

(i) Ordonnez ce **qu**$_i$**'** il vous   plaist [en t_i estre fait t_i].
     order   that which it you (DAT) pleased A CL to-be done
     'Order what you would like to be done.' (Melin. III, 204, cf. E. Stimming
     1915:166)

(ii) son fils **qu**$_i$**'** il me souvient [[t_i avoir dit [PRO$_i$ . . . estre parti]]
     his son which it me reminds   to-have said   to-be left
     'his son, of whom I remember that he had said that he had left' (Montchr., II, 227,
     cf. E. Stimming 1915:166)

47. The Ibero-Romance languages, which have never licensed ECM in CPs, allowed a parallel construction of (70) and (71) in their earlier stages. Consider the following examples from Old Spanish, Classical Spanish, and Classical Portuguese, respectively:

(i) Lo peor es . . . que **lo**$_i$ creen   [t_i ser asy].
     the worst is   that it (CL) (they) believe to-be so
     'The worst is . . . that they believe it to be so.' (Corb., 238.20; cf. González Muela
     1954:96)

(ii) **Le**$_i$ conoci [ser t_i extranjero].
     him (CL) (I) knew to-be   foreigner
     'I knew him to be a foreigner.' (Laz., 1554, 34v)

(iii) Conheci-**me**$_i$ não [t_i ter   conhecimento].
      (I) knew me (CL) not   to-have knowledge
      'I knew that I had no knowledge.' (Camões, Canç., 7, II, p. 320; cf. Otto 1991:
      378)

If clitics receive case in their X° adjunct positions, we might suppose that they do not incorporate into the head that bears the nominative feature (T°). In any case, as I argue in 5.2.2.2, clitics could incorporate into C° in earlier stages of Spanish and Portuguese, so it can be assumed that this unblocks C°'s opacity for ECM.

48. Lerch sees the origin of the most frequently attested to construction type, the adverbial infinitive clause introduced by final *pour,* in a kind of postposed explanation, in which the infinitive was placed after the sequence preposition + (pro)noun, whereas he explains the postverbal subject by assuming the inverse process, that a (pro)noun was added to *pour* + infinitive:

(i)   Donnez-moi un verre pour **moi** boire.
       give   me a glass for   me to-drink
       = 'Give me a glass for me, to drink.'

(ii)   quelque invention pour se   pouvoir entretenir **tous deux**
       some   invention for R CL can (INF) to-enjoy all two
       = 'some invention in order to enjoy themselves, both of them'

I include Lerch's explanations for the sake of completeness and to remind the reader of the phenomenon at issue. The explanation itself has to be rejected, of course. The interpretation of *pour moi boire* as deriving from something such as 'for me, namely for drinking' presupposes the grammaticalization of an expression like *pour moi, pour boire*, which is not attested to at all. In addition, the interpretation of the postverbal subject as an explanatory addition to the infinitive clause does not account for the accusative.

49. Note that there might still be a connection with ECM, the Latin A.c.I. construction, along the lines of Lewent (1925). Lewent's account presupposes that in some stage of the development from Latin to French a lexical C° would have been transparent for government. This should not be excluded by universal grammar because the properties of C° with respect to minimality are language-specific lexical properties.

50. Lerch (1929:158–59) makes a strict distinction between an earlier learned construction, which is archaic in Modern French, and a popular one. Lerch claims that a characteristic property of the learned variant is the use of the passive infinitive. It has to be observed, however, that this is irrelevant since the case-assigning properties are identical in both constructions. I assume that the lack of examples for passives in popular usage is only due to the fact that the passive is not very frequent in colloquial language. A speaker from Nancy whom I consulted did not exclude a sentence like the following:

(i)   ? Je t'   écris tout ça [pour **toi** être mis au courant].
       I you write all this for   you to-be put on current
       'I write all this to you in order for you to be kept informed of developments.'

51. It is probable that French does not allow nominative assignment by T° under government in finite constructions (against the assumptions made by Roberts 1993). This means that [+Tns] cannot license the subject in SpecVP. For this assumption, see my ideas about Modern Italian in note 8, keeping in mind that Modern French usually does not permit the word order $V° + DP_{subj} + DP_{obj}$, just like Modern Italian.

52. As an alternative to the interpretation given here, we could consider the existence of phonetically empty complementizers roughly corresponding to the overt complementizers *si* 'if' for modern French and *après que* 'after' in Middle French. We could then assume that these C° elements have a lexical [+Tns] feature that assigns nominative case under government. The latter assumption is not desirable, however, if we want to maintain the assumption made in note 51.

53. In addition, the results of this chapter provide a further argument against Dobrovie-Sorin's (1994) assumption that SpecAgrP is an A'-position in contemporary Romanian (cf. 4.3.3.1). I show that for the Old Romance varieties discussed, the A'-property of SpecAgrP yields the licensing of preverbal subjects in infinitive clauses. This is, however, not the case in Romanian.

54. This cannot be proved here because of the relatively small number of available examples. The word order in (81b) can be interpreted as incorporation of the participle in T°, which is similar to other languages, with the subject remaining in its base position (see also the situation of Sardinian that I am going to discuss). However, we could also consider that the subject is clause-final here. The fact that Old Neapolitan supported clause-final subjects in infinitive constructions can be observed in chapter 2, example (37c).

55. We could now even assume that the inflected infinitive of Portuguese and Galician has the same origin. Possibly, in Galician-Portuguese only T° was a valid case assigner in infinitive clauses, which is similar to most of the Romance languages (see my remarks at the end of section 6.3.1.3). However, the subject could move to SpecAgrP through A'-movement. This might have led, in the course of time, to a reanalysis of lexical agreement as functional agreement (now generated under Agr°). This, in turn, might have led to the grammaticalization of infinitival SpecAgrP as a case position and of Agr° as a nominative assigner.

Chapter 7

1. Chomsky (1995:174) reminds us that AgrSP and AgrOP—as, in general, all categorial labels—are only mnemotechnical terms. Both categories are of the same type, and they are only distinguished by their features: AgrSP possesses features for checking the subject, whereas the features of AgrOP serve to check objects. The upper agreement phrase (AgrSP) is not necessarily the position of the subject. It should be noted that Chomsky (1995:ch 4) suggests to eliminate agreement categories as projections without a semantic content. Here I assume a version of the minimalist program in which both AgrSP and AgrOP are present.

2. Given two trees, K and K', GT takes K, adds Ø, and then substitutes Ø by K', giving rise to a new tree K*. This is a recursive operation. In addition to the description provided by Chomsky (1992, 1995), see, among others, Kim et al. (1995:3).

3. As we see later in this chapter, this distinction between concrete and abstract material is crucial. Abstract material is deleted during the derivation. For inflection, this means that it is not sufficient to postulate the base generation of inflectional morphemes on the corresponding heads.

4. For the labels, I partially follow my own convention. See note 18.

5. [ϕD], [ϕV] represent feature complexes, such as [third person, SG, M].

6. In two converging derivations D_1 and D_2, the only difference between which is the fact that movement of an element α has been applied on LF (after spell-out) in D_1 and visibly (before spell-out) in D_2, D_1 is preferred to D_2.

7. This principle (cf. Lasnik 1993; Wilder and Cavar 1994) replaces the original principle, *greed*, formulated in Chomsky (1992).

8. Ambar (1994:18) argues that the assumption of this feature (already postulated by Raposo 1987) is confirmed by the following contrast, which she holds to be caused by the absence of the tense feature in constructions selected by volitional verbs:

(i)   Penso teres comprado ontem o livro.
(ii)   ★Quero comprar o livro ontem.

It has to be observed that the examples are not parallel (*teres comprado/comprar*); in addition it has to be noted that (i) is also possible with factive verbs like *lamentar*, without the word order facts typically found after declarative and epistemic verbs.

9. "Let us make the conjecture that through this relation the V-feature of AgrS is strong, while its N-feature becomes weak: Tense in Comp, being a +V (cf. Kayne 1982), will have no effects on +N elements" (Ambar 1994:19).

10. These grammaticality facts were not confirmed by the speakers I consulted in the course of Mensching (1997). For most speakers, all of these examples are ungrammatical, whereas some speakers accepted some examples with a question mark, there being no consensus that would confirm Ambar's judgments.

11. Kim et al (1995:2) mention the following restrictions from the earlier generative frameworks that are not supported by the minimalist program: (among others) general

restrictions that refer to indices, theta roles, feature percolation, case transmission, government, and binding.

12. In addition, [+Tns] is not a legitimate feature in the minimalist program. [Tns] is either strong or weak; in our case it should be weak because a strong [Tns] would trigger movement of the verb to C°.

13. For the Romance languages, Chomsky (1995) follows Pollock (1989) in assuming that the verb is usually located in T°. See chapters 3 and 5 for discussion.

14. This depends on whether auxiliaries are base-generated in V° or in T°. We do not discuss this issue here, but it seems that base generation in T° should be assumed from a minimalist perspective.

15. In Chomsky (1992), verb movement is motivated by [ϕV]. This is abandoned in Chomsky (1995:ch. 4, in particular pp. 349ff.) in favor of the categorial [V]-features; see section 7.4 for further discussion.

16. If no auxiliary is present, the ϕ-feature in C° cannot be deleted, given that the ϕ-features of V° are checked and deleted by the corresponding feature in AgrS°.

17. Consider Chomsky's (1995:198–99) remarks with respect to VSO languages.

18. For nominal categories, Chomsky (1995:ch. 4) distinguishes between [D]-features, in which the information on the type of category is encoded, and [N]-features, which belong to the ϕ-features and are responsible for agreement. According to Chomsky, the movement of subjects is triggered by the [D]-features. This is irrelevant here, the important thing being that AgrS° has some strong nominal feature.

19. The restrictions in Portuguese are discussed in the final section of this chapter.

20. At this point we have to recall that AgrSP and AgrOP are only mnemotechnical terms; see note 1. Since a complement is fronted here, the agreement phrase should probably be interpreted as AgrOP. I ignore this here.

21. Consider the following examples:

(i) affermando [mai sì bella   cosa non aver   veduta]
     stating   never such beautiful thing not to-have seen
     'stating that she had never seen such a beautiful thing' (Bocc. Dec., II, 7)

(ii) affermando ella [di mai   non volere   andare . . .]
     stating   she di never not to-want to-go
     'she stating that she never wanted to go . . .' (Bocc. Dec., II, 6)

References

Primary Sources

A. Ribeiro Arcanjo   Aquilino Ribeiro. *O Arcanjo negro*. Lisbon: Livraria Bertrand, 1960.

A. Ribeiro Mónica   Aquilino Ribeiro. *Mónica*. Lisbon: Livraria Bertrand, 1958.

Alberti Fam. *A*   Leonbattista Alberti. *Della Famiglia*, books 1–3. Florence: Carnesecchi, 1908.

Alberti Fam. *B*   Leonbattista Alberti. *Opere volgari*, vol. 1: *I Libri della Famiglia, Cena familiaris, Villa*, ed. C. Grayson. Bari: Laterza, 1960.

Alex.   *Libro de Alexandre*, ed. J. Cañas. Madrid: Cátedra, 1988.

ALF   *Atlas linguistique de la France*, ed. J. Gilliéron and E. Edmont, 7 vols. Paris: Champion, 1902–10.

ALGa (1990ff.)   See García Pérez et al. (1990ff.).

Alisc.   *Aliscans*, ed. C. Régnier, 2 vols. Paris: Champion, 1990.

Antonil   A. J. Antonil. *Cultura e Opulência do Brasil*. São Paulo: Melhoramentos, 1976.

APG   *Lettres achetées à l'Agence de Prisonniers de Guerre*. Geneva: International Red Cross, 1914ff.

Auberi   See Tobler (1870).

Augier L'hab. vert   Émile Augier. *L'habit vert: Proverbe en un acte en prose*. In *Théâtre complet de Émile Augier*, vol. 5, 239–79. Paris: Calmann-Lévy, 1929.

Bal.   Gui de Cambrai. *Balaham und Josaphas*, ed. C. Appel. Halle a. S.: Max Niemeyer, 1907.

Barlaão   *A Lenda dos Santos Barlaão e Josafate*, critical ed., ed. G. de Vasconcellos Abreu. Lisbon: Typ. da Academia Real das Sciencias, 1898.

Barros   João de Barros e Diogo de Couto. *Da Asia*, new ed., 24 vols. Lisbon: Regia Officina Typografica, 1778. Reprint Lisbon: Livraria Sam Carlos, 1973.

BDM   *Era Bouts dera Mountagno*. Saint-Gaudens: Imprimerie Abadie, 1905ff.

Belarmino   Ramón Pérez de Ayala. *Belarmino y Apolonio*. Madrid: Ediciones Saturnino Calleja, 1921.

Berceo, Mil. N.S.   Gonzalo de Berceo. *Los Milagros de Nuestra Sennora*, ed. C. García Turza. In Gonzalo de Berceo, *Obra Completa*, 553–795. Madrid: Espasa-Calpe, 1992.

Berceo, S. Mill.   Gonzalo de Berceo. *Vida de San Millán de la Cogolla*, ed. B. Dutton. In Gonzalo de Berceo, *Obra Completa*, 117–249. Madrid: Espasa-Calpe 1992.

Berceo, Sac.
Gonzalo de Berceo. *Del sacrificio de la misa,* ed. P. M. Cátedra. In Gonzalo de Berceo, *Obra Completa,* 933–1033. Madrid: Espasa-Calpe, 1992.

Bernat Metge
Bernat Metge. "Lo Somni." In *Documents pera la història de la Cultura Catalana mitgeval,* ed. A. Rubiò y Lluch, 2 vols., vol. 1. Barcelona: Institut d'Estudis Catalans, 1908–21.

Bestiario
"Il bestiario toscano", ed. M. S. Garver and K. McKenzie. *SR 8* (1912), pp. 1ff.

Biagi
See *Novellino.*

Bocc. Dec.
Giovanni Boccaccio. *Il Decameron,* critical ed., ed. A. Rossi. Bologna: Cappelli, 1977.

Botta
Carlo Botta. *Storia d'Italia dal 1789 al 1814,* books 8 and 9, Paris: Baudry, 1837.

Bovary
Gustave Flaubert. *Oeuvres complètes,* vol. 1: *Madame Bovary.* Paris, Quantin, 1885.

Brunetto Lat.
"Der Tesoretto und Favolello B. Latinos. Kritischer Text nebst einleitender Untersuchung über Handschriften und Sprache der Gedichte," ed. B. von Wiese. *ZRPh 7* (1883), 236–389.

BT
La Bouts de la Terre d'Armagnac, Biarn, Bigorre e Lanes, qui clame dus cops pèr mes. Pau: 1910–14.

Cal. e D. *A*
Calila e Dimna, ed. J. M. Cacho Blecua and M. J. Lacarra. Madrid: Editorial Castalia, 1984.

Cal. e D. *B*
"*Calila e Dymna* de Abdallah Ben Al-Mocaff." In *Escritores en prosa anteriores al siglo XV,* ed. P. de Gayangos, 11–78. Madrid: Hernando, 1928 (= BAE 51).

Cald.
P. Calderón de la Barca, *Obras completas,* 3 vols., 2nd ed. Madrid: Aguilar, 1991. (AQT = "Antes que todo es mi dama"; HD = "Hado y divisa de Leonido y Marfisa"; AH = "Armas de la Hermosura"; FD = "Fuego de Diós en el querer bien"; PC = "El Príncipe constante")

Calvin Lettres
Lettres de Jean Calvin, ed. J. Bonnet, 2 vols. Paris: Librairie de Ch. Meyrueis et Compagnie, 1854.

Camino
Miguel Delibes. *El camino.* Barcelona: Editorial Destino, 1963.

Camões
Luis de Camões. *Obras completas de Luis de Camões,* ed. J. Barreto and J. Monteiro, vols. 2 and 3. Hamburg: Langhoff, 1834.

Cantigas
Afonso X, O Sábio. *Cantigas de Santa Maria,* ed. W. Mettmann, 4 vols. Coimbra: Por ordem da Universidade, 1959–72.

Carducci
Giosuè Carducci. *Di alcuni giudizii su A. Manzoni. Tibulliana—Don Quixote— Critica ed Arte—Eterno Femminino regale,* 3rd ed. Bologna: Zanichelli, 1905.

Cast. de D. Sancho
Castigos e documentos para bien vivir, que don Sancho IV de Castilla dio a su fijo. In *Escitores en prosa anteriores al siglo XV,* ed. P. Gayangos, 79–234. Madrid: Hernando, 1928 (= BAE 51).

Cavalca
Domenico Cavalca. *Auswahl aus den 'Vite de Santi Padri, volgarizzamento'.* Milan: Silvestri, 1842.

Celest.	Fernando de Rojas. *Celestina: Tragicomedia de Calisto y Melibea,* ed. Miguel Marciales, with B. Dutton and J. F. Snow. Urbana: University of Illinois Press, 1985.
Chron. G. de C.	*La chronique du bon chevalier Messire Gilles de Chin,* ed. R. Chalon. Mons: Hoyois-Derely: 1837.
Cid	*Poema de mio Cid,* ed. C. Smith, 18th ed. Madrid: Cátedra, 1991.
Clareo	*Los amores de Clareo y Florisea y las tristezas y trabajos de la sin ventura Isea,* ed. M. A. Teijeiro Fuentes. Cáceres: Servicio de Publicaciones de la Universidad de Extremadura, 1991.
Claris	*Li romans de Claris et Laris,* ed. J. B. Alton. Tübingen: Litterarischer Verein in Stuttgart, 1884. Reprint Amsterdam: Rodopi, 1966.
Cleom.	*Les Oeuvres d'Adenet le Roi,* ed. A. Henry, 5 vols, vol. 5.1. Brussels: Éditions de l'Université de Bruxelles, 1951–71.
CLP	"Corpus da Língua Portuguesa." In Meyer-Hermann (1973).
Cod. Vor.	*Codicele Voroneţean,* ed. M. Costinescu. Bucharest: Editura Minerva, 1981.
Colletta	Pietro Colletta. *Storia del reame di Napoli,* books 3 and 4. Paris: Baudry, 1843.
Colón Diario	Cristóbal Colón. *Diario del descubrimiento,* ed. M. Alvar, 2 vols. Excmo. Cabildo Insular de Gran Canaria, 1976.
Commynes	Philippe de Commynes. *Mémoires.* Paris: Imprimerie Nationale, 1994.
Cond. Luc.	Don Juan Manuel. *El Conde Lucanor,* ed. A. I. Sotelo. Madrid: Cátedra, 1980.
Conti d'ant. Cav.	*Conti d'antichi Cavalieri,* ed. P. Fanfani. Florence: Baracchi, 1851.
Contos da Galiza	L. Carré Alvarellos. *Contos populares da Galiza.* Porto: Junta Distrital do Porto, 1968.
Corb.	Arcipreste de Talevera. *El Corbacho,* ed. C. Pérez Pastor. Madrid: Sociedad de Bibliófilos Españoles.
Corpus Oral	*Corpus oral de referencia de la lengua española contemporánea,* ed. F. Marcos Marín, with A. Ballester Carrillo et al. Madrid: Universidad Autónoma, 1992.
Costa, Solar	Augusto da Costa. *O Solar Desabitado,* Lisbon: Pereira, 1943.
Creangă	Ion Creangă. *Scrierile lui Ion Creangă* vol. 2: *Diverse.* Iaşi: 1892.
Cron.	Alfonso X, el Sabio. *Primera Crónica general de España,* new ed., ed. R. Menéndez Pidal. Madrid: Gredos, 1955.
CVC	"Carte volgari cagliaritane." In Solmi (1917:421–24).
Cygne	*La naissance du Chevalier au Cygne ou les enfants changés en Cygnes: French poem of the XIIth century,* ed. H. A. Todd. Baltimore: Modern Language Assoc., 1889. Reprint Ann Arbor, Mich.: Univ. Microfilms Internat., 1980.
Dante Conv.	Dante Alighieri. *Il Convivio,* critical ed., ed. M. Simonelli. Bologna: Pàtron, 1966 (= Testi e saggi di letterature moderni, Storia e testi 2).

Dante Div. Com.	Dante Alighieri. *La Divina Commedia*, ed. N. Sapegno. Milan: Riccardo Ricciardi Editore, 1957 (= La letteratura italiana, Storia e testi 4).
d'Aubigné	Th. Agrippa d'Aubigné. *Histoire universelle,* ed. A. de Ruble, 10 vols. Paris: Renouard, 1886–1909.
D'Azeglio	Massimo D'Azeglio. *Ettore Fieramosca.* Bibl. Naz. Economica, 1906.
Del Tuppo Lettera D.C.	"Lettera che precede l'edizione della Divina Commedia di Del Tuppo," ed. G. Persico Cavalcanti. *Rivista delle Biblioteche*, January 1898.
Desc. Pass.	René Descartes. *Les passions de l'âme,* introduction and notes by G. Rodis-Lewis. Paris: Librairie Philosophique J. Virin, 1955.
Devanceiros	X. Ferro Couselo. *A vida e a fala dos devanceiros: escolma de documentos en galego dos séculos XII ao XVI,* 2 vols. Vigo: Editorial Galaxia, 1967.
Diana	Jorge de Montemayor. *Los siete libros de la Diana.* Madrid: En casa de Francisco Sanchez, 1586.
Duarte Vencidos	Fausto Duarte. *Foram êstes os vencidos: Contos.* Lisbon: Inquérito, 1945.
DV	"Documenti vari." In Solmi (1917:425–36).
Erec	*Kristian von Troyes Erec und Enide*, new ed., ed. W. Foerster. Halle a. S.: Max Niemeyer, 1896 (= Romanische Bibliothek 13).
Esc.	Jean Renart. *L'Escoufle*, ed. F. Sweetser. Geneva: Lib. Droz, 1974.
Evast	Ramon Llull. *Llibre d'Evast e Blanquerna*, ed. M. J. Gallofré. Barcelona: Edicions 62, 1981.
Fenoglio: Il part.	Beppe Fenoglio. *Il partigiano Johnny*. Turin: Einaudi, 1968.
Ferreira de Castro	José M. Ferreira de Castro. *A lã e a neve*, 12th ed. Lisbon: Guimarães, 1985.
G. Chast.	Georges Chastellain. *Oeuvres*, vol. 1: *Chronique 1419–1422*, ed. K. de Lettenhove, 8 vols. Brussels: Heussner, 1863–66.
Galileo Mass. Sist.	Galileo Galilei. *Dialogo dei massimi sistemi.* In Galileo Galilei, *Opere*, ed. F. Flora. Milan: Riccardo Ricciardi Editore, 1953.
Gallucci	Luigi Gallucci. *Raccolta di poesie calabre.* Lugano: 1862. Reprint Cosenza: Tip. MIT, 1968.
Gar. l. Br.	Garin le Brun. *Eisenhamen* (= Bibliothèque Ambrosienne R. 71 sup., fol. 125c). See also Bartsch. *Chrestomatie provençale*, 4th ed. Elberfeld: R. L. Friderichs, 1880.
Garin Cronache	Eugenio Garin. *Cronache di filosofia italiana*, vol. 1. Rome: Laterza, 1966.
Garin le Lorrain	*Li romans de Garin le Loherain*, ed. P. Paris, 2 vols. Paris: Techener, 1833. Reprint Geneva: Slatkine Reprints, 1969.
Garin Storia	Eugenio Garin. *Storia della filosofia italiana*, vol. 1. Turin: Einaudi, 1966.
Gattopardo	G. Tomasi di Lampedusa. *Il Gattopardo*. Milan: Feltrinelli, 1961.

Gen. Est.	Alfonso X, el Sabio. *General Estoria*, electronic ed., ed. B. Dutton. Oxford: Oxford Text Archive.
Giord. Riv.	B. Giordano da Rivalto. *Prediche inedite*, ed. E. Narducci. Bologna: 1867 (= Collezione di opere inedite rare).
Giov. da Prato	Giovanni da Prato. *Paradiso degli Alberti*. Bologna: Romagnoli, 1867.
GO	Henri P. de Rochegude. *Essai d'un glossaire occitanien, pour servir à l'intelligence des poésies des troubadours.* Toulouse: 1819.
Gold. L'avv. on.	Carlo Goldoni. *L'avventuriere onorato*. In Carlo Goldoni, *Pamela nubile—Pamela maritata—L'avventuriere onorato—Un curioso accidente— La bottega del caffè—La casa nova*. Florence: Le Monnier, 1856.
Gozzi	Carlo Gozzi. *Memorie inutili*, vol. 1. Bari: Laterza, 1910.
Gozzi, Oss.	Gasparo Gozzi. *L'Osservatore*, 1st part. Florence: Barbèra, 1868.
Graf	Arturo Graf. *Foscolo, Manzoni, Leopardi*. Turin: Loescher, 1898.
Greg.	*Gregorii Turonensis opera*, ed. W. Arndt and B. Krusch. Hannover: Hahn, 1884 (= MGH Scriptores Rerum Merovingicarum, vol. I).
Grillo	Carlos Muñiz Higuera. *El Grillo*. Madrid: Ediciones Arión, 1957.
Guitt.	*Le lettere di Frate Guittone d'Arezzo*, ed. F. Meriano. Bologna: Commissione pei testi in lingua, 1922.
H.P.	Heitor Pinto. *Imagem da vida cristã*. Coimbra: 1562.
Joinv.	Jean de Joinville. *Vie de saint Louis*, ed. J. Monfrin. Paris: Garnier, 1995.
Laf.	Jean de la Fontaine. *Oeuvres*, ed. H. Regnier, 11 vols. Paris: Hachette, 1883–92.
Larivey Morf.	Pierre de Larivey. *Le Morfondu*. In *Les Comédies facecieves de Pierre de L'arrivey*. Rouen: Champenois, 1611.
Laz 1554	*La vida de Lazarillo de Tormes, y de sus fortunas y adversidades*. In *Los tres Lazarillos*, ed. J. M. Sola-Solé, vol. 1: *Textos*. Barcelona: Puvill Libros, 1987.
Leges et Cons.	*Portugalia Monumenta Historica a saeculo octavo post Christum usque ad quintum decimum iussu Academiae Scientiarum Olisiponensis edita*. Lisbon: 1866ff.
Leite de Vasc.	Leite de Vasconcelos. *Opúsculos*. Coimbra: Imprensa da Universidade, 1928–29.
Lorca	Federico García Lorca. *Obras completas*. Madrid: Aguilar, 1954.
Mach. Istorie	Niccolò Machiavelli. *Istorie fiorentine*, ed. P. Carli, 2 vols. Florence: Sansoni, 1927.
Mach. Principe	Niccolò Machiavelli. *Tutte le opere storiche e letterarie di Niccolò Machiavelli*, ed. G. Mazzoni and M. Casella. Florence: G. Barbèra Editore, 1929.
Mahom.	*Alixandre dou Pont's Roman de Mahomet: Ein altfranzösisches Gedicht des XIII. Jahrhunderts*, ed. B. Ziolecki. Oppeln: Franck, 1887. Reprint Geneva: Slatkine Reprints, 1974.

Malh. Épîtres — François Malherbe. *Les Épître de Sénèque.* In *Oeuvres de Malherbe*, ed. M. L. Lalanne, new ed., 5 vols. Paris: Librairie de L. Hachette, 1862–69.

Malispini — Ricordano Malispini. *Istoria fiorentina.* In *Rerum Italicarum Scriptores. Raccolta degli storici italiani dal Cinquecento al Millecinquecento*, ed. L. Muratori. Città di Castello: Lapi, 1900, vol. 8, 882ff.

Marg. de Nav. — Marguerite de Navarre. *Les dernières poésies*, ed. A. Lefranc. Paris: Colin, 1896.

Marot — Clément Marot. *Oeuvres*, ed. B. Pifteau, 2 vols. Paris: 1889.

Martí — Joan Martí i Castell, and Josep Moran. (eds.). *Documents d'història de la llengua catalana. Dels orígens a Fabra.* Barcelona: Editorial d'Empúries, 1986.

Melin — Melin de Sainct-Gelais: *Oeuvres complètes*, ed. P. Blanchemain. Paris: Daffis, 1873.

Mie prigioni — Silvio Pellico. *Le mie prigioni—I doveri degli uomini.* Milan: Hoepli, 1918.

Mir. N. D. — *Miracles de Notre Dame par personnages*, ed. G. Paris and U. Robert, 8 vols. Paris: F. Didot, 1866–93.

Miragres — "Miragres de Santiago," ed. J. L. Pensado. In *Anejo LXVIII de la Revista de Filología Española.* Madrid: Consejo Superior de Investigaciones Científicas, 1958.

Montaigne *A* — *Les essais de Montaigne,* according to the edition of 1588, with the notes from 1595, ed. H. Motheau and D. Jouhaust, 7 vols. Paris: Librairie des Bibliophiles, 1886.

Montaigne *B* — *Essais de Montaigne*, new ed., ed. M. J.-V. Leclerc. Paris: Garnier, 1925.

Montchr. — Antoyne de Montchrétien. *Traicté de l'oeconomie politique,* ed. Th. Funck-Brentano, Paris: M. Rivière, 1910.

Morelli — Giovanni di Pagolo Morelli. *Ricordi.*, ed. V. Branca, 2nd ed. Florence: Le Monnier, 1969.

Muchachos — Manuel Arce. *Oficio de muchachos.* Barcelona: Seix Barral, 1963.

N. D. Chartr. — Jehan le Marchant. *Le Livre des Miracles de Notre-Dame de Chartres,* ed. G. Duplessis. Chartres: Garmer, 1855.

Negruzzi — Constantin Negruzzi: *Scrierile lui Constantin Negruzzi,* vol. 1: *Păcatele tinereţelor.* Bucharest: Libraria Socec, 1872.

Novellino — *Le novelle antiche dei codici Panciatichiano-Palatino 138 e Laurenziano-Gaddiano 193*, ed. Guido Biagi. Florence: Sansoni, 1880.

Nunes, Crest. — José Joaquim Nunes. *Crestomatia Arcaica.* Lisbon: Portugal-Brasil Limitada, 1906.

O porco — Vicente Risco. *O porco de pé e outras narracións.* Vigo: Editorial Galaxia, 1972.

Orl. Fur. — Lodovico Ariosto. *Orlando Furioso*, ed. F. Ermini, 3 vols. Turin: Unione tipografica, 1928.

Osório, Ambições — Ana de Castro Osório. *Ambições,* 2nd ed. Lisbon: Paraceira A. M. Pereira, 1934.

P. mor. — "Poème Moral: Altfranzösisches Gedicht aus den ersten Jahren des XIII. Jahrhunderts," ed. W. Cloetta. *RF 3* (1887), 1–268.

Perceval	*The Continuation of the Old French Perceval of Chrétien de Troyes,* ed. W. Roach, 3 vols. Philadelphia: University of Pennsylvania Press, 1949–55.
Petr. Son.	Francesco Petrarca. *Canzionere,* critical ed., ed. G. Contini. Turin: Einaudi, 1964.
Pidal Romancero	Ramón Menéndez Pidal. *Romancero hispánico,* 2 vols. Madrid: Espasa-Calpe, 1953.
Pitrè	Giuseppe Pitrè. *Fiabe novelle e racconti popolari siciliani,* 4 vols. Palermo: Lauriel, 1870–1913. Reprint Bologna: Forni, 1968–69.
Promessi Sposi	Alessandro Manzoni. *I promessi sposi.* Milano: Hoepli, 1920.
Prosa	*La Prosa del Duecento,* ed. C. Segre and M. Marti. Milan: Riccardo Ricciardi Editore, 1959 (= La letteratura italiana. Storia e testi 3).
Prosas galegas	F. López Cuevillas. *Prosas galegas.* Vigo: Editorial Galaxia, 1971.
Quij.	Miguel de Cervantes Saavedra. *El ingenioso hidalgo Don Quijote de la Mancha,* part 2, critical ed., ed. V. Gaos. Madrid: Gredos, 1987.
Rabelais	François Rabelais. *Oeuvres complètes,* ed. J. Boulenger and L. Scheler. Paris: Editions Gallimard, 1955 (= Bibliothèque de la Pléiade 15).
Raimb. Vaqu.	Raimbaut de Vaqueiras. See Appel (1930:no. 41, 82).
Recontamiento	"Libro del rrekontamiento del rrey Ališandre." In Nykl (1929).
Redol, Gaibéus	Antonio A. Redol. *Gaibéus,* edição popular. Lisbon: Inquérito, 1945.
Ren. Montaub.	*Renaus de Montauban oder die Haimonskinder,* ed. H. Michelant. Stuttgart: Litterarischer Verein, 1862 (= Bibliothek des Litterarischen Vereins in Stuttgart 68).
Retablo	Ramón del Valle-Inclán. *Retablo de la avaricia, la lujuria y la muerte.* Madrid: Imprenta Rivadeneyra, 1927.
Revista	*Revista da Faculdade de Letras de Lisboa.*
Rime Scuola Sic.	*Le Rime della scuola siciliana,* critical ed., vol.1. Florence: Olschki, 1962 (= Biblioteca dell'Archivium Romanicum 65).
Rom. Ger.	*Romanceiro Geral Portuguêz,* ed. T. Braga, 2nd ed. Lisbon: Gomes, 1906–09.
Rui de Pina	*Chronica de El Rei D. Alfonso V.* Lisbon: Biblioteca de Clássicos Portuguêses, 1901.
Ruteb.	*Oeuvres complètes de Rutebeuf,* ed. E. Faral and J. Bastin, vol. 1. Paris: Editions A. et J. Picard, 1959.
Sacch. Nov.	Franco Sacchetti. *Novelle.* Milan: Sonzogno, 1874.
Santa Teresa, Vida	Santa Teresa de Jesús. *Libro de la Vida,* ed. D. Chicharro, 5th ed. Madrid: Cátedra, 1984.
Santillana Prov.	*Los prouerbios de D. Yñigo Lopez de Mendoça con su glosa.* Seville: 1494. Reprint Valencia: Artes Gráficas Soler, 1964.
Schiaffini	*Testi fiorentini del dugento e dei primi del trecento,* ed. A. Schiaffini. Florence: Sansoni, 1954.
Sercambi	Giovanni Sercambi. *Novelle.* Bologna: Romagnoli, 1871.

Serm. S. Bern.	"Li Sermon Saint Bernart: Älteste französische Überset-zung der lateinischen Predigten Bernhards von Clairvaux," ed. W. Foerster. *RF 2* (1886), 1–210.
Sette Savi	*Il libro dei Sette Savi di Roma: Tratto da un codice del sec. XIV*, ed. A. Cappelli. Bologna: Romagnoli, 1865 (= Scelta di curiosità letterarie inedite o rare dal secolo XIII al XVII, 64).
T. Coelho, Amores	Trinidade Coelho. *Os meus Amores*. Paris: Aillaud et Bertrand, 1928.
Testi non tosc. Qu.	*Testi non toscani del Quattrocento*, ed. B. Migliorini and G. Folena. Modena: Società Tipografica Modenense, 1953 (= Testi e manuali 39).
Textos arcaicos	*Textos arcaicos*, ed. José L. de Vasconcellos, 3rd ed. Lisbon: Teixeira, 1923.
Tigre	Ramón Pérez de Ayala. *Tigre Juan*. Buenos Aires: Colección Austral, 1946.
Tirant lo Blanc	Joanot Martorell. *Tirant lo Blanch,* ed. M. de Riquer, with M. J. Gallofré, 2 vols. Barcelona: Edicions 62, 1991.
Tratt. penit.	C. de Lollis. "Trattato provenzale di penitenza." In *Studi di filologia romanica 5* (1891); see also Appel (1930: no. 120, 185–87).
Unamuno	Miguel de Unamuno. *Recuerdos de niñez y mocedad.* Buenos Aires: Espasa-Calpe, 1946.
Valdés Dial.	Juan de Valdés. *Diálogo de la Lengua*, ed. Cristina Barbolani. Madrid: Cátedra, 1982.
Varchi	Benedetto Varchi. *Storia Fiorentina,* books 8–10. Trieste: Sezione Lett., 1858 (= Art. del Lloyd Austriaco).
Vieira Cartas	António Vieira. *Cartas,* ed. J. Lucio de Azevedo, 3 vols. Coimbra: Imprensa da Universidade de Coimbra, 1925–28.
Vieira Serm.	António Vieira. *Sermões,* ed. H. Cidade, 4 vols. Lisbon: Livraria Sá de Costa Editora, 1954.
Vulg.	*Biblia Sacra iuxta vulgatam versionem,* ed. R. Weber, 2 vols. Stuttgart: Württembergische Bibelanstalt, 1969.

Studies

Abney, S. (1987). "The English Noun Phrase in Its Sentential Aspect." Ph.D. diss., MIT, Cambridge, Mass.

Abraham, W. (ed.). (1985). *Erklärende Syntax des Deutschen*. Tübingen: Narr (= Studien zur deutschen Grammatik 25).

Abraham, W., W. Kosmeijer, and E. Reuland (eds.). (1991). *Issues in Germanic Syntax*. Berlin: Mouton de Gruyter.

Acquaviva, P. (1989). "Aspetti della complementazione frasale." Thesis, Università di Pisa.

Adams, M. (1987). "From Old French to the Theory of *pro*-Drop." *Natural Language and Linguistic Theory 5*, 1–32.

—— (1988). "Embedded *pro*." In Blevins and Carter (1988:1–21).

Alibèrt, L. (1976). *Gramatica Occitana segon los parlars lengadocians*, 2nd ed. Montpelier: Centre d'Estudis Occitans.

Alisova, T. (1967). *Strutture semantiche e sintattiche della proposizione semplice in italiano.* Florence: Sansoni.

Álvarez, R., H. Monteagudo, and X. L. Regueira. (1989). *Gramática Galega*, 2nd ed. Vigo: Editorial Galaxia.

Ambar, M. M. (1994). "'Aux to COMP' and Lexical Restrictions on Verb Movement." In Cinque et al. (1994:1–21).

Anderson, S., and P. Kiparski (eds.). (1973). *A Festschrift for Morris Halle.* New York: Holt, Rinehart & Winston.

Appel, C. (1930). *Provenzalische Chrestomatie*, 6th ed. Leipzig: Reisland. Reprint Hildesheim: Olms, 1971.

Badia i Margarit, A. M. (1962). *Gramática Catalana*, 2 vols. Madrid: Gredos.

Baker, M. C. (1988). *Incorporation: A Theory of Grammatical Function Changing.* Chicago: University of Chicago Press.

Barbaud, P. (1988). "De la modernité de la grammaire dans le style indirect: le cas de l'infinitif de narration." *Revue Québecoise de Linguistique Théorique et Appliquée 7.3*, 113–28.

Battistella, E. (1983). "Gerunds and Subject Case Marking." *Proceedings of the West Coast Conference on Formal Linguistics 2*, 1–10. Stanford, Calif.: Stanford University, Linguistics Dept.

Bayer, J. (1984). "Comp in Bavarian." *Linguistic Review 3*, 209–74.

Beardsley, W. A. (1921). *Infinitive Constructions in Old Spanish.* Reprint New York: AMS Press, 1966 (= Studies in Romance Philology and Literature 28).

Belletti, A. (1987). "Los inacusativos como asignadores de caso." In Demonte and Fernández Lagunilla (1987:167–230).

—— (1988). "The Case of Unaccusatives." *Linguistic Inquiry 19*, 1–34.

—— (1990). *Generalized Verb Movement: Aspects of Verb Syntax.* Turin: Rosenberg and Sellier.

Belletti, A., and L. Rizzi. (1981). "The Syntax of *ne*: Some Theoretical Implications." *Linguistic Review 1*, 117–54.

Belletti, A., and L. Rizzi (eds.). (1996). *Parameters and Functional Heads: Essays in Comparative Syntax.* New York: Oxford University Press (= Oxford Studies in Comparative Syntax).

Benincà, P. (ed.). (1989). *Dialect Variation in the Theory of Grammar.* Dordrecht: Foris.

Benucci, F. (1992). "Romance Infinitival Particles as Specifiers of CP." In Fava (1992:23–51).

Bergsträsser, G. (1928). *Einführung in die semitischen Sprachen: Sprachproben und grammatische Skizzen.* Reprint Darmstadt: Wissenschaftliche Buchgesellschaft, 1977.

Besten, H. den. (1981). "Government, syntaktische Struktur und Kasus." In Kohrt and Lenerz (1981:97–107).

Biedermann, A. (1908). "Zur Syntax des Verbums bei Antoine de la Sale." *RF 22*, 675–733.

Blasco Ferrer, E. (1986). *La lingua sarda contemporanea: Grammatica del logudorese e del campidanese.* Cagliari: Edizioni della Torre.

Blevins, J., and J. Carter (eds.). (1988). *Proceedings of NELS 18.* Amherst: GSLA, University of Massachusetts.

Blumenthal, P. (1980). *La syntaxe du message: Application au français moderne.* Tübingen: Niemeyer (= Beihefte zur ZRPh 180).

Blumenthal, P., G. Rovere, and C. Schwarze (eds.). (1996). *Lexikalische Analyse romanischer Sprachen.* Tübingen: Niemeyer (= Linguistische Arbeiten 353).

Bondre-Beil, P. (1994). *Parameter der Syntax.* Tübingen: Niemeyer (= Linguistische Arbeiten 324).

Bonet, E. (1989). "Postverbal Subjects in Catalan." Unpublished ms., MIT, Cambridge, Mass.

Bonet, S. (1986). *Sintaxi generativa catalana.* Barcelona: Enciclopèdia Catalana.

Bordelois, I. (1974). "The Grammar of Spanish Causative Constructions." Ph.D diss., MIT, Cambridge, Mass.

Bottari, P. (1991). "Structural Representations of the Italian Nominal Infinitive." In Fava (1992:71–96).

Brame, M. (1982). "The Head-Selector Theory of Lexical Specifications and the Non-Existence of Coarse Categories." *Linguistic Analysis 10.4,* 321–25.

Brandi, L., and P. Cordin. (1989). "Two Italian Dialects and the Null Subject Parameter." In Jaeggli and Safir (1989:111–42).

Breilmann-Massing, S. (1990). "Studien zum katalanischen Infinitiv." Ph.D. diss., Universität zu Köln.

—— (1995). "Klitische Personalpronomina in den iberoromanischen Sprachen: Eine kontrastive GB-Analyse für maschinelle Übersetzung." Unpublished ms., Universität zu Köln, Sprachliche Informationsverarbeitung.

Brumme, J. (1997). Praktische Grammatik der katalanischen Sprache. Wilhelmsfeld: Gottfried Egert Verlag.

Brunot, F. (1905). *Histoire de la Langue Française des origines à nos jours.* Paris: Armand Colin.

Burzio, L. (1986). *Italian Syntax: A Government and Binding Approach.* Dordrecht: Reidel.

Buyssens, E. (1975). *Les categories grammaticales du français.* Brussels: Editions de l'Université de Bruxelles.

Camproux, C. (1958). *Etude Syntaxique des Parlers Gévaudanais.* Paris: Presses Universitaires de France (= Publ. de la Fac. des lettres de l'Univ. de Montpellier 20).

Carstens, V., and K. Kinyalolo. (1989). "Agr, Tense, Aspect, and the IP Structure: Evidence from Bantu. "Paper presented at GLOW Conference, Utrecht.

Chomsky, N. (1980). "On Binding." *Linguistic Inquiry 11,* 1–46.

—— (1981). *Lectures on Government and Binding: The Pisa Lectures.* Dordrecht: Foris.

—— (1982). *Some Concepts and Consequences of the Theory of Government and Binding.* Cambridge, Mass.: MIT Press.

—— (1986a). *Barriers.* Cambridge, Mass.: MIT Press.

—— (1986b). *Knowledge of Language: Its Nature, Origin, and Use.* New York: Praeger.

—— (1989). "Some Notes on Economy of Derivation and Representation." In R. Freidin (1991:417–54).

—— (1992). "A Minimalist Program for Linguistic Theory." *MIT Occasional Papers in Linguistics 1,* 1–25.

—— (1993). "A Minimalist Program for Linguistic Theory." In Hale and Keyser (1993:1–52).

—— (1994). "Bare Phrase Structure." *MIT Occasional Papers in Linguistics 5.*

—— (1995). *The Minimalist Program*. Cambridge, Mass.: MIT Press.

—— (1998). "Minimalist Inquiries: The Framework." Unpublished ms., MIT, Cambridge, Mass.

Chomsky, N., and H. Lasnik (1977). "Filters and Control." *Linguistic Inquiry 8*, 425–504.

Chung, S., and J. McCloskey. (1987). "Government, Barriers, and Small Clauses." *Linguistic Inquiry 18*, 173–237.

Cinque, G. (1983). "Su una differenza tra italiano e inglese nelle costruzioni 'ad ellissi dell'oggetto'." *Rivista di Grammatica Generativa 8*, 127–51.

—— (1990). *Types of A'-Dependencies*. Cambridge, Mass.: MIT Press.

—— (1999). *Adverbs and Functional Heads: A Cross-Linguistic Perspective*. New York: Oxford University Press (= Oxford Studies in Comparative Syntax).

Cinque, G., J. Koster, J.-Y. Pollock, and L. Rizzi (eds.). (1994). *Paths Towards Universal Grammar: Studies in Honor of Richard S. Kayne*. Washington, D.C.: Georgetown University Press.

Contreras, H. (1991). "On the Position of Subjects." *Syntax and Semantics 25*, 63–79.

Cresti, D. (1990). "Italian Participle Absolutes and the Internal Subject Hypothesis." Senior Thesis, Board of Studies in Linguistics, University of California, Santa Cruz.

Dahmen, W., G. Holtus, J. Kramer, M. Metzeltin, W. Schweickard, and O. Winkelmann (eds.). (1998). *Neuere Beschreibungsmethoden der Syntax romanischer Sprachen: Romanistisches Kolloquium XI*. Tübingen: Narr.

Damourette, J., and E. Pichon. (1911–50). *Des mots à la pensée: Essai de grammaire de la langue française*, 7 vols. Paris: Collection des linguistes contemporains. Reprint Geneva: Slatkine Reprints, 1983.

Dardano, M. (1963). "Sintassi dell'infinito nei *Libri della famiglia* di L.B. Alberti." *Annali della Scuola Normale Superiore di Pisa: Lettere, Storia e Filosofia, Serie II, 32*, 83–135.

Demonte, V., and M. Fernández Lagunilla (eds.). (1987). *Sintaxis de las lenguas románicas*. Madrid: Ediciones El Arquero.

Diaconescu, I. (1977). *Infinitivul în limba română*, Bucharest: Editura ştiinţifică şi enciclopedică.

Diesing, M. (1990). "Verb Movement and the Subject Position in Yiddish." *Natural Language and Linguistic Theory 8*, 41–79.

Diez, F. (1882). *Grammatik der Romanischen Sprachen*, vol. 3, book 4: *Syntax*, 5th ed. Bonn: Weber.

Dittes, R. (1903). "Über den Gebrauch des Infinitivs im Altprovenzalischen: Syntaktische Studie." *RF 15*, 1–40.

Dobrovie-Sorin, C. (1987). "Syntaxe du roumain." Ph.D. diss., Université de Paris 7.

—— (1994). *The Syntax of Romanian:Comparative Studies in Romance*. Berlin: Mouton de Gruyter.

Draeger, A. (1881). *Historische Syntax der lateinischen Sprache*, 2nd ed. Leipzig: Teubner.

Duarte, I. (1989). "La topicalisation en portugais européen." In Rouveret and Sauzet (1980:275–304).

Dupuis, F. (1989). "L'expression du sujet dans les subordonnées en ancien français." Ph.D. diss., Université de Montréal.

Durante, M. (1981). *Dal latino all'italiano: Saggio di storia linguistica e culturale*. Bologna: Zanichelli.

Emonds, J. (1986). "Gerundios SV, infinitivos O y las modificaciones teóricas correspondientes." *Revista Argentina de Lingüística 2*, 183–208.

Fanselow, G. (ed.). (1993). *The Parametrization of Universal Grammar*. Amsterdam: Benjamins (= Linguistik aktuell 8).

Fanselow, G., and S. Olsen (eds.). (1991). *DET, COMP und INFL: Zur Syntax funktionaler Kategorien und grammatischer Funktionen*, Tübingen: Niemeyer (= Linguistische Arbeiten 263).

Fava, E. (ed.). (1992). *Proceedings of the XVII Meeting of Generative Grammar*, Trieste, February 22–24, 1991. Volume presented to Giuseppe Francescato on the occasion of his seventieth birthday. Turin: Rosenberg & Sellier.

Fernández Lagunilla, M. (1987). "Los infinitivos con sujetos léxicos en español." In Demonte and Fernández Lagunilla (1987:125–147)

Flasche, H. (1948). "Der persönliche Infinitiv im klassischen Portugiesisch (António Vieira 1608–1697)." *RF 60*, 685–718.

Fontana, J. (1993). "Phrase Structure and the Syntax of Clitics in the History of Spanish." Ph.D. diss., University of Pennsylvania, Philadelphia.

Franz, A. (1915). "Studien zur Wallonischen Dialektsyntax: Kapitel 4., Wallonische und galloromanische Dialektsyntax (Nach dem Atlas Linguistique de la France)." *ZfSL 18*, 113–53.

—— (1920). *Zur galloromanischen Syntax*. Jena: Verlag von Wilhelm Gronau (= Supplementheft 10 der *ZfSL*).

Frei, H. (1929). *La grammaire des fautes: Introduction à la linguistique fonctionnelle. Assimilation et différenciation, brièveté et invariabilité, expressivité.* Paris: Geuthner. Reprint Geneva: Slatkine Reprints, 1971.

Freidin, R. (ed.). (1991). *Principles and Parameters in Comparative Grammar*. Cambridge, Mass: MIT Press.

Fukui, N., and M. Speas. (1987). "Specifiers and Projections." *MIT Working Papers in Linguistics 8*, 128–72.

García de Diego, V. (1951). *Gramática histórica española*, Madrid: Gredos.

García Pérez, C., A. Santamarina, R. Álvarez Blanco, F. Fernández Rei, and M. González González (eds.). (1990ff.). *Atlas lingüístico galego*. Santiago de Compostela: Universidad de Santiago de Compostela, Instituto de la Lengua Gallega, La Coruña: Fundación "Pedro Barrie de la Maza, Conde de Fenosa."

García Turza, C., F. González Bachiller, and J. Mangado Martínez (eds.). (1998). *Actas del IV Congreso Internacional de Historia de la Lengua Española*, La Rioja, 1–5 de abril de 1997. Logroño: Universidad de la Rioja.

Gesenius, W. (1896). *Hebräische Grammatik*. 26th, ed. Leipzig: Vogel.

Gessner, E. (1893). "Das spanische Personalpronomen." *ZRPh 17*, 1–54.

Gili Gaya, S. (1985). *Curso Superior de Sintaxis Española*, 15th ed. Barcelona: Bibliograf.

Giorgi, A., and G. Longobardi (1991). *The Syntax of Noun Phrases: Configuration, Parameters and Empty Categories*. Cambridge: Cambridge University Press.

GLR. (1966). = *Gramatica Limbii Române*, new ed., 2 vols. Bucharest: Editura Academiei Republicii Socialiste România.

Godard, D. (1985). "Propositions relatives, relations anaphoriques et prédications." Thesis, Université de Paris 7.

Gondar, F. G. (1978). *O infinitivo conxugado en galego*. Santiago de Compostela: Secretariado de Publicaciones de la Universidad de Santiago.

González Muela, J. (1954). *El infinitivo en "El Corbacho" del Arcipreste de Talavera*. Granada: Universidad de Granada, Secretariado de Publicaciones.

Gougenheim, G. (1951). *Grammaire de la lange française du seizième siècle*. Lyon: IAC.

Graffi, G. (1994). *Sintassi*. Bologna: Il Mulino.

Greenberg, J. H. (1966a). "Some Universals of Grammar with Particular Reference to the Order of Meaningful Elements." In Greenberg (1966b:73–113).

—— (1966b). *Universals of Language*. Cambridge, Mass.: MIT Press.

Grewendorf, G. (1989). *Ergativity in German*. Dordrecht: Foris (= Studies in Generative Grammar 35).

Grewendorf, G., and W. Sternefeld (eds.). (1989). *Scrambling and Barriers*. Amsterdam: Benjamins (= Linguistik Aktuell 5).

Groß, P. (1912). "Die Konstruktion des doppelten Accusativobjekts im Französischen." Ph.D. diss., Universität Göttingen.

Guasti, M. T. (1989). "Romance Infinitive Complements of Perception Verbs." *MIT Working Papers in Linguistics 11*, 31–45.

—— (1996). "A Cross-Linguistic Study of Romance and Arbëresh Causatives." In Belletti and Rizzi (1996:209–38).

Haase, A. (1888). *Französische Syntax des XVII. Jahrhunderts*. Oppeln: Maske.

—— (1890). "Syntaktische Notizen zu Jean Calvin." *ZfSL 12*, 193–230.

—— (1965). *Syntaxe française du XVIIe siècle*, 5th ed. Paris: Librairie Delegrave and Munich: Max Hueber Verlag.

Haase, M. (1995). "Finite Infinitive. Portugiesisch, Rumänisch und Süditalien." In Schmitt and Schweickard (1995:129–49).

Haegeman, L. (1992). *Theory and Description in Generative Syntax: A case Study in West Flemish*. Cambridge: Cambridge University Press.

—— (1994). *Introduction to the Government and Binding Theory*, 2nd ed., Oxford: Blackwell.

—— (1995). *The Syntax of Negation*. Cambridge: Cambridge University Press.

Hale, K., and S. J. Keyser (eds.). (1993). *The View from Building 20: Essays in Linguistics in Honor of Sylvain Bromberger*. Cambridge, Mass.: MIT Press.

Hanssen, F. (1910). *Spanische Grammatik auf historischer Grundlage*. Halle a. S.: Max Niemeyer (= Sammlung kurzer Lehrbücher der romanischen Sprachen und Literaturen 6).

Harris, M. (1978). *The Evolution of French Syntax: A Comparative Approach*. London: Longman.

Hegarty, M. (1993). "The Derivational Composition of Phrase Structure." Unpublished ms., University of Pennsylvania, Philadelphia.

Heinz, S., and U. Wandruszka (eds.). (1982). *Fakten und Theorien. Beiträge zur romanischen und allgemeinen Sprachwissenschaft*. Festschrift für Helmut Stimm zum 65. Geburtstag. Tübingen: Narr.

Hellan, L., and K. Koch Christensen (eds.). (1986). *Topics in Scandinavian Syntax*. Dordrecht: Reidel.

Heny, F. (ed.). (1981). *Binding and Filtering*. London: Croom Helm.

Hernanz Carbó, M. L. (1982). *El infinitivo en español*. Bellaterra: Universidad Autónoma de Barcelona, Departamento de Filología Hispánica.

Hirschbühler, P., and K. Koerner (eds.). (1992). *Romance Languages and Modern Linguistic Theory*: *Papers from the 20th Linguistic Symposium on Romance Languages (LSRL XX)*, Ottawa, April, 10–14, 1990. Amsterdam: John Benjamins.

Hoekstra, E. (1984). *Transitivity: Grammatical Relations in Government-Binding Theory*. Dordrecht: Foris.

—— (1991). "X-bar Theory and Licensing Mechanisms." *Linguistic Review 8*, 47–73.

Hoinkes, U., and W. Dietrich (eds.). (1997). *Kaleidoskop der lexikalischen Semantik*. Tübingen: Narr.

Holtus, G., M. Metzeltin, and C. Schmitt (eds.). (1994). *Lexikon der Romanistischen Linguistik*, vol. 6.2. Tübingen: Niemeyer.

Hualde, J. I. (1992). *Catalan*. London and New York: Routledge (= Descriptive Grammars 14).

Huber, J. (1933). *Altportugiesisches Elementarbuch*. Heidelberg: Carl Winters Universitätsbuchhandlung.

Iatridou, S. (1993). "On Nominative Case Assignment and a Few Related Things." In Phillips (1993:II, 175–96).

Jaeggli, O., and K. Safir (eds.). (1989). *The Null Subject Parameter*. Dordrecht: Kluwer.

Jaeggli, O., and C. Silva-Corvalán (eds.). (1986). *Studies in Romance Syntax*. Dordrecht: Foris.

Jespersen, O. (1924). *The Philosophy of Grammar*. London: Allen & Unwin.

Johnson, K. (1988). "Clausal Gerunds, the ECP, and Government." *Linguistic Inquiry 19*, 583–609.

Jones, M. A. (1992). "Infinitives with Specified Subjects in Sardinian." In Laeufer and Morgan (1992:295–309).

—— (1993). *Sardinian Syntax*. London: Routledge.

Junker, M.-O. (1990). "L'effet V1: Le verbe initial en moyen français." *Revue Canadienne de Linguistique 35*, 351–71.

Junker, M.-O., and F. Martineau. (1992). "The Structure of Infinitives." *Probus 4*, 127–53.

Kailuweit, R., and H.-I. Radatz (eds.). (1999). *Katalanisch: Sprachwissenschaft und Sprachkultur*. Frankfurt: Vervuert.

Kaiser, G. (1992). *Die klitischen Personalpronomina im Französischen und Portugiesischen*. Frankfurt a. M.: Verfuert (= Editionen der Iberoamericana, Reihe III, Monographien und Aufsätze, 44).

Kato, M., and F. Tarallo. (1986). "Anything you can do in Brazilian Portuguese." In Jaeggli and Silva-Corvalán (1986).

Kaulen, F. (1904). *Sprachliches Handbuch zur biblischen Vulgata*, 2nd ed. Freiburg im Breisgau: Herdersche Verlagshandlung.

Kayne, R. S. (1975). *French Syntax: The Transformational Cycle*. Cambridge, Mass.: MIT Press.

—— (1977). *Syntaxe du français: Le cycle transformationnel*. Paris: Editions du Seuil.

—— (1981). "On Certain Differences between English and French." *Linguistic Inquiry 12.3*.

—— (1982). "Predicates ans Arguments, Verbs and Nouns." *GLOW Newsletter 8.24*.

—— (1983). "Chaines, Categories External to S, and French Complex Inversion." *Natural Language and Linguistic Theory 1*, 109–37.

—— (1984). *Connectedness and Binary Branching*. Dordrecht: Foris.

—— (1990). "Romance Clitics and PRO." *Proceedings of NELS 20*, 255–302.

—— (1991). "Romance Clitics, Verb Movement, and PRO." *Linguistic Inquiry 22*, 647–86.

—— (1994) *The Antisymmetry of Syntax*. Cambridge, Mass.: MIT Press.

Keenan, L. (1975). "Towards a Universal Definition of «Subject»." In Li (1975:305–33).

Kenesei, I. (ed.). (1987). *Approaches to Hungarian*. Vol. 2: *Theories and Analyses*. Szeged: Jate.

Keniston, H. (1937). *The Syntax of Castilian Prose: The Sixteenth Century*. Chicago: University of Chicago Press.

Kim, S.-S., H.-P. Kolb, G. Müller, and W. Sternefeld. (1995). *Minimalismus in der Syntax: Vorlesungsskript WS 94/95*. Tübingen: Seminar für Sprachwissenschaft der Eberhard-Karls-Universität Tübingen (= SfS Report 03-95).

King, L., and C. Maley (eds.). (1985). *Selected Papers from the 13th Linguistic Symposium on Romance Languages*. Amsterdam: John Benjamins.

Kohrt, M., and J. Lenerz (eds.). (1981). *Sprache: Formen und Strukturen, Akten des 15. Linguistischen Kolloquiums*, Münster, 1980, vol. 1. Tübingen: Niemeyer (= Linguistische Arbeiten 98).

Koopman, H. (1984). *The Syntax of Verbs: From Verb Movement in the Kru Languages to Universal Grammar*. Dordrecht: Foris.

Koopman, H., and D. Sportiche. (1988). "Subjects." Unpublished ms., UCLA.

Koopman, H., and D. Sportiche. (1991). "The Position of Subjects." *Lingua 85*, 211–58 (amplified version of Koopman and Sportiche 1988).

Körner, K.-H. (1983). "Wie originell ist der flektierte Infinitiv des Portugiesischen? Eine Studie zum Subjekt in den romanischen Sprachen." In Schmidt-Radefeldt (1983:77–103).

—— (1987a). "Anläßlich Chomskys Bemerkungen zum flektierten Infinitiv des Portugiesischen: Plädoyer für eine korrelative Sprachtypologie." In Körner (1987b:50–59).

—— (ed.). (1987b). *Korrelative Sprachtypologie: Die zwei Typen romanischer Syntax*. Stuttgart: F. Steiner Verlag.

Lachmund, A. (1878). "Über den Gebrauch des reinen und präpositionalen Infinitivs im Altfranzösischen." Ph.D. diss., Universität Rostock.

Laeufer, C., and T. Morgan (eds.). (1992). *Theoretical Analyses in Romance Linguistic: Selected Papers from the Nineteenth Linguistic Symposium on Romance Languages (LSRL XIX)*, Ohio State University, April, 21–23, 1989. Amsterdam: John Benjamins.

Lalande, J.-Y. (1997). *Verbstellung im Deutschen und Französischen unter Anwendung eines CAD-basierten Expertensystems*. Tübingen: Niemeyer (= Linguistische Arbeiten 365).

Lasnik, H. (1993). "Lectures on Minimalist Syntax." *University of Connecticut Working Papers 1*.

Lausberg, H. (1972). *Romanische Sprachwissenschaft*, vol. 3: *Formenlehre*, 2nd ed. Berlin: De Gruyter.

Ledgeway, A. (1998). "Variation in the Romance Infinitive: The Case of the Southern Calabrian Inflected Infinitive." *Transactions of the Philological Society 96*, 1–61.

Lemos Monteiro, J. (1994). *Pronomes pessoais: Subsídios para uma gramática do português do Brasil*. Fortaleza: EUFC.

Lenerz, J. (1984). *Syntaktischer Wandel und Grammatiktheorie: Eine Untersuchung an Beispielen aus der Sprachgeschichte des Deutschen*. Tübingen: Niemeyer (= Linguistische Arbeiten 141).

Leone, A. (1982). *L'italiano regionale in Sicilia: Esperienze di forme locali nella lingua comune*. Bologna: Società Editrice Il Mulino.

Lerch, E. (1929). *Historische Französische Syntax*, vol. 2. Leipzig: O. R. Reisland.

—— (1934). *Historische Französische Syntax*, vol. 3. Leipzig: O. R. Reisland.

Lewent, K. (1925). "Ein Kapitel aus der Geschichte des französischen Infinitivs." *ASNSL 148*, 221–45.

Li, C. N. (ed.). (1975). *Subject and Topic*. New York: Academic Press.

Lidforss, V. E. (1865). *Observations sur l'usage syntaxique de Ronsard et de ses contemporains*. Lund: Glerup.

Lieber, R. (1990). *On the Organization of the Lexicon*. New York: Garland.

Lightfoot, D. W., and N. Hornstein (eds.). (1994). *Verb Movement*. Cambridge: Cambridge University Press.

Lisio, G. (1902). *L'arte del periodo nelle opere volgari di Dante Alighieri e del secolo XIII*. Bologna: Zanichelli.

Lombard, A. (1936). *L'infinitif de narration dans les langues romanes: Etude de syntaxe historique*. Uppsala: Almquist & Wiksells, and Leipzig: O. Harrassowitz (= Skrifter utgivna av. K. Humanistika Vetenskaps-Samfundet i Uppsala, 30.1).

Loporcaro, M. (1986). "L'infinito coniugato nell'Italia centro-meridionale: Ipotesi genetica e ricostruzione storica." *Italia dialettale 49*, 173–240.

Lorian, A. (1973). *Tendances stylistiques dans la prose narrative française au XVIe siècle*. Paris: Klincksieck.

Marantz, A. (1984). *On the Nature of Grammatical Relations*. Cambridge, Mass.: MIT Press.

Martineau, F. (1990). "La montée du clitique en moyen français: Une étude de la syntaxe des constructions infinitives." Ph.D. diss., University of Ottawa.

Mascaro, J., and M. Nespor (eds.). (1990). *Grammar in Progress*. Dordrecht: Foris (= Studies in Generative Grammar 36).

Massam, D. (1985). "Case Theory and the Projection Principle." Ph.D. diss., MIT, Cambridge, Mass.

Maurer, T. E. (1968). *O infinito flexionado português: Estudo histórico-descritivo*. São Paulo: Editora Nacional e Editora da Universidade de São Paulo.

Mayerthaler, W., G. Fliedl, and C. Winkler. (1993). *Infinitivprominenz in europäischen Sprachen*, vol. 1. Tübingen: Narr (= Tübinger Beiträge zur Linguistik 390).

McCloskey, J. (1991). "Clause Structure, Ellipsis and Proper Government." *Lingua 85*, 259–302.

Meier, H. (1955). "Infinitivo flexional portugués e infinitivo personal español." *Boletín de Filología de la Universidad de Chile 8*, 267–91.

Menéndez Pidal, R. (1964). *Orígenes del Español: Estado lingüístico de la Península Ibérica hasta el siglo XI*, 5th ed. Madrid: Espasa-Calpe.

Mensching, G. (1994). *Einführung in die sardische Sprache*, 2nd ed. Bonn: Romanistischer Verlag.

—— (1995). "Kasustheorie und 'absoluter Infinitiv' in romanischen Sprachen." Paper presented at the '24. Deutscher Romanistentag', Münster (Germany). Unpublished ms., Universität zu Köln, Sprachliche Informationsverarbeitung.

—— (1996). "La sintaxis del infinitivo sardo a la luz de teorías generativistas recientes." Unpublished ms., Universität zu Köln, Sprachliche Informationsverarbeitung.

——— (1997) "Romanische Infinitivkonstruktionen mit explizitem Subjekt: Systematische Darstellung und syntaktische Analyse." Habilitation thesis, Universität zu Köln.

——— (1998). "Infinitivo con sujeto léxico en la historia de la Lengua española." In García Turza et al. (1998:I, 597–610).

——— (1999). "Infinitivkonstruktionen mit explizitem Subjekt im Katalanischen." In Kailuweit and Radatz (1999:191–217).

Mensching, G., and V. Popovici. (1997). "Constructions infinitives à sujet explicite en roumain." *Studii şi cercetări lingvistice 48*, 219–43.

Meyer-Hermann, R. (1973). "Zur Syntax des Infinitivs mit Person im gesprochenen Portugiesisch." Ph.D. diss., Universität zu Köln.

Meyer-Lübke, W. (1899). *Grammatik der romanischen Sprachen*, vol. 3: *Romanische Syntax*. Leipzig: Fues.

Millner, J.-C. (1980). "La prolepse en grec ancien." *Lalies 1*, 39–52.

Miremont, P. (1976). *La syntaxe occitane du Périgord*. Orlhac: Pierre Miremont.

Molho, M. (1975). *Sistemática del verbo español: Aspectos, modos, tiempos*, 2 vols. Madrid: Gredos.

Moritz, L. (1989). "Aperçu de la syntaxe de la négation en français et en anglais." Thesis, Université de Genève.

Motapanyane, V. (1988). "La position du sujet dans une langue à l'ordre SVO/VSO. Mémoire de pré-doctorat, Université de Genève." *Rivista di grammatica generativa 14*, 75–103.

——— (1994). "On Preverbal Positions in Romanian." *Revue Canadienne de Linguistique 39*, 15–36.

Müller, G. (1995). *A-bar Syntax. A Study in Movement Types*. Berlin: Mouton de Gruyter (= Studies in Generative Grammar 42).

Müller, N. (1993). *Komplexe Sätze: Der Erwerb von COMP und von Wortstellungsmustern bei bilingualen Kindern (Französisch/Deutsch)*. Tübingen: Narr.

Müller, N., and B. Riemer (1998). *Generative Syntax der romanischen Sprachen: Französisch, Italienisch, Portugiesisch, Spanisch*. Tübingen: Stauffenburg (= Stauffenburg Einführungen 5).

Nannucci, V. (1858). *Manuale della letteratura del primo secolo della lingua Italiana*, vol. 2, 2nd ed. Florence: Paggi, 1858.

Nykl, A. R. (1929). "Aljamiado Literature: El Rrekontamiento del Rrey Ališandere." *Revue Hispanique 77*, 466–611.

Nyrop, K. (1930). *Grammaire Historique de la langue française, vol. 6*. Copenhagen: Gyldendalske Boghandel, Nordisk Forlag; Leipzig: Otto Harrassowitz; New York: G. E. Stechert; Paris: Alphonse Picard.

Olsen, S. (1991). "Die deutsche Nominalphrase als 'Determinansphrase'." In Fanselow and Olsen (1991:35–56).

Ordóñez, F. (1994). "Postverbal Assymetries in Spanish." *GLOW Newsletter 32*, 40–41.

Otto, R. (1891). "Der portugiesische Infinitiv bei Camões." *RF 6*, 299–398.

Palmgren, V. (1905). *Observations sur l'infinitif dans Agrippa d'Aubigné*. Stockholm.

Par, A. (1923). *Sintaxi Catalana. Segons los escrits en prosa de Bernat Metge (1398)*. Halle: Niemeyer (= Beihefte zur ZRPh 66).

Pearce, E. (1990). *Parameters in Old French Syntax: Infinitival Complements*. Dordrecht: Kluwer.

Pesetsky, D. (1982). "Paths and Categories." Ph.D. diss., MIT, Cambridge, Mass.

Phillips, C. (ed.). (1993). *Papers on Case and Agreement*, 2 vols. Cambridge, Mass.: MIT (= MIT Working Papers in Linguistics 19).

Piera, C. (1987). "Sobre la estructura de las cláusulas de infinitivo." In Demonte and Fernández Lagunilla (1987:148–66).

Pittau, M. (1972). *Grammatica del sardo-nuorese*. Bologna: Pàtron.

Platzack, C. (1986). "COMP, INFL, and Germanic Word Order." In Hellan and Christensen (1986:185–234).

Platzack, C., and A. Holmberg. (1989). "The role of AGR and finiteness in Germanic VO languages." *Scandinavian Working Papers in Linguistics 43,* 51–76.

Pollock, J.-Y. (1989). "Verb Movement, Universal Grammar, and the Structure of IP." *Linguistic Inquiry 20*, 365–424.

Postal, P. M. (1974). *On Raising.* Cambridge, Mass.: MIT Press (= Current studies in linguistics 5).

Prado Coelho, J. do. (1950). "O infinito absoluto no romanceiro popular." *Boletim de Filologia 11*, 133–40.

Prein, A. (1921). *Syntaktisches aus französischen Soldatenbriefen.* Giessen: Romanisches Seminar (= Giessener Beiträge zur Romanischen Philologie 2).

Radford, A. (1988). *Transformational Grammar: A First Course.* Cambridge: Cambridge University Press.

—— (1997a). *Syntactic Theory and the Structure of English: A Minimalist Approach.* Cambridge: Cambridge University Press.

—— (1997b). *Syntax: A Minimalist Introduction.* Cambridge: Cambridge University Press.

Raposo, E. (1987). "Case Theory and Infl-to-Comp: The Inflected Infinitive in European Portuguese." *Linguistic Inquiry 18*, 85–109.

Raposo, E., and J. Uriagereka. (1990). "Long-distance Case Assignment." *Linguistic Inquiry 21*, 505–37.

Renzi, L., and G. Salvi. (1991). *Grande grammatica italiana di consultazione*, vol. 2: *I sintagmi verbale, aggettivale, avverbiale. La subordinazione.* Bologna: Il Mulino.

Reuland, E. J. (1983). "Governing -*ing.*" *Linguistic Inquiry 14,* 101–37.

Ribeiro, I. (1993). "Evidências para uma fase V2 do português antigo." In Roberts and Kato (1993).

Rizzi, L. (1981). "Nominative Marking in Italian Infinitives and the Nominative Island Constraint." In Heny (1981:129–57).

—— (1982). *Issues in Italian Syntax.* Dordrecht: Foris.

—— (1990a). *Relativized Minimality.* Cambridge, Mass.: MIT Press (= Linguistic Inquiry Monographs 16).

—— (1990b). "Speculations on Verb Second." In Mascaro and Nespor (1990:375–86).

Rizzi, L., and I. Roberts. (1989). "Complex Inversion in French." *Probus 1*, 1–30.

Roberts, I. (1993). *Verbs and Diachronic Syntax: A Comparative History of English and French.* Dordrecht: Kluwer.

—— (1994). "Two types of head movement in Romance." In Lightfoot and Hornstein (1994:207–42).

Roberts, I., and M. A. Kato (eds.). (1993). *Português brasileiro: Uma viagem diacronica: Homenagem a Fernando Tarallo.* Campinas (SP): Editora da Unicamp.

Rohlfs, G. (1949). *Historische Grammatik der italienischen Sprache und ihrer Mundarten*, vol. 2: *Formenlehre und Syntax.* Bern: Francke.

Rohrbacher, B. W. (1994). *The Germanic VO Languages and the Full Paradigm: A Theory of V to I Raising.* Amherst, Mass.

Rohrer, C. (ed.). (1981). *Logos Semanticos. Studia Linguistica in honorem Eugenio Coseriu (1921–1981),* vol. 4. Berlin: De Gruyter.

Rolshoven, J. (1996). "Lexikalisches Wissen in der maschinellen Übersetzung." In Blumenthal et al. (1996:85–100).

—— (1997). "Sprachliche Informationsverarbeitung." In Hoinkes and Dietrich (1997: 379–96).

—— (1998). "Bewegungen. GB und romanische Sprachwissenschaft." In Dahmen et al. (1998:363–95).

Rolshoven, J., J.-Y. Lalande, and G. Mensching. (1998). "Repräsentation und Evaluierung linguistischen Wissens zur Verbstellung in romanischen Sprachen in einem CAD-orientierten Expertensystem: Abschlußbericht vorgelegt bei der DFG." Unpublished ms., Universität zu Köln, Sprachliche Informationsverarbeitung.

Ronat, M. (1979). "Pronoms topiques et pronoms distinctifs." *Langue française 44,* 106–128.

Ronjat, J. (1937). *Grammaire Istorique des Parlers Provençaux Modernes,* vol. 3 (2nd part: *Morphologie et formation des mots;* 3rd part: *Notes de syntaxe*). Montpelier: Societé des Langues Romanes.

Roth, W. (1979). "Portugiesisch oder Brasilianisch? Zur Sprache Brasiliens als sprach- und literaturwissenschaftlichem Problem." *Iberoamericana 3,* 16–41.

Rouveret, A. (1980). "Sur la notion de proposition finie: Gouvernement et inversion. *Langages 60,* 75–107.

Rouveret, A., and P. Sauzet (eds.). (1989). *La structure de la proposition dans les langues romanes* (= Revue des Langues Romanes 93).

Rouveret, A., and J.-R. Vergnaud (1980). "Specifying Reference to the Subject: French Causatives and Conditions on Representations." *Linguistic Inquiry 11,* 97–202.

Rowlett, P. (1998). *Sentential Negation in French.* New York: Oxford University Press.

Saccon, G. (1992). "VP-internal arguments and locative subjects." Paper presented at NELS 22, University of Massachussets, Amherst.

Saco y Arce, J. A. (1967). *Gramática gallega,* 2nd ed. Orense.

Saenger, S. (1888). "Syntaktische Untersuchungen zu Rabelais.", Ph.D. diss., Universität Halle.

Said Ali, M. (1971). *Gramática Histórica da Língua Portuguêsa,* 7th ed. São Paulo: Edic. Melhoramentos.

Salvi, G., and L. Vanelli (1992). *Grammatica essenziale di riferimento della lingua italiana,* 3 vols. Novara: Istituto Geografico De Agostini; Florence: Le Monnier (= Strumenti per l'italiano 2).

Sandfeld, K. (1943). *Syntaxe du français contemporain,* vol. 3: *L'Infinitif.* Paris: Droz.

Sasse, H.-J. (1978). "Subjekt und Ergativ: Zur pragmatischen Grundlage primärer grammatischer Relationen.", *Fol. 12,* 219–52.

—— (1982). "Subjektprominenz." In Heinz and Wandruszka (1982:267–86).

—— (1987). "The Thetic/Categorical Distinction Revisited." *Linguistics 25,* 511–80.

Sauzet, P. (1989). "Topicalisation et prolepse en occitan." In Rouveret and Sauzet (1989:235–73).

Savj-Lopez, P. (1900). "Studi d'antico Napoletano: L'infinito coniugato." *ZRPh 24,* 501–4.

Schellert, D. (1958). "Syntax und Stilistik der Subjektstellung im Portugiesischen." Ph.D. diss., Universität Bonn.

Schmidt, C. M. (1992). "This Was Not about Agr(P): A reply to Iatridou (1990)." Unpublished ms., Universität zu Köln.

—— (1994). *Satzstruktur und Verbbewegung: Eine minimalistische Analyse zur internen Syntax der IP (Inflection-Phrase) im Deutschen.* Tübingen: Niemeyer (= Linguistische Arbeiten 327).

Schmidt-Radefeldt, J. (ed.). (1983). *Portugiesische Sprachwissenschaft.* Tübingen: Narr (= Tübinger Beiträge zur Linguistik 212).

Schmitt, C., and W. Schweickard (eds.). (1995). *Die romanischen Sprachen im Vergleich: Akten der gleichnamigen Sektion des Potsdamer Romanistentages.* Bonn: Romanistischer Verlag.

Schwendener, U. (1923). "Der accusativus cum infinitivo im Italienischen." Ph.D. diss., Universität Bern.

Scotti-Rosin, S. (1994). "Portugiesisch: Geschriebene Sprache und gesprochene Sprache." In Holtus et al. (1994;308–12).

Seelbach, D. (1978). Transformationsregeln im Französischen aus der Sicht der historischen und romanischen Syntax. Heidelberg: Winter.

Segre, C. (1991). *Lingua, stile e società.* Milan: Feltrinelli.

Sester, F. (1928). *Der Infinitiv im Neuportugiesischen auf Grund der Werke von Eça de Queiroz.* Ph. D. diss., Universität zu Köln.

Siebert, S. (1999). *Wortbildung und Grammatik: Syntaktische Restriktionen in der Struktur komplexer Wörter.* Tübingen: Niemeyer (= Linguistische Arbeiten 408).

Silva Dias, A. E. da. (1954). *Syntaxe historica Portuguesa.* Lisbon: A. M. Teixeira.

Skydsgaard, S. (1977). *La combinatoria sintáctica del infinitivo español,* 2 vols. Madrid: Editorial Castalia.

Skytte, G. (1983). *La sintassi dell'infinito in italiano moderno,* 2 vols. Copenhagen: Munksgaard Forlag.

Solmi, A. (1917). *Studi storici sulle istituzioni della Sardegna nel Medio Evo.* Cagliari: Società Storica Sarda.

Sportiche, D. (1988a). "Conditions on Silent Categories." Unpublished ms.

—— (1988b). "A Theory of Floating Quantifiers and Its Corollaries for Constituent Structure." *Linguistic Inquiry 19,* 425–49.

Stefanini, R. (1969). "Funzioni e comportamento di /e/ (e, e') proclitica nel fiorentino d'oggi." *Italia dialettale 42.*

Sten, H. (1952). "L'*infinitivo impessoal* et l'*infinitivo pessoal* en portugais moderne." *Boletim de Filologia 13,* 83–142, 201–56.

Steube, A., and G. Zybatow (eds.). (1994). *Zur Satzwertigkeit von Infinitiven, Small Clauses und Partizipialkonstruktionen.* Tübingen: Niemeyer (= Linguistische Arbeiten 315).

Stimming, A. (1886). "Verwendung des Gerundiums und des Partizip Präsens im Altfranzösischen." *ZRPh 10,* 526–53.

Stimming, E. (1915). *Der Accusativus cum Infinitivo im Französischen.* Halle a. S.: Niemeyer (= Beihefte zur ZRPh 59).

Strozer, J. R. (1976). *Clitics in Spanish.* Ann Arbor, Mich.: Xerox Univ. Microfilms.

Szabolcsi, A. (1983). "The Possessor that Ran Away from Home." *Linguistic Review 3,* 89–102.

—— (1987). "Functional Categories in the Noun Phrase." In Kenesei (1987:167–89).

Taraldsen, K. T. (1986). "Som and the binding theory." In Hellan and Koch Christensen (1986:149–84).

Thomas, E. W. (1969). *The Syntax of Spoken Brazilian Portuguese.* Nashville, Tenn.: Vanderbilt University Press.

Tobler, A. (1870). *Mittheilungen aus Altfranzösischen Handschriften,* vol. 1: *Aus der Chanson de Geste von Auberi nach einer vaticanischen Handschrift.* Leipzig: Hirzel.

—— (1921). *Vermischte Beiträge zur französischen Grammatik,* 1st series, 3rd ed. Leipzig: Hirzel.

Togeby, M. (1955). "L'énigmatique infinitif personnel en portugais." *Studia Neophilologica 27,* 211–18.

Treviño, E. (1992). "Subjects in Spanish Causative Constructions." In Hirschbühler and Koerner (1992:309–24).

Vallduví, E. (1992a). "Focus Constructions in Catalan." In Laeufer and Morgan (1992: 457–79).

—— (1992b). *The Informational Component.* New York: Garland.

Vater, H. (1990). "NP or DP—That's the Question." Unpublished ms., Universität zu Köln.

—— (1994). *Einführung in die Sprachwissenschaft.* München: Fink.

Vergnaud, J.-R. (1979). "Quelques éléments pour une théorie formelle des Cas." Unpublished ms., University of Massachusetts, Amherst.

—— (1982). *Dépendances et niveaux de représentation en syntaxe.* Ph.D. diss., Université de Paris 7.

—— (1985). *Dépendances et niveaux de représentation en syntaxe.* Amsterdam: Benjamins.

Vinet, M.-T. (1985). "Lexical Subjects in French Infinitives." In King and Maley (1985:407–23).

Vockeradt, H. (1878). *Lehrbuch der italienischen Sprache für die oberen Klassen höherer Lehranstalten und zum Privatstudium.* Berlin: Weidmannsche Buchhandlung.

Wagner, M. L. (1938–39) "Flessione nominale e verbale del sardo antico e moderno." *Italia dialettale 14,* 93–170 and *15,* 207–247.

—— (1980). *La lingua sarda,* 2nd ed. Bern: Francke.

Wandruszka, U. (1981). "Typen romanischer Subjektinversion." In Rohrer (1981:369–80).

Webelhuth, G. (ed.). (1995). *Government and Binding Theory and the Minimalist Program.* Cambridge, Mass.: Blackwell.

Wiese, B. (1928). *Altitalienisches Elementarbuch,* 2nd. ed. Heidelberg: Winter.

Wilder, C. (1995). "Derivational Economy and the Analysis of V2." *FAS Papers in Linguistics 1,* 117–56.

Wilder, C., and D. Cavar (1994). "Word Order Variation, Verb Movement, and Economy Principles." *Studia Linguistica 48,* 46–86.

Zubizarreta, M. L. (1980). "Remarks on Portuguese Infinitives." Unpublished ms., MIT, Cambridge, Mass.

Index

255